OXFORD MODERN LANGUAGES
AND LITERATURE MONOGRAPHS

Science and Structure in Proust's *A la recherche du temps perdu*

NICOLA LUCKHURST

CLARENDON PRESS · OXFORD

OXFORD
UNIVERSITY PRESS

Great Clarendon Street, Oxford, OX2 6DP
Oxford University Press is a department of the University of Oxford.
It furthers the University's objective of excellence in research, scholarship,
and education by publishing worldwide in

Oxford New York

Athens Auckland Bangkok Bogotá Buenos Aires Calcutta
Cape Town Chennai Dar es Salaam Delhi Florence Hong Kong Istanbul
Karachi Kuala Lumpur Madrid Melbourne Mexico City Mumbai
Nairobi Paris São Paulo Singapore Taipei Tokyo Toronto Warsaw
and associated companies in Berlin Ibadan

Oxford is a registered trade mark of Oxford University Press
in the UK and certain other countries

Published in the United States
by Oxford University Press Inc., New York

First published 2000

British Library Cataloguing in Publication Data

Data available

Library of Congress Cataloging in Publication Data

Luckhurst, Nicola.
Science and structure in Proust's A la recherche du temps perdu / Nicola Luckhurst.
p. cm. – (Oxford modern languages and literature monographs)
Includes bibliographical references and index.
1. Proust, Marcel, 1871–1922. A la recherche du temps perdu. 2. Literature and science.
I. Title. II. Series.
PQ2631.R63 A8287 2000 843'.912–dc21 99-048574
ISBN 0-19-816002-X

1 3 5 7 9 10 8 6 4 2

Typeset by Regent Typesetting, London
Printed in Great Britain
on acid-free paper by Biddles Ltd,
Guildford and King's Lynn

for Julian

ACKNOWLEDGEMENTS

This book was written during my research fellowship at Somerville College, Oxford; I am particularly grateful for the college's support.

Malcolm Bowie generously, supportively, and inspiringly supervised my work on Proust for the doctoral thesis from which this book was developed; I am immensely grateful to him for this and for subsequent conversations about Proust and science. Many thanks too are due to Ingrid Wassenaar, Jean van Altena, Kathy Laing, and Alice Staveley for their close readings of my work and invaluable suggestions. My father, Geoffrey Luckhurst, has patiently explained the nature of saturated, supersaturated, and suspended solutions and more. Finally, I owe much to Terence Cave, in particular for introducing me to the *moralistes*, the germ of this study.

CONTENTS

Faut-il en faire un roman, une étude philosophique, suis-je romancier?

. . . .

Mais je sens qu'un rien peut briser ce cerveau.

Proust, *Carnet de 1908*

Il meurt instantanément dans le particulier, et se remet immédiatement à flotter et à vivre dans le général. Il ne vit que du général, le général l'anime et le nourrit, et il meurt instantanément dans le particulier . . . Il est intermittent.

Proust, *Contre Sainte-Beuve*

INTRODUCTION

> j'ai en train:
> une étude sur la noblesse
> un roman parisien
> un essai sur Sainte-Beuve et Flaubert
> un essai sur les Femmes
> un essai sur la Pédérastie
> (pas facile à publier)
> une étude sur les vitraux
> une étude sur les pierres tombales
> une étude sur le roman
>
> Proust, Letter of 5/6 May 1908

Proust began work on *A la recherche* after a crucial period of hesitation between two genres, the essay and the novel:[1] 'Je voudrais, quoique bien malade écrire une étude sur Sainte-Beuve. La chose s'est bâtie dans mon esprit de deux façons différentes entre lesquelles je dois choisir. Or je suis sans volonté et sans clairvoyance.'[2]

Until this point Proust's writing can be broadly characterized as occupying both modes. *Contre Sainte-Beuve*, which he worked on from 1905 to 1909, is an essay, but couched in the form of a fictitious dialogue between himself and his mother. 'Non seulement cette indécision est profonde, mais encore elle est peut-être chérie,' Barthes proposes. And when the decision appears to be made in favour of the novel, *A la recherche du temps perdu*, both 'côtés' are still present, as if the *Contre Sainte-Beuve* solution had been turned inside-out. Rather than writing an essay which is also a novel, Proust writes a novel which includes the essayistic. At moments the narrator of *A la recherche* laments the loss of the straightforwardly general, of the essay—'Oui, j'ai été forcé d'amincir la chose et d'être mensonger' (iii. 696). According to the aesthetic which has been elaborated in its place, the particular is always infused with the general, or, as Proust exclaims: 'C'est à la cime même du particulier qu'éclôt le général.'[3] Yet this formula proves easily reversible, for there is such a variety of

[1] Barthes speaks thus about the desire to write in his essay 'Longtemps je me suis couché de bonne heure', in *Le Bruissement de la langue* (Paris: Seuil, 1984), 314.

[2] Letter to Mme de Noailles, towards mid-Dec. 1908, in *Correspondance*, ed. P. Kolb (Paris: Plon, 1970–93), viii. 320–1.

[3] Letter to Daniel Halévy, 19 July 1919, ibid. xviii. 334.

generality to be encompassed. *A la recherche* is not so much the story of a life as it is the story of the rapacious reflection of the desiring mind, whose narrator is 'à la fois enfant et adulte, *puer senilis*, passionné et sage, proie de manies excentriques et lieu d'une réflexion souveraine'.[4] Barthes terms the hybrid essay-novel which results 'une tierce forme'.

The decision between the two 'côtés' has proved less preoccupying for a critical tradition which has almost unfailingly opted for the novel, rejecting the simple sententious mode in favour of Proust's quintessentially abundant, lyrical, metaphor-laden sentence. The promotional tactics which *A la recherche* itself employs do little to relieve this bias. The infamous *madeleine* scene, together with the striking formula of *Le Temps retrouvé*, which might be parodied as 'involuntary memory translated via metaphor = Art!', serve only to reinforce the privileged critical preoccupations of metaphor, time, and memory. Yet, for the first readers of *A la recherche*, it was the presence of both maxim and metaphor which was striking, and indeed, strikingly modern. In 'Phases of Fiction' Virginia Woolf characterizes the modernity of Proust's 'tierce forme', or, as she terms it, his 'double vision':

> The mind of Proust lies open with the sympathy of a poet and the detachment of a scientist to everything that it has the power to feel. . . . It is as though there were two faces to every situation; one full in the light so that it can be described as accurately and examined as minutely as possible; the other half in shadow so that it can be described only in a moment of faith and vision by the use of metaphor. . . . And it is this double vision that makes the work of Proust to us in our generation so spherical, so comprehensive.[5]

Responses such as Woolf's permitted the full range of the Proustian sentence, embracing the abundant and the concise, the impressionistic and the analytic, or, to use Woolf's terms, the metaphor of the 'poet' and the maxim of the 'scientist'. Revisiting early reactions to the text already goes some way to restoring what one might think of as the unexpurgated version of *A la recherche*, and this is in part the aim of this study. Reading the neglected 'analytic' sentence means re-mapping the text against the grain of accumulated criticism; focusing on the maxims will restore the abundance of what Barthes calls the 'tierce forme'.

[4] Barthes 'Longtemps je me suis couché', 319.

[5] Virginia Woolf, 'Phases of Fiction', (1st pub. 1929), in *Granite and Rainbow* (New York: Harcourt Brace, 1958), 125 (first sentence) and 139.

The work of early critics such as Woolf certainly captures the excitement, the shock even, of *A la recherche*'s appearance. But what does it mean to read in this way? How does Proust's 'double vision' or 'tierce forme' signify? And why was it felt to be so meaningful by Woolf and others?

By examining the critical discourses which were emerging in response to *A la recherche*, we can begin to answer these questions. Of the approaches to the 'côté de l'Essai', two metaphors emerge strongly: first, that of Proust as moralist, and second, that of Proust as scientist. The former ties *A la recherche* back into a critical tradition which is peculiarly and proudly French; it suggests an intertextual approach to Proust's maxims. The second connects *A la recherche* rather differently, both more widely and contemporaneously into European modernist literature, but also with the scientific and epistemological questions of the early twentieth century. Although these two approaches may seem quite discrete, and the second rather more exciting than the first, it will be seen that they dovetail into one another in a curious and illuminating way.

Many studies of literature and science begin with the very abstract and theoretical question of how to study science and literature. Often this is fruitful. But I do not propose to rehearse that gesture here. Rather, I want to begin with literature, and focus quite specifically on Proust's maxims through an intertextual model, establishing the reading and writing practices which the sententious mode demands, and exploring Proust's own awareness of this literary mode of laying down the law. The very limits of this approach are revealing—for the intertextual model is exceeded by the range and setting of the maxims of *A la recherche*. They are unstable formulations, dynamically sprung within the text, subject to interaction with the *récit*, enunciated from various narrative positions and personae. As Proust states in a letter to Jacques Rivière, 'Cette évolution d'une pensée, je n'ai pas voulu l'analyser abstraitement mais la recréer, la faire vivre.'[6] Rather than presenting a collection of polished maxims, the end-products of sententiousness, the text displays the processes by which such formulations are reached, forming an enquiry into the desire for truths, performing an interrogation of intellectual method.

If the maxims of *A la recherche* do not lend themselves to collection in a commonplace book, if their excessive nature—they are both syntactically and quantitatively excessive—suggests that they plot

[6] Letter of 6 Feb. 1914, in *Correspondance*, xiii. 99.

only the desire, a very rigorous desire, for truth, then Woolf's metaphor, according to which the generalizing sentences of *A la recherche* are analogous to scientific law, may well prove more fruitful. The shift from the intertextual to the scientific model will work through the concept of law, considering how scientists and philosophers contemporary with Proust were also rethinking this concept in their own fields, questioning the justification, aesthetic or utilitarian, and the force and range of scientific law. The authority of science and scientific law is a key epistemological question of the 'modernist' period, and as such, it opens out on to related issues: How do hypotheses become theories? How do models, or metaphors, and theories interact? What is the personal involvement of the scientist in his experiment? What kind of work does the unconscious do in the pursuit of knowledge? And it will be seen that these issues are played out, now psychologically, now structurally, in *A la recherche.* For the narrator borrows from the sciences a range of metaphors. He posits himself as scientist, on the one hand observing the world around him as would a natural historian, on the other hand implicating others—particularly those he desires—in his speculation, experiment, and modelling, and recognizing his necessary and sometimes involuntary implication in these strategies. Science allows, as the initial intertextual enquiry does not, an exploration of the sententious mode as it interacts with other sentence types; in other words, it allows us to explore the 'tierce forme'. Inasmuch as science must be practised, and often performed, by 'the scientist', it also, unexpectedly, reveals the affective connections of the self: that is, the Proustian 'je'—the now authoritative, now brilliant, now needy utterer of maxims—with the sententious mode.

Put more simply, this study will begin with literature and the maxims, and move on to science and the 'tierce forme'. The very first sales strategies of the *Nouvelle Revue française* promoted *A la recherche* as a classical work in the finest French tradition, replete with profound maxims. Chapter I opens with a reading of this 'classical Proust', also known as 'Proust the *moraliste*', but discovers that there are fewer truths to be gleaned than Jacques Rivière had promised. Fortunately, Virginia Woolf's advice comes to the rescue of this first reading, and points the way to a 'double vision' which allows for the full force and range of the Proustian sentence. For Woolf, the sententious, or analytic, mode of *A la recherche* was 'scientific'. Yet, as in her own novels, where science does not simply lay down the law, so here, it models, it speculates—now playful, now ironic, now rigorously in earnest. Just as generality is various, so science and the self who constructs and is constructed by it are more diverse than at first appears.

1

MAXIMS

1.1 The Proustian critique

> Il y a des pages où il se fait moraliste; il légifère, son style change alors, sa phrase devient brève, linéaire et péremptoire, elle s'offre comme une maxime. Mais est-ce là le vrai Proust? Ne fait-il pas tort au romancier?
>
> Jean Rousset, *Forme et signification*

Reactions to the maxims of *A la recherche* tend to the extreme. Whereas Aldous Huxley delights in Proust's moralizing as 'La Rochefoucauld magnified ten thousand times',[1] Rousset questions its authenticity, as if Proust were writing out of character.[2] Huxley was, of course, one of Proust's first readers (he is named in *A la recherche* as the nephew of the biologist, 'l'illustre Huxley' (iii. 38)). The subsequent critical tradition, of which Rousset is a part, has privileged metaphor, time, and memory in *A la recherche*, and has not favoured its *sententiae*. This tradition is not peculiar to readings of *A la recherche*, for it represents a reluctance typical of criticism of the novel to explore, and even to acknowledge, sententiousness.[3] But if maxims are peculiarly anti-novelistic (peculiarly too because it would be inaccurate to describe sententiousness as a rare feature of the novel), then Proust's maxims might be thought of as particularly antagonistic to the style of their novelistic context. We do not expect to find sententiousness, the voice of narrative authority, in *A la recherche*; yet the Proustian self, this self-confessedly shifting, multiple, unreliable 'je', cannot help 'laying down the law', and picking it up again, and unpicking and refashioning it, and so on. For the maxims of *A la recherche* are variously and abun-

[1] Aldous Huxley, 'Books for the Journey', cited in Derek P. Scales, *Aldous Huxley and French Literature* (Sydney: Sydney University Press, 1969), 68.

[2] Jean Rousset, *Forme et signification* (Paris: Corti, 1962), 166.

[3] The tradition of hostility to the presence of *sententiae* in continuous prose is acutely analysed and documented by Geoffrey Bennington in *Sententiousness and the Novel* (Cambridge: Cambridge University Press, 1985). Bennington's study provides an invaluable analysis of both generalizing sentences and critical response to them. However, the typology he establishes to deal with eighteenth-century novels is not readily adaptable to the reading of such sentences in *A la recherche*.

dantly enunciated by a narratorial voice quite different from that of its authoritatively sententious nineteenth-century counterpart. That the Proustian 'je' is capable of—more than this, delights in—such 'moralizing' suggests that the sententious discourse of *A la recherche* is not merely a novelist's habit or an outdated mannerism, or even, as some critics have suggested, a stylistic error that Proust would have corrected had he lived longer. If *A la recherche* is regarded as a novel of transition—between the nineteenth and twentieth centuries, between realism and modernism—then this peculiarly Proustian sententiousness might represent less a fault than a fault-line between the two.

Once recognized, the sententious discourse of *A la recherche* is difficult to ignore. Indeed, maxims are so prolific throughout *A la recherche* as to be a characteristic feature of Proust's style—maxims such as 'Le temps dont nous disposons chaque jour est élastique; les passions que nous ressentons le dilatent, celles que nous inspirons le rétrécissent, et l'habitude le remplit' (i. 601); 'L'ivresse réalise pour quelques heures l'idéalisme subjectif, le phénoménisme pur; tout n'est plus qu'apparences et n'existe plus qu'en fonction de notre sublime nous-même' (ii. 173); 'Il faut aimer pour prendre souci qu'il n'y ait pas que des honnêtes femmes, autant dire pour s'en aviser, et il faut aimer aussi pour souhaiter, c'est-à-dire pour s'assurer qu'il y en a' (iii. 227); 'Nous trouvons de tout dans notre mémoire: elle est une espèce de pharmacie, de laboratoire de chimie, où on met au hasard la main tantôt sur une drogue calmante, tantôt sur un poison dangereux' (iii. 892); 'L'inconnu de la vie des êtres est comme celui de la nature, que chaque découverte scientifique ne fait que reculer mais n'annule pas' (iii. 893); 'L'être aimé est successivement le mal et le remède qui suspend et aggrave le mal' (iii. 228); 'Le témoignage des sens est lui aussi une opération de l'esprit où la conviction crée l'évidence' (iii. 694); 'Tout ce qui nous semble impérissable tend à la destruction . . . La création du monde n'a pas eu lieu au début, elle a lieu tous les jours' (iv. 247–8); 'Le regret comme le désir ne cherche pas à s'analyser' (i. 603); 'La résignation, modalité de l'habitude, permet à certaines forces de s'accroître indéfiniment' (i. 611); 'Il y a moins de force dans une innovation artificielle que dans une répétition destinée à suggérer une vérité neuve' (ii. 248); 'Notre personnalité sociale est une création de la pensée des autres' (i. 19); 'Des lois aussi précises que celles de l'hydrostatique maintiennent la superposition des images que nous formons dans un ordre fixe que la proximité de l'événement bouleverse' (ii. 211); 'On désire être compris parce qu'on désire être aimé, et on désire être aimé parce qu'on aime' (iv. 78); 'Même mentalement, nous dépendons des lois naturelles beaucoup plus que nous ne croyons et notre esprit possède d'avance comme certain cryptogame, comme telle graminée les particularités que nous croyons choisir' (ii. 246). If the maxim is a characteristic of Proust's style, its stylistic range, as these examples indicate, is strikingly diverse—from slight sententious clauses, to the precise and paradoxical sentence in the style of La Rochefoucauld, to the expansive and scholarly 'essai'.

Characteristically, the text gives its own account, and even justification, of sententiousness; but so deeply embedded is this in the aesthetic theorizing of *Le Temps retrouvé* that it is not a little overshadowed by Proust's 'metaphor and memory' manifesto. In these frequently quoted passages, the narrator's aesthetic revelation leads him to concoct a recipe for, as it were, how to write a balanced novel. You cannot write a novel from involuntary memory alone, he proposes, truths gained by the intellect must also be included, but only with the proviso that they are subordinate to the privileged experience of 'mémoire involontaire' and to its rhetorical counterpart, metaphor. The characterization of these 'truths' as the 'foule de vérités relatives aux passions, aux caractères, aux mœurs' (iv. 477) is key. The triplet 'caractères, passions, mœurs' clearly identifies the constituent truths as maxims belonging to a narrator–*moraliste* whose origin lies in the behavioural and psychological analyses of La Bruyère and La Rochefoucauld. The hierarchy which is suggested by this passage, then, places metaphors above maxims, the former being associated with the intuitive self, the latter with the intellect. Taking his cue specifically from the passage quoted, Tadié's summary in *Proust et le roman* spells out Proust's formula as follows: 'Tout se passe donc comme si l'œuvre organisait, autour d'un noyau intemporel, un réseau de vérités d'une valeur esthétique inférieure: les lois.'[4] That the aesthetic revelation of *Le Temps retrouvé* is the projection of an ideal work, that it is not an extra-textual template to be applied retrospectively to the novel, is clear. But we might still want to ask why Proust's narrator is manipulating one set of generalizing sentences (those proclaiming the aesthetic laws) to legislate against another (the *moraliste*-style maxims); and why he wants to package the sententious discourse of *A la recherche* (which is far too voracious to be classified as purely moralistic); and whether this is the whole story.

[4] Jean-Yves Tadié, *Proust et le roman* (Paris: Gallimard, 1971), 413.

Once the moment of revelation is past, once it has been translated into the striking hierarchy according to which metaphor and involuntary memory are superior to moralistic truths, so a looser, more speculative passage of aesthetic theorizing unwinds, in which the terms of what has become known as Proust's 'anti-intellectual' argument become difficult to distinguish. For while abstract intellectualizing is criticized, truths formed by the pressure of external sensual or physical force on the intellect are described by the narrator as a potential alternative, a supplementary aesthetic.

> Un homme né sensible et qui n'aurait pas d'imagination pourrait malgré cela écrire des romans admirables. La souffrance que les autres lui causeraient, ses efforts pour la prévenir, les conflits qu'elle et la seconde personne cruelle créeraient, tout cela, interprété par l'intelligence, pourrait faire la matière d'un livre . . . aussi beau que s'il était imaginé, inventé. (iv. 479–80)

The sensation of involuntary memory is similarly considered insufficient as a creative principle, unless interpreted: 'Il fallait tâcher d'interpréter les sensations comme *les signes d'autant de lois et d'idées*, en essayant de penser, c'est-à-dire de faire sortir de la pénombre ce que j'avais senti, de le convertir en un équivalent spirituel' (iv. 457; emphasis added). Both the lover's suffering and the experience of involuntary memory may produce a novel when fed into the formula: sensation (profound, physical, unconscious) + intellectual translation = Art. From these examples alternative hierarchies might be derived: the maxim after metaphor line-up would be refined by a categorizing of different kinds of maxim. The narrator's somewhat leisurely and authoritative generalizations, as, typically, the laws of homosexuality in *Sodome et Gomorrhe I*, would be ranked inferior to the 'Albertine maxims', by which I mean those hypothetical and temporary formulations through which the narrator pursues knowledge about Albertine's sexuality. This 'albertinage', more closely associated with the narrator-protagonist, is a desperate and sometimes comic grasping after truths to protect the self, an attempt to form a basis from which to construct for the self a plausible fiction. Caricaturing the solution offered in *Le Temps retrouvé*, we might deduce that some laws are better than others. These laws would not be judged on their own terms—were this the case, the 'older' narrator's more assured and even scholarly *sententiae* would be classed as superior—instead, the raw emotions from which the maxims of the narrator-protagonist result constitute their aesthetic justification.

But this picking over of what might be termed the finer points of the Proustian agenda—discriminating between competing sentence-types—runs the risk of repeating the narrator's own manipulation of maxims, and proving his point that metaphors are, on the whole, preferable. The discussion of sententiousness which takes place in *Le Temps retrouvé* seems both overly proscriptive and, once we read the small print, ambiguous. It is as if the narrator feels bound to hold to account what he describes variously as maxims, truths, and laws, but as the range of terms indicates, he cannot find a straight answer, or indeed a language, for doing so.

Turning our attention to the drama of the laws of metaphor and memory, which is, of course, where Proust wanted his readers' attention to be, it could be argued that so successfully did he stage this revelation that, from the publication of the final volume of *A la recherche*, the critical agenda had, effectively, been set, and that maxims were not its priority. By 1958, Rebecca West was commenting somewhat scathingly that Proust 'treated his madeleine's intellectual pretensions very seriously',[5] and, attempting to puncture these 'pretensions', she claims that the aesthetic theories of *Le Temps retrouvé* are at best commonplace: 'the whole of this theory which links up time and creation and memory is nonsensical'.[6] West's claim that Proust is a moralist is aggressively and plainly argued. Styled ironically as an attack on the author, her real concern is to question the tendency to accept *Le Temps retrouvé* as a 'mode d'emploi'. Unfortunately this strategy simply has the effect of polarizing possible readings: Proust is a moralist if you don't believe the involuntary memory theory, and a modernist if you do.

Reintroducing time, and specifically narrative time, into the discussion is helpful at this stage. These are the narrator's, not Proust's theories, and they grow out of, and belong to, the narrative which has gone before. They may describe an aesthetic which aspires to timelessness, but they remain set in the time of their narration. The story of how the narrator arrives at these theories is just one of many strands of narrative in which many kinds of maxims are formulated; *A la recherche* in effect describes and interrogates the affective relationship of the self with these maxims. What it becomes possible to say, in describing the narrative shape of this relationship, is that the narrator, having served his apprenticeship in the art of 'legislation' throughout

[5] Rebecca West, *The Court and the Castle* (London: Macmillan, 1958), 187.
[6] Ibid. 184–5.

the text, emerges in *Le Temps retrouvé* as the triumphant wielder and forger of aesthetic laws.

We need to think again about these maxims, laws, and theories, these sentences whose grammar lays claim to timelessness, as set in narrative time, to consider what their story is and how it is related to us. The later aesthetic maxims are less striking. They seem descriptive rather than prescriptive—this too is to do with their narration. The drama of involuntary memory and aesthetic recognition unwinds into reflection, description, and speculation about aesthetics. The authority of those initial laws depends on the style of their performance, and above all on its dramatic quality. We remember the aesthetic theories as bound up with involuntary memory and metaphor, because as readers we are made party to the experience of revelation. Proust might not so much have had what West called 'intellectual pretensions' as dramatic pretensions: the beginning and the end of *A la recherche* were written simultaneously, and collaborate to reinforce the final aesthetic revelation and theorization. Less memorable are the cogitations provoked by this. But thinking about the narration and performance of laws undermines the hierarchy and authority which have traditionally been accorded to some maxims over others. For now all such statements are bound up in the fictional texture of the novel, and none speaks from a position of superiority; indeed, they speak through a multitude of selves. While other characters are rarely allowed to formulate maxims, the narrator's status as enunciator is various and multiple. These are not Proust's maxims, but the narrator's, a narrator who is a writer and a would-be writer, a protagonist and a moralist, and so on. The rich variety of moralistic forms relates to the variety of narrative selves, but also to the needs of these selves as they construct and are constructed by the laws they enunciate. As Martha Nussbaum proposes in *Love's Knowledge*:

> Suppose one believes and wishes to state, as Proust's Marcel does, that the most important truths about human psychology cannot be communicated or grasped by intellectual activity alone: powerful emotions have an irreducibly important cognitive role to play. If one states this view in a written form that expresses only intellectual activity and addresses itself only to the intellect of the reader . . . a question arises. Does the writer really believe what his or her words seem to state? . . . Proust's text, by contrast, states in its form exactly what it states in its paraphrasable philosophical content.[7]

[7] Martha Nussbaum, *Love's Knowledge* (New York: Oxford University Press, 1990), 7.

This is to say that the narrator's perception of truth is dependent on an affective changing relationship—now needy, now authoritative, now riskily speculative—resulting in various moralistic forms: highly concentrated as the lover's speculations in the Albertine texts, revelatory in the aesthetic laws of *Le Temps retrouvé*, scattered in the opening pages of 'Combray', with vivid illustration, or as essay, in the opening of *Sodome et Gomorrhe.*[8]

The grammar of the maxim may lay claim to timelessness, yet it is set within a discourse which takes place in, and narrates the passage (whether backwards or forwards) of, time. In a letter to Jacques Rivière, Proust described this narration of what he calls 'the evolution of thought': 'Cette évolution d'une pensée, je n'ai pas voulu l'analyser abstraitement mais la recréer, la faire vivre. Je suis donc forcé de peindre les erreurs, sans croire devoir dire que je les tiens pour des erreurs.'[9]

The force of received readings has tended to deny what Woolf terms 'Proust's double vision'—the interplay of maxim and metaphor which is one of the fundamental paradoxes of *A la recherche*. And the common reader's experience, too, is pre-empted by a tradition which promotes a certain type of sentence, one which is abundant, lyrical, and often metaphor-laden, and bars entry to the more austere, analytical, and indeed moralistic Proust. Rebecca West's call to look at Proust's morals rather than his *madeleine* anticipates the opening pages of Malcolm Bowie's 'Proust, jealousy, knowledge', in which he calls for a reassessment of the 'supposed Proustian preferences . . . metaphors are superior to abstractions, art to science, being outside time to being inside it'.[10] Proust the moralist might seem distinctly less exciting than Proust the modernist. But one need not necessarily exclude the other. Looking at the moralizing Proust will allow a revision of how we define his modernist other. Indeed, writers such as West who have been neglected for their failure to fit the modernist

[8] See Gilles Deleuze's *Marcel Proust et les signes* (Paris: Presses Universitaires de France, 1964), in which a similar hierarchy of generalizing types is established. The hierarchy is chronologically organized, and moves from the world of 'Combray', where generality is established by ritual, to social signs and patterns, to the lovers' laws, and finally to the aesthetic maxims of *Le Temps retrouvé*. In fact, many key maxims are established in 'Combray' and 'Un amour de Swann', to be rehearsed and varied throughout the novel—rather than a succession of maxims leading towards ultimate 'truths', a repertoire is established.

[9] Letter of 6 Feb 1914, in *Correspondance*, xiii. 99–100.

[10] Malcolm Bowie, *Freud, Proust, and Lacan* (Cambridge: Cambridge University Press, 1987), 46.

category are currently the focus of a new criticism which seeks to question and redefine the received ideas which constitute the category.

This study will begin, however, with Proust the moralist, and with the promise of modernist redefinitions to come. This work of recovery involves schematic redescriptions of the maxims of *A la recherche*, as languages and models which may prove fruitful are explored. While such exploration is justified by the very lack of a discourse for speaking about sententiousness in the novel, the reader may wish to pass directly to the scientific model which will inform the majority of this study—for this reason and for general ease of use, the rest of this chapter is divided into subsections, science being introduced in Section 1.5. But first I want to focus quite specifically on readings of maxims and the intertextual connections between Proust and the *moralistes*.

1.2 Proust as *moraliste*

> Il faut être Pascal ou La Rochefoucauld pour concentrer en une phrase brève une grande richesse de vues (ce n'est point une comparaison que j'établis entre des auteurs mais deux tours d'esprit dont je marque la différence) le procédé est poli, mais un peu téméraire, même surtout chez de si grands esprits. Car ils renferment et condensent dans une maxime, une ample matière qui prête un fondement solide, et ouvre un vaste champ à des réflexions profondes.
>
> Louis Martin-Chauffier, *NRF* review of *Le Côté de Guermantes*

Proust's first French readers were to read his maxims as a hallmark of classicism, an indication that the literary pedigree of this vast modernist text could be found in the fragmentary writings of the seventeenth-century *moralistes*. This, at any rate, was the line taken by promoters of *A la recherche* such as Martin-Chauffier, who were concerned that readers might be discouraged by the novel's length and apparent lack of structure.[11] Proust himself uses a similar argument to defend *Du côté de chez Swann*. In a letter of 1914 to Henri Ghéon he quotes at length Francis Jammes's description of *Swann*: 'Cette

[11] Louis Martin-Chauffier, review of *Le Côté de Guermantes*, *La Nouvelle Revue française* (hereafter referred to as *NRF*), 16 (1 Feb. 1921), 204–5.

prodigieuse fresque toute fourmillante, qui s'accuse de plus en plus, cet inattendu des caractères, si *logique* dans son apparent illogisme, cette *phrase* à la Tacite, savante, subtile, équilibrée, voilà ce génie qui se dessine en teintes maîtresses', emphasizing the words 'logique' and 'phrase'.[12]

For Proust's promoters, linking *A la recherche* with the literature of French classicism rather than the classics solved two potential problems in one. Length, Martin-Chauffier argued, should not be equated with a lack of profundity. Where the *moralistes* condensed much wisdom into polished maxims, *A la recherche* reads as the expansion of such sentences; they provide the text with a foundation, 'un fondement solide'; they also allow for the development of further thought, 'des réflexions profondes'. Proust, as the modern inheritor of the moral discourse of Pascal, La Rochefoucauld, and La Bruyère, is both the writer and reader of maxims.

'On réunira sans doute un jour en un volume les réflexions psychologiques et morales qu'il a semées dans les pages de son œuvre, et l'on verra à quel point il se relie à la pure lignée des grands moralistes français,' writes Albert Thibaudet for *La Nouvelle Revue française*.[13] Jacques Rivière, in another *NRF* review, is also keen to stress this legacy, the classical, 'truth-telling' discourse of the *moralistes*: 'Notre littérature, un moment suffoquée par l'ineffable redevient ce qu'elle a toujours été dans son essence: "un discours sur les passions".'[14] Clearly these suggestions were not too fanciful, since readers outside the climate of Parisian reception also made the connection. In his essay 'Books for the Journey', Aldous Huxley declared: 'It is impossible to read Proust without being reminded of the *Maximes*, or the *Maximes* without being reminded of Proust . . . What are the love stories of *A la recherche du temps perdu* but enormous amplifications of these aphorisms?'[15]

Episodes of *A la recherche* may be read as the expansion not only of La Rochefoucauld's *maximes*, but also of certain of Pascal's *pensées*. *Pensée* 522 of the Lafuma edition, for example, sketches a scenario to suggest man's inconstancy: a man who has lost both wife and son forgets his mourning in the excitement of the hunt, a lapse that is taken as proof of his fallen condition. A similar anecdote and illustration of inconstancy is related in 'Combray', when the narrator as child

[12] Letter of 2 Jan. 1914, in *Correspondance*, xiii. 26.
[13] Albert Thibaudet, 'Marcel Proust et la tradition française', *NRF*, 20 (1 Jan. 1923), 137.
[14] Jacques Rivière, 'Marcel Proust et la tradition classique', *NRF*, 14 (1 Feb. 1920), 200.
[15] Cited in Scales, *Aldous Huxley*, 67–8.

is unable to understand how Swann's father can be so entranced by the beauty of the park as to forget the death of his wife. Read only in its immediate context, this episode does not have the resonance of the *pensée*: it is simply an anecdote from the narrator's childhood. Yet many of the opening events in 'Combray' establish the *topoi* of key maxims for the whole of *A la recherche*, and the *topos* of inconstancy will be replayed in the narrator's reaction to the death of his grandmother and to the real and fictional deaths and resurrections of Albertine, such that this apparently minor episode is also representative. The episode is both particular and general. Similar allusions and parallels between the work of Proust and Pascal have been traced by Margaret Mein in *A Foretaste of Proust*.[16] In thematic terms the exercise of matching *pensée* or *maxime* to Proustian episode is of limited interest—such connections could equally be made between Stendhal or Balzac and Proust (and such further readings are suggested by Mein, whose work does not focus exclusively on the *moralistes*). But connections such as these reveal the pervasiveness of sententiousness in *A la recherche*, such that we are led to read narrative events (the *récit*)—through their accompanying maxims and key terms—that is, both as narrative and as illustrative of a general law.

Explicit references to the *moralistes* in *A la recherche* display a keen awareness of reading practices—of how the particular gains general import, of how fragments become continuous text. The literature of the seventeenth century is prominent in *A la recherche*. Various characters are marked by strong reading relationships with writers of this period: the narrator's grandmother reads Mme de Sévigné, Charlus, Saint-Simon;[17] the 'jeunes filles' are examined on Racine, and scenes from Racinian tragedy are borrowed, often to comic effect, to stage episodes of *A la recherche*.[18] The *moralistes* alone are neither assigned as the favourite reading material of any one character, nor, save for the occasional reference, are they clearly signalled. Rather, there is a constant stylistic allusion in the narrator's own 'moralizing'.

These few exact references to the *moralistes* made in *A la recherche* reveal their ambiguous status in the text. Pascal is the *moraliste* most frequently named; yet these references tend to the comic or the ironic.

[16] Margaret Mein, *A Foretaste of Proust* (Farnborough: Saxon House, 1974).

[17] See Herbert de Ley, *Marcel Proust et le duc de Saint-Simon* (Urbana, Ill.: University of Illinois Press, 1966).

[18] Notably 'Comparaisons du personnel de l'hôtel et des chœurs de Racine' (iii. 170), and 'Les chasseurs et les jeunes israélites d'*Esther* et d'*Athalie*' (iii. 237). See also Bowie's reading of Racinian reference in *A la recherche*: *Freud, Proust, and Lacan*, 82–3.

The *Pensées* are invoked as the height of philosophical 'truth-telling' only to be undermined, sometimes explicitly, sometimes by the context of the reference. Françoise, for example, evaluates the standing of the Guermantes family 'à la fois sur le nombre de ses membres et l'éclat de son illustration, comme Pascal, la vérité de la religion sur la raison et l'autorité des Ecritures' (ii. 323); and the narrator, reassessing the loves of his youth, exclaims that 'l'abîme infranchissable que j'avais cru alors exister entre moi et un certain genre de petites filles aux cheveux dorés était aussi imaginaire que l'abîme de Pascal' (iv. 271). The revered arguments of the *Pensées* pertain at the level of the everyday, and vice versa. Proust's references to Pascal in effect make a moral argument about the nature of reading. Whereas Swann argues that the newspapers publish trivia, and would be advised to reprint 'les livres où il y a des choses essentielles', such as the *Pensées* (i. 25–6), the narrator concludes that the personal and contingent nature of reading is such that an advertisement for soap may be equally revealing:

> A partir d'un certain âge nos souvenirs sont tellement entre-croisés les uns sur les autres que la chose à laquelle on pense, le livre qu'on lit n'a presque plus d'importance. On a mis de soi-même partout, tout est fécond, tout est dangereux, et on peut faire d'aussi précieuses découvertes que dans les *Pensées* de Pascal dans une réclame pour un savon. (iv. 124)

It's not what you read, but the kind of reader you become, Proust's narrator seems to suggest; and this argument is key in his response to the *moralistes*.

Proust's reading of the *moralistes* is, then, somewhat dissimilar from that of his *NRF* promoters. In contrast to their reverential appropriation, he adopts a writerly approach to the moralistic discourse.[19] And subsequent criticism which follows Martin-Chauffier's lead seems to get no further than the Proust–*moraliste* connection, locating a stylistic paradox, but leaving it intact. Noémi Hepp, whose work most directly addresses this question, has suggested that the *moraliste* commentary may be the 'basis' of the novel, but is uncomfortable with this explanation: 'assertion paradoxale sans doute: quel rapport de la luxuriance et des chatoiements proustiens à la rigueur et à l'éclat de ceux dont nous prétendons le rapprocher?'[20] Already there is a contradiction between the notion of 'commentary', established after

[19] See Annie Barnes, 'Proust lecteur de Pascal', *Bulletin de la Société des amis de Marcel Proust*, 27 (1977), 392–409, which documents Proust's marginal notes on Pascal.

[20] Noémi Hepp, 'Le dix-septième siècle de Marcel Proust dans *La Recherche du temps perdu*', *Travaux de linguistique et de littérature*, 17/2 (1974), 139.

the (textual) event, and the maxims as foundation, prior to this 'event', and on which the narrative depends. Moreover, readings such as these seem to refer to the writing of *A la recherche*, to the process of composition. They imply that Proust is, to quote Barthes, 'un artisan penché sur l'établi du sens et choisissant les meilleures expressions du concept qu'il a antérieurement formé', that he began from a theoretical grid which was then expanded, illustrated, and 'novelized'.[21] Fraisse and Raimond, however, describe Proust's compositional method as a dialectic between theory, the maxims, and narrative, the 'romanesque':

> D'un côté, en nourrissant la partie romanesque d'épisodes nouveaux, Proust voit surgir de nouveaux articles théoriques, et chaque fois un feuillet ou une note vient grossir le dossier final; de l'autre, le théoricien a l'idée d'une belle conclusion répondant à un début d'histoire qui n'existe pas encore.[22]

Once the question of Proust's moralistic writing is formulated in this way—that is, as speculation about writing practice—it is better and more accurately addressed by genetic criticism. The work of Almuth Grésillon and Claudine Quémar, for example, goes some way towards addressing the place of maxims in the genesis of the text.[23] But to consider how the maxims work in *A la recherche*, rather than prior to it—that is, to pursue the notion that the text both reads and writes maxims—requires a different approach.

1.3 Writing La Bruyère and rewriting

The influence of seventeenth-century literature is striking in Proust's early writing. The development of his readings of the *moralistes*, and in particular of La Bruyère, illustrates the shift from a readerly to a writerly approach. Barthes's distinction between the readerly and the writerly is defined in *S/Z*: 'Ce qui peut être aujourd'hui écrit (ré-écrit): le scriptible. Pourquoi le scriptible est-il notre valeur? Parce que

[21] Barthes describes the compositional process expected of an 'auteur classique': 'que l'auteur conçoit d'abord le signifié (ou la généralité) et lui cherche ensuite, selon la fortune de son imagination, de "bons" signifiants, des exemples probants' (*S/Z* (Paris: Seuil, 1970), 179).

[22] Luc Fraisse and Michel Raimond, *Proust en toutes lettres* (Paris: Bordas, 1989), 23.

[23] See Claudine Quémar's article 'Autour de trois avant textes de l'"Ouverture" de *la Recherche*', *Bulletin d'informations proustiennes*, 3 (1976), 7–29. See also the essay collection *Proust à la lettre*, edited by Almuth Grésillon, Jean-Louis Lebrave, and Catherine Viollet (Tusson: Du Lérot, 1990).

l'enjeu du travail littéraire (de la littérature comme travail), c'est de faire du lecteur, non plus un consommateur, mais un producteur du texte.'[24] Barthes's own interest in the reading and writing of fragments—in his work on Michelet[25] and in the later *Fragments d'un discours amoureux*, for example, as well as in *S/Z* itself—makes him a frequent point of reference in this introductory and intertextual exposition of Proust's maxims. And it will be seen that the terms set up by Barthes's opposition are particularly well suited to a discussion of Proust's writing and reading of the *moralistes*.

A readerly approach is the starting-point of 'Fragments de comédie italienne', a section of Proust's first published book, *Les Plaisirs et les jours* (1896). The title, suggesting the grotesque masks and caricatures of the *commedia dell'arte*, already links the 'Fragments' to the theatre of seventeenth-century France—and what follows is in fact a pastiche of La Bruyère's *Caractères*.[26] The 'Fragments' are for the most part elaborated around a single line or *pointe*, which, in the style of La Bruyère, usually forms the conclusion of the sketch. A limited range of themes is covered, which may be broadly characterized as love, society, truth, and literature. The effect, typical of the *moralistes*, is that of demasking social strategies and motivations, revealing the paradox of situations, which again tend to be those favoured by the *moralistes*. The characters of each scenario have precious names—Fabrice, Cléanthe, Doris, Myrto. The modes of the 'Fragments' include the scenario, anecdote, *pensée*, and dialogue, all of which are used by La Bruyère. Narrative technique is also reminiscent of the *Caractères*—sometimes an introduction is given (fragment ii); often the fragment begins *in medias res* (i, iii); the impersonal *pensée* is used in v and parts of x to present paradoxes; fragment vii uses the technique of defamiliarization, 'si vous n'étiez pas du monde . . .'; while in viii the *moraliste* enters into dialogue with the character criticized. The *topos* of society as theatre and the use of *commedia dell'arte* figures in the final two

[24] Barthes, *S/Z*, 10.

[25] His early phenomenological criticism of Michelet's work (Roland Barthes, *Michelet par lui-même* (Paris: Seuil, 1954)), makes of 'Michelet's writing a series of spectacular fragments, associating the interest of writing not with continuity, development, structure—all understandable qualities of Michelet's work as a historian—but with the pleasure of textual fragments' (Jonathan Culler, *Barthes* (Glasgow: Fontana, 1983), 44).

[26] Proust, *Les Plaisirs et les jours*, ed. P. Clarac and Y. Sandre (Paris: Gallimard, 1971), 5–178. The introduction-dedication to this piece contains several allusions and references to seventeenth-century literature. Proust, for example, praises Robert de Montesquiou's style as 'cette éloquence sentencieuse et subtile, cet ordre rigoureux qui parfois chez lui rappellent le XVIIe siècle' (p. 5). Referring to his own situation as writer, he speaks of the 'grâce' of ill health, and cites *Phèdre* (p. 7).

fragments are typical of La Bruyère's satire of the court. These sketches in turn presage many episodes and concerns of *A la recherche*. The relationship between the various salons visited by the narrator is condensed in the second fragment: Marcel's reaction to Albertine's intellectual development (i); Swann and Charlus as potential but failed artists (viii); childhood memories and reading the book of the self (xi).

The fragmentary form and the maxim are also used in the section of *Les Plaisirs et les jours* entitled 'Les Regrets, rêveries couleur du temps'. Here lyrical passages on, for example, 'Tuileries', 'Versailles', or 'Promenade' (sections i–iii) are interspersed with passages of reflection—commentary on the nature of society, for example, or a critique of female dilettantism. The *topoi* of *A la recherche* are already suggested here in highly condensed form, as in section x, 'source des larmes qui sont dans les amours passées', which considers the interplay of reason and sentiment, and the opposition between love and indifference. Similarly condensed in section xii are the themes of death and inconstancy, 'Nous avons oublié ce matin la tragédie qui hier . . .', and in section xxi, the *topos* of death as an analogy for forgetting: 'L'être qui après nous avoir tant fait souffrir ne nous est plus rien, est-ce assez de dire, suivant l'expression populaire, qu'il est "mort pour nous?" . . . Il est plus que mort pour nous.'

'Les Regrets' argues that discontinuity is mimetic of the mind. If memory consists of a sequence of 'tableaux', representing the past 'comme une suite, coupée de lacunes, il est vrai, de petits tableaux pleins de vérité heureuse et de charme sur lesquels le temps a répandu sa tristesse douce et sa poésie' (p. 131), writing must translate these images into self-contained fragments: 'Les paroles dont j'ai perdu le sens, peut-être faudrait-il me les faire redire d'abord par toutes ces choses qui ont depuis si longtemps un chemin conduisant en moi, depuis bien des années délaissé, mais qu'on peut reprendre et qui, j'en ai la foi, n'est pas à jamais fermé' (p. 144).

Both sentiment and satire are expressed discontinuously in these early texts. The 'tableaux' of the 'Regrets' are fragmented by nostalgia, the 'Fragments de comédie italienne' are the *aperçus* of the *moraliste*; whereas the memories and *caractères* of *A la recherche* are the property of a desiring, self-justifying narrator, a narrator who both reads and writes maxims, and for whom writing is to be mimetic of a different kind of memory, one which is involuntary and continuous. As Genette notes: 'Chaque apparition de ses personnages, chaque "état" de sa société, chaque épisode de son récit pourrait faire la matière d'une page de Balzac ou de La Bruyère, mais tous ces éléments traditionnels sont emportés par une irresistible force d'érosion.'[27] The less stylized *caractères* of *A la recherche*, as just one of a range of techniques—*sententiae*, mythological references, exempla from the text or drawn from other literary sources—, are caught up in the expansive generalizing movement elaborated by the narrator.

When La Bruyère is next read within a *caractère* of the narrator's own, the preoccupation with continuity and discontinuity, the readerly and the writerly, is explicit:

'Les hommes souvent veulent aimer et ne sauraient y réussir, ils cherchent leur défaite sans pouvoir la rencontrer, et, si j'ose ainsi parler, ils sont contraints de demeurer libres.' (iv. 473)[28]

In this scenario, which is again part of the aesthetic theorizing of *Le Temps retrouvé*, the unsuccessful lover discovers this maxim of La Bruyère's, and is consoled by it. His reading is, according to the narrator's critique, based on unthinking identification, the appropriation of a rhetorical ornament: 'la belle pensée d'un maître . . . réduit [les hommes] tout de même à n'être que la pleine conscience d'un autre' (iv. 473). This lover's readerly approach makes him unlikely to 'maximize' on a soap advertisement.[29] Moreover, the narrator is able to perform his critique and assert his superiority by rewriting the maxim: 'il faudrait "être aimés" au lieu d'"aimer" ', he suggests parenthetically.

A similar scenario is already anticipated in Proust's essay 'Sur la lecture' (1905),[30] written on reading and translating Ruskin. Again Proust's reader figures as lover (p. 171), and Martin-Chauffier's review would have tempted this character who reads because he desires to cull truths. He is disappointed. Books are found not to contain truths, Pascalian reflections, or indeed 'l'univers et la destinée'. Instead, each represents just part of a library, one of a range of perspectives from the *Journal de modes illustré* to *La Géographie d'Eure-et-Loir* (p. 171). Proust goes on to argue that the skilful reader, unlike the reader of La Bruyère, will see truths not as collectable, 'une chose matérielle, déposée entre les feuillets des livres comme un miel tout préparé' (pp. 180–1), but as

[27] Gérard Genette, 'Proust Palimpseste', in *Figures I* (Paris: Seuil, 1966), 53.

[28] Jean de La Bruyère, 'Du cœur', in *Les Caractères*, ed. R. Garapon (Paris: Classiques Garnier, 1962), 139.

[29] I use 'maximize' in the sense of to formulate maxims on, while also retaining the common usage of 'to make as high or great as possible'—hence, 'maximize on': to draw the highest yield of maxims from a topic.

[30] Later entitled 'Journées de lecture', in *Contre Sainte-Beuve*, ed. P. Clarac and Y. Sandre (Paris: Gallimard, 1971), 160–94.

created by the interaction of reader and text: 'c'est là, en effet, un des grands et merveilleux caractères des beaux livres . . . que pour l'auteur ils pourraient s'appeler "Conclusions" et pour le lecteur "Incitations" ' (p. 176).

According to this reading practice, texts no longer offer up *sententiae* of a decorative eloquence ripe for appropriation. Rather than the reduction of a continuous text to a collection of ornamental truths, the reader is to expand even the continuous text, which now has the status of fragment: 'C'est une Vénus collective, dont on n'a qu'un membre mutilé si l'on s'en tient à la pensée de l'auteur, car elle ne se réalise complète que dans l'esprit de ses lecteurs' (iv. 150).[31] And this reading practice, as the latent violence of the phrase 'membre mutilé' suggests, will also serve to justify more negative and dubious forms of reading 'truth' as they are enacted in *A la recherche* once the subject is no longer metaphorically, but literally, a lover who reads people rather than books.[32]

Proust's concern with continuity and ideal interactive reading scenarios is shared by other writers whose discussion of poetics includes a consideration of sententiousness. The danger of discontinuity caused by excessive use of *sententiae* is noted, for example, in Quintilian's *Institutio Oratoria*.[33] Too many 'reflections' will, he argues,

[31] Note Montaigne's similar use of this figure (*Essais*, ed. A. Micha (Paris: Flammarion, 1979), iii. essai 5): 'Que Martial retrousse Vénus à sa poste, il n'arrive pas à la faire paroistre si entière. Celui que dict tout, il nous saoule et nous degouste, celuy qui craint à s'exprimer nous achemine à penser plus qu'il n'en y a.'

[32] Reading in such episodes is often replaced by different metaphors expressing the activity of interpretation. The narrator-lover's obsessive interpretation of Albertine is, for example, described in scientific rather than aesthetic terms: 'Albertine ne racontait jamais de faits pouvant lui faire du tort, mais d'autres qui ne pouvaient s'expliquer que par les premiers, la vérité étant plutôt un courant qui part de ce qu'on nous dit et qu'on capte, tout invisible qu'il soit, que la chose même qu'on nous a dite' (iii. 482–3). Here the metaphor of truth as an electric current which the narrator alone is able to see and whose origin he can identify, suggests isolation and mistrust rather than dialogue and creative collaboration. Similarly, when Marcel pays a call on Gilberte, the *maître d'hôtel*'s message that she is out is interpreted as unwittingly revealing: 'Ces paroles, de la sorte qui est la seule importante, involontaires, nous donnant la radiographie au moins sommaire de la réalité insoupçonnable que cacherait un discours étudié, prouvaient que dans l'entourage de Gilberte on avait l'impression que je lui étais importun' (i. 577).

[33] I paraphrase here Bennington's argument, 'Quintilian: standing out' (Quintilian and Lamy are both cited in this section), *Sententiousness and the Novel*, 44–5. Bennington argues that poetic treatises have not developed the synthetic approach which an understanding of the sententiousness of continuous prose demands. Rather, the generalizing sentence has been regarded as contained within, and therefore subordinate to, its prosaic container. Discussed according to this 'poetics of continuity', *sententiae* tend to become 'broken sentences', opposed to narrative and discursiveness (Francis Bacon, *The Advancement of Learning* (1605), cited ibid. 47).

cause the text to be read as a collection of fragments, rather than as a coherently argued whole. *Sententiae* are likened to a patch or stripe on a dress, ornamental additions to be used in moderation if they are to retain their decorative effect: 'A purple stripe appropriately applied lends brilliance to a dress, but a dress decorated with a quantity of patches can never be becoming to anybody.' Bernard Lamy, in *La Rhétorique, ou l'art de bien parler* (1675), adopts the same figure: 'Ces pensées détachées sont comme des pièces cousues et rapportées, qui étant d'une couleur différente du reste de l'étoffe, font une bizarrerie ridicule.' Again, *sententiae* are desirable for their concision and ingenuity, 'qui par un tour non commun excitent l'attention', for those very qualities which make them 'stand out', but which also render them a threat. *Sententiae* must, according to the rhetorical prescriptions of both Quintilian and Lamy, be 'extravagant' and 'artificial', yet used excessively, they threaten the continuity of the text. Accompanying these rhetorical considerations, we find a moral argument: writers who make too great a use of extravagant *sententiae* are not guided by the desire for truth but by 'amour-propre': they wish to dazzle their readers or listeners with formal brilliance, rather than persuade with coherent—in other words, continuous—argument.

The maxims of *A la recherche* are certainly abundant, but the effect is not one of discontinuity, for they do not aim to stand out in the spectacular sense envisaged by both Lamy and Quintilian. Such surface brilliance would, in any case, be undesirable given the Proustian theories of reading discussed above. Indeed, Lamy's moral argument bears a close resemblance to the Proustian critique of the appropriative readings of *sententiae*. Far from resembling a patch, the maxims of *A la recherche* are woven into the very fabric of the text. The syntax and structure of the maxim, so highly prized by the poetic treatise, as well as by renowned stylists such as Gracián and La Rochefoucauld, is often interrupted by metaphor and example; conversely, narrative sentences may be interrupted by the most brief and understated of maxims. It is this which makes the maxims of *A la recherche* difficult to extract; for, unlike the independent *sententiae* feared by Lamy and Quintilian, these sentences remain reflexive and provisional. An example of this is the tendency to reformulate—whether refining through subordinate clauses a maxim occupying a single sentence, or whether rewriting the initial maxim, producing a group of variations around a single point. The maxims of *A la recherche* display too an organic insistence, with narrative sentences almost imperceptibly turning into generalizing propositions, a move unthinkable for the composer of showy, outstanding *sententiae*. Nor are the maxims fiercely self-sufficient; they may collaborate with metaphors—those of medicine and sickness in particular—or with anecdotes and exempla: 'Je travaillerais auprès d'elle [Françoise], et presque comme elle . . . car, épinglant ici un feuillet supplémentaire, je bâtirais mon livre, je n'ose pas dire ambitieusement comme une cathédrale, mais tout simplement comme une robe' (iv. 610). In comparing his activity as writer to Françoise's work as seamstress, the narrator suggests that his art is a craft quite different from the artful ornamentation described by Lamy and Quintilian. Proust's 'patch' is no ornamental addition to the finished article, but plays an integral role in the construction of the fabric of the text.

Attempts to unpick *A la recherche* to a commonplace book of sorts reveal the extent to which Proust's patching was successful. While Ronald and Odette Cortie collect Proustian *topoi* for their *Marcel Proust on Life, Love and Letters* (1988), Justin O'Brien (*The Maxims of Marcel Proust* (1948)) describes his use of a 'scalpel' to extract maxims from *A la recherche*. In the light of Proust's analogy, whereby reading is the making complete of the broken Venus, O'Brien's metaphor is ironically appropriate. His technique involves the suppression of certain figures and even name-changes (Elstir becomes Manet and Renoir, while Vinteuil is turned into Debussy). He attempts to make the maxims clearer and more general, a process which involves some 'tidying' of syntax and structure. By cutting maxims loose from the 'restrictive' fabric of the novel, they are to become more representative of Proust as part of the 'belle époque'. O'Brien's compilation nears that of an anthology of misquotations, where the value of the Proustian hallmark is paramount. Moreover, compilations of this kind tend to adopt a thematic organization which conflicts with the purposeful lack of system favoured by most aphorists, and which is the natural result of aphorisms scattered throughout the novel. As Barthes indicates in his essay on La Rochefoucauld, reading a single maxim may be revelatory or 'éclatant'; reading a collection of such sentences as if they formed in themselves a continuous text is more likely to be 'étouffant', suppressing the reader's response, revealing instead a catalogue of the author's (or editor's) obsessions.[34]

[34] This is particularly striking in the case of La Rochefoucauld. The current Folio edition of the *Maximes* also includes the maxims of Mme de Sablé. De Sablé's *maximes* were first published in 1678 in this format. However, subsequent editions simply included her work under La Rochefoucauld's name. They did not appear separately until the 1870 edition,

A reductive and anthologizing reading, albeit to a lesser extent, is latent in the reading begun here of Proust and the *moralistes*, since this approach tends to view the maxims of *A la recherche* as if they were simply one genre set within another. The connections between the maxims of *A la recherche* and the fragmentary writings of the seventeenth-century *moralistes* are thematically and stylistically interesting. As a 'discours sur les passions', the maxims of *A la recherche* revisit the concerns and language of the *moralistes*, exploring the human condition through a specific, often physiological terminology and series of fictional experiments, in which the notion of the 'unconscious' or 'amour-propre' is fundamental.[35] Indeed, in connecting the seventeenth- and twentieth-century terms for the instinctive or non-rational,[36] Proust's claim (made in the drafts of *A la recherche*) that the only book worth writing would 'lift the veil of the unconscious on the laws of *amour-propre*' (iii. 1270) suggests an updating of the *moralistes*' project. As Anne-Marie Desfougères notes: 'cette zone cachée où se trament les combinaisons de l'imagination et de l'amour-propre, c'est l'inconscient dont Freud a étudié la formation, les contenus et la valeur dynamique.'[37]

More revealing in stylistic terms are the limitations which become apparent when making such connections, and to which Proust himself

published by Jouaust in the Cabinet du Bibliophile. As Lafond notes in his edition of the *Maximes* (Paris: Gallimard, 1976): 'Sur l'amitié, sur le paraître, sur la sagesse toute relative de l'homme, les conclusions sont pourtant les mêmes et plusieurs réflexions sont parallèles' (p. 304).

[35] As W. G. Moore argues in 'Scientific Method in the French Classical Writers', La Rochefoucauld's 'method of presentation and of argument is curiously parallel to the inductive methods of the scientist. His book is a questioning of the current notions of vice and virtue by means of accumulated observation' (*Literature and Science*, ed. L. A. Bisson (Oxford: Blackwell, 1955), 153). With the establishment in the seventeenth century of the experimental method (the theory–experiment dialectic), science first began to distinguish itself from other forms of knowledge. See A. R. Hall, 'Le XVIIème siècle et nous', in *Destins et enjeux du XVIIème siècle*, ed. Y.-M. Bercé (Paris: Presses Universitaires de France, 1985), 253–60; and J. Roger, 'Actualité de la science du XVIIème siècle', ibid. 261–70. Relations between the literary world and the world of the new science were very close in seventeenth-century Paris, as is illustrated by J. S. Spink, 'Form and Structure', in *Literature and Science*, ed. Bisson, 144–50; and Hugh M. Davidson, *Pascal and the Arts of the Mind* (Cambridge: Cambridge University Press, 1993).

[36] 'Tous les actes de notre entendement par lesquels nous pouvons parvenir à la connaissance des choses sans aucune crainte d'erreur; il n'y en a que deux: l'intuition et la déduction' (Descartes, *Œuvres et lettres*, ed. A. Bridoux (Paris: Gallimard, 1952), 43). Herbert de Ley, *The Movement of Thought* (Urbana, Ill.: University of Illinois Press, 1985) considers notions of reason and intuition in seventeenth-century French texts.

[37] Anne-Marie Desfougères, 'Des moralistes à la psychanalyse', in *Destins et enjeux*, ed. Bercé, 245.

draws attention, both in his essay on reading and in the allusions to and readings of the *moralistes* practised in *A la recherche* itself. For to read back and forth between the maxims of *A la recherche* and those of Pascal, La Bruyère, and La Rochefoucauld is to become aware again and again of the excessive nature of the former. To explore Proust's maxims only through the *moraliste* connection is to neglect the force and persistence of their variety. *A la recherche* performs what might be termed the workshop activity of the *moralistes*; for its maxims are always in the process of being formulated, of being desired in time—that is, the time of the narrator's desire. A model which maps the dynamics of this process and takes into account the full scope of the sententiousness of *A la recherche* is needed.

1.4 Concluding our reading of maxims

> Eine gute Sentenz ist zu hart für den Zahn der Zeit und wird von allen Jahrtausenden nicht aufgezehrt, obwohl sie jeder Zeit zur Nahrung dient: dadurch ist sie das große Paradoxa in der Literatur, das Unvergeßliche inmitten des Wechselnden, die Speise, welche immer geschätzt bleibt, wie das Salz, und niemals, wie selbst dieses, dumm wird.
>
> (A good aphorism is too hard for time's teeth and will not be consumed by the passing of thousands of years, although it serves every age as nourishment: and so it is literature's greatest paradox, unforgettable in the midst of all change, the dish which will always be prized, as salt is, but which never, as even salt does, becomes insipid.)
>
> Nietzsche, *Menschliches, Allzumenschliches*

What Proust identifies as a reading problem—the distinction between 'bad' readings of texts, involving their appropriation (or their rejection), and 'good' readings, in which texts are subject to expansion and personalization—is all the more acute when that text consists of maxims. This is a reading problem which, clearly, has something to say about Proust's desire—as a writer—to move from an aesthetic of discontinuity to one of continuity, but I want to step aside from these concerns to consider for a moment other possible models of reading and writing sententiousness. Roland Barthes's critique has thus far accompanied and illuminated this discussion of Proust as *moraliste*. Now I want to allow the two writers to diverge; to move away from

Proust's rather anxious prescriptions, and to review Barthes's arguments about *maximes*, about reading and writing, the continuous and discontinuous, in an attempt to develop a model for mapping sententiousness in *A la recherche*.

Lacking context, laying claim to the authority of the universal proposition, the maxim challenges the reader's response—at once tightly constructed, thick with meaning, it is also hollow, requiring readers to supplement its abstraction, to bring to it their particular experience, so providing a context and testing its generality. The maxim appears to thrive when it finds a reading community. This community may practise the appropriation or expansion of maxims: that is, to take up Barthes's distinction, it may favour a readerly or a writerly approach. Examples of the former include the valorization of the maxim as a vehicle of knowledge, the laws of a stable scientific community; or as a vehicle of religious dogma (biblical proverbs); or as an aesthetic ornament (the compilation of florilegia in sixteenth-century France, for example). All these practices can and have been reversed; the laws of the scientific community are also subject to interrogation, reinterpretation, or replacement. Nietzsche's *Also sprach Zarathustra* parodies and suggests an alternative to religious—in this case Christian—dogma, as indeed does the aphorism cited above. Similarly, the reading and writing of *maximes* by La Rochefoucauld and other *habitués* of the late seventeenth-century salons might be seen as an extension of the culling of 'beaux lieux',[38] but here the rewriting sets the rhetoric of the maxim against conventional morality.[39]

Barthes schematizes these reversible reading practices according to a distinction between doxal and paradoxal *sententiae*:

Doxa/paradoxa

Formations réactives: une doxa (une opinion courante) est posée, insupportable, pour m'en dégager, je postule un paradoxe, puis ce paradoxe s'empoisse, devient lui-même concrétion nouvelle, nouvelle doxa, et il me faut aller plus loin vers un nouveau paradoxe.[40]

[38] See Claudie Balavoine, 'Bouquets de fleurs et colliers de perles', in *Les Formes brèves de la prose et le discours discontinu*, ed. J. Lafond (Paris: Vrin, 1984), 51–71.

[39] 'Une lecture appelée à privilégier certains aspects discontinus du discours a conduit lentement à une écriture discontinue.' See Lafond, 'Les formes brèves de la littérature morale aux XVIe et XVIIe siècles', ibid. 101–22 for a detailed discussion of this shift in the reading and writing of sentences in sixteenth- and seventeenth-century France.

[40] Roland Barthes, *Roland Barthes par Roland Barthes* (Paris: Seuil, 1975), 75; and, in the same text, 'Méduse. La doxa, c'est l'opinion courante, le sens répété, comme si de rien n'était. C'est Méduse: elle pétrifie ceux qui la regardent. Cela veut dire qu'elle est évidente. Est-elle vue? Même pas: c'est une masse gélatineuse qui colle au fond de la rétine' (pp. 126–7). Other references to doxa include pp. 51, 73, 141–2.

Sententiae representative of the doxa express generally accepted truths, the truths which a community shares unquestioningly, and which operate according to an economy of general circulation. Theirs is the order of convention, clarity, morality, plausibility, certainty, and communal truth.[41] The doxal *sententiae* of the everyday figure as proverbs; and in science might be described as those laws commonly accepted in the practice of 'normal science'.[42] Yet the two orders are held together by a generative, reciprocal resistance. Paradox depends for its effect on a reaction against a body of received wisdom, yet is equally prone to itself becoming the common currency of a group of readers—to becoming, in effect, their doxa.

The paradoxal order, according to Barthes's definition, is characterized by its instability; it is individual, amoral, relativizing. The paradoxal *sententiae* of a literary text may exploit rhetoric to undermine the authority of the doxa, effectively setting up a new order of truth over plausibility; as, for example, La Rochefoucauld's analysis of the passions, which, in displaying the arbitrariness of language, questions and ultimately undermines moral conventions. However, even the paradoxical, individualistic sentences of the *moralistes* might be said to represent the doxa of their reading and writing community. In both literature and science, the doxal and paradoxal are difficult to keep apart: one may provoke or flow over into the other.

Common to these approaches is the notion that the maxim is open to two extremes of reading, and that these are extreme precisely because such sentences make excessive demands of the reader. The maxim, whether free-standing or as part of a continuous text, has an ambiguous authority. It draws attention to itself, appears self-contained, knowing, yet tends to be defined in opposition to a real or imaginary background of continuity. Maxims encourage both appropriative and heuristic readings.[43] If we look to a potential origin of the

[41] Bennington (*Sententiousness and the Novel*, 14) uses 'paradoxal' in the eighteenth-century sense, as defined by Diderot: 'Le paradoxe n'est donc qu'une proposition contraire à l'opinion commune.'

[42] I refer to 'normal science' here in the sense established by Thomas Kuhn in *The Structure of Scientific Revolutions*, 2nd edn (Chicago: University of Chicago Press, 1970) as the acceptance by a scientific community of certain stable paradigms which it then explores further and refines. Kuhn's mapping of the genesis of scientific law might be redescribed in Barthesian terms: during the 'pre-paradigmatic period', the previous laws of 'normal science' are undermined to such an extent that new—or 'paradoxal'—formulations must be found; certain of these new formulations will in turn gain acceptance by the scientific community and, in taking the place of its previously accepted laws, become doxal.

[43] Both critical opinion on Joubert's *Pensées* and the author's own reflections on his work point up these particular contradictory features. Blanchot, in his essay 'Joubert et l'espace',

genre, we find only a repetition of these ambiguities. Heraclitus (521–487 BC)—whose vision of eternal flux suggests the impossibility of attaining certain knowledge, promoting instead a kind of oracular wisdom—seems the most likely contender.[44] Only quotations, paraphrases, and reports remain of the original continuous text. After 1901, the standard arrangement of these hundred or so quotations was that established by Diels, who listed the fragments in alphabetical order, according to the author citing them.[45] Any arrangement according to subject-matter would have meant imposing a personal interpretation. Diels's edition calls attention to 'the aphoristic style of the fragments, to their resemblance to the sayings of the Seven Sages, and, with Nietzsche's *Zarathustra* in mind, Diels suggested that these sentences had originally been set down in a kind of notebook or philosophical journal, with no literary form or unity linking them to one another.'[46] Kahn's argument is that Heraclitus's contemporaries (Pindar and Aeschylus) provide better models than does Nietzsche for understanding the former's style; his arrangement is made with the assumption that these are fragments of a continuous and ordered discourse. 'I think we can best imagine the structure of Heraclitus' work on the analogy of the great choral odes, with their fluid but carefully articulated movement from image to aphorism, from myth to riddle to contemporary allusion.'[47] Heraclitus's style may give the impression that his was the first commonplace book, and, clearly, Diels's reading of the fragments as aphorisms was persuasive, but the proverbial mode is now known to have been only one of his many literary styles. What appears as an origin is in fact determined by a long history of reception (the citation and rewriting of Heraclitus's original text) and of reading trends (the privileging of aphorism by Diels, the speculative reconstruction of the continuous text by Kahn).[48] At the origin of the

describes Joubert placing a single maxim on a 'sea of white paper', to be read diagrammatically, acting as an emblem or hieroglyph 'où tout serait dit à la fois'. Yet, as Kinloch indicates, Joubert himself stresses the constant process of research, seeing creation as act rather than result, and the manuscripts—innumerable, often illegible pages crammed with maxims—bear witness to this. See D. P. Kinloch, *The Thought and Art of Joseph Joubert 1754–1824* (Oxford: Clarendon Press, 1990), 196–7.

[44] See Charles H. Kahn, *The Art and Thought of Heraclitus* (Cambridge: Cambridge University Press, 1979).

[45] *Herakleitos von Ephesos* (Berlin, 1901). For details see Kahn's introduction.

[46] Kahn, *Art and Thought of Heraclitus*, 6.

[47] Ibid. 7.

[48] Indeed, according to Kahn's reconstruction, the place of aphorism in Heraclitus's text resembles the digressive order of *A la recherche*. Heraclitus's experience of the emergence of the first recognizably scientific world-view in sixth-century Miletus ('the creation of a new

genre is a characteristic ambiguity which is dependent on reception. The publication of Proust's unfinished text itself exposes the vagaries of reception, with editors preferring a continuous or discontinuous aesthetic. Thierry Laget's edition of *La Fugitive* is more drawn to the moralistic qualities of Proust's writing than is the Pléiade's *Albertine disparue*, edited by Anne Chevalier; and Raffalli's introduction to Laget's edition, in which he remarks that 'la richesse de la matière [qui] rayonne à travers l'inachèvement même, comme il s'est trouvé pour les *Pensées* de Pascal', makes this preference clear.[49]

These antitheses could be used to identify both how maxims are read within the text and how we, as readers of the novel, respond to them. *A la recherche* presents maxims of what could be termed 'the Heraclitean order': the opening pages of 'Combray' could be reduced to the formula: 'the world is in a state of flux, to be fixed only by the desiring subject'. But present also are the 'truths' perceived by this desiring subject, the narrator, whether they be maxims about the nature of that desire or about its object: about society, for example, or homosexuality. From a sceptical basis, according to which generalizing is at worst an impossible activity and at best a kind of necessary therapy, the narrator establishes a body of Hippocratic laws[50] shared by various communities (the lovers, the homosexuals, the Guermantes . . .).[51]

For the reader, the striking maxims of *A la recherche* may not lend themselves to appropriation, but they do provide a set of commonplaces—the novel's doxa. These commonplaces take on a structural rather than a purely decorative value in helping readers find their way about the text. Certain *sententiae* might play a key structural role with-

paradigm of theoretical explanation, with the peculiar distinction that this world view is the first one to be recognizably scientific' (ibid. 16)) also bears a striking affinity to Proust's background of 'scientific revolution', as will be discussed later.

[49] Bernard Raffalli, *La Fugitive* (Paris: Laffont, 1987), 333.

[50] Hippocrates is also cited as a potential 'origin' of the free-standing maxim as genre: yet the Hippocratic treatise *On Regimen*, probably dating from the fifth century BC, shows a systematic attempt to imitate the enigmatic, antithetical style of Heraclitus's prose (Kahn, *The Art and Thought of Heraclitus*, 4).

[51] Barthes describes the therapeutic function of maxims: 'La maxime. Il rôde dans ce livre un ton d'aphorisme (nous, on, toujours). Or la maxime est compromise dans une idée essentialiste de la nature humaine, elle est liée à l'idéologie classique: c'est la plus arrogante (souvent la plus bête) des formes de langage. Pourquoi donc ne pas la rejeter? La raison en est, comme toujours, émotive: j'écris des maximes (ou j'en esquisse le mouvement) pour me rassurer: lorsqu'un trouble survient, je l'atténue en m'en remettant à une fixité qui me dépasse: "au fond, c'est toujours comme ça": et la maxime est née. La maxime est une sorte de phrase-nom, et nommer, c'est apaiser. Ceci est au reste encore une maxime: elle atténue ma peur de paraître déplacé en écrivant des maximes' (*Roland Barthes par Roland Barthes*, 181).

out ever being voiced—these are the text's laws, the maxims of love, habit, and jealousy. For such laws there is no *single* quotable instance, but many formulations whose underlying sense is none the less clear. In this case 'sententiousness becomes no longer so much a "type of sentence" as a force in texts, of which the type of examples remarked by anthologies are only the spectacular surface manifestations'.[52] But the most abundant *sententiae* of *A la recherche* are those which we have described as resisting appropriation, those tentative, speculative, fragmentary maxims whose characteristic is a forward-reachingness which desires to find the right formulation, to clinch the perfect maxim or law, and which begins to tell a story of its own.

This survey has taken us some way from the original point of comparison, the connection with the *moralistes*. Awareness that the maxims of *A la recherche* exceed the model of their seventeenth-century counterparts has led to a discussion of reading and writing practices, informed by Proust and Barthes. Both writers invoke oppositional pairs—doxal–paradoxal, *éclatant–étouffant*, continuous–discontinuous—to describe the textual dynamic of maxims, how they are written and read; but this movement is not always a dialectic. A different dynamic, represented by the undercurrent of legal terms and phrases (the key example being 'laying down the law'), has informed this exposition, and indicates the importance of the maxims as a power discourse. The narrator both inflicts and suffers under the force of a law which is by turns speculative and prescriptive. The question of the affective dynamic between the subject and sententiousness eludes the *moraliste* connection, but is addressed by another contemporary response to *A la recherche*.

1.5 Proust as scientist

> The mind of Proust lies open with the sympathy of a poet and the detachment of a scientist to everything that it has the power to feel. . . . It is as though there were two faces to every situation; one full in the light so that it can be described as accurately and examined as minutely as possible; the other half in shadow so that it can be described only in a moment of faith and vision by the use of metaphor. . . . And it is this double vision that makes the work of Proust to us in our generation so spherical, so comprehensive.
>
> Virginia Woolf, 'Phases of Fiction'

[52] Bennington, *Sententiousness and the Novel*, 62.

Woolf's reading in 'Phases of Fiction' is striking, because it notices the at-once-ness of Proust's prose. She identifies, but does not isolate, his maxims. Her interpretation acknowledges Proust as poet and as scientist in a gesture similar to that made by Barthes when he describes *A la recherche* as a 'tierce forme'. For Woolf and for many of her contemporaries ('in our generation') it was this very quality of 'double vision' which made *A la recherche* so compelling. Their reading permitted the full range of the Proustian sentence—from metaphor to moral or, indeed, scientific law. Moreover, Woolf's analogy, 'Proust the scientist',[53] suggests an alternative to the more conservative, literary 'Proust the *moraliste*' of Rivière and others.

The originality of Woolf's formulation lies in its synthetic approach to Proust as at once scientist and poet.[54] Other critics who use the metaphor are more concerned with defining what this science might be, and their analogy, 'Proust as scientist', informs two significantly differing interpretations. First, critics such as Rivière, who had originally promoted Proust as the inheritor of the classical *moraliste* tradition, focus on the 'truths', the 'psychological laws', supposedly uncovered in *A la recherche*: 'Les découvertes qu'il a faites dans l'esprit et dans le cœur humains seront considérées un jour comme aussi capitales et du même ordre que celle de Kepler en astronomie, de Claude Bernard en physiologie ou d'Auguste Comte dans l'interprétation des sciences.'[55]

Ramon Fernandez, one of the few critics who shares Woolf's sense of the synthetic potential of *A la recherche*—'Par son travail de romancier, de psychologue, de moraliste, il a jeté un pont entre la littérature d'expression et de connaissance'[56]—also suggested that

[53] Woolf's use of the adjective 'scientific' can be read simply as synonymous with 'analytic'. The use of science in her own writing, however, particularly that of the new physics in *The Waves* and of Darwin in *Between the Acts*, suggests that her opposition—the poet, the scientist—at once allows a striking characterization, but is also more complex than it at first appears, and that science may involve more than sententiousness. On Woolf and the new physics see Michael Whitworth, 'Physics and the Literary Community 1905–1939' (Oxford, unpub. D.Phil. thesis, submitted 1994); on Woolf and Darwin, Gillian Beer in *Arguing with the Past* (London: Routledge, 1989).

[54] Ernst-Robert Curtius describes the difficulty of analysing individual elements of *A la recherche*: 'On peut considérer à part dans son œuvre la psychologie, la poésie, la science, l'observation, l'émotion. Mais ce sera toujours procéder à un isolement artificiel et qui fausse la vérité. Tous ces éléments que l'analyse tâche de séparer forment chez lui non pas un mélange, pas même une fusion, mais l'épanouissement d'une expérience identique, primordiale, et indivise' ('Marcel Proust', *NRF*, 20 (1 Jan. 1923), 264).

[55] Jacques Rivière, Obituary notice of Proust, *NRF*, 19 (1 Dec. 1922), 641–2.

[56] Ramon Fernandez, 'Note sur l'esthétique de Proust', *NRF*, 31 (1 Aug. 1928), 274. Compare Edmund Jaloux's eulogy of *A la recherche* as an 'ideal' synthesis: 'Jamais œuvre

Proust himself took a literal view of the scientificity of his work. Proust, he argues, believed that art could literally make discoveries, could discern the laws of human psychology and behaviour:

[La croyance de Proust] la plus essentielle est que l'art, en retrouvant et en fixant, bref en exprimant les impressions concrètes de notre vie passée, nous permet, par un travail de comparaison, par une sorte d'algèbre de l'imagination, de connaître les lois générales qui constituent l'essence de l'être. . . . Autrement dit, l'artiste ferait, pour les sentiments et les actes de l'homme, ce que le savant fait pour les phénomènes physiques et naturels.[57]

The alternative to this literal approach reads Proust not so much for his wisdom, the results, or 'découvertes' as Rivière terms them, as for the text's enactment or even dramatization of the scientific imagination. This second approach is sensitive to the *dynamics* of analysis. Middleton Murry notes that 'though M. Proust is in a sense applying a theory to experience, he is doing so by the strikingly novel method of describing the process by which the theory was gradually and inevitably formed in the consciousness which applies it'.[58] The maxims of *A la recherche* are described as a 'poetry of analysis',[59] or, as Conrad suggests, an analysis pushed to the point of creativity:

One critic goes so far as to say that Proust's great art reaches the universal, and that in depicting his own past he reproduces for us the general experience of mankind. But I doubt it. . . . The important thing is that whereas before we had analysis allied to creative art, great in poetic conception, in observation, or in style, his is a creative art absolutely based on analysis.[60]

Benjamin Crémieux's characterization of the dynamics of analysis in *A la recherche* argues that Proust

Loin d'abstraire, de schématiser le résultat intellectuel auquel il aboutit, de l'exprimer sous forme générale d'aphorisme, il exige de la pensée qu'elle reste étroitement liée à la sensation qui lui a donné naissance. . . . Il entend nous faire

littéraire ne s'est approchée autant de la science; elle fait penser au beau mot prophétique de Claude Bernard: "Je suis persuadé qu'un jour viendra, où le physiologiste, le poète et le philosophe parleront la même langue et s'entendront tous" ' ('Sur la psychologie de Marcel Proust', *NRF*, 20 (1 Jan. 1923), 159).

[57] Fernandez, 'Note sur l'esthétique de Proust', 274.

[58] Middleton Murry, *Discoveries: Essays in Literary Criticism* (1922), cited in Leighton Hodson, *Marcel Proust, the Critical Heritage* (London: Routledge, 1989), 196.

[59] Albert Thibaudet, review of *La Prisonnière*, in *L'Europe Nouvelle*, 9 Feb. 1924, cited in Hodson, *Marcel Proust*, 265.

[60] Conrad, 'Proust as Creator' (1923), cited in Hodson, *Marcel Proust*, 253.

suivre tout le parcours que sa sensibilité et son intelligence ont suivi pour arriver au but.[61]

As the later volumes of *A la recherche* were published, Crémieux began to criticize its increasing number of passages of reflection and speculation; yet his critique still operates through the scientific metaphor. Reviewing *Albertine disparue*, he proposes that this volume is not the work of an experimental scientist, but the ideal reconstruction of a practised consultant: 'La reconstitution idéale, paléontologique (à la façon de Cuvier et de sa vertèbre) de ce que seraient cette douleur et les progrès de l'oubli chez un être idéalement doué pour éprouver.'[62] He notes the rehearsal of stereotypically Proustian themes: 'il s'agit de variations, de fugues psychologiques écrites avec une virtuosité, une maîtrise, on dirait presque une gratuité incomparables'. In the later volumes theory does indeed dominate, but with an urgency which puts in question Crémieux's notion of an 'ideal reconstruction'. Moreover, the metaphor used in his review predicts, and is also corrected by, a formulation which figures amongst the 'aesthetic laws' of *Le Temps retrouvé*, according to which the scientist is painfully implicated in a repeated experiment on the self: 'Certes nous sommes obligé de revivre notre souffrance particulière avec le courage du médecin qui recommence sur lui-même la dangereuse piqûre' (iv. 484). Although the Proustian commonplaces *are* revisited in these later Albertine texts, the perspective, as this metaphor suggests, has changed. No longer an objective spectator and formulator of laws, the narrator feels their force acutely—it is here that the affective relationship with the law is at its most evident—as will be discussed in Chapter 7.

The identification of the maxim with the laws of science made through both the literal and the dynamic readings is suggestive. The normative laws of *A la recherche* can, on the one hand, be read as such. The most lawlike of the maxims, those Proustian *topoi*, on lying, desire, jealousy, habit, which Rivière claims are truly discoveries about human nature, might be described according to a structural model as lying nearest the surface of the text, but also as deeply embedded in it. Repeatedly they seem to pull the *récit* down to the status of example;

[61] Benjamin Crémieux, 'Le sur-impressionisme de Proust', from *Vingtième siècle* (1924), in *Les Critiques de notre temps et Proust*, ed. J. Bersani (Paris: Garnier, 1971), 35.

[62] Crémieux, 'Nouveauté d'*Albertine disparue*', *NRF*, 26 (1 Feb. 1926), 217. Crémieux relates the analyses of *A la recherche* both to the laws of science and to the style of what he terms the 'classic' *moraliste* texts of Racine and Marivaux.

for these *topoi* are obsessively pursued and rehearsed. The particular may prove to be just another example of a Proustian norm. And yet these laws coexist with the speculative 'maximes en mouvement'. These maxims may announce themselves in sententious style, but their hypothetical nature soon becomes apparent, both in their syntax and in their interaction with other types of sentence. Such maxims are restless, seek reformulation. They may develop into an argument in their own right, so that the *récit* which provoked them is reduced to the status of example. They create sets of stylistic variations, in which alternatives are formed which have no apparent advantage over their predecessors. Alternative fictions are sketched out, then abandoned, as the narrator continues to formulate still more maxims, or, satisfied, returns to the *récit*. Maxims may even collaborate with metaphor, thus collapsing the standard maxim–metaphor opposition—and this opposition will be redescribed, as the collaboration of hypothesis and model, in Chapters 4 and 5. Analysing these 'maximes en mouvement' introduces a dimension absent from the readerly models of the previous section, notably the interaction of the particular and the general—what allows a maxim or law to gain general validity? Maxims may be speculative encounters with, or prescribe, the real in the world of *A la recherche*.[63] The text now gathers, now disperses, its pool of generality.

This kind of interaction can be seen in the discussion of Vinteuil's music in *A l'ombre* (i. 520). From this narrative 'event', Odette's performance of the Vinteuil sonata, the narrator opens a discussion of the reception of music and the function of memory in such reception. This leads to a reflection on the brevity of memory, which in turn yields a fictional example, almost a *caractère* in the style of La Bruyère: 'aussi brève que la mémoire d'un homme qui en dormant pense mille choses qu'il oublie aussitôt, ou d'un homme tombé à moitié en enfance qui ne se rappelle pas la minute d'après ce qu'on vient de lui dire'. Such 'examples' allow the development and often amplification of the argument. And in this case, once the argument (or 'series of reflections') is established, the *récit* is allowed to intrude, but with the

[63] See the entry 'loi', in Lalande's *Vocabulaire technique et critique de la philosophie*, 8th edn (Paris: Presses Universitaires de France, 1960): 'Formule générale (constative non impérative) telle qu'on puisse en déduire d'avance les faits d'un certain ordre . . . Le mot, en ce sens, se dit exclusivement: 1. des "lois de la nature" suggérées et vérifiées par l'expérience, et des lois de la vie mentale, considérées comme analogues aux lois naturelles: "La loi de l'habitude".' The ease with which this analogy can be made will be seen to be questioned by the syntax and structure of the 'laws' of *A la recherche*.

function now of specific illustrative example. The argument resumes, moving from the individual's reception of music to the recognition of the general public. The maxim 'Ce qu'on appelle la postérité, c'est la postérité de l'œuvre' (i. 522) is the central point of a series of reflections on this topic, into which 'real' examples—Beethoven, Hugo, Molière—are introduced. A set of maxims bearing on the question of the accuracy of prediction (i. 523) closes this passage of reflection, and the *récit* is taken up again. 'Mme Swann me joue la Sonate de Vinteuil', 'Les chefs-d'œuvre ne nous livrent pas d'emblée ce qu'ils ont de meilleur' (i. 1532), read the editors' unwittingly ironic résumés of the various reflections generated by this episode.

The notion of closure, however, is as questionable as the résumé cited above. An argument of sorts has been developed, but one without a beginning, middle, or, indeed, an end. The reflections stop—but they might equally have carried on, for we find no *point*, no resounding maxim, whose authority might conclude and resolve the discussion. And the various topics covered by this series of reflections are, of course, recognizably 'Proustian'. Aesthetic reception, memory, posterity have already been, and will be further, meditated on and generalized by the text, reaching a climax in the 'aesthetic laws' of *Le Temps retrouvé.*

When the force of the generalizing sentence, of its concision, *is* felt, maxims resurface, as subordinate or parenthetical, disturbing the flow of the sentence, sending the reader back to a body of ideas rehearsed more fully, or perhaps more obsessively, elsewhere. A pre-rehearsed memory is created for the reader. As Spitzer describes: 'C'est un mécanisme de langage qui requiert un cicerone (le spécialiste de stylistique) pour quiconque ne veut pas s'y égarer—un mécanisme de langage qui répond au mécanisme psychique auquel croit Proust.'[64]

One might take the example of a key term such as 'habitude', which is already introduced in the opening pages of 'Combray'. Here, as later, it is significant for its effect on perception. The narrator attempts to control his surroundings by using habit as a tool which will numb the painful sharpness of fresh perceptions and calm his anxiety. First introduced subordinately into the sentence, 'habitude' is then the subject of exclamation as it is established as a concept, and, of course, *topos* of the Proustian repertoire:

L'habitude! aménageuse habile mais bien lente et qui commence par laisser

[64] Leo Spitzer, 'La complexité dans l'appréhension du monde', in *Les Critiques de notre temps et Proust*, ed. J. Bersani (Paris: Garnier, 1971), 47.

souffrir notre esprit pendant des semaines dans une installation provisoire; mais que malgré tout il est bien heureux de trouver, car sans l'habitude et réduit à ses seuls moyens il serait impuissant à nous rendre un logis habitable. (i. 8)

Habit is a 'bon ange de la certitude'. And when, in this same episode, habit is painfully interrupted by the magic lantern's projections on to the bedroom walls, the term's initial definition is further refined by a medical analogy, 'l'influence anesthésiante de l'habitude' (i. 10). Habit is a key player too in the 'drame du coucher', where the narrator has 'l'habitude, le besoin' of his mother's goodnight kiss (i. 13). By virtue of the continued usage, refinement, and variation of this term throughout the text, it accumulates a certain force.[65] When, in *Albertine disparue*, the narrator first expresses the significance of Albertine's departure, it is through 'l'habitude', such is the weight of the maxims which have accrued to it: 'J'avais une telle habitude d'avoir Albertine auprès de moi, et je voyais soudain un nouveau visage de l'Habitude' (iv. 4). From the maxim (in the style of La Rochefoucauld), 'il est du reste à remarquer que la constance d'une habitude est d'ordinaire en rapport avec son absurdité' (iii. 553), it has become a 'pouvoir annihilateur', then a 'divinité redoutable' (iv. 4). As the narrator subsequently becomes accustomed to the loss of Albertine, so a tamer, more scholarly mode of habit is invoked: 'L'habitude d'associer la personne d'Albertine au sentiment qu'elle n'avait pas inspiré me faisait pourtant croire qu'il était spécial à elle, comme l'habitude donne à la simple association d'idées entre deux phénomènes, à ce que prétend une certaine école philosophique, la force, la nécessité illusoires d'une loi de causalité' (iv. 85).

The force of this *topos* is such that Beckett can 'maximize' on 'Proust's' own maxims. His parodic variations, which suggest a reversal of the traditional Proustian hierarchy, are worth quoting extensively:

The laws of memory are subject to the more general laws of habit. Habit is a compromise effected between the individual and his environment, or between the individual and his own organic eccentricities, the guarantee of a dull inviolability, the lightning-conductor of his existence. Habit is the ballast that chains the dog to his vomit. Breathing is habit. Life is habit.[66]

[65] As, for example, with reference to the narrator's perception of Albertine, 'Ces effigies gardées intactes dans la mémoire, quand on les retrouve, on s'étonne de leur dissemblance d'avec l'être qu'on connaît; on comprend quel travail de modelage accomplit quotidiennement l'habitude' (iii. 576). The 'habitudes' of living with Albertine are repeatedly the subject of reflection in *La Prisonnière* (iii. 594; 607).

[66] Samuel Beckett, *Proust* (New York: Grove Press, 1931), 7–8.

The use of such maxims is obsessive—but in Proust, unlike Beckett, these sentences work variously: they may be concise and prescriptive, but they may also open up a discursive, now playfully, now painfully, speculative space.

The laws of *A la recherche* are both hypothetical and normative. In terms of the reader's initiation into the text (which they effect), they can also be described as dogmatic. Key maxims, on topics such as jealousy or habit, promote a backwards/forwards reading, establishing for the reader a rehearsed and prompted memory. Sententiousness supplies the commonplace book of *A la recherche*, but also constitutes, as it were, the text's living skeleton. The maxims of *A la recherche* may be just as sinuous, and as abundant, as the highly imaged sentences which are termed 'Proustian'.

1.6 Poincaré's science and method

The literal and dynamic-metaphoric readings of Proust's science already point to the rich variety of law statements in *A la recherche*, the co-presence of the hypothetical and the normative which we have read in the above passages. The model which has begun to emerge from the notion of 'Proust as scientist' maps cognition in the text, it also exposes the power structures of knowledge, and explores the subject's affective relationship with these. But can this model be fine-tuned by taking into account the conceptualizations of similar questions by philosophers and scientists contemporary with Proust?

The question 'How does science view sententiousness?' may seem anachronistic, all the more since the current work of leading exponents in the rhetoric of science is often felt to be suspect, even reprehensible.[67] Yet 1908 saw the publication of *Science et méthode*, in which the philosopher and mathematician Henri Poincaré describes and

[67] Alan G. Gross's *The Rhetoric of Science* was first published in 1990. The recent second edition (Cambridge, Mass.: Harvard University Press, 1996) includes a defensive preface justifying the style of the book, and claiming that what was needed at the time of its first publication was 'not a monograph, but a manifesto' (p. viii). Philosophers of science too have attempted to reconceptualize the monolithic notion of 'scientific law'. As Norwood Russell Hanson (*Patterns of Discovery* (Cambridge: Cambridge University Press, 1958)) argues, there is no single 'law of inertia': 'the first law sentence can express as many things named "The Law of Inertia" as there are different uses to which the sentence can be put . . . law sentences are used sometimes to express contingent propositions, sometimes rules, recommendations, prescriptions, regulations, conventions, sometimes a priori propositions (where a falsifying instance is unthinkable or psychologically inconceivable), and sometimes formally analytic statements (whose denials are self contradictory)' (p. 98).

analyses the function and rhetoric of scientific law.[68] Poincaré's text is unusual for its direct focus on the process of scientific work and on the scientific imagination, where most popular scientific writers tend to describe the latest and more spectacular advances of the field, or to consider how these results might impact on society.

Science et méthode can in part be understood as a response to the climate of scientific discovery in which Poincaré himself was working.[69] Physics and mathematics were the site of science's most spectacular advances: the 'new physics', the new scientific power discourse.[70] Yet, paradoxically, these advances also undermined science's philosophical basis, problematizing, for example, the notion of progress. Maxims from ancient philosophy regained scientific currency as modern physics was perceived as 'in some way extremely near to the doctrines of Heraclitus. If we replace the word "fire" [for Heraclitus the basic element] by the word "energy", we can almost repeat his statements [about the dynamic nature of reality] word for word from our modern point of view.'[71] The concept of scientific law itself needed rethinking as Heisenberg's comparison between legal philosophy and science's powers of legislation proposes:

[68] Henri Poincaré (1865–1912) was both a mathematician and a philosopher of science. His work and that of fellow 'conventionalists' provided 'the foundation for the mathematical shape of much of the new twentieth-century physics of relativity and the quanta' (Jerzy Giedymin, *Science and Convention* (Oxford: Pergamon, 1982), p. vii).

[69] In physics, the widely accepted paradigm of normal investigation, developed by Newton, no longer provided an adequate explanation, and Maxwell's theory, although Newtonian in origin, had precipitated a crisis of explanation. The eventual shift from Newtonian to Einsteinian mechanics represents not only a 'displacement of the conceptual network through which scientists view the world', but, more widely, a shift from the materialistic and deterministic attitude derived from Newton to the attitudes of relativity and quantum mechanics. See Kuhn, *Structure of Scientific Revolutions*, 102 and 66–76. Richard Sheppard's 'The Problematics of European Modernism', in *Theorizing Modernism: Essays in Critical Theory*, ed. S. Giles (London: Routledge, 1993), 1–51, gives an excellent account of the scientific revolution and its relations with literary modernism.

[70] Conversely, in the field of biology, we find a 'power vacuum' created by Darwin's theory of evolution. This theory had been seen as a classic example of scientific method, the ideal model of investigation, and between the 1860s and the 1880s studies in morphology had sought to establish the evolutionary relationships between species and members of species. By the end of the nineteenth century, however, biologists were turning away from this approach and posing instead a new set of questions. These questions involved experimental embryology and, through plant breeding, the theory of mutation in evolution. Darwin's theory had not been displaced as such, but in providing a schema so general, it allowed and, indeed, begged refinement, and reinterpretation. Turn-of-the-century Darwinian modes are described in Henri Bergson, *L'Évolution créatrice* (1st pub. 1907, Paris: Presses Universitaires de France, 1994). For a historical survey see Ernst Mayr, *The Growth of Biological Thought* (Cambridge, Mass.: Belknap Press, 1982).

[71] Cited in Sheppard, 'Problematics of European Modernism', 15.

Many legal philosophies assume that while Law always exists, each new case generally involves a new discovery of law, and that the written law can be relevant only to limited realms of life and that it cannot be binding for ever. The exact sciences also start from the assumption that in the end it will always be possible to understand nature, even in every new field of experience, but that we may make no a priori assumption about the meaning of the word 'understand'.[72]

Scientific laws, which had been accepted as universal truths, now seemed to be conventional; and problems and disputes in the history of science which had appeared substantive and empirical were seen to result 'from the existence of observationally equivalent theories based on different conventions'.[73] Scientists recognized that 'the new mathematical formulae no longer describe nature itself but our knowledge of nature', yet the *aim* of science remained 'that same great framework of natural laws'.[74]

Contemporaneous with the developments of the new physics was a proliferation of the fields of enquiry termed 'scientific', to encompass much science and pseudo-science on the subject of 'man', and in particular his sexuality.[75] This 'science of man' provided material which was borrowed by literary texts, and, curiously, the reverse was also true. This two-way exchange resulted, literally, in a self-perpetuating fiction, as will be discussed later.

The power of science to lay down the law extended from the everyday to the limit cases of human 'nature', and from the experiential everyday, to intangible, even unimaginable meta-worlds. Equally, what was meant by scientific law had to be re-evaluated.

Poincaré's texts aim to take account of what he saw as the necessarily conventional nature of the laws of science, while resisting the

[72] Werner Heisenberg, *The Physicist's Conception of Nature*, trans. A. J. Pomerans (1st pub. 1955, London: Hutchinson, 1958), 27–8.

[73] 'The result of the conviction widespread at the time among mathematicians and philosophers, that the discovery of non-Euclidean geometries, strengthened later by metageometrical results as well as by research into the origin and functioning of space perception in man and animals emanating from the theory of evolution, physiology, and the psychology of perception, made the orthodox Kantian view of space and geometry untenable' (Giedymin, *Science and Convention*, 2).

[74] Heisenberg, *Physicist's Conception of Nature*, 25–6.

[75] See Christopher Robinson, *Scandal in the Ink* (London: Cassell, 1995); Jonathan Dollimore, *Sexual Dissidence* (Oxford: Clarendon Press, 1991), Julius Edwin Rivers, *Proust and the Art of Love* (New York: Columbia University Press, 1980), and also his article 'The Myth and Science of Homosexuality in *A la recherche*', in *Homosexualities and French Literature*, ed. G. Stambolian and E. Marks (Ithaca, NY: Cornell University Press, 1979). Lilian Faderman, *Surpassing the Love of Men* (New York: Women's Press, 1981) and Bram Dijkstra, *Idols of Perversity* (New York: Oxford University Press, 1986) consider specifically the science of 'woman'.

nominalist extremes to which such a view could be taken: namely, the belief in the absolute conventionality of scientific law. This reflection on the nature and justification of the laws of science was to preoccupy Poincaré throughout his career: his last publication, *Dernières pensées*, begins with a consideration of the evolution of laws. The earlier *Science et méthode* focuses on the variety of scientific law, and on the strategies and apparatus which may be used to establish it. Although dealing exclusively with developments in mathematics and physics, Poincaré's reflection necessarily involves speculation about cognitive process, speculation which in turn derives from biology and from the new 'science of man'.

Poincaré's four principal philosophical-cum-popular texts, *La Science et l'hypothèse* (1902), *La Valeur de la science* (1905), *Science et méthode* (1908), and *Dernières pensées* (1913), are articulated in response to this specific context of debate. Yet they also address timeless philosophical and scientific questions with great clarity and eloquence, and enjoyed a considerable general readership. Poincaré is the only contemporary scientist referred to in *A la recherche*. As Saint-Loup reminds the narrator, 'rappelle-toi le grand mathématicien Poincaré, il n'est pas sûr que les mathématiques soient rigoureusement exactes' (ii. 414). Writing in 1922 for the *NRF*, Camille Vettard suggested a comparison between Proust and Poincaré:

> M. Hadamard a dit un jour . . . que 'les idées de Henri Poincaré se présentaient si *naturellement* qu'on avait peine à comprendre qu'elles n'eussent pas germé plus tôt dans l'esprit des hommes'. Ce n'est pas, je l'espère, ma faute, si ayant lu Proust et Poincaré, je ressens à la lecture de l'un comme de l'autre cette impression de naturel.[76]

Both Proust and Poincaré claim a creative impulse common to the artist and scientist. In *La Valeur de la science*, Poincaré describes both the capacity of mathematics to help the philosopher to 'approfondir les notions de nombre, d'espace, de temps' and the aesthetic enjoyment—'des jouissances analogues à celles que donnent la peinture et la musique'—which mathematicians derive from their work (p. 139). Poincaré is fascinated by the 'mécanisme psychologique de l'invention',[77] regardless of whether the 'savant à l'œuvre' is working in the arts or the sciences, and in the mental landscape of *Science et méthode*, as of *A la recherche*, laws come into being under the force of the unconscious, their translation involving questions of form and rhetoric.

[76] Camille Vettard, 'Correspondance: Proust et Einstein', *NRF*, 19 (1 Aug. 1922), 250.
[77] Henri Poincaré, *Science et méthode* (1st pub. 1908, Paris: Flammarion, 1920), 2.

Science et méthode opens with an accessible and eloquent account of scientific law. Poincaré contrasts the abundance of nature, the countless 'petits faits' which are potentially available to the scientist for investigation, with the paucity of data he is able to uncover and work with: 'pendant que le savant découvre un fait, il s'en produit des milliards de milliards dans un millimètre cube de son corps'.[78] Yet this apparently chaotic abundance is, Poincaré argues, shot through with regularities. These are nature's 'analogies intimes', and the scientist acts, in effect, as their translator: 'La meilleure expression de cette harmonie, c'est la Loi; la Loi est une des conquêtes les plus récentes de l'esprit humain.'[79] While the argument concludes with the notion of law as a 'conquest', it is worth noting that this is not the stereotypical scientific conquest of nature. Rather, a psychological advantage has been won: the ability to formulate law is 'une des conquêtes les plus récentes de l'esprit humain'. Moreover, the lexical drift of the argument, from 'regularity' to 'analogy' to 'harmony' to 'law', suggests a new, more tentative relationship between the scientist and the natural world. This is no Baconian science, seeking 'by its "virile" power . . . to bind Nature to man's service and make her his slave',[80] but a science which requires sensitive and acute perception and translation of Nature's aesthetic qualities. Invoking aesthetics makes the scientist's work seem a good deal more subjective, a matter of taste even—and it is to address this question that Poincaré draws speculative arguments from evolutionary and psychological theory. This speculation will be considered in detail in the final chapter; for the moment I want to focus instead on the method and dynamics of aesthetic-scientific law.

Economy, Poincaré proposes, as well as aesthetics, must inform scientific method. The economy of scientific thought demands that the scientist, like the historian, operate selectively. If the scientist's choice is to encompass the abundance of nature, it must be that of the most general law, general laws in turn constituting the building-blocks of science. Yet this generality may be established in a number of

[78] Ibid. 9. Subsequent page references refer to *Science et méthode* unless otherwise indicated.

[79] Poincaré, *La Valeur de la science* (1st pub. 1905, Paris: Flammarion, 1914), 7. Poincaré also stresses, however, that these analogies are not crudely sensual, but are 'véritables, profondes' and must be divined by reason. In this the mathematician's work is similar to that of the artist (p. 146).

[80] Evelyn Fox Keller, *Reflections on Gender and Science* (New Haven: Yale University Press, 1985), 7.

different ways, and the general law which results cannot be considered absolute in any straightforward sense. A law might be derived simply from observable frequency, from the noting of repetition. But the limit areas of scientific knowledge may also be used to establish 'le fait simple', since the infinitely large and the infinitely small often have the effect of reducing natural abundance to simplicity and similarity. The legal—that is, the permitted—techniques for establishing laws are various. The law may stem from the everyday, from the directly accessible, or from meta-worlds, inaccessible to the senses and even to the imagination.

Laws which are variously established may conflict. The paradox(ic)al discoveries of the new physics, such as relativity, or four-dimensional space, encounter resistance in what might be termed the scientific laws of the everyday. For the latter, Poincaré argues, both appeal to our physical experience of the world and are rooted in our biological inheritance, so constituting a powerful body of established communal truths:

> Une association nous paraîtra d'autant plus indestructible qu'elle sera plus ancienne. Mais ces associations ne sont pas, pour la plupart, des conquêtes de l'individu, puisqu'on en voit la trace chez l'enfant qui vient de naître; ce sont des conquêtes de la race. La sélection naturelle a dû amener ces conquêtes d'autant plus vite qu'elles étaient plus nécessaires. (p. 107)

Poincaré draws a stark comparison between the pragmatic origins of science, when man's survival depended on the explanations he found for his experience of the world, and its modern aestheticized counterpart. Modern science is motivated by the desire to find similarities of pure form—'différentes par la matière, elles se rapprochent par la forme, par l'ordre de leurs parties' (p. 14). This evolutionary sketch of scientific law suggests that science has broken free of its original pragmatic constraints (at least in the field of physics), and has styled itself as science for science's sake, the primary motivation, methodology, and justification being aesthetic.

But this is not simply a promotion of aesthetics over pragmatics; Poincaré's argument is also the declaration of a new aesthetic, outlining a scientific manifesto. *Science et méthode* contrasts two orders of natural beauty: a beauty perceived by the senses and related to the profusion and diversity of nature and a beauty which is perceived by the intellect alone and is related to form and structure:

> Cette beauté plus intime, qui vient de l'ordre harmonieux des parties, et qu'une

intelligence pure peut saisir. C'est elle qui donne un corps, un squelette pour ainsi dire aux chatoyantes apparences, qui flattent nos sens, et sans ce support, la beauté de ces rêves fugitifs ne serait qu'imparfaite parce qu'elle serait indécise et toujours fuyante. (p. 15)

The language used by Poincaré here to describe the aesthetics of scientific law already sounds Proustian. The terms 'fugitifs' and 'fuyante', in particular, recall the 'êtres de fuite' (iii. 599–601) whose pursuit generates both the extended metaphors of *A l'ombre* and the skeletal laws of jealousy and desire which, in the later Albertine texts, become increasingly prominent. But to describe this development as a shift across the span of *A la recherche* from lyricism to law is too simplistic. Poincaré's laws are both 'un corps' and 'un squelette'. Proust's laws appear to serve as a skeletal frame, but often, rather than simply supporting the body of the text, the *récit*, or metaphor, they are dynamic. Maxims interact, are fleshed out by the narrator, or reformulated. Occasionally they generate an experiment in miniature, a fiction styled in the manner of the *Caractères* of La Bruyère. They seem to push towards the perfect law, the generalization whose order will encompass all other such statements,[81] and in such passages, the *moralité* becomes the *récit*—that is, the story of these reflections. When the narrator desires to pursue both fiction and speculation, the text is at once mobile and various; his desire to formulate laws implies the opposite tendency, a paring down. If the law becomes too dominant, if its formulation is too true, then a reflex—often unannounced or awkward—sends the text back to the *récit*.

For Poincaré, the concept of the ideal formulation of law checks the possible multiplication of theories. The scientist is looking for an 'analogie profonde, mais cachée' (p. 22); the law is termed 'l'âme du fait'. The *elegance* of the successful formulation allows a glimpse of both resemblance and difference; its beauty results from 'je ne sais quelle adaptation entre la solution que l'on vient de découvrir et les besoins de notre esprit' (p. 26). Again, aesthetics introduces an element—a very necessary element—of subjectivity. The solution is elegant

[81] Barthes's essay on La Rochefoucauld, also using the metaphor of the skeleton, describes this tendency of the *maximes* towards an irreducible ideal law: 'il y a dans cet édifice *profond* un vertige du néant; descendant de palier en palier . . . on n'atteint jamais le fond de l'homme, on ne peut jamais en donner une définition dernière, qui soit irréductible; quand l'ultime passion a été désignée, cette passion elle-même s'évanouit . . . la maxime est une voie infinie de déception; l'homme n'est plus qu'un squelette de passions, et ce squelette lui-même n'est peut-être que le fantasme d'un rien' ('La Rochefoucauld: "Réflexions ou Sentences et Maximes"', in *Le Degré zéro de l'écriture* (Paris: Seuil, 1972), 84).

because it at once solves the problem and is intellectually satisfying. Poincaré's phrase 'je ne sais quelle adaption' suggests the mysterious nature of this harmonious connection between the material and the intellectual world.

Such an extreme concern with 'l'harmonie des diverses parties, leur symétrie, leur heureux balancement' (p. 25) recalls the preoccupations of particularly formalist aphorists such as Gracián and La Rochefoucauld, whose priority is what Barthes terms 'cet ordre verbal, fort archaïque, qui règle le dessin de la maxime'.[82] Poincaré describes the effect of this structure as heuristic: the law may cause the unexpected and creative juxtaposition of certain elements; the simplicity of the formulation may contrast with the complexity of the original problem, so provoking further thought.[83] The resultant movement is a narrowing to a point of stasis (the maxim or law is formed), followed by a widening as the law is applied and tested, leading to new formulations.

Once laws have been rigorously established, they may become concise, repeatable *sous-entendus*, thereby achieving science's aim of concentrating 'beaucoup d'expérience et beaucoup de pensée sous un faible volume, et c'est pourquoi un petit livre de physique contient tant d'expériences passées et mille fois plus d'expériences possibles dont on sait d'avance le résultat' (p. 15). This sense of the predictable, of a reaching out towards both past and present, extending from these nodes of truth which are the scientific laws, also suggests an analogy for the structure and dynamic of generalization in *A la recherche*. The text's maxims articulate a wealth of material. Fundamental laws are laid down in the opening passages of the novel; these are the novel's repeatable *sous-entendus*, or commonplaces. Their application or demonstration—but also their variation—extends to past, present, and future experience. The analysis of 'habitude' above is an example of this pattern. Another example is the classic demonstration of the laws of jealousy and desire provided by Swann's story. In the following quotation, Charlus's story is seen as a 'limit case' of these same laws. The baron, who has fallen in love with Aimé, writes a letter which is

A cause de l'amour antisocial qui était celui de M. de Charlus, un exemple plus frappant de la force insensible et puissante qu'ont ces courants de la passion . . . Sans doute l'amour d'un homme normal peut aussi, quand l'amoureux par l'invention successive de ses désirs, de ses regrets, de ses déceptions, de ses

[82] Barthes, *Le Degré zéro de l'écriture*, 70.

[83] See ch. 2 of *Science et méthode*, 'L'Avenir des mathématiques'.

projets, construit tout un roman sur une femme qu'il ne connaît pas, permettre de mesurer un assez notable écartement de deux branches de compas. (iii. 382)

Charlus's experience as lover here allows him to be yoked back into the repertoire of maxims on desire and into the community of lovers. His homosexuality means only that he constitutes a more striking example of the law, the law here being the disparity between reality and the passionate imaginings of the lover. (Elsewhere the laws of homosexuality are so formulated as to distinguish this group.) The subsequent comparison with heterosexual desire, 'l'amour d'un homme normal', in turn connects with the later aesthetic maxims of *Le Temps retrouvé.* In this passage, then, the maxims have a powerful corroborative and unifying effect; elsewhere the exception may disprove the rule: 'Un seul petit fait, s'il est bien choisi, ne suffit-il pas à l'expérimentateur pour décider d'une loi générale qui fera connaître la vérité sur des milliers de faits analogues' (iv. 95). This is a classic example of the frailty of the maxim in *A la recherche.* An unreliable eyewitness report provides the one 'petit fait' capable of cutting through the multiple layers and many pages of sophisticated analysis and speculation preceding it. The reader is led along these Proustian paths of hypothesis, persuaded to follow the twists and turns of generalization, but equally made aware of their shortcomings, of their frailty in the face of the slightest piece of empirical evidence. This is a central paradox of the narrator's now magisterial, now speculative-desirous, now needy relationship with the sententious discourse. Both the regulative and speculative styles of maximizing have a cumulative, knock-on effect, by which further *moraliste* style or self-referential case-studies are provoked. Yet, equally, the fragility of these maxims, of their tentative relationship with the real, is exposed.

Poincaré's schematization suggests that the scientist's art lies in articulating this tension between the singular and the general, between abundance and parsimony. In this respect, the formulation of the law is of prime importance, condensing the abundance of nature, containing its own potential 'fécondité' for further theory and experiment. A profusion of laws, demonstrations, and explanations may threaten mathematical elegance. Yet, under the aesthetic mandate of contemporary science, sterility seems to be Poincaré's principal fear for the law—fear of the sterility which the too perfect law of specialization may bring. For the simplicity of scientific law to be meaningful, it has to relate to a parallel order of complexity and abundance.[84] 'Rapprochements inattendus' are the key to advancing knowledge:

> Les grands progrès du passé se sont produits lorsque deux de ces sciences se sont rapprochées, lorsqu'on a pris conscience de la similitude de leur forme, malgré la dissemblance de leur matière, lorsqu'elles se sont modelées l'une sur l'autre, de telle façon que chacune d'elles pût profiter des conquêtes de l'autre. (p. 35)

Poincaré's own scientific career was exemplary in this respect. In 1905 he held simultaneously the posts of Professor of Mathematical Physics, of Astronomy, and of Celestial Mechanics at the University of Paris. Yet he was aware of, and warned against, the tendency towards specialization in the face of the increasing complexity of modern science: 'A mesure que la science se développe, il devient plus difficile de l'embrasser tout entière; alors on cherche à la couper en morceaux, à se contenter de l'un de ces morceaux: en un mot, à se spécialiser. Si l'on continuait dans ce sens, ce serait un obstacle fâcheux aux progrès de la Science.'[85] The speed and diversification of modern science meant that it was increasingly difficult to sustain proficiency in more than one area. What had become problematic for the formulation of scientific law was not so much the abundance of nature as the abundance of science itself: 'Nos richesses ne tarderaient pas à devenir encombrantes et leur accumulation produirait un fatras aussi impénétrable que l'était pour l'ignorant la vérité inconnue' (p. 20).

Reading *Science et méthode*, a comparison between Proust and Poincaré emerges which is peculiarly pertinent to formal questions: the process of formulating laws, the dialectic between abundance and concision, between law and nature. Poincaré characterizes scientific law not as absolute, but as dependent on the period of history in which it is formulated, the use to which it is put—heuristic or pragmatic—and the method by which it is established. Throughout his argument, aesthetics is key in both the methodology and the justification of contemporary science. Poincaré wants his metaphor, the aesthetics of science, to signify an impersonal, formal rigour. Yet the comparison at once asserts a new scientific certainty, and also admits uncertainties of a different kind. Primarily, aesthetics raises the question of subjec-

[84] 'In the report on the Bolyai Prize of the Hungarian Academy of Sciences (awarded in 1905), Poincaré was described as "incontestably the foremost and most powerful researcher of the present time in the domain of mathematics and mathematical physics"' (Gerald Holton, *Thematic Origins of Scientific Thought*, rev. edn (Cambridge, Mass.: Harvard University Press, 1988), 202–3).

[85] Poincaré, *Science et méthode*, 34–5.

tivity, the scientist's implication in his work. If aesthetics sets the new standard, who is to arbitrate in matters of aesthetic-scientific taste?

Poincaré's discussion of scientific law, then, provides a model for reading the variety of law statements in *A la recherche*. First, it allows a formal—that is, a structural—analysis. Secondly, Poincaré's recognition of the insufficiency of a purely formal approach allows *Science et méthode* a psychological and historical take on scientific law which addresses those questions which have troubled the various readings of maxims explored earlier in the chapter: namely, the recognition of the narrator's affective relationship with the laws of the text.

Grave incertitude, toutes les fois que l'esprit se sent dépassé par lui-même; quand lui, le chercheur, est tout ensemble le pays obscur où il doit chercher et où tout son bagage ne lui sera de rien. Chercher? pas seulement: créer. Il est en face de quelque chose qui n'est pas encore et que seul il peut réaliser, puis faire entrer dans sa lumière. (i. 45)

The narrator's recognition of the self as both subject and object of science echoes Poincaré's belief that science needs to examine the conditions of its own production: 'D'une part, la science mathématique doit réfléchir sur elle-même et cela est utile, parce que réfléchir sur elle-même, c'est réfléchir sur l'esprit humain qui l'a créée' (p. 31). The extent to which Proust's and Poincaré's epistemological reflections on the nature of creativity overlap or resonate is largely due to the belief of leading scientists at this time that for science to become self-reflexive could only benefit the discipline (and indeed benefit further knowledge in other areas, notably psychology). These questions will be considered in more detail in the final chapter.

'Proust's science' seen through 'Poincaré's science' is no longer simply a body of laws, but an imaginative and speculative process—the *desire* to cast experiments, to hypothesize and model, the *need* to formulate and to justify the formulation of laws—which underlies creativity in both art and science.[86] For the metaphoric support system of *Science et méthode* suggests an openness to literature which, as the next chapter explores, is the mirror image of Proust's own metaphoric take on science.

[86] 'Once Proust's fictional enactment of the problems of knowledge in these inner volumes has been fully examined and pondered, his attitudes to the scientific or analytic intelligence may perhaps finally be credited with their full discriminateness and complexity' (Bowie, *Freud, Proust, and Lacan*, 70).

2

CORRESPONDENCE BETWEEN ART AND SCIENCE

> Tout ce qui peut aider à découvrir des lois, à projeter de la lumière sur l'inconnu, à faire connaître plus profondément la vie, est également valable.
>
> Proust, *Correspondance*

> La vérité, même littéraire, n'est pas le fruit du hasard . . . Je crois que la vérité (littéraire) se découvre à chaque fois, comme une *loi* physique. On la trouve ou on ne la trouve pas.
>
> Proust, *Correspondance*

There is a serious scientific—indeed, a legislative—impulse in Proust's conception of *A la recherche*. Sometimes these justificatory borrowings take the form of a conceit, as in the following letter to Jacques-Émile Blanche, in which Proust dismisses the special illustrated edition of *Swann*: 'La rareté en un mot ne me semble pas être dans l'édition mais se faire dans l'esprit, comme le phosphore etc. se font du pain et de la viande que nous avons mangés et non en introduisant directement des substances chimiques dans notre alimentation.'[1] But science is also used literally and dogmatically to defend the activity of the novelist or artist, and the 'truth' of their creation. Art, too, uncovers laws and truths, Proust asserts, and these truths are just as necessary as those of physics or chemistry. Such arguments seem, paradoxically, to predate the concerns of scientists such as Poincaré, in that they describe scientific law not only as stable, but also as unproblematically revealing truths as if they were latent in nature. By implication, Proust's rhetoric of science also suggests a reversion to the desire of nineteenth-century novelists for science's prestige. The characterization of Elstir as triumphant scientist-cum-creator, 'l'atelier d'Elstir m'apparut comme le laboratoire d'une sorte de nouvelle création du monde' (ii. 190), echoes Claude Bernard's vision of the scientist as creator, 'un inventeur de phénomènes, un véritable contremaître de la création'.[2]

[1] Letter to Jacques-Émile Blanche, end Mar./Apr. 1918, in *Correspondance*, xvii. 156.

[2] Claude Bernard, *Introduction à l'étude de la médecine expérimentale* (1st pub. 1865, Paris: Flammarion, 1984), 48.

What distinguishes the Proustian argument are the notions of independence and process. Literature must make claims on its own terms. The two cultures, literature and science, are equally valid—for both go in search of truth, and both have the power to lay down the law.

Proust's correspondence is rich in such claims. In an exchange with Lionel Hauser on the nature of moral action,[3] for example, Proust claims that actions of the 'highest' order are 'bienfaisant', not because they are directed towards others, but because they focus exclusively on the accomplishment of the action itself. As the following passage makes clear, what Proust terms 'actions of the highest order' include those of the artist, the writer, and the scientist, all of whom are pursuing an 'inner truth':

> Tout le bien qui a été fait sur la terre par des artistes, par des écrivains, par des savants l'a été d'une façon non pas à proprement parler égoïste (puisque leur objet n'était pas la satisfaction de désirs personnels, mais l'éclaircissement d'une vérité intérieure entrevue) mais enfin sans s'occuper des autres. L'altruisme, pour Pascal, pour Lavoisier, pour Wagner, n'a pas consisté à interrompre ou à fausser un travail solitaire pour s'occuper d'œuvres de bienfaisance.[4]

Literary truth is equated with scientific truth, and defended as such. The equation is naturally very much in the artist's favour. It protects him from a questioning readership, since he is not concerned with accommodating the vagaries of public taste, but rather, as is the scientist, with uncovering laws, discerning truths (although the qualification of this truth as 'intérieure' suggests that the parity between the two might not be as straightforward as Proust's comparison suggests). Swann may become less sympathetic, Proust explains teasingly; but since the particularity of Swann is itself related to the general laws of character, there is nothing that he, as the author, can do about it: 'Je ne suis pas libre d'aller contre la vérité et de violer les lois des caractères. "*Amicus Swann, sed magis amica veritas.*" '[5] A similar point is made, but in a more serious vein, to Daniel Halévy:

> Les mystérieuses lois qui président à l'éclosion de la vérité esthétique aussi bien que de la vérité scientifique sont faussées, si un raisonnement étranger intervient d'abord. Le savant qui fait le plus grand honneur à la France par les lois qu'il met

[3] Letter to Lionel Hauser, 28 Apr. 1918, in *Correspondance*, xvii. letter 83.

[4] Ibid. xvii. 216.

[5] Letter to Mme Schiff, 2 July 1919, ibid. xviii. 296. Proust rewrites the Latin proverb 'Platon m'est cher, mais la vérité me l'est davantage' (Aristotle, *Nicomachean Ethics*).

en lumière, cesserait de lui faire honneur s'il le cherchait et ne cherchait pas la vérité seule, ne trouverait plus ce rapport unique qu'est une loi.[6]

Written in 1919, this letter is also a response to the post-war pressure on French writers to engage politically, to write with patriotic sentiment. Proust defends the artist's freedom, not only by pointing out how absurd it would be to expect scientists to produce patriotic laws of nature, but also by describing the two 'cultures' as processes which have a common language.

Scientific justification is in part prompted by the reception of *A la recherche* (the reviews cited in the previous chapter being one example of this); author and readers, or at least reviewers, speak through the same metaphor. But readers were also making the kind of fashionable connection with the new physics that Proust himself did not. *Du côté de chez Swann* was published in 1913, at which time Einstein's theories were becoming widely known. Relativity was a resonant and fruitful analogy for redescribing such characteristic Proustian features as the depiction of time and space, or relative point of view.[7] Edmund Wilson's *Axel's Castle* of 1931 describes the 'moral schema' of *A la recherche* through one such comparison with relativity:

For Proust, though all his observations seem relative, does, like Einstein, build an absolute structure for his world of appearances. His characters may change from bad to good, from beautiful to ugly, as Einstein's measuring-rods shrink and elongate . . . yet as Einstein's mathematical apparatus enables us to establish certain relations between the different parts of the universe, in spite of the fact that we do not know how the heavenly bodies are moving . . . so Proust constructs a moral scheme out of phenomena whose moral values are always shifting.[8]

Camille Vettard's article 'Proust et Einstein' proposes that *A la recherche* is 'en même temps qu'une œuvre d'art, une œuvre de science', and that Proust and Einstein have 'le sens, l'intuition, la compréhension des grandes lois naturelles'.[9] The comparison, despite its modishness,

[6] Letter to Daniel Halévy, 19 July 1919, *Correspondance*, xviii. 334–5. For further examples of 'scientific' justification see ibid. xviii. letter 219, and xx. letter 174.

[7] See also John D. Erickson, 'The Proust–Einstein Relation', in *Marcel Proust*, ed. L. B. Price (Urbana, Ill.: University of Illinois Press, 1973), which examines the problematics of setting up a comparison between Proust and Einstein. Erickson's strategy is to determine what theoretical bases their work might have in common. However, Proust's depiction of relative time and space might also be traced to science fiction. The Pléiade notes indicate a probable allusion to H. G. Wells, *The Time Machine*. The narrator describes the disorienting experiences of sleep and waking and the 'fauteuil magique [qui] le fera voyager à toute vitesse dans le temps et dans l'espace' (i. 5).

[8] Edmund Wilson, *Axel's Castle* (1st pub. 1931, New York: Macmillan, 1991), 162–3.

[9] Vettard, 'Correspondance', 247.

is couched in sufficiently general terms to echo Proust's own justificatory use of science. Yet his response is dismissive: 'On compare deux valeurs (la mienne fort mince) incommensurables et de nature si différentes que le moindre point de contact semble impossible à trouver.'[10] Elsewhere in his correspondence, Proust does, however, recommend the article, and in a letter to Crémieux is even happy to use the language of relativity in self-defence.[11] The ambivalence of his response to the comparisons between *A la recherche* and the new physics, or, more precisely, between himself and Einstein, can perhaps be located in his own arguments for the independence of the two cultures.

In fact, Proust claims to know little of contemporary scientific developments and to understand still less. He appears not to have studied the contemporary and revolutionary developments in physics, which would have been accessible in various forms; he also seems not to share the general excitement about the new physics. Whereas Valéry, for example, devotes himself to the study of relativity,[12] Proust's encounter with Einstein occurs in the work of admiring critics of *A la recherche*. In the preface to *Dates* (1921), Jacques-Émile Blanche compares writer and scientist in hyperbolic style: 'Herr Einstein, déjà si fameux avant la guerre par son principe de la *relativité*, nous ferait croire aujourd'hui que Newton s'est trompé. Vous saurez plus tard, vous, Marcel Proust, si Einstein est aussi grand que vous . . . Car vous nous avez déjà fait connaître une dimension nouvelle.'[13] Proust does cite Einstein, but as a rather different kind of justification. Having failed to attend an engagement at the Guiches, Proust writes to apologize, offering as an excuse that not until five in the morning

[10] Letter to Gaston Gallimard, shortly before 5 Aug. 1922, ibid. xxi. 400.

[11] In a letter to Crémieux of 6 Aug. 1922 (ibid. xxi. 403), Proust denies that chronological discrepancies are present in *Le Côté de Guermantes*, and speaks instead of breaks in the chronology 'à cause de la forme aplatie que prennent mes êtres en révolution dans le temps'.

[12] One might usefully contrast the position of Paul Valéry, who engages with the study of modern science. Valéry, conversant with the shift from the continuous to the discontinuous interpretation of the observer's relation to the physical world, tries to incorporate this in his own work: '*La distance . . . entre la théorie et l'expérience est telle,– qu'il faut bien trouver des points de vue d'architecture*', exclaims his Einstein in *L'Idée fixe* (1932), in *Œuvres*, ed. J. Hytier (Paris: Gallimard, 1960), ii. 264. See Christine Crow, *Paul Valéry: Consciousness and Nature* (London: Cambridge University Press, 1972), 39–41.

[13] Cited in Proust, *Correspondance*, xx. 70. Paul Souday makes the same comparison, but in rather less laudatory terms: 'Et voilà que je commence à craindre moi-même de n'être pas sensiblement plus clair que M. Marcel Proust, qui est ici un Bergson ou un Einstein de la psychologie romanesque, et à qui certaines idées un peu subtiles imposent presque inévitablement parfois un langage un peu abstrus' (*Le Temps*, 12 May 1921; cited in Proust, *Correspondance*, xx. 260–1.

did he feel sociable, by which time, even given relativity's deformation of time, he would probably not have been welcome: 'malgré Einstein je ne pouvais croire qu'il fût cinq heures du matin rue Hamelin, et deux heures de l'après-midi rue de la Faisanderie'.[14] Guiche, who was a pioneer in the field of aerodynamics, writes back to Proust, informing him that in London, those with intellectual pretensions speak of only two things: 'Les scientifiques vous parlent d'Einstein, bien entendu. Les littéraires de "Prrrr...oust".'[15] Some months later, Proust confesses to Guiche that, despite these and more serious comparisons, he understands nothing of Einstein: 'Que j'aimerais vous parler d'Einstein! On a beau m'écrire que je dérive de lui, ou lui de moi, je ne comprends pas un seul mot à ses théories, ne sachant pas l'algèbre. Et je doute pour sa part qu'il ait lu mes romans. Nous avons paraît-il une manière analogue de déformer le Temps.'[16] Proust does then make some attempt to read about relativity (the text is not specified, although the letter suggests that it may have been Einstein's own paper, rather than a popularizing account), but claims that 'dès la première ligne je suis arrêté par des "signes" que je ne connais pas'. Guiche responds immediately, sending the next day a 'brochure' on relativity, including 'une note qui remonte à quelques années, alors qu'Einstein n'était pas encore à la mode'.[17] In his covering letter he cites a typically modish, humorous anecdote 'illustrating' relativity (and which in fact recalls Proust's own 'relative' apology to Guiche, cited above): 'Deux Marseillais se disputent sur la vitesse des autos, des avions[,] de l'électricité etc . . . "Bien mieux dit l'un d'eux; tu es sur la Canebière; je couche avec ta femme à Pékin—*instantanément* tu es cocu!" Eh bien, ça n'est pas vrai.' Guiche also assures Proust that even Einstein had difficulty in understanding relativity, and describes a conversation in which, 'de temps à autre, Einstein se prend la tête à deux mains et s'écrie: "ce ne doit pas être la vérité, c'est trop compliqué", et ajoute Fabry, "il a peut-être raison, en tout cas, je ne le suis pas dans ses calculs!! ["]'.[18]

Proust also approaches Camille Vettard for advice on what to read.

[14] Letter to Guiche, 16 June 1921, *Correspondance*, xx. 342.

[15] Letter from Guiche, 6 July 1921, ibid. xx. 388.

[16] Letter to Guiche, 9/10 Dec. 1921, ibid. xx. 578. The claim also made in this letter that Guiche is not appreciated just in his role as 'vulgarisateur des vérités scientifiques' suggests that Proust may have appealed to him frequently for information on scientific matters.

[17] 'Sur le principe de la Relativité', in *Essai d'aérodynamique du plan* (1913).

[18] Charles Fabry, described by Guiche as 'probablement le plus grand physicien français vivant', was a colleague of Einstein's at the Zürich Polytechnicum (letter of 11 Dec. 1921, in *Correspondance*, xx. 580).

Significantly, he wants to know which books have 'renewed Vettard's vision of the world': 'Je serais bien content (si toutefois j'étais capable de les comprendre) de savoir quels sont ces livres de Sciences qui ont renouvelé votre vision des choses'—to which Vettard replies, 'qu'il s'agissait des spéculations sur le hasard d'un Maxwell, d'un Boltzmann et d'un Gibbs, et des théories relativistes d'Einstein, qui n'étaient pas encore à la mode'.[19]

It seems unlikely, and is also difficult to establish, that Proust followed up Vettard's recommendations. His descriptions of the deforming effect of time and, in the following extract from *A la recherche*, the expression of subjective time in spatial terms, do, however, suggest that he knew more about relativity than he admitted:

> [La matinée] était . . . une vue optique des années, la vue non d'un moment, mais d'une personne située dans la perspective déformante du Temps . . . un être qui se déforme tout le long de son trajet dans l'abîme où il est lancé, abîme dont nous ne pouvons exprimer la direction que par des comparaisons également vaines, puisque nous ne pouvons les emprunter qu'au monde de l'espace, et qui, que nous les orientions dans le sens de l'élévation, de la longueur ou de la profondeur, ont comme seul avantage de nous faire sentir que cette dimension inconcevable et sensible existe. (iv. 504)

What fascinates Proust is not so much the science but, rather, the revolutionary and revelatory effects which science can have on perception, 'votre vision des choses'. Yet this is not how he uses science to discuss and theorize his own work. Proust's rhetoric of scientific justification seems curiously indifferent to the spectacular developments of the early part of the twentieth century. Where contemporary science was questioning precisely such notions as the viability and validity of general laws, Proust's science depends on them: 'Ce que je fais je l'ignore, mais je sais ce que je veux faire; or j'omets (sauf dans les parties que je n'aime pas) tout détail, tout fait, je ne m'attache qu'à ce qui me semble (d'après un sens analogue à celui des pigeons-voyageurs[ )] . . . déceler quelque loi générale.'[20] His concern is almost exclusively with the laws of science, on the one hand because scientific law acts as a locus for various justifications for the independent status of art, on the other because science provides a language for describing artistic creativity.

If Proust's correspondence weaves a supporting net of justificatory

[19] Letter shortly after 22 Oct. 1920, ibid. xix. 554 and, for Vettard's response, ibid. n. 5.

[20] Letter to Louis de Robert, cited in Léon Pierre-Quint, *Proust et la stratégie littéraire* (1st pub. 1930, Paris: Correâ, 1954), 60.

arguments about literature's 'scientific' status, it is also true that science appears at many of the key moments of literary empowerment in *A la recherche.* Many of the novel's best-known 'statements of purpose' are couched in a scientific language which would seem to be transparent, so much has it been overlooked. Even the infamous characterization of style as metaphor is qualified by a reference to scientific law: 'La vérité ne commencera qu'au moment où l'écrivain prendra deux objets différents, posera leur rapport, analogue dans le monde de l'art à celui qu'est le rapport unique de la loi causale dans le monde de la science, et les enfermera dans les anneaux nécessaires d'un beau style' (iv. 468). The truth of metaphoric connection is analogous to that of the law of causality. Causality implies that only one sequence of connection is possible; metaphor, similarly, is to establish the only possible relationship (between two different objects). Metaphor itself is not law, but is informed by the—very Proustian—law of metaphoric connection.

Radiography is another point of reference for the narrator of *Le Temps retrouvé* on the way to artistic revelation. In fact, it is part of what begins as a mock apology for the narrator's *inability* to become an artist and concludes, with the help of scientific metaphors drawn from geometry and radiography, as a triumphant statement of a new aesthetic. Having read a page (or rather a pastiche) of the Goncourt brothers' *Journal*, the narrator doubts that he will ever become a writer. Whereas the Goncourts capture reality by noting superficial detail, the narrator is unable to perceive such 'qualités sensibles'. His vision is analogous to that of the geometer, who recognizes only the underlying forms and structures of human behaviour, 'leur substratum linéaire'. The narrator's apparent inability is then redescribed as a conscious and rather intellectual attempt to discern generalities, or truths, about human behaviour and character: 'c'était un objet qui avait toujours été plus particulièrement le but de ma recherche' (iv. 296). As the narrator warms to his theme, so he is metamorphosed from geometer to surgeon—'comme un chirugien qui, sous le poli d'un ventre de femme, verrait le mal interne qui le ronge'. Now the metaphor of the surgeon suggests a rather different involvement with the subject than that of the objective abstracting vision afforded by geometry. Moreover, while the peeling back of the woman's stomach to reveal her 'mal interne' suggests the art of anatomical drawing or modelling, the very next sentence specifies that the surgeon is in fact using radiography: 'J'avais beau dîner en ville, je ne voyais pas les convives, parce que, quand je croyais les regarder, je les radiographiais' (iv. 297), a comparison which serves to make more objective and powerful the narrator's 'scientific' vision. Woolf, too, uses radiography to suggest the bones of passion fleshed over by convention:[21]

> Lily Briscoe knew all that. Sitting opposite him could she not see, as in an X-ray photograph, the ribs and thigh bones of the young man's desire to impress himself lying dark in the mist of the flesh—that thin mist which conversation had laid over his burning desire to break into the conversation.[22]

What makes Proust's metaphor so striking is the slippage between disciplines and techniques, from geometry to surgery to radiography, a slippage which suggests an uncertainty about the human implications of the artist's vision. The image of the surgeon brings to mind the cartoon in which Flaubert holds up for inspection the bleeding heart of Emma Bovary; the phrase 'qui le ronge' also suggests the delight with which the artist-surgeon inspects his suffering subject. Moreover, whereas Woolf simply uses the metaphor to express the artist Lily Briscoe's perception, Proust's narrator bases a new aesthetic of the general on such a perception, one which other writers have been unable to achieve—indeed, which other writers have not been able to desire.

Involuntary memory is also subject to scientific redescription. Again, a quintessentially Proustian aesthetic moment is reformulated, this time through chemistry: 'Car nous trouvons de tout dans notre mémoire: elle est une espèce de pharmacie, de laboratoire de chimie, où on met au hasard la main tantôt sur une drogue calmante, tantôt sur un poison dangereux' (iii. 892). Here the narrator as scientist is at work in the laboratory. The formulation of laws has been replaced by an interior chemistry, over which he has little control. The 'pharmacie', in which beneficial drugs are prescribed by the authority of the chemist, is not usually a place of experiment. The lime-flower tea of Combray, whose serendipitous effects produce the first instance of involuntary memory and, we are told, the novel which follows, is taken on prescription, and the narrator exclaims at the 'charmante prodigalité du pharmacien'.[23] In this passage from *La*

[21] See Malte Herwig's discussion of radiography in Thomas Mann's *Zauberberg*, in 'Exakte Literatur und schöne Wissenschaft' (Oxford, unpub. M.Phil. thesis, submitted 1998), 65–86.

[22] Virginia Woolf, *To the Lighthouse* (1st pub. 1927, London: Granada, 1985), 85.

[23] 'Si ma tante se sentait agitée, elle demandait à la place sa tisane et c'était moi qui étais chargé de faire tomber du sac de pharmacie dans une assiette la quantité de tilleul qu'il fallait mettre ensuite dans l'eau bouillante' (i. 50).

Prisonnière, however, the therapeutic effect is threatened by elements of chance and ignorance (the narrator cannot distinguish the various potions). The pharmacy becomes a laboratory in which drugs are chosen randomly. 'Memory—[is] a clinical laboratory stocked with poison and remedy, stimulant and sedative.'[24] Research into Albertine has led to an experimentation on the self, on the narrator's own memory. Memories triggered by this scrutiny may be acutely painful or pleasurable, but none provides the answer, only more uncertainty, bringing the narrator to the sceptical conclusion that 'L'inconnu de la vie des êtres est comme celui de la nature, que chaque découverte scientifique ne fait que reculer mais n'annule pas' (iii. 893).

These key instances—metaphor–causality, artistic vision–radiography, involuntary memory–chemistry—stand out amongst the overwhelmingly prolific scientific metaphors of *A la recherche*: 'it seems safe to say that no writer has ever made more varied and skilful use of metaphors from science than Proust. This is the more remarkable because *A la recherche du temps perdu* is better known for the allusions to painting and music than for the allusions to science.'[25] Reino Virtanen's article 'Proust's Metaphors from the Natural and the Exact Sciences' provides a helpful catalogue of facts and figures. He claims to have listed well over 300 scientific metaphors, and of these a large proportion involve the exact sciences. 'Including electricity, photography, and optics, the number for physics is about 100; astronomy, over 50; chemistry, some 30; geology, about 12.' Mathematical, chemical, and zoological analogies are evenly distributed; medical analogies are concentrated in *Du côté de chez Swann*, less numerous in the last part of *A l'ombre* and *Le Côté de Guermantes*, and numerous again from *Sodome et Gomorrhe* onwards. Astronomical analogies are rare in *Du côté de chez Swann*, and increase over the remaining volumes, peaking in *Le Temps retrouvé*. Virtanen quotes a number of these metaphors, and his list, as does Victor Graham's in *The Imagery of Proust* (1966), reveals the range and subtlety of scientific reference.[26]

Medical metaphor in *A la recherche* constitutes a conceptual web which exceeds that of any other science; or, as Woolf puts it, 'there must be a volume or two about disease scattered through the pages of

[24] Beckett, *Proust*, 22.

[25] Reino Virtanen, 'Proust's Metaphors from the Natural and the Exact Sciences', *PMLA*, 69 (1954), 1038–59. See also Georges Cattaui, 'Proust et les sciences', in *Literature and Science*, ed. Bisson, 287–92.

[26] See also Victor Graham, 'Proust's Alchemy', *MLR*, 60 (1965), 197–206.

Proust'.[27] By conceptual web I mean to indicate that patterns of echo and repetition among the scattered medical metaphors of *A la recherche* allow such references to signify differently. In the same way that the key term 'habit' is established, then repeated with variations, so the invalid (alongside the traveller and the lover) is introduced as a Proustian archetype, who then illustrates an amplified, or even heightened, experience of the text's commonplace laws (of jealousy, habit, desire, imagination)—in this case a heightened physical experience, or 'drama of the body'.[28] As the son and brother of eminent physicians, Proust was not only in close contact with medical science; he also constituted a likely subject for scientific study. In Adrien Proust's medical milieu, the purely nervous character of asthma was held to be indisputable; indeed, the first in a series of guides to 'practical hygiene', edited and introduced by Proust's father,[29] was Édouard Brissaud's *L'Hygiène des asthmatiques* (1896). Adrien Proust's contribution to the series, in collaboration with Gilbert Ballet, was a guide to neurasthenia, *L'Hygiène du neurasthénique* (1897). Proust was familiar with these guides, and studied many other such books in an attempt to cure himself which was more than unsuccessful. Such links have been documented by several studies of Proust and medicine.[30]

School reports describe Proust as a 'literary' pupil, talented, but rather lazy: 'ses faiblesses ne viennent pas de son manque d'aptitudes, mais d'une insuffisante application. Il a de mauvais résultats dans les disciplines techniques: en mathématiques, en physique et aussi en allemand.'[31] Yet he did win the natural history prize at the Lycée Condorcet. His biology teacher Georges Colomb was later to become known by the punning pseudonym 'Christophe Colomb' as the author of *L'Idée fixe du savant Cosinus* (1899) and *Les Facéties du sapeur Camember* (1896), forerunners of the comic strip. Possibly as a result of

[27] Virginia Woolf, 'On Being Ill' (1930), in *The Moment* (London: Hogarth Press, 1947), 14.

[28] Ibid. 15.

[29] Adrien Proust held a chair in hygiene at the Paris Faculty of Medicine; the series was a forerunner of the modern 'Living with' guides, and its seventeen volumes 'entassaient en désordre des idées à la mode, des affirmations gratuites, des principes de morale, les fantasmes de l'auteur et . . . le peu de science alors disponible' (François-Bernard Michel, *Proust et les écrivains devant la mort* (Paris: Éditions Grasset et Fasquelle, 1995), 29). See also Roger Duchêne, *L'Impossible Marcel Proust* (Paris: Éditions Robert Laffont, 1994), 'Le Professeur Adrien Proust', 50–7.

[30] Serge Béhar, *L'Univers médical de Proust* (Paris: Gallimard, 1970); L. A. Bisson, 'Proust and Medicine', in *Literature and Science*, 292–8; Michel, *Proust et les écrivains devant la mort*; and Robert Soupault, *Marcel Proust du côté de la médecine* (Geneva: Plon, 1967).

[31] Duchêne, *L'Impossible Marcel Proust*, 103.

the influence of Colomb's witty and non-conformist approach to the discipline, Proust's letters to friends are scattered with caricatural drawings of people as plants or animals; 'il aimera aussi peindre les hommes comme s'ils étaient des plantes ou des animaux.'[32] Proust retained an active interest in botany. His knowledge and speculation in this field are so prevalent in *A la recherche* that it constitutes an alternative lens through which the human world of the novel can be viewed.

For metaphors drawn with any degree of complexity from other scientific fields, Proust depended on the knowledge of friends. This exchange in turn depended on his ability so to characterize an aspect of human behaviour that friends and acquaintances could draw on their expertise to find an appropriate analogy.[33] (This technique will be considered in detail in Chapter 5.) Not all metaphors require specialist knowledge—those drawn from the field of mathematics, and principally geometry, are frequently and straightforwardly used to express the lover's ever frustrated desire for accuracy (Albertine is like an equation which the narrator cannot solve, and so on). More sophisticated metaphors draw on relativity, as does the extract from the 'matinée des Guermantes' cited above, to express subjective time in spatial terms, and in the following passage, to contrast 'flat' psychology with 'depth' psychology which takes account of time:

> Ainsi chaque individu—et j'étais moi-même un de ces individus—mesurait pour moi la durée par la révolution qu'il avait accomplie non seulement autour de soi-même, mais autour des autres, et notamment par les positions qu'il avait occupées successivement par rapport à moi . . . il faudrait user, par opposition à la psychologie plane dont on use d'ordinaire, d'une sorte de psychologie dans l'espace. (iv. 608)

Strikingly, the episode in which the narrator succeeds in kissing Albertine is also described as the revolution of a solid: 'Etait-ce parce que nous jouions (figurée par la révolution d'un solide) la scène inverse de celle de Balbec . . . qu'elle me laissa prendre . . . ce qu'elle avait refusé jadis?' (ii. 661). The key term of revolution in these images might be read as indicating the revolutionary scientific developments from which the metaphors are drawn; it might also indicate the renewed vision which Proust felt to be the result of such developments—hence his question to Vettard 'which books on science have

[32] Duchêne, *L'Impossible Marcel Proust*, 96.

[33] Proust's curiosity about mathematics is described by Robert de Billy in *Marcel Proust, lettres et conversations* (Paris: Éditions des portiques, 1930), ch. 16.

renewed your vision of reality?'; but perhaps most simply, the figure of the revolving solid indicates how Proust manipulates scientific metaphor to make the two-dimensional world of any theory tangible.

Culling direct references to the sciences in this way gives immediate access to what might be called the text's 'top layer' of science. This, after all, is where one might expect a study of science in literary texts to begin: that is, with the text's scientific 'pictures', images, or metaphors, rather than with what we might term the cognitive structure of the text, its maxims. Observing science through the metaphors of *A la recherche* reveals a layer of scattered and fragmented debate, in which recurrent patterns become evident. Scientific metaphors are, rather like the maxims, difficult to extract. References to science are contaminated by comparisons with other areas of intellectual enquiry and creativity. The metaphors of *A la recherche*, often simply by virtue of syntactical compression, cross and blur boundaries between art and science. 'Proust's book is a gigantic dense mesh of complicated relations: cross references between different groups of characters and a multiplication of metaphors and similes connecting the phenomena of infinitely varied fields—biological, zoological, physical, aesthetic, social, political and financial.'[34]

Beyond noting its interconnectedness, we can begin to make sense of the science of *A la recherche* by characterizing its style. This is a science which often flaunts itself, then cloaks its audacity or preciosity with ironic disclaimers. The extended, baroque botanical analogy which opens *Sodome et Gomorrhe* is, for example, termed: '(simple comparaison pour les providentiels hasards, quels qu'ils soient, et sans la moindre prétention scientifique de rapprocher certaines lois de la botanique et ce qu'on appelle parfois fort mal l'homosexualité)' (iii. 9). This coy disclaimer itself provides the underpinning for what is the text's key presentation of sexuality and science. Elsewhere, in a parody of the style of scientific popularizers, concerned that their audience might be frightened by jargon and technical terms, the narrator lards his description of friendship with specialist vocabulary, all the while claiming that he is avoiding terminology the reader may not understand:

Les défauts d'une simple connaissance, et même d'un ami, sont pour nous de vrais poisons, contre lesquels nous sommes heureusement 'mithridatés'. Mais, sans apporter le moindre appareil de comparaison scientifique et parler d'anaphy-

[34] Wilson, *Axel's Castle*, 158.

laxie, disons qu'au sein de nos relations amicales ou purement mondaines, il y a une hostilité momentanément guérie, mais récurrente par accès. (iii. 60)

These pointed and teasing non-disclaimers question the use which literary predecessors made of science's prestige; for, in practice, Proust's science is far from the literal application we find in nineteenth-century novelists such as Balzac or Zola. The justificatory rhetoric of the correspondence about the absolute and intuited nature of scientific law is tailored to the claims which Proust makes for literature as epistemologically equal to, but independent of, science. Science often mediates key moments of literary empowerment in *A la recherche*, yet the text also displays a wariness about this tradition, a questioning of just how literature might hook up to science. Proust's pastiche of Balzac indicates an awareness that his use of science is writing him into a tradition of scientific-literary relations: Talleyrand becomes, for example, 'ce Roger Bacon de la nature sociale', and the narrator claims that 'un physicien du monde moral qui aurait à la fois le génie de Lavoisier et de Bichat—le créateur de la chimie organique—serait seul capable d'isoler les éléments qui composent la sonorité spéciale du pas des hommes supérieurs'.[35] Moreover, studies of the novel's genesis show that the drafts contain explicit scientific material which, in the final version, is transposed into metaphor.[36] *A la recherche*, rather than taking science substantially or discursively, manipulates its images and rhetoric on the one hand to aesthetic ends, the justification of art, on the other to parodic, ironic, or surreal effect.

Discounting doctors, as Proust's narrator so frequently does, there are no scientists in *A la recherche*. Vington, a natural historian, is replaced in the later drafts by Vinteuil, a composer.[37] Much of the Vington/Vinteuil narrative remains unchanged: Vington's unfinished experimental research is completed by his daughter's lover, as will be Vinteuil's compositions. The only trace of his scientific origins in *A la recherche* is found in Swann's exclamation:

'Ô audace aussi géniale peut-être, se disait-il, que celle d'un Lavoisier, d'un Ampère, l'audace d'un Vinteuil expérimentant, découvrant les lois secrètes d'une

[35] 'Pastiches et mélanges', in *Contre Sainte-Beuve*, 8. Balzac, who drew metaphors from the natural sciences, magnetism, and mechanics, recognized in such applications a substantial, rather than formal, correspondence between, say, physical energy and will, or magnetism and hypnotism.

[36] See Alison Winton's *Proust's Additions* (Cambridge: Cambridge University Press, 1977). Later descriptions draw increasingly and more boldly on botanical and zoological imagery, a technique already present in the drafts.

[37] See Esquisses LI and LII (i. 796–805).

force inconnue, menant à travers l'inexploré, vers le seul but possible, l'attelage invisible auquel il se fie et qu'il n'apercevra jamais!' (i. 345)

Swann's exclamation reads as a euphoric version of similar descriptions in Proust's correspondence. Again, the focus is on the creative processes of art and science, and again, both are characterized by their search for laws.

Metaphor transforms a range of quite disparate characters into scientists—Vinteuil, Elstir, and Bergotte; Françoise and Aunt Léonie; Swann and the narrator himself. Each of these three groups in turn might be said to practise a rather different kind of science, of which the first is the most admirable, and also closest to the sentiment of Proust's correspondence. Only in conclusion does the narrator gain access to this group, as the above discussion of science and literary empowerment indicates; but already in *A l'ombre des jeunes filles en fleurs* his aesthetic awareness is mediated through a scientific model. Elstir's studio is 'le laboratoire d'une sorte de nouvelle création du monde' (ii. 190). By *Le Côté de Guermantes* this metaphor has become a Proustian law of aesthetics—'le monde . . . n'a pas été créé une fois, mais aussi souvent qu'un artiste original est survenu' (ii. 623)—of which Bergotte's novels are just one illustration.

The narrator's encounters with both Elstir and Bergotte are informed by this maxim, and develop a discussion of the nature of progress in art and science: 'J'arrivais à me demander s'il y avait quelque vérité en cette distinction que nous faisons toujours entre l'art, qui n'est pas plus avancé qu'au temps d'Homère, et la science aux progrès continus' (ii. 624). In the case of Bergotte, a geological metaphor describes aesthetic progress: the new world of the artist's creation 'durera jusqu'à la prochaine catastrophe géologique que déchaîneront un nouveau peintre ou un nouvel écrivain originaux' (ii. 623).

The discussion of Elstir's work, while exploring similar notions of progress and perspective, develops rather differently. Whereas discussions of Bergotte appeal not to literary examples, but to the history of the visual arts, the description of Elstir's creativity is more straightforwardly and strikingly visual. As the narrator enters the artist's studio, he is overwhelmed not by the purely painterly qualities of Elstir's work, but by the possibility of a poetic knowledge—'une connaissance poétique, féconde en joies, de maintes formes que je n'avais pas isolées jusque-là du spectacle total de la réalité' (ii. 190).

The qualification of this knowledge as an ecstatic recognition of the rich variety of nature is also couched in a language more scientific than artistic. The narrator in fact speaks not of nature, but of 'the sum spectacle of reality', and the forms which he will be able to distinguish in it are to be 'isolated' as if they were to be subject to experimentation and further investigation. In the 'Cahier Manuscrit', this sum spectacle is dramatically extended to encompass those areas of reality which science has made known but not visible to the eye, and the narrator desires that Elstir might isolate the microscopic and even invisible scientific phenomena, such as 'les ondes électriques qui nous entourent, et dont j'aurais tant voulu qu'un Elstir, de son regard subtil et révélateur . . . eût fixé pour m'apprendre à les reconnaître' (iii. 1268).

The narrator's subsequent analysis of Elstir's work in the passage from *A l'ombre des jeunes filles* adopts the more commonplace form of an argument about the nature of progress in art and science: 'Bien qu'on dise avec raison qu'il n'y a pas de progrès, pas de découvertes en art, mais seulement dans les sciences . . . il faut pourtant reconnaître que dans la mesure où l'art met en lumière certaines lois, une fois qu'une industrie les a vulgarisées, l'art antérieur perd rétrospectivement un peu de son originalité' (ii. 194). Elstir's originality lies in his depiction of things not as we know them to be, but according to the optical illusion of our first impressions; the theory which emerges from this approach is the law of perspective. Photography's subsequent reproduction of this technique has the effect of banalizing it; Elstir's work seems, in retrospect, less original. Yet the narrator's subsequent descriptions of the paintings suggest that his conclusion isn't quite so simple as that. The seascape described is at once lyrical and scientific. The laws of perspective literally emerge from the sensual detail of the canvas, 'd'autres lois se dégageaient de cette même toile' (ii. 195). The description enacts the 'connaissance poétique', the lyric knowledge whose possibility is glimpsed by the narrator's own first impressions on entering Elstir's studio.

A less admirable science is practised by Françoise and Léonie. Their 'research' is characterized neither by the qualities of vision and progress, nor by the clichéd scientific qualities of logic and rationality. Instead, these women work by intuition, jealousy, and revelation. Françoise's 'connaissance instinctive et presque divinatoire' is compared to the science of the Ancients (ii. 654), and is suspiciously applied to the narrator's relationship with Albertine. Françoise herself is the subject of Aunt Léonie's rigorously suspicious and instinctive investigations, investigations which prove fruitless until 'une révélation d'Eulalie—comme ces découvertes qui ouvrent tout d'un coup un champ insoupçonné à une science naissante et qui se traînait dans l'ornière' (i. 116). This science is at once primitive and the foundation of modern approaches. Both Françoise and Plato have preconceived ideas which limit their research; both pursue knowledge in such a way that they are not limited by lack of material resources, and similarly, 'de nos jours encore les plus grandes découvertes dans les mœurs des insectes ont pu être faites par un savant qui ne disposait d'aucun laboratoire' (ii. 654). These comic shifts of register and time link Françoise with ancient philosophy, the beginnings of Western science, and one of its more recent manifestations, the work of naturalist Henri Fabre. And it is this sliding scale which indicates the epistemological awareness of Proust's text. These connections might say something important about the nature of scientific investigation, but they might also mockingly undermine it. Nowhere is this point more dramatically made than in the spectacular scientific pretensions of the third group, the lovers of *A la recherche*: 'Devant les pensées, les actions d'une femme que nous aimons, nous sommes aussi désorientés que le pouvaient être devant les phénomènes de la nature, les premiers physiciens (avant que la science fût constituée et eût mis un peu de lumière dans l'inconnu)' (i. 576). The lovers of *A la recherche* figure most frequently and comically as scientists—as a community, they might be said to share certain laws and methodologies. When the narrator-protagonist writes a letter to Swann, which expresses his admiration, and is designed to give him access to Gilberte, Swann reads it according to the maxims of experience which Marcel has yet to acquire: 'peut-être simplement Swann savait-il que la générosité n'est souvent que l'aspect intérieur que prennent nos sentiments égoïstes quand nous ne les avons pas encore nommés et classés' (i. 483). The narrator, already sharing—and attributing to Swann—knowledge of these maxims, predicts the repetition which will characterize the lover's experience. His prediction is couched in a highly technical language: 'Je ne pouvais partager ses prévisions, car je n'avais pas réussi à abstraire de moi-même mon amour, à le faire rentrer dans la généralité des autres et à en supputer expérimentalement les conséquences' (i. 483).

Yet, while the lovers might be said to share a body of experiential laws, they can gain access to these only in retrospect, in, as it were, the third person. This is the Proustian version of being wise after the event. In love, unable to tap into the commonplace (of which being wise after the event is a part), the lover develops a more desirous and speculative relationship with the truth, in which scientific metaphors tend to express the difficulty of establishing any form of knowledge. The narrator's 'passionate astronomy', for example, evolves from his attempts to work out the movements and habits of the 'jeunes filles': 'Combien d'observations patientes, mais non point sereines, il faut recueillir sur les mouvements en apparence irréguliers de ces mondes inconnus avant de pouvoir être sûr . . . que nos prévisions ne seront pas trompées, avant de dégager les lois certaines, acquises au prix d'expériences cruelles, de cette astronomie passionnée!' (ii. 188). The jealousy of Swann, the archetypal lover of *A la recherche*, also leads him to a 'passion' for the truth: 'Mais d'une vérité, elle aussi, interposée entre lui et sa maîtresse, ne recevant sa lumière que d'elle, vérité tout individuelle qui avait pour objet unique, d'un prix infini et presque d'une beauté désinteressée, les actions d'Odette, ses relations, ses projets, son passé' (i. 269). The rationalization of a truth which is 'individual', of a beauty which is almost 'disinterested', points up Swann's awareness of his rather dubious interest in the particular; and accordingly, he proceeds to cloak it in yet more scientificity. Swann's 'methodology'—gossip, eavesdropping, shadowing—is closely related to that of Léonie and Françoise, but finds its justification in claiming to be an *intellectual* pursuit: 'des méthodes d'investigation scientifique d'une véritable valeur intellectuelle et appropriées à la recherche de la vérité' (i. 270). As Malcolm Bowie describes, 'All in a sudden exhilarating access of self-awareness he [Swann] has been promoted, within the intellectual community, from day-labourer to polymathic hero. And all because he urgently wishes to know whether his mistress is alone.'[38]

The narrator becomes the arch-investigator in this 'field' of research. Like Swann, he imagines casting women within experiments, and is comically overwhelmed by the language of science—catching sight of a country girl from Mme de Villeparisis's carriage, he exclaims, 'j'étais désespéré de ne pas pouvoir faire dans des conditions uniques, ne laissant aucune place à l'erreur possible, l'expérience de ce que nous offre de plus mystérieux la beauté qu'on désire' (ii. 155). Later, on approaching the 'jeunes filles', the precision of experiment is no longer idealized; instead, the narrator revels in his power as experimenter: the responses of the 'jeunes filles' are '[des] propos auxquels je

[38] Bowie, *Freud, Proust, and Lacan*, 50.

pouvais attribuer une valeur d'autant plus grande que par mes questions je les provoquais à mon gré, les faisais varier comme un expérimentateur qui demande à des contre-épreuves la vérification de ce qu'il a supposé' (ii. 300). But the irony of this pretence to disinterested scientific activity, to 'recréer expérimentalement le phénomène qui diversifie l'individualité d'un être' (ii. 660), is finally undermined by the narrator's attempt to kiss Albertine. What might be termed the scientist's 'physical involvement' in the experiment effectively wards off the subject, and the laws which result are digressions on natural history and photography, not the laws of Albertine. The lover's desire to approach his mistress and be empowered by experiment is frustrated.

Save for its scale, the science of the lovers, this third group of scientists, would seem scarcely to differ from that practised by Léonie and Françoise. What distinguishes the latter is that they are unconcerned with justifying their activities. Whereas the narrator uses science briefly to characterize Léonie and Françoise's cunning and trickery, their desire for knowledge, the lovers, the narrator and Swann are for ever manipulating science. As their very interested desire for knowledge of Albertine and Odette increases, so their pretence to disinterested scientific investigation becomes ever greater. The scientific staging of these desirous investigations ('Vous devriez me le dire, cela m'intéresserait pour me faire connaître une loi d'histoire naturelle humaine' (iv. 228), the narrator imagines persuading a potential Albertine) is in turn threatened by foreknowledge of a different order of maxim, the inevitable law of indifference: 'L'importance scientifique que je voyais à savoir le genre de désir qui se cachait sous les pétales faiblement rosés de ces joues . . . s'en irait sans doute quand je n'aimerais plus du tout Albertine ou quand je n'aimerais plus du tout cette jeune femme' (iv. 229).

That such metaphors were suggestive to those critics who read Proust's maxims as 'scientific' is clear. Far more complex is the nature of this science. Science is used to justify art in both Proust's correspondence and *A la recherche* itself, whether the art is that of the narrator, or of Vinteuil, Elstir, or Bergotte. Their science is a pure, disinterested activity which uncovers universal truths. Yet science is also repeatedly and ironically staged to justify the sly and obsessive investigations of the lovers.

This contradiction is the mirror image of the tension expressed in Poincaré's aesthetic justification of scientific law. The metaphors of science and aesthetics (as used by Proust and Poincaré respectively) assert old certainties—indeed, they express the desire for these certainties, for laws to be universal and truths to be expressed—yet they also admit new uncertainties—that science might also be impure, that aesthetics might be highly subjective.

In this review of Proust's science we note both the metaphoric science of *A la recherche* and its legislative impulse. The text delights in its abundance of metaphor, the jostling of disparate frames of reference, yet also desires for itself the stability of law. Proust's science is at once 'just' another self-justificatory move in a history of such strategies used by literature to claim for itself the prestige of a lawlike, objective Newtonian science, and also an interrogation of the very basis and justification of a science which, according to Heisenberg's definition, 'no longer confronts nature as an objective observer, but sees itself as an actor in this interplay between man and nature'.[39]

[39] Heisenberg, *Physicist's Conception of Nature*, 29.

3
RETRODUCTION

> C'est à la cime même du particulier qu'éclôt le général.
>
> Proust, *Correspondance*

> A propos de son refus de la 'spécialisation':
> 'N'ayant jamais pu atteindre à cette sagesse, j'accepte joyeusement d'être réduit à l'universalité.'
>
> Nicolas Landau, *Aphorismes*

The 'retroduction' of this chapter aims to reconnect the images of 'Proust's science' with the rhetoric of sententiousness discussed at the end of Chapter 1. Retroduction will, in effect, reconnect metaphor and maxim. The dynamic and literal readings of the maxims of *A la recherche* can already be seen to parallel the ambiguities of the legislative and performative science of the text's metaphors. The generalities or commonplaces at the heart of the text constitute, according to the literal reading, 'scientific' discoveries about human nature, the Proustian 'laws'. These *topoi*, to which the text repeatedly returns, have a regulatory effect. Yet this central regulatory body also dilates, so that the text reaches out to speculate over different areas, to experiment with metaphor, to explore the possibilities of connecting with the general, to reflect on the individual's affective relation with the law. The term 'retroduction' will allow a closer examination of this interaction of the speculative and the regulative, through metaphor and maxim. But before passing to this close analysis, I want to introduce 'retroduction' by way of a brief methodological digression.

Establishing a study of science and literature, of how science is written into a literary text, is methodologically tricky.[1] The presence of

[1] The introductory chapter of Whitworth's 'Physics and the Literary Community 1905–1939' gives a useful survey of the state of the field. George S. Rousseau's article 'Literature and Science', *Isis*, 69/249 (1978), 583–91, locates the origin of such study in the 1940s, when scholars provided glosses of scientific vocabulary for a literary audience. The study of science and literature grew as it was increasingly recognized that scientific ideas could not be isolated in this way. For Rousseau, the advent of structuralism seemed to have blocked this developing field. Structuralism's 'scientific' methodology divided scholars: humanists who had studied science and literature wanted nothing more to do with it; while, for structuralists, the concept of 'influence' was not valid. As the work of scholars such as Beer, Levine, Jordanova, Christie, and Shuttleworth, has shown, Rousseau's article was unduly

science in *A la recherche* is indisputable. An abundance of scientific imagery, ranging over botany, zoology, physiology, geometry, magnetism, physics, and astronomy, is dispersed throughout *A la recherche*. Emblematic of the progressive fragmentation and refiguration of science in the novel is the metamorphosis of Vington, a natural historian in earlier drafts, into Vinteuil, composer. In the earlier drafts scientific metaphors are extended, more discursive, and linked to stronger statements of purpose than those which survive in the final text. In his correspondence, but also at key moments of literary empowerment in *A la recherche* itself, Proust claims for literature a serious scientific purpose.

A traditional study of science in literature would take these characteristics and attempt to find their origin. The beginnings of such a study are sketched in the previous chapter at those moments where we move away from the text itself, and the kind of science that can be read there, to consider where that science might have come from and how it might have been received by the author. Tracking influence in this way can involve seeking out biographical information, an approach which is often problematic, as the general bias of literary study towards internal histories means that contacts with science are not always recorded; biographies make similar omissions, and information easily goes lost. Precise biographical connections *are* enabled when an author is perceived to be—as Proust was not—scientifically engaged, as, for example, Paul Valéry[2] or Robert Musil.[3]

Alternatively, influence might be sketched in more general terms, as the scientific discourses available during a period through, for example, radio broadcasts and reports in newspapers, periodicals, and other texts popularizing science; influence is also perceptible in the filtering down of scientific discovery into technology. William Carter's *The Proustian Quest* takes this last approach, and explores how Proust's frequent analogies from technology—optical devices, machines of transportation, and inventions relating to communica-

pessimistic. Recent studies have questioned the monolithic opposition between science and literature, and have focused on, for example, the textuality of scientific writing. N. Katherine Hayles's essay, 'Deciphering the Rules of Unruly Disciplines', in *Literature and Science*, ed. D. Bruce and A. Purdy (Amsterdam: Rodopi, 1994), 25–48, is of particular interest on recent methodologies in the study of literature and science.

[2] Christine Crow, *Paul Valéry: Consciousness and Nature.*

[3] David S. Luft, *Robert Musil and the Crisis of European Culture 1880–1914* (Berkeley: University of California Press, 1980); Peter D. Smith, 'German Literature and the Scientific World-View in the Nineteenth and Twentieth Centuries', *Journal of European Studies*, 27 (1997), 389–415.

tion—are used to describe new kinetic experiences. This more general approach to science in literature has the advantage of replacing the mechanistic cause/effect notion of influence with the metaphor of the 'field of force'.[4] As Michael Whitworth describes, the concept of influence might be revised according to a scientific model: authors and ideas, rather than being viewed as Newtonian matter in motion, linked by particular collisions, are instead considered as part of a 'field'. Stephen Kern's study *The Culture of Time and Space*, for example, ranges across the arts and sciences (both taken in the widest sense), and the account is structured by considering connections through a field, rather than by way of direct causality. At this point, however, 'field' begins to sound suspiciously like 'Zeitgeist' creeping back in scientific guise—and the danger of working with this more general notion of influence is that it risks leaving the author bathed in the scientific atmosphere of their time. Even if 'atmosphere' is re-described, and, as it were, rehabilitated, as the set of epistemological possibilities available, an account of how the text connects with these still needs to be given.

The biographical and general scientific connections as sketched in the previous chapter might be summarized as follows:

(1) Proust's contact with medicine through his father, brother and their colleagues. This is documented and analysed by various studies of Proust and medicine, including Serge Béhar, *L'Univers médical de Proust*; L. A. Bisson, 'Proust and Medicine'; François-Bernard Michel, *Proust et les écrivains devant la mort*; and Robert Soupault, *Marcel Proust du*

[4] The concept of causality has itself undergone a series of revisions, as the account given by Hanson in *Patterns of Discovery* of the reception of Newton's *Principia* describes (pp. 90–1). Newton's theory of motion was at first regarded as abstract, as merely mathematical; it was not held to provide a satisfactory physical explanation of particle motion and interaction. Newton himself declined to supply the mechanical illustrations required. Yet, as the *Principia* won over physicists' thinking and became the model for every other field of enquiry, it ceased to be a purely mathematical aid to the prediction of how bodies behave, and became *the* system of mechanics. Mechanics became the paradigm of a causal theory. Consequently, 'causal' and 'mechanical' became identified with 'picturable', and the attempt to fit developments in late nineteenth-century science to this style of model proved impossible: '*Principia* became the archetype of picturability. Maxwell's field equations for electrodynamical phenomena were criticized for not being picturable. Many attempts were made to supplement his theory with a mechanical model' (p. 91). The 'field of force' was one aspect of the electromagnetic theory developed by Faraday and Maxwell in response to these developments, and is identified by Heisenberg as the beginning of 'the crisis of the materialist conception': 'Interactions between fields of force without any matter to propagate the force were very much more difficult to understand than the materialist picture of atomic physics' (*Physicist's Conception of Nature*, 13).

côté de la médecine. In terms of the legal rhetoric of science, one might say that Proust experiences the laws of medicine as descriptive, but also overwhelmingly as prescriptive—as a neurasthenic and homosexual, Proust is both the victim of and censured by this law.

(2) Contact with friends/acquaintances, some of whom are scientists. Proust sometimes 'models' phenomena for them, asking them to find a scientific equivalent.

(3) Proust's active interest in botany, and more generally in natural history.

(4) General background of scientific revolution. The effects of science through technology. Abundance of popularizing texts and periodicals. We have no evidence that Proust read any general publications popularizing science, save those on natural history and medicine. Similarly, more general periodicals which Proust is known to have read include items on science, but letters and other records do not document his direct reaction to these.

This, then, is the atmosphere—or perhaps 'ether' is the more accurate description—in which Proust was immersed. Medicine and botany/natural history are the strongest points of contact. Otherwise, science is mediated by friends and acquaintances in response to Proust's requests for scientific metaphors. Often, as the final point indicates, the connections are extremely tenuous.

Returning to *A la recherche* at this stage, we return to the underlying question of what it is that makes meaningful the textual characteristics of science in *A la recherche*, notably its abundant metaphoric, speculative, and regulatory presence. Perhaps this 'evidence' could be arranged to connect with some aspect of the state of science contemporary with Proust. It might also be possible to begin with the scientific context, taking this as a guide to *A la recherche*, one which might in turn be 'proved' by the facts of the text. Neither of these inductive or deductive gestures is particularly helpful or indeed applicable here. Were it possible to locate exact points of contact between the author and science, and term these 'influence'—'the influence of the new physics on the depiction of time and space in *A la recherche*', for example—the operation would certainly appear more straightforward, more plausible even. It would cover up awkward questions such as, 'What is it that patterns the description? Is it inductive or deductive?' But even so, such questions would continue to lurk beneath the account. In the case of Proust and *A la recherche*, where direct influence is, for the most part, lacking, some kind of delicate negotiation between the three areas (science as presented by the text, Proust's scientific culture, the scientific context) is required.

The delicate negotiation between science in the text and extra-textual scientific material requires that narratives of causal influence and 'Zeitgeist' alike be avoided. In the place of such narratives one might attempt to give an account in which a different, perhaps non-linear, order of events were presented. This account would work simultaneously with our reading of science in *A la recherche* and with a hypothesis about what was patterning this reading. Why should some features of the novel stand out? Hypotheses formulated in answer to this question would be both about the nature of science in the novel, but also about the notion of extra-textual science contemporary with Proust. If this process—which is not so revolutionary, since it in fact describes the general pattern of how researchers work—is redescribed in terms borrowed from the philosophy of science, it would be said to involve an attempt to hold at once the general and the particular, the nascent theory, or hypothesis, and the data. A dialectical relationship is established between these two terms, between the interested observation of phenomena and an intuition, formulated as a hypothesis, of what it is that makes them interesting, that makes some features stand out. This process was described by Aristotle in the *Prior Analytics* as the third type of inference, after deduction and induction. The term 'retroduction' was then coined from a translation of this text by philosopher Charles S. Peirce.[5] It is from this last type of inference that, Peirce claims, 'all the ideas of science come; it consists in studying the facts and devising a theory to explain them. Its only justification is that if we are ever to understand things at all, it must be in that way.'[6]

In the 1950s, Norwood Hanson further developed the concept of retroductive inference, in which 'the dawning of an aspect and the dawning of an explanation both suggest what to look for next'.[7] His basic explanation is worth rehearsing:

(1) Some surprising phenomenon P is observed.

[5] Charles S. Peirce, 'Principles of Philosophy', in *Collected Papers of Charles Sanders Peirce*, I, ed. C. Hartshorne and P. Weiss (Cambridge, Mass.: Belknap Press, 1931), 65. Peirce also calls this type of inference 'by the otherwise quite useless name of Abduction' (*Collected Papers*, v. 144) or 'hypothesis'. See Susan Howe, 'Renunciation is a P[ei]rcing Value', in *Profession 1998* (New York: MLA, 1998), 51–61.

[6] Peirce, 'Pragmatism and Pragmaticism', in *Collected Papers*, v. 145.

[7] Hanson, *Patterns of Discovery*, 86.

(2) P would be explicable as a matter of course if [hypothesis] H were true.

(3) Hence there is reason to think that H is true.

H cannot be retroductively inferred until its content is present in (2). Inductive accounts expect H to emerge from repetitions of P. H-D (hypothetico-deductive) accounts make P emerge from some unaccounted-for creation of H as a 'higher-level hypothesis'.[8]

In other words, the hypothesis does not *just* result from the statistical processing of a certain quantity of observed phenomena; nor is the hypothesis *just* thought of, and the phenomena deduced from it. Instead, the phenomena are distinguished as worthy of observation because they seem to form a certain pattern, and what makes us notice this pattern is an intuition of its theorization, of law. The two are worked at simultaneously. And once the pattern as a whole is understood, so new details become explicable within it. 'Grasping this plot makes the details explicable.'[9] This account of retroduction maps sensitively (as the accounts of induction and deduction do not) the *workings* of the creative imagination. 'The struggle for intelligibility (pattern, organization) in natural philosophy has never been portrayed in inductive or H-D accounts.'[10]

There is great potential in the concept of 'retroduction' for answering the methodological concerns raised by this study of science and structure in *A la recherche*. 'Retroduction' both rescues Proust from the ether of *general* scientific influence and, as an alternative to tracking causal chains of connection, might be described as epistemologically better suited to this particular study. Looking beyond methodological concerns, this type of inference is also peculiarly appropriate to *A la recherche*. Retroductive accounts describe the birth of theory—at this stage, theory is still hypothesis, an intuition of the patterns of intelligibility, caught up in a dialectic between data suggesting a certain organization and the intuition of a theory which traces and makes meaningful such patterns. And this dialectic suggests an apt description of the structure and dynamics of *A la recherche* itself, of the interaction of maxim–metaphor and *récit*.

Retroduction, then, allows for the initial 'embarrassment' of negotiating between facts and theories, or hypotheses; but, significantly, it constitutes itself a hypothesis about the interaction of *récit* and maxim–metaphor in *A la recherche*. 'Retroduction', unsurprisingly, is not in common usage among scientists. Retroductive accounts of

[8] Hanson, *Patterns of Discovery*, 86. [9] Ibid. 87. [10] Ibid.

science would have to be pieced together from conversations, notebook jottings, accounts of experiments in process.[11] Such accounts have no place in public or formal scientific rhetoric. Science requires accounts which operate in the context of justification, not of discovery. And these justificatory narratives operate in retrospect, telling a different story according to a linear plot, clearing up the mess of negotiation between observation, hypothesis, and intuition, forgetting or masking the all-at-once-ness of the inference.[12]

The non-linear narrative of *A la recherche* re-exposes the retroductive order. The laws of *A la recherche* rarely cap a series of observations. They are either pre-established, the Proustian commonplaces, or speculative, tending to reformulate, to proliferate, producing clusters of lawlike statements—as occurs most characteristically in the Albertine texts. These dynamic law statements might be described as pulsing according to a system of systole and diastole; contracting around the key regulatory maxims of desire, love, jealousy, and habit, dilating outwards, speculatively, over a range of topics. Moreover, in this dilatory mode, maxims do not necessarily precede or follow on from case history or metaphor or episode in the *récit*. Metaphors jostle as if in competition, for the outcome will determine the resultant law. Conversely, law may determine metaphor or anecdote ('case history'), which in turn has the potential to produce a subset or higher set of the original theory.

The relation between the general and the particular is fraught; the one is infused with, and constantly suggesting, the other.[13] As Adorno describes, 'The particular is the general, and vice versa, with each mediated through the other, so the whole, resistant to abstract outlines, crystallizes out of intertwined, individual presentations.'[14] There

[11] Holton distinguishes between science in its public, institutional aspect and science as a 'personal struggle'; see *Thematic Origins of Scientific Thought*, 6–20.

[12] Hanson's discussion of Newton draws attention to these two possible narrative styles: 'For Newton the law, as it was first retroduced, did not simply "cap" a cluster of prior observations. . . . Rather it was discovered as that from which the observations would become explicable as a matter of course. Newton was not an actuary who could squeeze a functional relationship out of columns of data; he was an inspired detective' (*Patterns of Discovery*, 107).

[13] Crémieux, misled by Proust's notion of mapping the *evolution* of thought, reads this dialectic as a one-way narrative: 'Proust ne se contente pas de nous tendre les deux bouts de la chaîne: la sensation qui est à l'origine, la pensée qui est au point d'arrivée. Il entend nous faire suivre tout le parcours que sa sensibilité et son intelligence ont suivi pour arriver au but. Parcours que l'imagination de Proust rend particulièrement riche; c'est par la voie d'observations précises, de comparaisons, d'analogies, d'associations d'idées, de métaphores imprévues que, partis de l'impression, nous atteignons la pensée centrale' ('Le surimpressionisme de Proust', 35).

[14] Trans. S. W. Nicholsen in *Notes to Literature* (New York: Columbia University Press,

is a pull at once towards the particular and the general. For, according to this aesthetic, parsimony falsifies:

Du reste, si nous n'étions pas pour l'ordre du récit obligé de nous borner à des raisons frivoles, combien de plus sérieuses nous permettraient de montrer la minceur menteuse du début de ce volume où, de mon lit, j'entends le monde s'éveiller, tantôt par un temps, tantôt par un autre! Oui, j'ai été forcé d'amincir la chose et d'être mensonger, mais ce n'est pas un univers, c'est des millions, presque autant qu'il existe de prunelles et d'intelligences humaines, qui s'éveillent tous les matins. (iii. 696)

For this dialectic to become apparent, I will read retroduction in three short passages. The first two indicate moments at which the Proustian commonplaces are dominant and exercise a regulatory effect; the third, the Rivebelle restaurant scene, is a passage of dilatory exchange between maxim and metaphor.

Qu'on dise si dans la vie en commun que mènent les idées au sein de notre esprit, il est une seule de celles qui nous rendent le plus heureux qui n'ait été d'abord, en véritable parasite, demander à une idée étrangère et voisine le meilleur de la force qui lui manquait. (i. 472–3)

The above maxim is itself the final clause of a variety of generalized examples. We have been introduced to such figures from the very first pages of *A la recherche*, where we find 'le malade', 'un homme qui dort', 'le voyageur'. In this particular series we find the artist, the lover, and the traveller. Its generalizing impulse is apparently generated by the young narrator's response to La Berma's performance as Phèdre (i. 472–3). As Marcel reads the critics' reviews, however, his initial disappointment gives way to exaltation. Our reaction as readers to this transformation—we may doubt Marcel's sincerity—is pre-empted by the narrator's reflection which begins, 'qu'on songe plutôt à tant

1991), 174. Adorno, 'Kleine Proust-Kommentare' in *Noten zur Literatur*, vol. 2 (Frankfurt: Suhrkamp, 1961), 95: 'Das Besondere sei das Allgemeine und umgekehrt, beides sei durcheinander vermittelt, so kristallisiert sich das Ganze, allem abstrakten Umriß abhold, aus den ineinandergewachsenen Einzeldarstellungen.' German critics or, rather, German-speaking critics of Proust (notably Spitzer, Curtius, and Benjamin) seem particularly sensitive to this relation between the particular and the general. Wladimir Weidlé (*Die Sterblichkeit der Musen*, trans. K. A. Horst (Stuttgart: Deutsche-Verlags-Anstalt, 1958), 27) addresses the relation through the analogy of 'Proust the scientist': 'Für Proust kam es also so weit, daß er sich als einen Erforscher von Gesetzen, als einen Beweis führenden Darsteller, daß er sich—mit einem Wort—als einen Wissenschaftler betrachtete, zu dem es denn auch durchaus paßt, ein Ereignis als Musterfall einer bestimmten Kategorie von Ereignissen herauszustellen' ('Proust's case was so extreme that he saw himself as a discoverer of laws, whose depictions had the force of demonstration; in short, he saw himself as a scientist, for whom it is quite appropriate to single out an event as exemplary of a certain category of events').

d'écrivains'. This is the first example. The writer who, disappointed by his own work, then reads an article praising the genius of Chateaubriand or hums to himself a phrase of Beethoven when writing, and retrospectively assimilates these to his own text. The lover's experience is then added as another example of this same law, 'qu'on se rappelle tant d'hommes qui croient en l'amour d'une maîtresse de qui ils ne connaissent que les trahisons'. The example is varied, and that of the artist briefly reintroduced, before the introduction of the final figure, the traveller: 'qu'on pense encore aux touristes qu'exalte la beauté d'ensemble d'un voyage dont jour par jour ils n'ont éprouvé que de l'ennui'. It is at this point that we reach the concluding generalization cited above. This is the variety of law—and we are made to feel it all the more strongly through the containment of this range of examples within a single sentence. Each example could be, and indeed is, 'filled out' over the course of the novel, whereby, stepping down from its generality, it becomes an episode in the *récit* in its own right. Here, however, the examples serve as potent illustrations, grouped by the same underlying dynamic, their cumulative force eventually releasing the law, which, it is worth noting, though psychological, is itself expressed through a physiological model.

The illustrations of *A la recherche* rarely remain well-behaved demonstrations. The swelling scale of generalization from its initial particular point may occur to comic effect. In the passage cited above, the illustrations are generalized and recognizably Proustian *topoi*; they culminate in the expression of the law which was also their motivator. But we also find instances in which an apparently limited law grows far beyond its original application. The young narrator's meeting with M. de Norpois (i. 468–9) is a case in point. In the narrator's response as Norpois offers to mention him to Gilberte and Odette there is already an effect of comic generalization through myth—transformed into 'une divinité de l'Olympe qui a pris la fluidité d'un souffle ou plutôt l'aspect du vieillard dont Minerve emprunte les traits', the narrator is able to gain access to the salon of Mme Swann. He almost moves to thank Norpois by kissing his hands, then checks himself. The perception of this gesture by the narrator and by Norpois triggers the movement of generalization: 'Il est difficile en effet à chacun de nous de calculer exactement à quelle échelle ses paroles ou ses mouvements apparaissent à autrui.' The belief that our gestures go for the most part unnoticed and unremembered by others is compared to the mistaken attitude of the criminal, who in the belief that no comparison will be made with what he has said previously, will recount a slightly different version of events. 'Même en ce qui concerne la vie millénaire de l'humanité', claims the narrator, as the scale of the generalization increases; the journalist whose philosophy is that all is sentenced to oblivion is likely to be proved wrong. The paper which reports on one page a supposedly ephemeral event or work of art may include on the very next a report from the Académie française which discusses a poem from the time of the Pharaohs, and a second-rate one at that, 'un poème de peu de valeur, qui date de l'époque des Pharaons et qu'on connaît encore intégralement' (i. 469).

The narrator then returns to the original episode in the *récit* and its conclusion some time in the future, when he discovers that not only had Norpois recognized his gesture; he had also remembered it, and was still recounting it to others.

> Ce 'potin' m'éclaira sur les proportions inattendues de distraction et de présence d'esprit, de mémoire et d'oubli dont est fait l'esprit humain; et je fus aussi merveilleusement surpris que le jour où je lus pour la première fois, dans un livre de Maspero, qu'on savait exactement la liste des chasseurs qu'Assourbanipal invitait à ses battues, dix siècles avant Jésus-Christ. (i. 469)

The original slight and comic Norpois anecdote motivates analogical examples which touch on collective memory and the retelling of ancient history. As Phyllis Rose proposes, 'This small, well-observed transaction becomes the subject of a discourse on the effects of magnification'[15]—a discourse which, in considering the nature of perception and memory, touches on fundamental concerns of *A la recherche*. And while this passage may grow from an anecdote which the narrator tells against himself, the digression is so manipulated as to work in the text's own interests to suggest the still greater posterity of art. The Egyptian poem may persist, but 'peut-être n'en est-il pas tout à fait de même pour la courte vie humaine' (i. 469).

The Rivebelle restaurant scene of *A l'ombre des jeunes filles en fleur* (ii. 166–73), our final example of reading retroduction, is also the most extended and spectacular instance of this maxim–metaphor–*récit* interaction.

The restaurant scene is one of the set pieces of *A la recherche*, read as a classic example of Proustian metaphor. According to this reading, the restaurant becomes a solar system, the tables planets with the

[15] Phyllis Rose, *The Year of Reading Proust* (London: Vintage, 1998), 20.

waiters in orbit around them. But this is just one of the metamorphoses which takes place, and the passage might instead be read as a comic example of retroduction. The scene, viewed by the narrator through a number of different analogies, is framed by a theorization of the desire to write. The passage begins with the *topos* of habit. The *topos* is not named as such, because the reader is already sufficiently versed in its laws to recognize its markers—in this case the narrator's acute sensory awareness is the result of habit broken, 'me trouvant dans cette zone différente où l'exceptionnel nous fait entrer après avoir coupé le fil, patiemment tissé depuis tant de jours, qui nous conduisait vers la sagesse' (ii. 166). Yet, instead of causing suffering, it precipitates the loss of certain fears and desires: 'je ne savais plus la peur de tomber malade, la nécessité de ne pas mourir, l'importance de travailler' (ii. 166). The narrator experiences a heightened sense of the present—his older and wiser counterpart rarely intrudes to comment on this episode—, a sense of physical well-being, even of euphoria. When the theoretical frame closes in on the scene, this experience of the moment is equated with the loss of the time of desire—that is, of a sense of past and future, and so with the time of writing (ii. 172–3).

The narrator is 'un homme nouveau', whose by now intoxicated vision connects and metamorphoses the spectacle of the restaurant. At first it is a racecourse. The waiters are 'lâchés entre les tables', hence 'ce genre de courses' and 'malgré le galop'; with a closer focus on the scene, one of these waiters is transformed from racehorse to exotic bird, 'emplumé de superbes cheveux noirs, la figure fardée d'un teint qui rappelait davantage certaines espèces d'oiseaux rares que l'espèce humaine' (ii. 167). As the narrator calms down, the 'spectacle' too becomes more comprehensible, 'plus noble et plus calme', and his vision encompasses the whole restaurant in the metaphor of planetary motion. The 'tables rondes' are like so many planets; the behaviour of the diners is explained in terms of force fields: 'une force d'attraction irrésistible s'exerçait entre ces astres divers et à chaque table les dîneurs n'avaient d'yeux que pour les tables où ils n'étaient pas' (ii. 168). The waiters are in unceasing revolution around these 'astral' tables, 'leur course perpétuelle entre les tables rondes finissait par dégager la loi de sa circulation vertigineuse et réglée' (ii. 168), and the 'caissières' become magicians, involved in the calculation and prediction of possible disturbances in this 'voûte céleste conçue selon la science du Moyen Age'.

The narrator then turns briefly to the subject of his own vision, the power of analogy which has effected these transformations. This is described as the practice of 'sectionnement qui nous débarrasse de [l'] apparence coutumière [des objets] et nous permet d'apercevoir des analogies' (ii. 168), and constitutes the *sous-entendu* of this episode. But the process does not stop at this point. It is already richer than received readings suggest, as various metaphors are proposed before the full exposition of the planetary scene—there follows an even less likely analogy, between the restaurant and industrial chemistry: 'pareil à ces industries chimiques grâce auxquelles sont débités en grandes quantités des corps qui ne se rencontrent dans la nature que d'une façon accidentelle et fort rarement, ce restaurant de Rivebelle réunissait en un même moment plus de femmes' (ii. 169). This notion of industrial chemistry provides an ironic counterpart to the alchemical reactions of the 'tilleul' and involuntary memory. The mass production of women is at this point just a subordinate clause prefacing the more intoxicating delights of the restaurant music—waltzes, operettas, café-concert songs. But the music itself provides a figure for woman desired, and reintroduces the *topos* of jealousy (ii. 169). Returning from his reflections to the restaurant setting, the narrator observes women taking tea in the glassed gallery as shining fish: 'on aurait dit un réservoir, une nasse où le pêcheur a entassé les éclatants poissons qu'il a pris, lesquels à moitié hors de l'eau et baignés de rayons miroitent aux regards en leur éclat changeant' (ii. 170); and as the light fades, these are replaced by the vegetation of 'un pâle et vert aquarium géant à la lumière surnaturelle'. The 'planets' of the dining room retain their attractive and deflective forces, but now a physiological model is introduced. The dinner parties consist of corpuscles: 'il arrivait souvent qu'au moment du passage tel dîner en marche abandonnait l'un ou plusieurs de ses corpuscules, qui ayant subi trop fortement l'attraction du dîner rival se détachaient un instant du leur' (ii. 171).

Throughout these transformations, the restaurant has acted as container. We see with the narrator the patterns and dynamic of its spectacle, staged as a gamut of flora and fauna (racehorses, birds, fish, underwater vegetation), as chemicals or cells (industrial chemistry, corpuscles), as an astrological tableau, whose theoretical underpinning is a maxim on the power of analogy. Now, as the narrator returns from the restaurant, the text returns to the initial preoccupations of the frame, namely habit, work—that is, writing—and death: 'l'ivresse réalise pour quelques heures l'idéalisme subjectif, le phénoménisme pur; tout n'est plus qu'apparences et n'existe plus qu'en fonction de notre sublime nous-même' (ii. 173).

The spectacular show of metaphor seems to exist here free of the restraining fears and desires of the text, governed only by the law of analogy. Yet, many of these metaphors have echoes and counterparts elsewhere, while the scene as a whole reminds us of another classic example of extended metaphor, the aquarium/opera scene (ii. 337–58). And even here, through the music of the restaurant, surface momentarily the irresistible laws of desire and jealousy, accompanied by a generalized illustration ('chaque fois que dans notre vie nous avons déplu à une femme' (ii. 169–70)). This is the illustration which links the frame (theorizing on the effects of drunkenness) back to the *récit* ('je ne connaissais aucune des femmes à Rivebelle'), and 'proves' the maxim that 'cette mathématique du lendemain, la même que celle d'hier et avec les problèmes de laquelle nous nous retrouverons inexorablement aux prises, c'est celle qui nous régit même pendant ces heures-là, sauf pour nous-même' (ii. 174).

This is the characteristic texture which the scientific mapping of the text will explore. Retroduction allows close stylistic analysis, but it will also be developed to examine the text at the level of the *récit*: namely, to consider its narratives of intuition and cognition.

The retroductive model represents the schematized and untroubled version of Poincaré's reflections on scientific creativity. For retroduction depends on, but more importantly states, what had been for Western science a tacit belief—namely, that man is in harmony with nature and therefore able to intuit its laws. As Peirce proposes: 'It is certain that the only hope of retroductive reasoning ever reaching the truth is that there may be some natural tendency toward an agreement between the ideas which suggest themselves to the human mind and those which are concerned in the laws of nature.'[16]

Intuition becomes problematic once it becomes necessary to formalize it as part of a scientific discourse. Poincaré's speculation about the retroductive dialectic, couched as an interrogation of the role of intuition or the unconscious in scientific work, will be revisited to consider involuntary memory, the dominant narrative of creativity in *A la recherche* and its most spectacular form of intuition, but also to analyse the text's backdrop of more speculative and sometimes fearful accounts of revelation, intuition, and memory.

The speculative style, and indeed the performance of speculation in

[16] Peirce, 'Principles of Philosophy', 1. 81.

A la recherche, will be the subject of the next chapter. This style has been eloquently characterized as a 'rich prose [which] fuses into a highly sensuous and simultaneous present within which the possible explanations and possible effects of any gesture multiply to infinity';[17] and this, in a sense, is to describe in aesthetic terms what we have more technically named 'the expansive, dilatory movement of retroduction'. Both characterizations omit the subject and object of speculation, thereby evading the key question of the relation of self to hypothesis, to intuition and law, but also to the real. These relations might be redescribed as the performance of speculation.

[17] Roger Shattuck, *Proust's Binoculars* (London: Chatto and Windus, 1964), 122–3.

4
HYPOTHESIS

> Je crois en un monde en soi, monde régi par des lois que j'essaie d'appréhender d'une manière sauvagement spéculative.
>
> Einstein, letter to Max Born

> Rôle de l'hypothèse.—Toute généralisation est une hypothèse; l'hypothèse a donc un rôle nécessaire que personne n'a jamais contesté. Seulement elle doit toujours être, le plus tôt possible et le plus souvent possible, soumise à la vérification. Il va sans dire que, si elle ne supporte pas cette épreuve, on doit l'abandonner sans arrière-pensée. C'est bien ce qu'on fait en général, mais quelquefois avec une certaine mauvaise humeur.
>
> Poincaré, *La Science et l'hypothèse*

When the text at its most legislative 'maximizes' on science, we learn that science and art are equally creative processes, that an intuitive approach to science yields the best results, that metaphor in literature is like causality in science, and so on. What is the force of these, and countless other, maxims? Literal readings accord them the status of law; mapping through the notion of 'retroduction' reveals them to be a good deal more speculative than that. To avoid collapsing the dynamics of law to the commonplace statements, we need to explore their locus as they are formulated both by the narrator's desiring personae—the self staged as lover, as would-be artist, as traveller—and by the narrator as producer of those selves. The narrator's claims—both overt and implied—that he is now a natural historian, occasionally a physicist or a mathematician, engaged in research will be tested by tracking him as he devises experiments, proofs, and hypotheses.

Speculation greatly preoccupies the narrator—indeed, the Albertine volumes might be described as one single relentless hypothesis about the nature of Albertine's sexuality. If hypothesis about the particular makes of the narrator a detective and motivates plot, hypotheses about the general inform the text at the stylistic, retroductive level; for the maxims of *A la recherche* appear now speculative, now to bear the authority of the law. 'Toute généralisation est une hypothèse.'[1] Poincaré's slogan goes to the heart of the hypothesis debate. His *La Science et l'hypothèse* illuminates the epistemological anxiety which this term arouses in both *A la recherche* and in the practice and philosophy of science at the turn of the century.

This chapter will trace the 'scientific activity' of *A la recherche* at its most speculative, through *hypothèse* and its derivatives. When plotted and psychologized, the hypotheses of *A la recherche* are fundamental to the *expérience* of the narrator as scientist, artist, and lover, for he is now constituted, placed, by them; now in control, disposing of and playing with speculation at his whim. Generally, women appear as the desired object of study—the duchesse de Guermantes, the 'jeunes filles' of *A l'ombre*, Albertine in the later volumes. These women are, for the narrator, a puzzling and tantalizing 'natural phenomenon'. In the earlier volumes they appear in their natural habitat, and the narrator attempts to decipher them as an elemental part of the rural landscape or seascape. In later volumes, displaced from the countryside to Paris, they are more elusive; and, more troubling still, they are no longer simply the increasingly inaccessible object of the narrator's speculation, but also a *subject* with knowledge of itself. The ever more desirous relations of the narrator with Albertine or, rather, with his hypothesis about her ultimately defines both the power and the impotence of his speculation.

Writing about hypothesis describes desire. The desire for knowledge (manifest in the imagery drawn from the sciences, but also through a range of scientific and cognitive vocabulary) is the lover's desire, the web of hypotheses he casts to pin the other down. Now, there is a book of desire which is *A la recherche*, a slim commonplace book encapsulating not hypotheses, but laws. The narrator's account of his desire for Gilberte is so punctuated by maxims on love, forgetting, resignation, regret, that it might be described as an essay of which the *récit* is simply an illustration. Some of the shorter, more extractable maxims include: 'Le temps dont nous disposons chaque jour est élastique; les passions que nous ressentons le dilatent, celles que nous inspirons le rétrécissent, et l'habitude le remplit' (i. 601): 'Le regret comme le désir ne cherche pas à s'analyser' (i. 603); 'La résignation, modalité de l'habitude, permet à certaines forces de s'accroître indéfiniment' (i. 611): 'On désire une joie, et le moyen matériel de l'atteindre fait défaut. "Il est triste, a dit La Bruyère, d'aimer sans une

[1] Poincaré, *La Science et l'hypothèse*, 'Les hypothèses en physique', 165.

grande fortune" ' (i. 613); 'La personne que nous aimons doit y être reconnue seulement à la force de la douleur éprouvée' (i. 619); 'Ceux qui souffrent par l'amour sont, comme on dit de certains malades, leur propre médecin. Comme il ne peut leur venir de consolation que de l'être qui cause leur douleur et que cette douleur est une émanation de lui, c'est en elle qu'ils finissent par trouver un remède' (i. 620); 'On construit sa vie pour une personne et quand enfin on peut l'y recevoir, cette personne ne vient pas, puis meurt pour nous et on vit prisonnier, dans ce qui n'était destiné qu'à elle' (i. 623). So classic are these maxims that the narrator even breaks his own rules, enlisting and quoting La Bruyère (see pp. 20–1).

By *La Prisonnière* the narrator is noting the repetition of his maxims: 'Pour nos sentiments, nous en avons parlé trop souvent pour le redire, bien souvent un amour n'est que l'association d'une image de jeune fille . . . avec les battements de cœur inséparables d'une attente' (iii. 574–5). In *Albertine disparue*, however, such *topoi* are revisited with greater urgency. Here too the text is at its most lawlike when the narrator, as lover, is most desirous. The set of commonplaces about desire still pertains; yet the law is, as it were, remobilized, interrogated—the narrator rails against these Proustian commonplaces, he also speculates not just about the nature of his desire (as in the Gilbertine extract), but about that of Albertine. The proliferation of maxims has as its counterpoint the binary hypothesis which attempts to uncover not some general law, but the particular: Is Albertine lesbian or not? The text repeatedly rehearses a reductive gesture, back towards the law, back towards the origins of these spectacular surface manifestations of desire in sexuality.[2] Yet these origins are themselves complex and multiple, as, for example, the botanical/racial/mythic origins of homosexuality (*Sodome et Gomorrhe I*) or the metamorphoses of the 'jeunes filles' in their elemental setting. Albertine is often presented as the figure of such oppositions, between depth-origins and surface-speculation. Her 'centre' is inaccessible, only ever visible by the layers which, like snow on a stone, have accumulated around it, allowing its form, roughly, indistinctly, to emerge (iv. 22). Her 'depth' is labyrinthine, elemental but complex, represented by the canals of Venice, which are in turn internalized by the narrator: 'Je pouvais

[2] And criticism may mime this gesture. See Kaja Silverman's analysis of the narrator's attempt to kiss Albertine in the chapter 'A woman's soul enclosed in a man's body: femininity in male homosexuality' (*Male Subjectivity at the Margins* (New York: Routledge, 1992), 339). My discussion of this passage (Sect. 4.3) may be usefully contrasted with Silverman's.

bien . . . caresser [Albertine], passer longuement mes mains sur elle, mais, comme si j'eusse manié une pierre qui enferme la salure des océans immémoriaux ou le rayon d'une étoile, je sentais que je touchais seulement l'enveloppe close d'un être qui par l'intérieur accédait à l'infini' (iii. 888).

The text's self-exposure is perhaps most striking in *Albertine disparue*, where reduction is plotted. Here the pursuit of Albertine's sexuality is structured around the hypothetical pair: is she gay or straight? This mode of hypothesizing appears superficially to be opposed to the delight in multiplicity and diverse speculation, and indeed to the overt disdain for narrow hypothesis displayed in earlier texts. Yet, this earlier speculative energy is not so much reduced as compressed, ultimately spilling out of the confines of the insoluble binary hypothesis and channelled into every available space. Hypotheses proliferate: 'Albertine ne gagnait pas moins à être ainsi transportée de l'un des deux mondes où nous avons accès et où nous pouvons situer tour à tour un même objet, à échapper ainsi à l'écrasante pression de la matière pour se jouer dans les fluides espaces de la pensée' (iii. 565).

The following episode in *La Prisonnière* is one of many occasions on which the narrator speculates about Albertine's sexuality, but in which this desire to reduce provokes digressions on a range of topics, from the apparently slight and everyday to the world of science and questions of the novelist's art. Albertine lies about why she has returned home late; she claims to have visited Bergotte (iii. 693), a fact which the narrator accepts at the time and comes to question only later, on discovering its impossibility. Even at this stage, the narrator formulates a digressive generalization, triggered by the observation that he no longer sees Bergotte for his own pleasure, but for that of Albertine: 'Ces cas sont fréquents; parfois, celui ou celle qu'on implore non pour le plaisir de causer de nouveau avec lui, mais pour une tierce personne' (iii. 694). The death of this writer, whom the narrator had held in high esteem, now signifies only in that it allows him to discover Albertine's lie, and thereby to progress in his research about her sexuality. From this minor digression, he moves from speculation about the particular to a more confident sententious mode. Albertine's lie becomes the next subject for digression, and this is introduced in a manner similar to that of the scholarly exordium of *Sodome et Gomorrhe*: 'Il y aurait du reste beaucoup à discuter ce mot de fausseté' (iii. 694). Here, however, the topic of the digression, lying, leads swiftly to vast generalizations on the nature of vision—

'L'univers est vrai pour nous tous et dissemblable pour chacun' (iii. 694)—before feeding back into, and articulating, a discussion of the reliability of what others report that they have seen and of our own sensory perception. An imaginative experiment is devised to test the proposal that eyewitness reports cannot be relied upon, that only by witnessing events oneself can one be certain of their validity. In this hypothetical situation, Albertine claims to be late, because she has been walking outside with a woman friend. The narrator imagines verifying the claim. What if he had been outside and seen that this was not true? 'On peut imaginer pourtant qu'une telle hypothèse n'est pas invraisemblable' (iii. 694). But this too must be modified; the hypothesis is redundant, for it cannot be tested: the narrator's faith in Albertine's statement might cause him to believe that he saw the situation wrongly, just as his scepticism might lead him to ignore the woman's presence. Lying proves to be a subset of a general law of false perception according to which any hypothesis about observable reality proves impossible to verify.

The narrator's account of the difficulties of seeing Albertine echoes Bertrand Russell's anecdotal illustration of 'seeing Jones', in which a similar point about the subjectivity of perception is made. What we think we see, Russell argues, is somewhat different from what is actually observed:

> The point is that Jones is a *convenient hypothesis* by means of which certain of your own sensations can be collected into a bundle; but what really makes them belong together is not their common hypothetical origin, but *certain resemblances* and *causal affinities* which they have to each other. These remain, even if their *common origin is mythical*.[3]

Russell redescribes the process in scientific terms (atoms, light waves, quanta, and optic nerves), but stresses that such terminology cannot pin down the nature of vision: the brain's reception of images is not absolute, but always dependent on perspective. 'The connection of "seeing Jones" with Jones is a remote, roundabout causal connection. Jones himself [as does Albertine] remains wrapped in mystery', or, as the narrator concludes: 'Le témoignage des sens est lui aussi une opération de l'esprit où la conviction crée l'évidence' (iii. 694).

This maxim appears to resolve the episode, encapsulating the laws of subjectivity, of relative point of view. But the energy of the initial hypothesis (about Albertine) still animates the text. The narrator is

[3] Bertrand Russell, *The Scientific Outlook* (London: George Allen and Unwin, 1931), 78.

incorrigible, delighting in further examples of false perception, those of mishearing and mispronunciation as demonstrated by Françoise and Aimé, then returning again to the key hypothetical situation and to his sense that, had he been able to go outside and check Albertine's statement, he would not have seen the woman, but would have assumed this to be an error on his part, an optical illusion. Vision for the narrator, as for Russell, is conditioned by the mythical, by the stories woven around the object we are trying to see: 'car le monde des astres est moins difficile à connaître que les actions réelles des êtres, surtout des êtres que nous aimons, fortifiés qu'ils sont contre notre doute par des fables destinées à les protéger' (iii. 696). This explanation leads once again to a case of the extreme dialectic between the general and the particular, here moving to a comparison between astronomy and psychology, which recalls the claimed scientific status of the narrator's research. Knowledge is prevented by necessary fictions, those fables which, sustained by the lover-scientist's own desire, mask and protect the beloved. The lover, the scientist and . . . 'fable' triggers the third member of this desiring group, the novelist, whose reflections on the ethics and aesthetics of abundance account in retrospect for the movement of the passage which has provoked them:

> Du reste, si nous n'étions pas pour l'ordre du récit obligé de nous borner à des raisons frivoles, combien de plus sérieuses nous permettraient de montrer la minceur menteuse du début de ce volume où, de mon lit, j'entends le monde s'éveiller, tantôt par un temps, tantôt par un autre! Oui, j'ai été forcé d'amincir la chose et d'être mensonger, mais ce n'est pas un univers, c'est des millions, presque autant qu'il existe de prunelles et d'intelligences humaines, qui s'éveillent tous les matins. (iii. 696)

Here the academic, narrating 'nous' speaks of the narrated 'je'—and this in turn gives way to an authorial 'je', reflecting on his novel. Just as the lover recognizes and rails against the single perspective to which he is restricted, so does the writer react to the confines of the novelistic form. Truth cannot be expressed by a linear narrative, 'l'ordre du récit': this paring down falsifies, 'minceur' is 'menteuse'. Yet the movement of this passage, and more generally of the text, from *récit* to generalization of varying degrees to textual illustration to speculative example performs what is desired: that is, an aesthetic of complete representation.

This exclamation is far from the text's plotted reductionism, far too from the commonplace book—for there is such a variety of generality to be encompassed! The ideal of universality is represented by the drive to generalization, to the emblem, to ground in the literary, mythic, and scientific, as a substitute for the impossible aesthetic of absolute inclusion. The 'je' here is placed as particular and as general, as it is from the beginning of the novel, and even from the very first drafts of 'Combray', in which the two modes are confused.[4] This art of placing so as to be propitious to generality—'Or si au cours de cet ouvrage, j'ai eu et j'aurai bien des occasions de montrer comment la jalousie redouble l'amour, c'est au point de vue de l'amant que je me suis placé' (iii. 697)—provokes the return to the *récit* and to Albertine's lies.

Hypotheses about the particular, which are neither verifiable nor falsifiable, trigger this mode of speculative generality. The dialectic between the particular and the general is generated around the narrator's jealous 'hypothèse', whose evolution will be described over the following pages. Such rhetorical performances are always simply reducible, whether to the commonplace or to their 'origins' in sexuality. The possibility of reduction is, of course, implicit in the retroductive model of contracting and dilating generality, and it is perceived by the narrator both as empowering and as a threat: 'ces particularités de caractère, pareilles à ces petits losanges d'épiderme dont les combinaisons variées font l'originalité fleurie de la chair. Notre radiation intuitive les traverse et les images qu'elle nous rapporte ne sont point celles d'un visage particulier mais représentent la morne et douloureuse universalité d'un squelette' (ii. 249).

In the case of the passage from *La Prisonnière* analysed above, the reduction in fact moves towards an epistemological maxim: namely, that it is impossible to establish the truth of the particular. The narrator cannot discover whether Albertine is lying or not; he cannot trust the view of others, nor can he trust his own. The significance of this conclusion for hypothesis—or at least for hypotheses about the particular—is that it must always operate imaginatively, speculatively, in the narrator's mind. Hypothesis can never be verified or falsified by reference to the real. Yet the real is, as it were, an incitement to the narrator's speculation. Tracing the web of this speculation allows a

[4] See Claudine Quémar, 'Autour de trois avant textes de l'"Ouverture" de la *Recherche*', *Bulletin d'informations proustiennes*, 3 (1976), 7–29. Such slippage also occurs in the final text, as e.g. iii. 788–9, where the narrator, describing Brichot's memories, slips from 'je' to 'il' to 'nous'. Gilbert Gaston (*Proust, l'homme des mondes* (Paris: Kimé, 1993), 209) terms this 'Le *Je* pénétrant dans les profondeurs du *Il* donne, si l'on peut dire, naissance au *Nous* qui, dans cette phrase si signicative, prolifère'.

mapping of the complex, affective relationship between the particular and the general. With Poincaré's 'toute généralisation est une hypothèse' in mind, generality will be caught at those moments when it is still in the process of negotiation with the particular.

4.1 Tracing hypothesis—abundance

> C'est dans la moule de l'action que notre intelligence a été coulée. La spéculation est un luxe tandis que l'action est une nécessité.
>
> Bergson, *L'Évolution créatrice*

The hypotheses of *A la recherche* follow two quite distinct patterns and two apparently distinct aesthetics, the first of which might be characterized as luxuriant speculation. This mobile, diverse speculation which constantly defers contact with the object(s) of desire is above all the mode of *A l'ombre des jeunes filles en fleur*. Although, as Kaufmann's *Post Scripts* reveals, it bears a curious resemblance to Proust's own financial and epistolary speculation, which is also characterized by a deflected contact with the real: 'Proust spends his life gambling on others and on their thoughts and desires. Instead of asking for something, he tries to win it. Speculation (which is, fundamentally, a work of the imagination) is Proust's favourite means of communication with others, while words and speech are repeatedly rejected or qualified.'[5] Or, in the narrator's words, 'par nature le monde des possibles m'a toujours été plus ouvert que celui de la contingence réelle' (iii. 533).

In *A l'ombre* the narrator is initally a botanist, roaming the countryside in search of new specimens, country women in their natural habitat. His speculative research is punctuated by epistemological reflections. On glimpsing a girl from Mme de Villeparisis's carriage, for example, Marcel at once regrets that he will not be able to meet her, yet recognizes that her absence sustains his speculative desire: 'Et alors, tout effort pour pénétrer dans sa vie m'eût semblé soudain impossible. Car la beauté est une suite d'hypothèses que rétrécit la laideur en barrant la route que nous voyions déjà s'ouvrir sur l'inconnu' (ii. 73). Not only does the value of this—very unscientific—hypothesis lie in its untestability, but it would be endangered by any engagement with the real. The aesthetic of the purely speculative

[5] Vincent Kaufman, *Post Scripts*, trans. D. Treisman (Cambridge, Mass.: Harvard University Press, 1994), 83.

imagination is at once stimulated and threatened by the desire for such an engagement, and the passage to which this maxim is the conclusion itself enacts this mode of speculation.

'Fleurs de la belle journée', the passage opens with the narrator's exclamation, 'mais qui ne sont pas comme les fleurs des champs, car chacune recèle quelque chose qui n'est pas dans une autre et qui empêchera que nous puissions contenter avec ses pareilles le désir qu'elle a fait naître en nous' (ii. 71). His commonplace analogy vainly attempts to divest the girl of her particular attraction by restoring her to her natural habitat. As desire for the particular reasserts itself, so generalizations on the nature of desire are introduced, illustrated by metaphors of ingestion. Within these metaphors the narrator becomes 'un enfant né dans une prison ou dans un hôpital et qui ayant cru longtemps que l'organisme humain ne peut digérer que du pain sec et des médicaments, a appris tout d'un coup que les pêches, les abricots, le raisin, ne sont pas une simple parure de la campagne, mais des aliments délicieux et assimilables' (ii. 71). The peaches, apricots, and grapes—the 'filles de campagne'—are too exotic for the narrator's delicate constitution. In this episode the narrator's convalescence effectively prevents him from meeting the women he spies from his carriage, as he is accompanied by Mme de Villeparisis and his grandmother. Later, sickness will be feigned, and deterministic metaphors used independently, to suggest the preference for operating in a hypothetical imaginary where 'un désir nous semble plus beau, nous nous appuyons à lui avec plus de confiance quand nous savons qu'en dehors de nous la réalité s'y conforme, même si pour nous il n'est pas réalisable' (ii. 71–2).

This digression through metaphor to generality is brought comically back to the particular as the narrator returns to the *récit* only to sight another country girl. Again, he is attracted by her particularity: she is a 'créature unique, consciente et volontaire'. The narrator's first reaction is to aestheticize, 'son individualité . . . se peignait en une petite image prodigieusement réduite, mais complète', before returning to a more detailed botanical metaphor—which, significantly, anticipates the description of homosexual courting of the opening of *Sodome et Gomorrhe*—to characterize his own physical response: 'Aussitôt, mystérieuse réplique des pollens tout préparés pour les pistils, je sentais saillir en moi l'embryon aussi vague, aussi minuscule, du désir de ne pas laisser passer cette fille' (ii. 72). This desire is analysed, through maxims and analogous cases formulated in terms of

Proustian archetypes—notably the traveller, whose sickness or poverty prevents him from visiting a country, and who therefore finds that it is this country above all which he desires to visit. The final maxim ('l'imagination est entraînée par le désir de ce que nous ne pouvons posséder') attempts to conclude the analysis, but, requiring refinement, turns ineluctably to a metaphor which evokes a mythological landscape and remobilizes the chain of speculation:

> Pour peu que la nuit tombe et que la voiture aille vite, à la campagne, dans une ville, il n'y a pas un torse féminin, mutilé comme un marbre antique par la vitesse qui nous entraîne et le crépuscule qui le noie, qui ne tire sur notre cœur, à chaque coin de route, du fond de chaque boutique, les flèches de la Beauté, de la Beauté dont on serait parfois tenté de se demander si elle est en ce monde autre chose que la partie de complément qu'ajoute à une passante fragmentaire et fugitive notre imagination surexcitée par le regret. (ii. 73)

The Proustian *topos* according to which the woman desired is an unknown country is reworked here, so that 'we' are racing through a crepuscular landscape, peopled with indistinct female torsos. Like statues from antiquity, these indistinct figures appear mutilated, and the latent violence of this image anticipates the model of reading and writing presented in *Albertine disparue*: 'C'est une Vénus collective, dont on n'a qu'un membre mutilé si l'on s'en tient à la pensée de l'auteur, car elle ne se réalise complète que dans l'esprit de ses lecteurs' (iv. 150). Here the *text* is a mutilated Venus, again a broken statue from antiquity, which the reader's participation can bring to completion. Once the metaphor becomes textual, the possibility of completion and of communication arises. In the metaphor of *A l'ombre*, however, the narrator is suspicious of the fragment, suspicious that 'the arrows of Beauty' shot at him by the female torso might instead originate in his own imagination. The textual model of the broken Venus states the necessity of collaboration; the hypotheses of *A l'ombre* exclude the possibility of engagement or dialogue. The misprision of speculation is creative, but it is also fragile, mistrustful, fearful. The narrator's desirous hypothesis leaves him reaching out to a particular woman whose existence he can barely admit, only to recoil, fearfully, through maxim and metaphor, before reaching out and recoiling again. The process is knowingly and comically solipsistic: the original hypothesis with which this passage begins both describes its fear of an engagement with reality, its hostility to verification/falsification, and also enacts the desires of the speculative imagination. The digressive movement which results works through aesthetics to botany, to metaphors of digestion, and finally to notions of space—woman as unknown country, woman within mythological landscape. Each of these stages offers the possibility of generalization, sustaining the speculative order; each is threatened by a desire for the particular. The narrator's final desire to enter and define the consciousness of one particular girl is frustrated by her sudden emergence as landscape, and as only one of many fragmentary figures within a further mythological space. The mobility and fragility of this speculation suggest not so much that hypothesis is successful in preserving an order free from the constraints of engagement with the particular, as the narrator claims, but rather that the potential for such an engagement both endangers and sustains the digressive, speculative response.

Speculation involving notions of space, science, reading, and consumption occurs repeatedly throughout *A l'ombre*, and in particular around the term 'hypothèse'. Common to these four modes of speculation is that they allow the narrator to maintain an independence from the restrictions of the particular. In allowing not only speculation about the desired object, but also reflection about the nature of that desire, these four modes further facilitate the mobility of 'la beauté [qui] est une suite d'hypothèses' (ii. 73). Reading is a form of (creative) misprision; consumption is always deferred. Spatial patternings both suggest the narrator's desire to map an unknown territory and quite simply allow a physical distance between the narrator and the object desired. Science is the most ambiguous mode of speculation. Intended to enable an objective categorization, one which tends to suppress the self, science also expresses the reverse. The botanical model allows a categorization of the countrywomen, but the narrator's own desire draws him into, and is explicable by, the very object of his study, a close-up analogy of plant fertilization. The ambivalence which operates more widely in *A la recherche* between what we have tagged as Newtonian and Heisenbergian philosophies of science is condensed in such instances. The lawlike, objective science controlled by the narrator is the flip side of a science in which subjectivity is key, in which he is part of every phenomenon he attempts to understand.

When the narrator's hypothesis about the social status of the 'jeunes filles' proves mistaken, he returns to first principles, to account scientifically for the characteristics of the group: 'une liaison invisible, mais harmonieuse comme une même ombre chaude, une même atmosphère, faisant d'eux un tout aussi homogène' (ii. 151). In the earlier passage, the women are mute, and do not return the narrator's gaze; the torsos of the mythological landscape are undifferentiated, standing simply for Beauty. Now, as the narrator becomes the object of Albertine's gaze, his speculation is reconfigured: 'Si elle m'avait vu, qu'avais-je pu lui représenter? Du sein de quel univers me distinguait-elle? Il m'eût été aussi difficile de le dire que lorsque certaines particularités nous apparaissent grâce au télescope, dans un astre voisin' (ii. 152). Science is no longer a sufficient means of classification and characterization, as a yawning astronomical space opens between the narrator and Albertine, necessitating a reconfiguration of the spatial mapping of his desire:

> C'était par conséquent toute sa vie qui m'inspirait du désir; désir douloureux, parce que je le sentais irréalisable, mais enivrant, parce que ce qui avait été jusque-là ma vie ayant brusquement cessé d'être ma vie totale, n'étant plus qu'une petite partie de l'espace étendu devant moi que je brûlais de couvrir, et qui était fait de la vie de ces jeunes filles, m'offrait ce prolongement, cette multiplication possible de soi-même, qui est le bonheur. (ii. 152)

The narrator is in effect reduced to the status of fragment, while Albertine becomes a figure of totality, a plenitude which he can enter by way of hypothesis, moving from the original constriction of the 'désir douloureux' to a pleasurable expansion, the prolongation and multiplication of the self. The molecular movement of osmosis describes the narrator's desire for the 'jeunes filles' to become conscious of him: 'la supposition . . . que ces yeux . . . pourraient jamais par une alchimie miraculeuse laisser transpénétrer entre leurs parcelles ineffables l'idée de mon existence' (ii. 153). His spatial modelling is replaced by a scientific-aesthetic redefinition of the 'jeunes filles', in which the languages of art and science themselves might be said to merge according to 'some miraculous alchemical process'. The narrator wishes to be part of 'la théorie qu'elles déroulaient le long de la mer', where 'théorie' signifies 'procession', but might also be read as 'theory'. The 'jeunes filles' figure as an ancient fresco inaccessible to the narrator; but, more tantalizing still, they present what he terms 'an insoluble contradiction', whose equation or theory he might yet deduce.

As in the previous passage, hypothesis implies movement towards the desired object, but whereas before this threatens to collapse the speculative order, here the movement of the object itself, the 'jeunes filles', 'extrait de la fuite innombrable de passantes' (ii. 154), is seen in slow motion. The implicit failure to read the female torsos of the previous passage is replaced by a recognition of reading as a faulty interpretative model: 'ces déchiffrages rapides d'un être qu'on voit à la volée nous exposant ainsi aux mêmes erreurs que ces lectures trop rapides où, sur une seule syllabe et sans prendre le temps d'identifier les autres, on met à la place du mot qui est écrit, un tout différent que nous fournit notre mémoire' (ii. 155). The narrator chooses to escape the creative misprision of the haphazard reading-writing model by adopting the language of science, of proof rather than hypothesis, and, it is implied, by suppressing the self. He desires to observe the 'jeunes filles' from various perspectives: 'pour que je pusse faire soit la rectification, soit la vérification et la "preuve" des différentes suppositions de lignes et de couleurs que hasarde la première vue, et pour voir subsister en eux, à travers les expressions successives, quelque chose d'inaltérablement matériel' (ii. 155). The insistence upon rectification, verification, *and* proof (to which still more attention is drawn, as if the force of the three alone were insufficient), upon an exact scientific reading, gives way to aesthetic concerns, the 'lignes et couleurs'. The 'jeunes filles' are now the 'most favourable hypothesis', favourable not to free speculation but to the specification of desire, staged as rigorous science: 'c'était presque pour des raisons intellectuelles que j'étais désespéré de ne pas pouvoir faire dans des conditions uniques, ne laissant aucune place à l'erreur possible, l'expérience de . . .' (ii. 155). This stress on an exact language of science seems to presage a new order of speculation, just at that point when the desire for the particular becomes more pressing. The very use of such terms as 'preuve' suggests the need for an approach at once more rigorous and more neutral than the botanical model, but one which is at this stage still competing with claims made by a quite different type of speculation. These claims are described in the following maxim:

> Il faut que l'imagination, éveillée par l'incertitude de pouvoir atteindre son objet, crée un but qui nous cache l'autre, et en substituant au plaisir sensuel l'idée de pénétrer dans une vie, nous empêche de reconnaître ce plaisir, d'éprouver son gôut véritable, de le restreindre à sa portée. (ii. 154)

This initial order of hypothesis delights in the free play of a speculation which never meets with reality, is neither verifiable nor falsifiable. Typically, the proposition quoted above, which describes the narrator's speculative practice, is not the end-point, the conclusion of a series of reflections; instead, a metaphor follows, and takes the idea further. This metaphor uses a *topos* associated with hypothesis, the consumption of food, phrased as an ironic antidote to the high register of scientific and aesthetic language of the preceding passage:

Il faut qu'entre nous et le poisson qui si nous le voyions pour la première fois servi sur une table ne paraîtrait pas valoir les mille ruses et détours nécessaires pour nous emparer de lui, s'interpose, pendant les après-midi de pêche, le remous à la surface duquel viennent affleurer, sans que nous sachions bien ce que nous voulons en faire, le poli d'une chair, l'indécision d'une forme, dans la fluidité d'un transparent et mobile azur. (ii. 154)

From its comic and mundane opening—the fish on the table, ready for consumption—the image traces back through the process of deferral, the 'mille ruses', to an aesthetic of fluidity and uncertainty, one which is close to the patterning of the 'jeunes filles'. Resolution is found in metaphor, not because anything is effectively concluded beyond the proposition of its partner maxim, but because the fish on its plate and the reductive maxim can only be consumed. The sinuous syntax of the metaphor interrupts and constantly defers the initial imperative 'Il faut que . . .', so enacting the movement and wiles of the imagination which it describes. Whereas the maxim ends negatively—sensual pleasure cannot be experienced directly, cannot be tasted—the metaphor develops the 'but qui nous cache l'autre', and allows this 'goal' to emerge gradually, indistinctly, and sensually, as does the fish described, from the sentence.

The expansive, metaphoric order of hypothesis is restless, textually rich in its switching between the general, as maxim and metaphor, and the particular, the *récit*. One might even say that there is a porosity by which each is infused with the other. (Recounting his first introduction by Elstir to Albertine, the narrator generalizes the episode, reducing his particular experience to the status of illustration: 'Au moment où notre nom résonne dans la bouche du présentateur, surtout si celui-ci l'entoure comme fit Elstir de commentaires élogieux' (ii. 227)). This mobile speculation knowingly resists engagement with the real, knowingly because many of its maxims are self-reflexive, describing the nature of knowledge and desire. A generative fear persists that any engagement with the desired particularity threatens to limit the speculative order, 'ces hypothèses merveilleuses'. Again, the example is taken from the narrator's introduction to Albertine:

Mais, aussi agiles que ces ciroplastes qui font un buste devant nous en cinq minutes, les quelques mots que l'inconnue va nous dire préciséront cette forme et lui donneront quelque chose de définitif qui exclura toutes les hypothèses auxquelles se livraient la veille notre désir et notre imagination. (ii. 227–8)

Knowledge, in opposition, figures as contraction, impoverishment, loss: 'cette connaissance se faisait par soustraction, chaque partie d'imagination et de désir étant remplacée par une notion qui valait infiniment moins' (ii. 228). The meeting with Albertine is the point of transfer to this area in which the second order of hypothesis comes into play.

4.2 The hypothetical norm

The narrator's fear that knowledge will limit the free play of his speculation might be read as an inversion of science's fear that hypothesis could limit scientific knowledge: 'L'hypothèse est le rudiment de la science. Elle y est souvent aussi un impédiment.' The *Larousse grand dictionnaire universel du XIXe siècle* (1873), from which this quotation is taken, gives some idea of the normative view of hypothesis and of the debates surrounding it at this time. The basic definition is a 'supposition sur laquelle on base un raisonnement ou un développement', the first step in a logical, reasoned process. The legitimacy of hypothesis is then discussed; it is valid only if its application is strictly regulated. Only verifiable hypotheses should be applied, 'des hypothèses susceptibles d'être réduites de l'état de conjecture à l'état de fait', and these should not be allowed to proliferate; only useful hypotheses are permissible. The dangers of hypothesis are then outlined: many hypotheses are nebulous and superfluous, applied by certain scientists to insoluble problems which would be better handled by a metaphysician than a physicist or a chemist.

This strictly legislative view, which begins with a grudging admission of the usefulness of speculation, tends in its concluding stages to the hysterical. Little space remains for the creative imagination in this entry, which nevertheless seems to recognize that it is legislating against the very nature of hypothesis—they *do* proliferate, all are *not* verifiable[6]—and, still worse, that certain eminent scientists, Chevreul and Claude Bernard, actively promote them: 'Nous ne sommes de

[6] As the entry confesses, not all hypotheses are empirically verifiable, they are justified instead by the claims of theoretical necessity ('Ils sont dans la voie logique'), and still play 'un grand rôle dans l'histoire des sciences'.

l'avis ni de M. Chevreul ni de M. Claude Bernard. Les hypothèses à quelque titre qu'on les emploie sont plus nuisibles qu'utiles dans les sciences.' Even the current, regulated use of hypothesis, the entry concludes, is only a provisional stage. Hypothesis has no lasting place in scientific methodology, for, when all laws are known, 'quand on en saura l'enchaînement régulier et nécessaire', it will become redundant.

This restrictive definition in fact condenses a complicated historical debate on the value of hypothesis, famously expressed in Newton's 'Hypotheses non fingo' ('I do not feign hypotheses'). Newton's hostility to hypotheses is also expressed in the first paragraph of the *Opticks*: 'My design in this Book is not to explain the Properties of Light by Hypotheses, but to propose and prove them by reason and experiments.'[7] Koyré, in his study of hypothesis and experience in Newton's scientific thought, places such statements in the context of a debate between Newton and his 'continental adversaries', notably Descartes and Leibniz. Descartes insisted on a divorce between the truth and the 'hypothetical' premisses which he advanced: 'I will suppose here several [hypotheses] which I believe to be false', though 'their falsity does not at all prevent what may be deduced from being true'.[8] The binary terms of this debate effectively exclude discussion of the nature and function of hypothesis.

Koyré's more general definition of hypothesis proposes that 'All meanings have this in common, that they attenuate (or suppress) provisionally (or definitively) the affirmative character and the relation to truth (or reality) of the "hypothetical" proposition.'[9] This characterization becomes polemical only when hypothesis breaks loose from its methodological moorings. Claude Bernard's account in his *Introduction à l'étude de la médecine expérimentale* (1865), for example, hooks up hypothesis to the experimental method, as the 'point de départ nécessaire de tout raisonnement expérimental'.[10] Hypothesis, or the 'idée expérimentale' as Bernard renames it, must be experimentally verifiable. The fear that hypotheses might in any way be arbitrary informs Bernard's statement of the importance of their very origin: hypotheses may not be drawn from the imagination; rather, they must be drawn from observation of the phenomena under study. Yet this account is

[7] Newton, *Opticks* (1704), cited in Alexandre Koyré, *Newtonian Studies* (Chicago: University of Chicago Press, 1968), 25.

[8] Descartes, *Principia philosophiae*, cited in Koyré, *Newtonian Studies*, 34.

[9] Koyré, *Newtonian Studies*, 32.

[10] Bernard, *Introduction*, 65.

not as categorical as it pretends. Already in the following paragraph we see that the origin of hypothesis is less easily tamed or held in place by Bernard's method. Hypothesis may also be the result of intuition, making a spontaneous, even serendipitous appearance: 'l'idée neuve apparaît alors avec la rapidité de l'éclair comme une sorte de révélation subite'.[11] The conflict between two apparently competing claims, Bernard's desire for hypothesis to appear respectable (by way of the experimental method which subsequently ties it down) and its unrespectably intuitive character, is resolved by the claim that 'nous avons dans l'esprit l'intuition ou le sentiment des lois de la nature, mais nous n'en connaissons pas la forme. L'expérience peut seule nous l'apprendre.'[12]

For scientists working at the turn of the century, such as Henri Poincaré, the origin of hypotheses in 'intuition' is less readily dismissed. The scientist's task, Poincaré argues, is better performed if he tries to understand such intellectual or intuitive work, and this activity in turn is considered to be his principal instrument for arriving at a solution (a claim which will be discussed in the final chapter). The harmony between the mind and nature which Bernard states as fact is also open to question. In *La Science et l'hypothèse* (1902), Poincaré proposes that Euclidean geometry is conventional and relative: it is neither an a priori nor an experiential ordering of external space. When the scientist operates on a scale which exceeds experiential reality, non-Euclidean geometries become more convenient. In this discussion of hypothesis, simplistic references to observation and experiment no longer pertain. The term 'convenient' in itself suggests a new, more speculative relationship between science and nature. Such concerns were expressed in Poincaré's first published article of 1887, and represent 'the conviction, widespread at the time among mathematicians and philosophers, that the discovery of non-Euclidean geometries, strengthened later by meta-geometrical results as well as by research into the origins and functioning of space perception in man and animals emanating from the theory of evolution, physiology and psychology of perception, made the orthodox Kantian view of space and geometry untenable'.[13]

An extreme liberty was accorded to hypothesis by many of Poincaré's contemporaries, who believed quite literally that 'toute généralisation est une hypothèse'. The tenets of these 'nominalists' or 'extreme conventionalists' were summarized in an article by Édouard

[11] Ibid. 67. [12] Ibid. [13] Giedymin, *Science and Convention*, 2.

Le Roy (a pupil of both Bergson and Poincaré) entitled 'Un positivisme nouveau' (1901), and include pan-theoreticism, the view that there is no essential difference between facts and theories; the claim that all scientific laws and theories are conventions (which may change); and finally, that science is meaningful only from the perspective from which it is constructed.[14] Poincaré was wary of the absolute scepticism of the nominalists, and contested their views in both *La Science et l'hypothèse* and *La Valeur de la science*,[15] arguing that the traditional methodology of science remained the only possible means by which we might understand nature. His bravura 'toute généralisation est une hypothèse' is qualified by the need for hypothesis to be verified: 'Il va sans dire que, si elle [l'hypothèse] ne supporte pas cette épreuve, on doit l'abandonner sans arrière-pensée.'[16] And the account of scientific speculation in *La Science et l'hypothèse* attempts to avoid polemical oppositions: hypotheses *may* be verifiable, and, once confirmed by experience, become fruitful truths ('des vérités fécondes'); they may *also* serve usefully to fix our thoughts: 'les autres [hypothèses], sans pouvoir nous induire en erreur, peuvent nous être utiles en fixant notre pensée'; and a third category, found above all in mathematics, appear to be hypotheses, but are, in fact, definitions or conventions in disguise.[17] This third category—potentially the most 'hypothetical' in the worst sense of arbitrary, unfettered by experience—reflects badly on the other forms of 'hypothesis', and triggers a discussion which returns to the traditional terms of the debate.

Where Bernard and others seek to justify hypothesis by way of an innate 'harmony' between mind and nature, Poincaré suggests a power relation: 'L'expérience nous laisse notre libre choix, mais elle le guide en nous aidant à discerner le chemin le plus commode. Nos décrets sont donc comme ceux d'un prince absolu, mais sage, qui consulterait son Conseil d'Etat.'[18] This is, on the one hand, a pragmatic solution: 'if scientific knowledge were merely conventional, it would be powerless'. Poincaré also side-steps the excessive nominalist view by adopting an evolutionary model of scientific development. Such development is, he argues in *La Valeur de la science*, comparable to the

[14] Le Roy's article lists representatives of what he terms the 'nouvelle critique des sciences', including Poincaré and Duhem. Le Roy's own work combined elements of 'Bergsonian irrationalism, evolutionism and voluntarism' with extreme conventionalism. See Giedymin, *Science and Convention*, 3–5.

[15] Poincaré, *La Science et l'hypothèse*, 24–5.

[16] Ibid. 165.

[17] Ibid. 24.

[18] Ibid.

evolution of zoological types, which, changing ceaselessly, become unrecognizable to common sight, yet, to the expert eye, still bear traces of their previous forms. Hence, as Toulmin describes, Einstein's work did not prove Newton's laws of motion to be untrue: 'It accounted for some limits, which had hitherto been unexplained . . . but it superseded Newton's mechanics only for the most refined theoretical purposes, and could only whimsically be said to prove the older laws of motion untrue.'[19]

Yet such arguments are the uneasy partners of the belief of Poincaré and others that science does not attain nature itself, 'les choses elles-mêmes', but the relations between things in nature. For what is to guide the scientist who operates according to scales which exceed the pragmatic and experiential—scales according to which, for example, non-Euclidean geometry might be preferable because it is more convenient, and might be replaced by a still more convenient ordering? The conventionalism of this area of science—of which Poincaré was an eminent researcher—sits uneasily with what Giedymin terms his 'main philosophical aim': 'to examine changes in science and to show that there is continuous progress in spite of rapid apparently disruptive changes in theories'. Moreover, Poincaré's discussion of nominalism served in a sense only to popularize those aspects he most wished to critique in an otherwise specialist debate. 'Nous savons bien qu'il n'y a aucune relation, sauf dans notre sensibilité, entre les étoiles qui le composent selon les lignes virtuelles créées par nous,' concludes Paul Valéry from his reading of Poincaré's *La Valeur de la science*.[20] Despite Poincaré's best attempts, hypothesis is left somewhere between being a useful tool and, in place of scientific law, the fundament of modern science.

The speculative mode of *A la recherche* reveals concerns strikingly similar to those of contemporary science. The fear of scientists such as Poincaré, who were working in the early years of the twentieth century, focuses on the possible conventionality of all scientific law: that is, on the dangers of hypothesis and experience diverging. Once detached from experience or 'nature' in this way, who or what was to be the arbiter in the passage from hypothesis to law? Whereas Claude Bernard's account allows for the possibility of the 'spontaneous generation' of hypotheses, because ultimately they will be

[19] Stephen Toulmin, *The Philosophy of Science* (1st pub. 1953, London: Hutchinson, 1960), 70.

[20] Valéry, *Cours de poétique*, cited in Crow, *Paul Valéry: Consciousness and Nature*, 83–4.

subject to experimental testing, the areas in which Poincaré was working did not necessarily admit of such testing. (Einstein's general principle of relativity, for example, was formally announced in 1916, but not 'proved' as such until the eclipse observation made by Eddington and his colleagues in May 1919.) The question—where do hypotheses come from?—demanded attention, and focused on the *nature* of intuition, of those seemingly involuntary, or unconscious, hypotheses. These concerns are both enacted and reflected upon in the speculations of *A l'ombre* which are mapped in the first part of this chapter. Irresponsible, proliferating hypothesis creates its own rich imaginary order. Contact with the real is deferred, but through speculation about the possibilities of such contact, self-reflexive maxims on the nature of knowledge and desire are formulated. These maxims have a digressive energy, for, unlike the straightforward speculation which provokes them, they are sustained by interaction with metaphor. Consequently, the narrator is able to generalize—speculatively—without concern for verification or falsification, or indeed any notion of testing or experimental proof. In this, the narrator's hypothetical maxims would seem to have more in common with the view of current philosophers of science: namely, that hypotheses are justified in 'that they have a hold on our imagination and that they help us to deal with experience'.[21] And yet the initial speculative mode described by *A la recherche* is not quite as independent as it might like to believe. Hypothesis is provoked by a desire for, and fear of, the particular; botanical modelling exists alongside the language of geometric accuracy; and while the text may declare and enact a movement of deferral, hypothesis actually draws the narrator ever closer to the object of desire, until speculation becomes fraught: 'Nous connaissons le caractère des indifférents, comment pourrions-nous saisir celui d'un être qui se confond avec notre vie, que bientôt nous ne séparons plus de nous-même, sur les mobiles duquel nous ne cessons de faire d'anxieuses hypothèses, perpétuellement remaniées?' (ii. 248–9). This is the mode of the Albertine texts wherein 'scientific' accuracy and verification become imperative.

[21] Holton, *Thematic Origins of Scientific Thought*, 20. Holton's fascinating study has as its premiss this concept of deep-going hypotheses, or 'themata', which is then used as a means of analysing scientific work. Holton defines the new 'methodological themata' of modern science as '*hypotheses fingo*': 'This—a new methodological thema reinforced by the scientific advances of the first two decades of our century—was precisely what Lodge, Larmor, Poincaré, and so many others could not accept. Poincaré, who was perhaps technically the best-prepared scientist in the world to understand Einstein's relativity theory of 1905, did not deign to refer to it once' (ibid).

4.3 'A propos des deux hypothèses *essentiel*'

The speculation of the Albertine texts is structured around a basic binary opposition: is Albertine gay or straight? This may in turn generate other pairs: absence/presence, or amorality/morality. The two hypotheses of the Albertine texts have precedents in, for example, Swann's speculations about Odette; he wonders similarly whether she is gay or not, whether she is with Forcheville or not, and so on. But in the case of the Albertine 'enquiry', they have become 'essentiel' (iii. 1058), the parameters of an investigation which points up, again and again, the failure of speculation to connect with experience:

> Pour ce qui concerne l'hypothèse d'une vertu absolue (hypothèse à laquelle j'avais d'abord attribué la violence avec laquelle Albertine avait refusé de se laisser embrasser et prendre par moi et qui n'était du reste nullement indispensable à ma conception de la bonté, de l'honnêteté foncière de mon amie), je ne laissai pas de la remanier à plusieurs reprises. Cette hypothèse était tellement le contraire de celle que j'avais bâtie le premier jour où j'avais vu Albertine! (ii. 292)

Analysing Albertine's refusal to kiss him (his false interpretation of her invitation, his failure to understand her reaction), the narrator directs his hypothesis towards moral and psychological questions unexplored in *A l'ombre*. In the passage which follows there is a constant move to generalize, as if the drive to resolve the original problem is expressed in maxims which digress from this topic. Returning to the *récit*, the narrator describes how Albertine, disappointed at having hurt him, gives him a gold pencil—'par cette vertueuse perversité des gens qui . . .' (ii. 293). The narrator's explanation is supplemented by two examples in the style of La Bruyère: 'Le critique dont l'article flatterait le romancier l'invite, à la place à dîner, la duchesse n'emmène pas le snob avec elle au théâtre, mais lui envoie sa loge pour un soir où elle ne l'occupera pas.' Having generalized with assurance this aspect of Albertine's behaviour, the unresolved hypothesis is returned to as *récit*. Albertine explains her moral position, to which the narrator responds by condoning heterosexuality and condemning lesbianism. This response is apparently unprovoked. Albertine's moral argument, which has nothing to do with sexual orientation, has been reformulated according to the two hypotheses which will come to structure the narrator's enquiry. Albertine is either moral and heterosexual or amoral and lesbian. Indeed, the narrator's response goes beyond a straightforward restructuring; he rails against the terms of his own opposition, claiming that lesbianism is 'inventé . . . improbable, impossible' (ii. 294). His response seems explicable only in terms of Montjouvain, but in fact prefigures the revelation which will later link Albertine with Mlle Vinteuil's lover. Albertine still replies within the frame of a purely heterosexual code, reasserting her moral position within it, frustrating the terms of the opposition.

The free speculation of *A l'ombre* results in spatial expansion; the oppositional hypotheses here cause Albertine to figure as a knot. This is not the neat opposition of expansion and contraction, of 'originalité fleurie' and 'universalité d'un squelette', but 'un sentiment presque familial, ce noyau moral': 'Pour le moment, cet embryon d'estime morale, d'amitié, restait au milieu de mon âme comme une pierre d'attente' (ii. 294). The complexity of origins resists the narrator's schema, and the figure recurs, with variations, so that, under similar pressures, Albertine becomes a crystal, or a stone covered in snow (iv. 22–3). Here the origins of the figure are suggested: it is embryonic, a 'pierre d'attente', that is a stone left at the angles of a building so as to allow further linked construction; or, figuratively, 'chose qu'on ne regarde que comme un commencement et qui doit avoir une continuation.'[22] Albertine becomes a figure of condensed complexity, triggering the narrator's response in time and space:

> Je me demandais quelle table de logarithmes il constituait pour que toutes les actions auxquelles il avait pu être mêlé, depuis un poussement de coude jusqu'à un frôlement de robe, pussent me causer, étendues à l'infini de tous les points qu'il avait occupés dans l'espace et dans le temps, et de temps à autre brusquement revivifiées dans mon souvenir, des angoisses si douloureuses. (iii. 862)

From the expansive speculative movement of *A l'ombre*, a new representation of hypothesis is introduced, as a concentrated and sensitized space, which may through sudden and seemingly infinite expansion cause pain. And in the face of such an expansion, such complexity, the reflex is back towards the simple hypothetical pair. Already in *La Prisonnière* the odds are on the second hypothesis, that Albertine is lesbian; the narrator describes his sense of 'une autre hypothèse qui expliquait bien plus de choses et avait aussi cela pour elle que, si on adoptait la première, la deuxième devenait plus probable' (iii. 849). And yet, only fourteen pages later the problem is posed again, as a choice between two equally plausible theories: 'Laquelle des deux hypothèses était la vraie?' demands the narrator (iii. 863).[23]

[22] See entry for 'pierre d'attente' in the *Larousse grand dictionnaire du XIXe siècle*.

[23] The narrator continues to describe this hypothesis about Albertine's sexuality as if it

Tel nénuphar à qui le courant au travers duquel il était placé d'une façon malheureuse laissait si peu de repos que . . . il n'abordait une rive que pour retourner à celle d'où il était venu, refaisant éternellement la double traversée. Poussé vers la rive, son pédoncule se dépliait, s'allongeait, filait, atteignait l'extrême limite de sa tension jusqu'au bord où le courant le reprenait, le vert cordage se repliait sur lui-même et ramenait la pauvre plante à ce qu'on peut d'autant mieux appeler son point de départ qu'elle n'y restait pas une seconde sans en repartir par une répétition de la même manœuvre. (i. 166–7)

The movement of the water-lily, tugged inexorably by the current from one shore of the Vivonne to the other, is described as analogous to the habits of neurasthenics. While the narrator has his Aunt Léonie in mind, the movement also suggests a model for his own involuntary binary speculation. For when the narrator next glimpses Albertine's possible lesbianism, the parameters of his research, the two hypotheses, remain unchanged—and there is something scandalous about this shock of recognition the second time around.

The division between the two speculative modes is, of course, not the whole story. The narrator's second attempt to kiss Albertine results in speculation which is rather in the style of *A l'ombre des jeunes filles*. Triggered this time by the possibility of a very sensual contact with the real, the result is a passage of comically inflated speculation. The narration of this 'event' moves through an extraordinary range of digressions as Marcel moves towards Albertine's cheek. These focus primarily on the topic of perspective. The narrator, protesting that his physical desire for Albertine is diversified and amplified by more spiritual wishes, describes his use of various optical instruments to detach her from her setting. She is reified, becomes emblematic of his technique: 'cette image, on peut la détacher, la mettre près de soi, et voir peu à peu son volume, ses couleurs, comme si on l'avait fait passer derrière les verres d'un stéréoscope' (ii. 658). The narrator's 'scientific' pleasure becomes a relativistic coolness; Albertine is just one of many objects which may be viewed in this way—'les connaître, les approcher, les conquérir, c'est faire varier de forme, de grandeur, de relief l'image humaine' (ii. 658). But the detached, authoritative tones are belied by a desire for lip rather than visual knowledge, 'connaissance par les lèvres'. And this desire is comically frustrated, since, as the narrator-natural historian digresses, man has not developed an organ capable of this: 'l'homme, créature évidemment moins rudi-

were involuntary; he tells her that the women in the hotel have paid them little attention, 'peut-être dans l'hypothèse, que je n'envisageais pourtant pas d'une façon consciente, où Albertine eût aimé les femmes' (iii. 198).

mentaire que l'oursin ou même la baleine, manque cependant encore d'un certain nombre d'organes essentiels' (ii. 659). His lips meet 'la clôture de la joue impénétrable', allowing only a visual close-up of the cheek. But far from this causing textual closure, the notion of the close-up allows a return to the previous topic of perspective and a digression on developments in photography, which are compared to the kiss for their production of new perspectives at high speed—'pour recréer expérimentalement le phénomène qui diversifie l'individualité d'un être' (ii. 660). From object of scientific study to mythological being, Albertine, now in her general role as 'woman desired', becomes a 'déesse à plusieurs têtes', before the narrator returns to the *récit* and his well-rehearsed maxim on physical pleasure and the loss of desire. The failure of the narrator's first kiss is truly spectacular, the spectacle of the hypotheses comically obfuscating the disappointing contact with the real.

Both modes of speculation, abundant and binary, absorb Albertine. Hypothesis may revolve around her physical or sexual absence, but it may also render her absent, as in the above passage. Swann's example is another means of absorbing the particularity of Albertine into the general. Indeed, hypothesis is first introduced through Swann.

'Il continuait à tâcher d'apprendre ce qui ne l'intéressait plus, parce que son moi ancien parvenu à l'extrême décrépitude, agissait encore machinalement, selon des préoccupations abolies' (i. 515). Swann no longer desires Odette, the subject of his jealous speculation in 'Un amour de Swann', yet is still inhabited by the desire for knowledge of her. His is no cool application by the single subject, but the dramatized language of the passions. Swann's controlled research is replaced by a state in which he is subject to hypothesis, misled by it. It acts as a drug, a sedative, 'en somme bienfaisante puisque, tant qu'avait duré sa maladie amoureuse, elle avait diminué ses souffrances en les lui faisant paraître imaginaires' (i. 514). Hypothesis seems to act independently, to inhabit the subject. It functions according to its own whims and desires long after speculation is actively promoted by the subject. The subject is the site of many competing passions (this is expressed in terms close to those of La Rochefoucauld's *Maximes*), and hypothesis may be a function of one of these, such as reason; or be required emotively; or live on independently within the subject.

This complex distribution of hypothesis through its simple introduction in Swann as emblematic lover is repeated when the narrator speculates about Albertine. Here too the language of the passions is physical; the denial of hypothesis acts as a medicinal palliative, calming the narrator's jealous sickness: 'la jalousie appartenant à cette famille de doutes maladifs que lève bien plus l'énergie d'une affirmation que sa vraisemblance' (iii. 227). And as the hypothesis is undermined, there is a pull towards the general, releasing a concise epistemological reflection: 'Il faut aimer pour prendre souci qu'il n'y ait pas que des honnêtes femmes, autant dire pour s'en aviser, et il faut aimer aussi pour souhaiter, c'est-à-dire pour s'assurer qu'il y en a' (iii. 227).[24]

As in the case of Swann, so for the narrator, hypothesis is personified, it seems to act independently of, to inhabit the subject: 'Je continuais à vivre sur l'hypothèse qui admettait pour vrai tout ce que me disait Albertine. Mais il se peut qu'en moi pendant ce temps-là une hypothèse toute contraire et à laquelle je ne voulais pas penser ne me quittât pas' (iii. 848). But in this case hypothesis is not simply one of many competing expressions of the passions, it is the dominant representation of desire. The narrator chooses to live according to one hypothesis, while being inhabited by another. Whereas Swann speculates generally about Odette, the narrator's speculation is reduced to two possible hypotheses, of which the latter, the involuntary, is the more compelling.

The repetition of the inexorable 'deux hypothèses' is far from the earlier speculative model of expansion or perspectivism, still further from the actual gaining of knowledge as impoverishment or loss. The desirous pursuit of knowledge reduces to two effects, again expressed in physiological terms, 'l'être aimé est successivement le mal et le remède qui suspend et aggrave le mal' (iii. 228), and to the two hypotheses. The relationship is purely affective. And the narrator explicitly draws on Swann's story as a model through which Albertine assumes Odette's guilt:

> Au fond si je veux y penser, l'hypothèse qui me fit peu à peu construire tout le caractère d'Albertine et interpréter douloureusement chaque moment d'une vie que je ne pouvais pas contrôler tout entière, ce fut le souvenir, l'idée fixe du caractère de Mme Swann, tel qu'on m'avait raconté qu'il était. (iii. 199–200)

Recognized as both necessary and inappropriate, Swann's example imposes itself on the narrator again and again: it becomes part of the

[24] This is one of the few Proustian sententiae which almost achieves the elegance of La Rochefoucauld's *Maximes*—almost, were it not for the parentheses 'autant dire . . .', 'c'est-à-dire . . .', both of which indicate the *desire* to formulate such generalizing statements.

two hypotheses repetition, triggering the narrator's 'sickness', his fear of the verification of hypothesis. He hesitates between the two readings, prompted now by Swann's example, now by his own affective response: 'J'aurais donc commis une faute de raisonnement aussi grave—quoique inverse—que celle qui m'eût incliné vers une hypothèse parce que celle-ci m'eût fait moins souffrir que les autres' (iii. 228).

The binary hypothesis becomes, in the Albertine texts, an involuntary phenomenon—as the deterministic language of the passions suggests—which divests the narrator of all responsibility.

> Oui, c'est cela qu'elle a voulu, c'est cela l'intention de son acte, me disait ma raison compatissante; mais je sentais qu'en me le disant ma raison se plaçait toujours dans la même hypothèse qu'elle avait adoptée depuis le début. Or je sentais bien que c'était l'autre hypothèse qui n'avait jamais cessé d'être vérifiée. Sans doute, cette deuxième hypothèse n'aurait jamais été assez hardie pour formuler expressément qu'Albertine eût pu être liée avec Mlle Vinteuil et son amie. Et pourtant, quand j'avais été submergé par l'envahissement de cette nouvelle terrible, au moment où nous entrions en gare d'Incarville, c'était la seconde hypothèse qui s'était trouvée vérifiée. (iv. 6–7)

Reason, yet again, is undermined by its presentation, its personification here in dialogue with the narrator's sensibility. Reason places and adopts hypotheses, whereas the narrator himself is inhabited by speculation, and above all inhabited by the sense that the 'second hypothesis' is constantly verified. But this verification is not some active process on the part of the narrator (note the use of the passive); nor is the hypothesis bold enough to formulate itself and its consequences. Knowledge is not gained by the narrator; rather, he is overcome by it, 'submergé par l'envahissement de cette nouvelle terrible'. The second hypothesis is verified by intuition: 'cette réalité dépassait les chétives prévisions de ma deuxième hypothèse, mais pourtant les accomplissait. Cette deuxième hypothèse n'était pas celle de l'intelligence' (iv. 7). Speculation seems to be part of an 'intellectual method', whose slogan, 'Foi expérimentale', demands that, while the scientist-artist-lover must begin with the application of reason, resolution demands the abdication of the intellect. Yet even this conclusion is only temporary; the 'deux hypothèses' raised up in mutual opposition pre-date Albertine, and are ultimately insoluble.

The binary hypothesis is, however, also a creative principle, triggering the negative copiousness of this new speculative order.

Represented here is the apparent pursuit of knowledge which, through hypothesis, repeatedly defers the intuited conclusion, sustaining the desire which produces what might be termed a 'negative copiousness'. Or as Gaston, in *Proust, l'homme des mondes*, describes: '[Aux yeux de Proust] le pont reliant l'homme à la nature ne relève pas d'une approche conceptuelle. L'intelligence spéculative ne dépassera pas le stade du questionnement circulaire, qui revient toujours au même point et ne connaît pas d'issue.'[25] When the narrator speculates about Albertine's departure, he soon leaves her behind to generalize about why women in such situations do leave. *Topoi—habitude, souvenir*, and so on—are rehearsed; a scenario is imagined as an example, but is interrupted by the exclamation 'Que d'hypothèses possibles! Possibles seulement. Je construisais si bien la vérité, mais dans le possible seulement, que . . .' (iv. 10). Unable to deal with the particular, and under the force of the two hypotheses, the speculative imagination is driven to sententious pronouncements, exempla, and digressions, which move around the object pursued. However much the narrator may 'raisonner', 'pronostiquer', 'chercher la vérité' about Albertine's moral and sexual nature, he is drawn to the sententious conclusion that 'L'inconnu de la vie des êtres est comme celui de la nature, que chaque découverte scientifique ne fait que reculer mais n'annule pas' (iii. 893).

The hypothesizing of the Albertine texts may appear superficially to conform to the normative view discussed earlier, yet it is far more insidious. Veiled as the pursuit of knowledge of the particular, the two hypotheses enable—indeed, energize—the text to create its own independent speculative order around the desired but inaccessible object. The narrator recognizes the impossibility of establishing as fact either of the hypotheses. What knowledge there is seems to be involuntary: it is either suppressed or poorly handled by 'reason'. The non-verifiable speculation of *A la recherche* suggests that 'toute généralisation est une hypothèse'. Hypothesis operates only in the realm of the affective imaginary. Indeed, this second mode of hypothesizing is still further removed from even the slight contact with the real which triggered the initial speculative mode. Holding Albertine captive within his apartment, letting her out only under the supervision of others, the narrator is himself the eponymous 'prisonnière' of this volume. His self-confinement is designed to prevent that contact with the real which results in painful speculation. The narrator's feigned illness,

[25] Gaston, *Proust, l'homme des mondes*, 148.

which keeps him in convalescence, itself taps the physiological model of the mind: letting others keep watch over Albertine is described as anaesthetizing his speculation, this practice 'ankylosait en moi, rendait inertes tous ces mouvements imaginatifs de l'intelligence' (iii. 533). He desires a supervisor not only for Albertine, but also for his own imagination: this supervisor, who might be 'un préfet de police, un diplomate à claires vues, un chef de la Sûreté', would exercise logic, deductive reasoning, and judgement, thereby reducing the spectrum of proliferating hypothesis to four principal points, and ultimately to the only possible outcome. Instead, deprived even of those points of contact, 'la vie extérieure', which might trigger speculation, the narrator's imagination, 'la vie intérieure', provides a substitute: 'les hasards rencontrés dans les réflexions que je faisais seul me fournissaient parfois de ces petits fragments de réel qui attirent à eux, à la façon d'un aimant, un peu d'inconnu qui, dès lors, devient douloureux' (iii. 534). The physical absence at the 'heart' of the narrator's hypotheses facilitates and energizes the production of maxims.

The aesthetic potential of hypothesis does not go unnoticed by the text. In a *mise en abyme* of the speculative aesthetic described in this chapter, Vinteuil's musical compositions are described as 'les éternelles investigations de Vinteuil, la question qu'il se posa sous tant de formes, son habituelle spéculation, mais aussi débarrassée des formes analytiques du raisonnement que si elle s'était exercée dans le monde des anges' (iii. 760).

Through Vinteuil's hypothesizing we glimpse his origins as a scientist. The description of his speculation as habitual and as freed of analytical forms of reasoning (both of which suggest that marker of aesthetic truth in *A la recherche*, the involuntary) might equally be applied to the narrator's hypotheses. Yet Vinteuil's speculation is qualified as 'eternal', rather than compulsive, and its displacement to the 'monde des anges' suggests not that it is unable to make contact with the real, but that it is lifted out of it. Hypothesis is not only recognized by the text, but justified in this image of aesthetic redemption.

The narrator's speculative impulse is, by contrast, plot-bound, and its narration will be considered further in Chapter 6. But first we should consider the counterpart of speculation. For neither mode of hypothesis in *A la recherche* is recourse to the real a possibility; both are sustained by the narrator's imaginary: 'Ma jalousie naissait par des images, pour une souffrance, non d'après une probabilité' (iii. 534). The locus of this richer, imaged form of speculation depends on the collaboration of maxim and metaphor which is modelling.

5
MODELLING

Nicht alles an diesem Leben ist musterhaft, exemplarisch aber ist alles.
(This is not a model life in every respect, but everything about it is exemplary.)

Walter Benjamin, 'Zum Bilde Proust's'

Il y a moins de force dans une innovation artificielle que dans une répétition destinée à suggérer une vérité neuve.

(ii. 248)

There is throughout *A la recherche* a strange sense of the not-quite-ness of repetition. In the same way that maxims repeat, rehearse themselves, and undergo reformulation; in the same way that the digressions try to illustrate, yet always exceed, the law; so we are constantly made aware that the narrator's experience is simply a repetition and also something more. It is, most strikingly, a rewriting of Swann's story—now with the comfort of revisiting the familiar, now with the anxiety that Swann's example is inappropriate, but somehow necessary, instinctive, and then again with the recognition, after the event, of a difference beyond repetition.

When, in conclusion (the conclusion of *Le Temps retrouvé*) the narrator theorizes—or, at least, accounts for—repetition, he does so through an analogy with the visual arts which ignores this experience, shared by both reader and narrator-protagonist, of not-quite-ness: 'Et plus qu'au peintre, à l'écrivain, pour obtenir du volume et de la consistance, de la généralité, de la réalité littéraire, comme il lui faut beaucoup d'églises vues pour en peindre une seule, il lui faut aussi beaucoup d'êtres pour un seul sentiment' (iv. 486). The writer is compared to the artist who copies from a series of models;[1] the 'volume' and 'consistency' of his portrayal are paratactically equated with generality and 'literary reality'. This is a process both of enrichment—

[1] Fernand Vandérem, in 'Les lettres et la vie', *La Revue de France*, 7 (15 June 1921), 845–9, corrects this analogy to suggest a more scientific form of modelling: 'J'avais tort de le comparer à un peintre devant le modèle. C'est un savant au laboratoire. Il ne me rappelle ni Tolstoï ni Hervieu, mais bien plutôt Lubbock penché sur ses fourmis, Huxley sur ses écrevisses' (p. 848).

the use of many models to obtain the true picture—and of condensation—a movement from many models to the representation of just the one, whether church or 'sentiment'. We might also say that the writer, unlike the painter, is repeating himself. For it is the writer's sensitivity to his own repetition which allows him to perceive generality. 'Literary realism' depends upon this perception and its subsequent expression. By noting what is common to each case, the writer will give a true psychological portrayal. But a typically Proustian twist motivates this modelling scenario. The narrator is not so much copying from the models—noting resemblances which they share—as attempting to track the self. Tracking self-repetition results in a particular kind of generality which might be defined as the laws of psychology.

But how valid is this argument? Moving further back to the painterly origins of the analogy, one might ask why it should be necessary to see many churches in order to represent just the one?[2] If anything, the reverse might be true. Phrasing the question differently, one might ask instead what *kind* of art requires many churches to be seen in order to paint just one? Such a representation would bring out characteristics common to all churches—structural similarities, for example. The resulting representation, in reducing the many to one, would amount to a schematic redescription, one which would convey information about churches as such. The reduction of people according to this method might result in an anatomical drawing (rather than the cubist-style portraiture of multiple selves with which critics have often compared Proust's characterization). Yet the Proustian twist has revealed that the 'je' is observing not the models but the self. As Jacques-Émile Blanche comments of Proust's work: 'ce qui constitue un des caractères de votre génie et, peut-être, avec votre langue, votre principale originalité,—c'est cette dualité de peintre et de modèle'.[3] The many 'êtres' are to be reduced, but also internalized, to one single 'sentiment'. They are simply the stimulants of an affect, their presence registered in the narrator's repetitive response. Further, for the analogy to work, we have to accept that, in the same way that there is an underlying structure common to all churches which

[2] Later we will see that this argument is used in a letter to Jacques de Lacretelle of 20 Apr. 1918 simply as a disclaimer against the reading for 'clefs'—no one church was 'borrowed' for *A la recherche*, Proust argues; no one acquaintance served as a model for any of his characters (*Correspondance*, xvii. 194–5); but rather, many churches and people constitute what are effectively composite fictions.

[3] Preface to *Dates*, cited in *Correspondance*, xx. 69–70.

permits reductive representation, so affective responses are also reducible, the same response being repeated under different circumstances. The narrator's repetition of self is at once a demonstration and a guarantee of psychological laws.

The painterly analogy wants to suggest the deepening, enriching qualities of repetition, as if the reductive process it describes were a recipe for intensifying the flavour of a sauce. Instead, the models are stimulants only to self-repetition and self-representation. The resulting representation is schematic and designed to appeal cognitively (it will tell us something about churches or about psychology) rather than sensuously. Yet this sounds unlike the representation of knowledge, whether about psychology or about churches, in *A la recherche* itself. For once the repetitious material is thrown into time and redistributed among various characters, and indeed among the various selves of the narrator—that is, when the movement from many to one is reversed—'not-quite-ness' necessarily sets in. Both the schematic mode of representation and the enriching layering of generality suggested by the painterly analogy are equally far from the text's narratives of repetition, far from the interrupted rhythms—forwards and backwards—which the narrator indicates, and which constitute our reading experience. The child's anguish in 'Combray' is already the anguish of the adult lover, Swann; Swann as lover stands as example for the narrator's own later experience; and Swann is seen not just as prefiguring, but also as determining, the direction this later experience will take: 'Je me dis que s'il était juste de faire sa part au pire, non seulement quand, pour comprendre les souffrances de Swann, j'avais essayé de me mettre à la place de celui-ci, mais maintenant qu'il s'agissait de moi-même, en cherchant la vérité comme s'il se fût agi d'un autre' (iii. 228).

Modelling here does not involve representation, so much as a jostling between some kind of polluted original and its copies. In terms of the text's genesis, drafts reveal the degree of drift between the narrator and the other characters, and indeed between the particular and the general, as if a kind of transfer were in operation whereby the 'je' 's'accapare d'autres personnes, s'approprie d'autres expériences—comme si tout devenait intersubjectivement identique, interchangeable, relativisé'.[4] As a result of this redistribution, Swann is

[4] Almuth Grésillon, Jean-Louis Lebrave, and Catherine Viollet, 'Quand tous mes autres moi seront morts . . .', in *Proust à la lettre*, 125. This article also describes Proust's practice of drawing on 'pre-written' pieces, 'les insérer à sa guise, transplanter des épisodes en les appli-

given a story which makes him an origin(al)—he is the narrator's point of reference when the latter comes to experience love, desire, jealousy, the *topoi* of the lover's maxims. Yet both Swann's story and image are ambiguously located, the former temporally and authorially, the latter by reference to Tissot's painting 'Le Cercle de la rue Royale' (iii. 704). Ironically presented as both origin and copy, Swann is the character most closely, incestuously, confusedly related with the narrator.

There is a tension, then, between the painterly representation of repetition as the empirical evidence supporting a law and its narration, a tension between the pleasure of noting similarity and the need for difference, for repetition to be not quite such that it might be narrated—cast over time as the experience of different characters. Common to these scenarios of modelling is the ambiguous relationship between artist and model (most clearly in the painterly analogy, but also between the narrator and the other characters in the drafts of the novel, and between the narrator and Swann) in which both parties threaten to reveal themselves as the same Proustian self. This is a variation of the law–*récit* tension which sets the narrator's *recognition* of repetition (and consequently of the laws governing this phenomenon) against his affective involvement with the *experience* of repetition. Once 'Marcel' finds himself within this scenario, he does not want Swann's story to become his own, does not wish to become an example of his own law. As readers, we feel this tension in the competing claims made on us to recognize now similarity, now difference—this is our experience of the not-quite-ness of repetition.

The narrator's desire for precision (often expressed through the language of mathematics and geometry), and for generality in a world where nothing ever repeats itself *quite*, makes of modelling in *A la recherche* an uneasy, almost dishonest technique. General laws rarely grow from a repeated particularity, but are styled variously according to their affective enunciation. The formulation of maxims above scant evidence appears, as was shown in the previous chapter, speculatively detached from the particular; in the form of the text's commonplaces, maxims seem to prefigure and even determine narrative events, certainly to provide a taxonomy for them. In this second case the law may be desired by the narrator to predict and ward off the flux and chaos of the 'not quite'; but, alternatively, the narrator's sense of

quant à d'autres protagonistes et, notamment, à ce "je", flottant entre la singularité et l'universalité' (p. 127).

entrapment and his need to assert the particularity of his own story may lead him to challenge, reformulate, or even abolish the law.

The explanation of *Le Temps retrouvé*, that this is painterly modelling whereby repetition proves and allows a distillation of laws, or 'truths', attempts to cover up a process which is constantly expressed and described as problematic. But modelling need not be threatened by 'not-quite-ness'; indeed, scientific models depend upon it.

A scientific model is a cognitive tool, at once a means of representation and speculation—a partner to hypothesis. For modelling, as a means of gaining knowledge, is an imaginative exercise which, through the perception of a certain similarity, maps the known or familiar on to the unknown.[5] Unlike the mimetic relationship of, say, the scale model, reproducing as accurately as possible the original in miniature, or of the painterly model, reproducing in response to conventions or convictions, aesthetic and personal, the scientific model aims to reproduce the structure of the original. In contrast to the Proustian representation of churches, however, structure here indicates not the lowest common denominator, but the characteristics of interest in the original. Max Black terms this scientific model an 'analogue model', and defines it as 'some material object, system, or process designed to reproduce as faithfully as possible in some new medium the *structure* or web of relationships in an original'.[6] In redescribing the original through a relatively unproblematic, more familiar, or simply better-organized secondary domain, statements can be translated back to provide corresponding information about the original. In other words, a model is a kind of analogy, bringing 'two separate domains into cognitive relation by using language directly appropriate to the one as a lens for seeing the other'.[7] It could also be described as an intuitive caricature, intuitive inasmuch as the user must have a close understanding, a 'feel for' the model's

[5] Roger Paultre's study, *Marcel Proust et la théorie du modèle* (Paris: Nizet, 1986), considers *A la recherche* in its entirety as model—i.e. as the author's means of understanding and representing the world. According to this view, any work of art might be considered a model: 'Toute connaissance, au sens à la fois le plus large et le plus vague du terme, comporte toujours une première démarche qui est d'ailleurs rarement consciente de sa part d'arbitraire et de relativité, celle qui consiste à construire avec les meilleurs moyens dont les sens et la technique disposent, une image simplifiée mais correcte d'une réalité dont la complexité et la diversité est a priori rebutante. Nous l'appellerons le modèle' (p. 12). My study looks at modelling as it is dramatized and discussed by the text, regarding this self-conscious display as peculiar to *A la recherche*.

[6] Max Black, *Models and Metaphors* (Ithaca, NY: Cornell University Press, 1962), 222.

[7] Ibid. 236.

capacities if inferences are to be drawn from it.[8] Scientific models, rather than acting simply as illustrative analogies of the kind often found in popularizing scientific texts, are also predictive metaphors, rich in their potential for extension—that is, for further hypothesis and speculation.

But this is a speculative business, and there are risks involved. A model is only ever partially applicable, indeed, it must necessarily be unfaithful in some respects, since the perfect model would elide with its subject and cease to be informative. The danger lies in the work of intuition. Whereas Proust's painter of churches is looking for what is common to each, the gaze of the analogue modeller is theory-laden and intuitive. If the modeller's feel for the capacities of his analogy is exaggeratedly optimistic, if his knowledge of the known domain is faulty in some way, he may extend the model too far, or not far enough. Even once successful parallels with a sense of story or sequence are established (and it is worth noting that narrative necessarily emerges from this kind of modelling as it does not in the painterly modelling scenario), these may be precarious and risk diverging. The process, then, carries 'the risks of fallacious inference from inevitable irrelevancies and distortions in the model'.[9] Only with subsequent factual verification/falsification will this be recognized. Such back-up mechanisms, as we have seen in the previous chapter, are not available to the narrator who both fears contact with the real and sees always the partiality and manipulability of empirical evidence. Revelation, as will be discussed in the following chapter, is the only guarantee of the real; and since the authenticity of this guarantee depends on the involuntary nature of knowledge, it is not subject to the narrator's conscious modelling and speculation, his active enquiry. The narrator is, in one sense, a 'modeller of nebulae'.[10] Yet his noting of the not-quite-ness of repetition, which does not quite permit him to establish the law inductively, may also manifest itself as a delight in the potential of such difference, which ultimately informs a more speculative relationship with the law.

Expressed in *A la recherche* is the desire for the generality of an idealized aesthetic modelling. This occurs at the level of plot, where modelling appears to be imposed on the narrator, through Swann, and is partnered by a generality composed of Proustian common-

[8] Black terms this 'Gestalt knowledge' (ibid. 232).

[9] Ibid. 223.

[10] Bowie, *Freud, Proust, and Lacan*, 59. The narrator describes 'la joie que donnait les premières fois à mon esprit ce travail de modelage d'une nébuleuse encore informe' (iii. 874).

places. Yet, were the Proustian community overly law-abiding in its adherence to the commonplaces, repetition might threaten the *récit.* The anxiety that nothing ever repeats itself quite is replaced by an anxiety that the not-quite-ness might disappear. By redescribing this not-quite repetition as the difference necessary to scientific modelling access opens up to a more speculative generality. Unlike aesthetic modelling, this 'scientific' process, as manipulated by the narrator, thrives on difference. Operating through metaphor into theory, its most spectacular appearance is the botanical model, focused in *Sodome et Gomorrhe I*, but fragmented and extended throughout the novel.

Over the following pages I want to reflect further on these three modelling scenarios—the aesthetic, the mimetic (Swann as model), and the scientific—in order to explore some key concepts and structures: repetition and reproduction, sameness and difference, law and *récit*, affective and objective relationships with the law. These pairs are all variations generated by the self–model pair, and offer different perspectives on the dialogue between the particular and the general in *A la recherche.*

5.1 Modelling aesthetics

The discourse of modelling in *Le Temps retrouvé* is primarily aesthetic. Once the first rush of involuntary memory and its theorization as metaphor have subsided, the narrator gets down to the problem of what else and, more importantly, how else to write. After intuition, what sort of *work* is involved? The analogy with the painter and his models is developed, as we have seen, to account for a different style of writing, whose attribute is not metaphor, but maxim and, specifically, psychological law: 'Peut-être les êtres que nous connaissons, les sentiments que grâce à eux nous éprouvons sont-ils pour le psychologue ce que sont pour le peintre des modèles. Ils posent pour nous. Ils posent pour la souffrance, pour la jalousie, pour le bonheur' (iv. 864). In this allegorical representation of the passions, the models serve only to stimulate a repertoire of suffering, jealousy, happiness—elements which in turn feed into the text's abundance of pre-established laws, the Proustian commonplaces. This passage is part of the Esquisse XXXVII, cahier 57 (composed in 1916–17), and develops the painterly passages of *Le Temps retrouvé* (notably iv. 480–7). In the final version, the models are played down still further; indeed, the narrator claims that once generality is formulated, the particular can be discarded: 'Ces substitutions ajoutent à l'œuvre quelque chose de désintéressé, de plus général, qui est aussi une leçon austère que ce n'est pas aux êtres que nous devons nous attacher, que ce ne sont pas les êtres qui existent réellement et sont par conséquent susceptibles d'expression, mais les idées' (iv. 487). The sententious tone of this final version, with its 'leçon austère', is rather different from the speculative 'peut-être' of the drafts. Speculation about artistic instinct frames the earlier passage in which, significantly, the analogy is drawn not between painter and writer, but between painter and psychologist. Whereas in the ideal aesthetic model of *Le Temps retrouvé* the particular can simply be discarded, the drafts maintain the tension between the particular and the general—the force of generality must in fact be felt through personal experience: 'A quoi bon nous dire "ce n'est qu'une Odette, qu'une Albertine", puisque pour que l'Amour, la Jalousie, la Souffrance se manifestent à nous, il faut qu'ils fassent leur entrée dans notre vie derrière quelque petit corps féminin qui en lui-même n'a aucune importance' (iv. 865).

This kind of modelling involves both a valorization and a denigration of the particular, of the physical. In this passage the psychological repertoire is formalized, the passions capitalized, while the women, rather than being simply *an* Odette, *an* Albertine, become allegorical figures, with the same symbolic weight as, say, 'a Judith' or 'an Apollo'. Access to generality as an 'étoffement' of the personal might appear, as it does in the final version, unproblematic, modelling being simply a process of enrichment through repetition: 'Parfois, quand un morceau douloureux est resté à l'état d'ébauche, une nouvelle tendresse, une nouvelle souffrance nous arrivent qui nous permettent de le finir, de l'étoffer' (iv. 484). Yet it is only through the particular and an affective contact with it that modelling can take place and laws be formulated. This is a less triumphalist version of Proust's 'c'est à la cime même du particulier qu'éclôt le général'.[11] The 'petit corps féminin', the woman's body, not only gives access to generality; it forces the narrator to step inside the law, to feel the legislative force of the maxims he has formulated: 'Malheureusement il est plus malheureux qu'il n'est méchant: quand il s'agit de ses propres passions, tout en en connaissant aussi bien la généralité, il s'affranchit moins aisément des souffrances personnelles qu'elles

[11] Letter to Daniel Halévy, 19 July 1919, in *Correspondance*, xviii. 334.

causent' (iv. 480). Outside the law, as an observer and gatherer of evidence, the narrator seems to generalize with consummate ease; within the law the personal reasserts itself, affranchisement is 'moins aisé' than its aesthetic counterpart suggests.

This is the double bind, the characteristically Proustian twist: the passions of the individual lead to a 'souffrance' anterior to a recognition of law; suffering in turn provokes the need for soothing generalities, for a kind of re-recognition. Reduced to the status of example and of individual, of a 'petit corps féminin' even, the narrator struggles frantically back towards his masterly position as artist-scientist. Now he is at once artist and model, subject and object, mind and body, masculine and feminine. And so this characteristically curious texture is created; for the narrator desires the evidence of the particular, his own story, not Swann's, etc., as a means of escaping the text's seemingly pre-established laws; yet he is equally driven to reformulate—as if for the first time—the original maxims on the passions, and beyond these to conjure up quite new *sententiae* on diverse subjects, as the energy of a specific generalizing force is diffused throughout the surrounding text. 'Souffrance'—the affective experience of the particular—energizes the law. Rather than enrichment, there is a frantic repetition, revisiting, reformulation of previous maxims, narratives, hypotheses, which results from the tight dialectic between 'corps' and 'esprit': 'La raison ne les calme pas car l'esprit s'abstrait de la douleur mais n'arrive pas à entraîner le corps avec lui' (iv. 865).

The aesthetic model has been interiorized, but not assimilated; the most vigorously corporeal writing, the language of the 'petit corps féminin' and of 'souffrance', will produce the most rigorous laws, or at least lay claim to this. The spectacular effects of the law are scored, not modelled, on the body.

5.2 Swann's story

The writer's technique of modelling is troubled also by the paradoxical notion of an original model—as the narrator proposes: 'En somme, si j'y réfléchissais, la matière de mon expérience, laquelle serait la matière de mon livre, me venait de Swann' (iv. 493–4). This suggestion of the fictional autobiographical origins of the novel parodies Montaigne's 'je suis moi-même la matière de mon livre'.

Where Montaigne's gesture is to ground the *Essais* in the physical particularity of the self, the author of the book, *A la recherche* claims for itself the generality of a fictional model.[12] Swann is, most simply, a model for the narrator-protagonist's experience. Yet he is also projected for the reader as the origin of many laws (or at least their original illustration). His first appearance in 'Combray' is, for example, interpreted by the narrator as demonstrating that 'notre personnalité sociale est une création de la pensée des autres' (i. 19). Swann, then, would seem to be a filling out, a vessel for the narrator's desiring and legislative imagination.

Still closer links between the two are revealed in the *avant texte* (notably cahier 4):

> J'ai / peut'être / déjà trop parlé de M. Swann et je n'ai pourtant donné encore qu'un aspect de sa personne, le moins intéressant certainement. D'autres traits de sa nature, que j'ai peut'être reconstitués plus tard par les récits des miens plus que je n'ai été à même de les observer, me sont si sympathiques, si voisins en un certain sens de ma nature que je veux leur donner quelques mots. (f° 60r°)[13]

This sounds less like modelling than some kind of incestuous doubling. And once, by the final text, Swann has been all but shed, he does literally become the 'matière' of the book. Swann is subject for and subjected to the narrator's reflections, enabling the latter to escape the stifling dialectic of 'corps'–'esprit'. Rather than the spectacular maxims of 'souffrance', the laws of the community are reinforced. This is the community of jealous lovers, of those who desire to know, over which the narrator, as legislator, presides. Yet, despite this reordering, the luxuriant abundance of variation in *A la recherche* is still haunted by the *notion* of origins, enthralled by its own origin in repetition. And this is enacted stylistically at the close of *Du côté de chez Swann*, where metaphor and variation suddenly fall away, revealing that 'le lac n'était qu'un lac'.[14] Over the following pages, I will revisit the

[12] 'Ils [les invertis] cherchent la ressemblance de ce qu'ils ressentent moins dans la peinture de l'amour de Musset pour Georges Sand, que dans celle de l'amitié de Montaigne pour La Boétie, image de ceux de leurs amours inexaucés pour des amis différents d'eux' (var. *d* Esquisse IV (iii. 1810)).

[13] Swann and the narrator share the 'désir d'aller bravement au fond de ce que la réalité nous offre . . . [Swann] en usait, au moins avant son mariage, d'une façon évidemment choquante, mais [qui] se rattache étroitement et étrangement à plusieurs de mes idées [sur] le plaisir et sur la vie; si bien qu'en essayant de raconter les siennes, c'était les miennes aussi que je m'am/enais pendant / ces longues nuits à m'exposer à moi-même' (addition to f°. 61v°). Both extracts are from cahier 4 (1908–9), cited in Julia Kristeva, *Le Temps sensible* (Paris: Gallimard, 1994), 46–7.

[14] The passage reads: 'au-dessus du moulin factice le vrai ciel était gris; le vent ridait le

narrator's strategies for warding off the threat that 'le narrateur n'était qu'un Swann'.

Lest Swann become too true an original model, his origins are described by further artifice. Despite his function as the projection of an origin, Swann's death figures retrospectively. The narrator reads about it in the newspaper, but neglects to inform the reader until some time after the event. When he does so, it is as a return to an origin apparently beyond the text, Swann's 'real-life' counterpart Charles Haas. This strategy of stepping outside the fictional texture, whereby the author, Marcel Proust, rather than the narrator 'Marcel', speaks occurs rarely; it is unique here in that it operates through an extra-textual referent, the model for Swann. Yet neither Marcel Proust nor Charles Haas are ever named as such. The real names are indirectly suggested by reference to Tissot's painting 'Le Cercle de la rue Royale'. 'Et pourtant, cher Charles Swann' is the narrator's initial address to his fictional character, as if the latter were already Charles Haas. The address—'Si on parle tant de vous'—then continues, but is directed to Haas's portrait in Tissot's painting, to the unnamed Haas, the named Charles Swann, who is sitting alongside General Galliffet, Prince Edmond de Polignac, and Gaston de Saint-Maurice. And this brief glimpse of the (anonymous) original, Swann's real-life counterpart, is pointedly and provocatively abandoned in favour of the textual 'copy'. For Swann, unlike Charles Haas, and indeed unlike Tissot's representation of him—the narrator claims—gives access to 'des réalités plus générales' (iii. 705).[15]

Swann's story is told because of its potential to yield truths. Its telling is triggered by the narrator's childhood experience—that is, by his experience *already* of the fundamental Proustian laws of jealousy, habit, and desire. Yet, between the 'Swann a connu une angoisse semblable à la mienne' of 'Combray' and the faith in modelling, with Swann as origin, of *Le Temps retrouvé*, it is the failure of such repetition, of such analogies, which is expressed constantly—and always with surprise. There is the occasional 'Comme Swann, je me figure que

Grand Lac de petites vaguelettes, comme un lac; de gros oiseaux parcouraient rapidement le Bois, comme un bois' (i. 419).

[15] 'Le mythe généalogique est . . . la forme première de la réflexion historique', claims Léon Poliakov in *Le Mythe aryen* (Paris: Calmann-Lévy, 1971). And, citing André Leroi-Gourhan, 'La recherche du mystère des origines et les sentiments complexes sur lesquels elle se fonde sont nés sans doute avec les premières lueurs de la réflexion' (p. 15). *A la recherche*'s reflection on, and figuring of, its own origin leads teasingly full circle back into artifice and further models.

la mort d'Albertine supprimerait ma douleur', but this is soon supplanted by 'J'ai connu un bonheur et un malheur que Swann n'avait pas connus', and further, 'Rien ne se répète exactement: la principale opposition (l'art) ne s'est pas manifestée encore'.[16] Similarly, the narrator's love for Gilberte sets a precedent for his relationship with Albertine: the former's sensual and wilful character is described as migrating into the latter's body. The narrator perceives 'des analogies profondes' (iv. 84) between the two women; yet Gilberte's model does not allow the prediction of Albertine: 'A l'aide de Gilberte j'aurais pu aussi peu me figurer Albertine et que je l'aimerais, que le souvenir de la sonate de Vinteuil ne m'eût permis de me figurer son septuor' (iv. 84).

Repetition does, certainly, enforce the Proustian commonplace book, as does slight variation. As readers, we are drawn now to the likeness, now to the not-quite-ness (hence the involuntary comedy of the editorial summaries quoted above). This response might be described simply as the pleasurable recognition of a theme and its variations were it not for the epistemological loading which repetition and difference are accorded by the text. The tension between these two terms ends up reading less like the theme–variation interplay and more like, say, the tension experienced by Darwin between the pleasures of taxonomy, on the one hand, and of the luxuriant abundance—'the tangled bank'—of nature, on the other. In the following passage, repetition is, we are told, not a drawback for the reader, but an advantage as it uncovers new truths:

> Une certaine ressemblance existe, tout en évoluant, entre les femmes que nous aimons successivement, ressemblance qui tient à la fixité de notre tempérament. . . . De sorte qu'un romancier pourrait au cours de la vie de son héros, peindre presque exactement semblables ses successives amours et donner par là l'impression non de s'imiter lui-même mais de créer, puisqu'*il y a moins de force dans une innovation artificielle que dans une répétition destinée à suggérer une vérité neuve.* (ii. 248, emphasis added)

In other words, the innovation which holds the reader's attention is to lie in the law rather than in the *récit*, the maxims rather than the stories. Empirical evidence—and it is the function of the *récit* to provide this—is allowed to fall slightly short of its role as guarantor of the law, since narrative conventions require that it fails to repeat exactly—'peindre *presque* exactement', '*tout en* évoluant'. Proustian

[16] For these summaries, see iv. 1477–8.

conventions, however, ensure that it will repeat sufficiently still to connect with the desired generality.

When the narrator is placed within his own story, the already epistemologically loaded terms of repetition and difference are experienced with great anxiety. This in itself is a different kind of narrative: the story of how the narrator, seemingly locked within his own narratives and their commonplaces, begins to question their validity. Why should a law be based on repetition? Why should the mind instinctively register this, rather than explore difference? And what is the validity of this instinct in the first place?

As we saw in the previous chapter, the narrator's pursuit of Albertine, structured around two hypotheses (Albertine is heterosexual and innocent, or lesbian and guilty), summons up Swann's example as a model recognized as both necessary and inappropriate. Despite the fact that Albertine is not Odette, the narrator still reads the former according to 'Un amour de Swann', and does so while fully cognizant of what he terms his 'faute de raisonnement':

> Au fond si je veux y penser, l'hypothèse qui me fit peu à peu construire tout le caractère d'Albertine et interpréter douloureusement chaque moment d'une vie que je ne pouvais pas contrôler tout entière, ce fut le souvenir, l'idée fixe du caractère de Mme Swann, tel qu'on m'avait raconté qu'il était. (iii. 199–200)

Such modelling seems, as does hypothesis, to impose itself on the narrator. It suggests another dimension to Benjamin's description of 'Proust's frenetisches Studium, sein passionierter Kultus der Ähnlichkeit' ('Proust's frenetically studying resemblances, his impassioned cult of similarity').[17] Beyond the simple noting of analogy, there is a sense in which this modelling appears instinctive, compulsive, a blindness to difference rather than an acute perception of similarity. The narrator's construction and interpretation of Albertine's character according to Swann's well-worn story—one which he knows we know he 'put about' himself—is a fearful response to 'une vie que je ne pouvais pas contrôler tout entière'. We might say that this is a kind of needy repetition, that, suffering from within the law, the narrator desires its therapeutic vantage-point, wishes that Albertine could just be 'une Albertine' or 'une Odette'. The difference results not so much from the story—we might also call it a case history—as from the perspective on the law. For now the narrator is inside the law, suffering from one of the passions, rather than noting how similar it is

[17] Benjamin, 'Zum Bilde Prousts', 75; Zohn's translation, *Illuminations*, 200.

to the last experience of it. The narrator's knee-jerk rehearsal of Swann's story admits of a recognition of both similarity and difference—the originality of the narrator's story is of course this stepping inside the law, this affective experience of the passions as if for the first time. Everything is the same as before, but different.

Swann and the narrator are closely aligned in their desirous relation with knowledge, with the lover's laws. In the drafts Swann is the narrator's double, becoming, in *A la recherche*, his puppet—his mascot. The narrator's attempt to rid himself of Swann is not so much a 'shedding' of 'matière' as the *infusoire*-like splitting which we see in process in the drafts (the *infusoires*, microscopic unicellular water creatures, the lowest and most mutatable life-form in *A la recherche*, reproduce by self-division[18]). This does not result in the subject–object separation by which the narrator is to master and elude the law. Instead, according to the specific law of such reproduction, a copy is produced, another *infusoire*. Difference, then, must be imposed by force, or at least by artifice—the artifice according to which the narrator is both artist and model, subject and object, Swann and self.

Exact repetition is dangerous. The lake might just be a lake, the narrator just a Swann. Gilberte's origins, unlike her father's, are described by a scientific rather than an aesthetic analogy: she is the product of the complex combinations of 'l'hérédité morale'. This moral heredity is described as a natural history of the passions which has existed since time began, 'depuis que le monde dure':

> Les égoismes accumulés . . . prendraient une puissance telle que l'humanité entière serait détruite, si du mal même ne naissaient, capables de le ramener à de justes proportions, des restrictions naturelles analogues à celles qui empêchent la prolifération infinie des infusoires d'anéantir notre planète, la fécondation unisexuée des plantes d'amener l'extinction du règne végétal, etc. (iv. 165)

The cumulative effect of repetition is fatal, whether of the passions or, moving back to the field of biology from which the analogy is taken, of a single species. This proliferation from self-fertilization occurs at the

[18] 'Infusoire (m.): Grande classe du règne animal, renfermant les animaux les plus simples, qu'on trouve ordinairement dans les infusions . . . des animaux aquatiques, très petits, non symétriques, sans sexes distincts, sans œufs visibles, sans cavité digestive déterminée ou permanente, ayant toute une partie de leur corps sans tégument résistant, et se propageant par division spontanée ou *par quelque mode encore inconnu* (Dujardin) . . . La forme des *infusoires* est extrêmement variée et ne paraît, du reste, nullement permanente dans les mêmes espèces: il en est de sphériques, d'ovoïdes, de cylindriques, de filiformes, de coniques, de discoïdes, de vermicules. Quelques-uns affectent des formes de vases, de fleurs, d'étoiles diversement radiées' (*Larousse grand dictionnaire universel du XIXe siècle*).

expense of the whole—'notre planète', 'le règne végétal'. Difference is necessary to enforce natural restrictions and true proportions. The apocalyptic vision of the annihilation of the planet, the destruction of the human race, the extinction of all plant life, hysterically indicates the dangers of reproduction as repetition.

The *infusoires* make a similarly apocalyptic reappearance in the discussions of the First World War which occur in *Le Temps retrouvé*. The passage is revealing both for its repetitiousness—the fear again that extinction might result from reproduction as infinite repetition—and for its sense of repetition of the particular as revealing and proving patterns of human behaviour on a large scale or, in other words, as proving the laws of psychology. The passage begins with the second approach to repetition. The narrator claims that his experience of Albertine and Françoise lying during his quarrels with them has led him to distrust the claims and promises made by heads of state whose countries are at war. On the one hand, the narrator argues, it could be said that this reasoning is false, because personal disputes concern only 'la vie de cette petite cellule spirituelle qu'est un être' (iv. 350). The use of the phrase 'spiritual cell' already indicates the move in scale which is to occur, a move which will connect the particular and the general ('petit corps féminin'/'petite cellule spirituelle'—'c'est à la cime même du particulier qu'éclôt le général') through an argument couched in the language of the natural historian. Just as, the argument runs, the bodies of animals and people are made up of groups of cells, 'des assemblages de cellules', so nations are made up of 'd'énormes entassements organisés d'individus', and the life of these masses (of cells or of people) 'ne fait que répéter en les amplifiant la vie des cellules composantes'. There is no sense here that amplification might distort the laws which pertain at the most microscopic level, no sense that individuals might behave quite differently once absorbed into 'the mass'—and this is puzzling given that Proust was writing at a time when research into mass psychology was not only coming to prominence in the media, but was also a subject for literary exploration. The effect of mass behaviour is simply to amplify; the response to this amplification is aesthetic—for the expert psychologist, 'le maître de la psychologie des individus', which these extreme perspectives allow the narrator to become, such large-scale reproduction is sublime: 'ces masses colossales d'individus conglomérés s'affrontant l'une l'autre prendront à ses yeux une beauté plus puissante que la lutte naissant seulement du conflit de deux caractères' (iv. 350). Two perspectives are suggested. The first is microscopic; the psychologist is himself simply one of thousands of cells constituting the body of the state, his view is 'à l'échelle où verraient le corps d'un homme de haute taille des infusoires dont il faudrait plus de dix mille pour remplir un cube d'un millimètre de côté'. The second is sublime; the war may be like a boxing match, but it is a match between giants, 'de géants assemblages', and so, from a human perspective (rather than the initial microscopic perspective), it becomes a conflict between immense natural forces which shape coastlines and smash mountains:

> La querelle prenait des formes immenses et magnifiques, comme le soulèvement d'un océan aux millions de vagues qui essaye de rompre une ligne séculaire de falaises, comme des glaciers gigantesques qui tentent dans leurs oscillations lentes et destructrices de briser le cadre de montagnes où ils sont circonscrits. (iv. 351)

—in other words an amplified elemental conflict figured through a sublime landscape.

The movement from the micro- to the macroscopic is also a movement from nature as the subject of minute scientific study to nature outpacing and overwhelming man; this involves a dramatic shift in the temporal scale, from the relatively short life span of man to the ages over which landscapes are broken and reformed. In drawing up the first perspective, the microscopic, Proust's use of 'infusoire' appears misplaced.[19] *Infusoires* are microscopic water creatures, not the constituent cells of animals or people. In fact, his usage constitutes the literal application of a scientific model: late nineteenth-century biologists had begun to use *infusoires* as an analogy for the reproduction of human cells, and indeed for all forms of life—their work anticipated the study of genetics. The *infusoires* were regarded as both the origin and also, analogically speaking, the building-blocks of life: 'Les organismes unicellulaires, tels que les Rhizopodes et les Infusoires, se multiplient en se divisant . . . Tous les individus de ces espèces unicellulaires, qui vivent de nos jours sur la terre, sont donc plus âgés que la race humaine prise dans son ensemble; ils sont presque aussi âgés que la vie terrestre l'est elle-même.'[20] Proust's application of the

[19] Remy de Gourmont uses a similar illustrative analogy to explain the constitution of multicellular life-forms: 'C'est par cette notion de colonie que l'on explique les êtres complexes, et même les animaux supérieurs, en les considérant comme des réunions primitives d'êtres simples qui se seraient différenciés en restant solidaires, se partageant le travail physiologique. Les colonies de protozoaires sont formées d'individus à fonction identiques, vivant en égalité parfaite' (*Physique de l'amour* (1st. pub. 1904), in *Œuvres*, vol. 3 (Paris: Mercure de France, 1930), 24).

[20] August Weismann, 'De l'hérédité', trans. Henry de Varigny, in *La Découverte des lois de l'hérédité*, ed. C. Lenay (Paris: Presses Pocket, 1990), 171–2.

analogy reveals the essential preoccupations of his argument—notably the preoccupation with what is most singular (the smallest independent unit of life) and what is eminently repeatable. The application also connects the primitive to the sophisticated—the most primitive life form, the *infusoire*, is at the origin of life itself, yet fundamental to apparently advanced forms of human civilization, such as, in this case, nation-states and their political disputes.

The *infusoires* are also the link into the subsequent paragraph which would seem to explore a different aspect of the war. In spite of the dramatic, large-scale changes which the conflict threatens to impose, the daily lives of 'bien des personnages qui ont figuré dans ce récit', in particular Charlus and the Verdurins, continue almost unaffected. The danger of such indifference is described by the following maxim–metaphor couplet:

> Les gens vont d'habitude à leurs plaisirs sans penser jamais que, si les influences étiolantes et modératrices venaient à cesser, la prolifération des infusoires atteignant son maximum, c'est-à-dire faisant en quelques jours un bond de plusieurs millions de lieues, passerait d'un millimètre cube à une masse un million de fois plus grande que le soleil, ayant en même temps détruit tout l'oxygène, toutes les substances dont nous vivons; et qu'il n'y aurait plus ni humanité, ni animaux, ni terre. (iv. 351)

This apocalyptic use of the *infusoires* clearly mirrors that of the passage analysed above. But where the previous analogy with the reproduction of *infusoires* and single sex plants trails provocatively into an *et cetera*, which threatens to exhaust itself through the repetition of such metaphors, here the sense of closure comes by balancing the threat of the microscopic with that of the macroscopic: 'une irrémédiable et fort vraisemblable catastrophe pourra être déterminée dans l'éther par l'activité incessante et frénétique que cache l'apparent immutabilité du soleil' (iv. 351). What unites these 'cosmic threats' is their invisibility to the human eye. The emphasis here is on the naïvety of man's reliance on a precarious natural balance, his indifference making danger invisible to him, rather than, as in the earlier passage, on nature's self-regulation, 'les influences étiolantes et modératrices' (iv. 351), the 'restrictions naturelles' (iv. 165).

Both *infusoire* passages draw on Michelet's *La Mer*, which gives a similarly hyperbolic account of reproduction, restriction, and annihilation:

> Pleine de vie à la surface, la mer en serait comble si cette puissance indicible de production n'était violemment combattue par l'âpre ligue de toutes les destruc-

tions. Qu'on songe que chaque hareng a quarante, cinquante, jusqu'à soixante-dix mille œufs! Si la mort violente n'y portait remède, chacun d'eux se multipliant en moyenne par cinquante mille, et chacun de ces cinquante mille se multipliant de même à son tour, ils arriveraient en fort peu de générations à combler, solidifier l'Océan, ou à le putréfier, à supprimer toute race et à faire du globe un désert.[21]

Here the reproducing culprit is the herring, but in this same text Michelet also gives a less dramatic account of the reproduction of *infusoires*, which are, he claims, the origin of both plant and animal life.[22] Proust's suggestion of the precarious harmony of nature, of the ever-present threat of extinction, and of a chaotic co-presence of different life-forms at various stages in the evolutionary chain, rather than nature following 'a law of universal progress, tending to the production of organisms more and more perfect from the point of view of complexity of structure',[23] is also indebted to Elie Metchnikoff's *Études sur la nature humaine: essai de philosophie optimiste* (1903).[24]

Nature threatens to stifle itself by too easily and abundantly reproducing—and in *A la recherche* the agents of reproduction are creatures or plants which reproduce independently by budding or splitting, by what might be termed 'self-repetition'. Proust's use of metaphor to tap in and out of different evolutionary stages and life-forms suggests that similar laws of nature govern these and human behaviour—a suggestion which is, in scientific terms, often simply untrue. The apocalyptic *infusoire* analogies imply that their reproductive pattern informs both human heredity and behaviour—certainly it threatens to do so in *A la recherche*.[25] Similarly, what holds the 'cosmic threat' of repetition/reproduction in all these scenarios in place is nature's self-regulation, but, as Gourmont points out in his *Physique de l'amour*,

[21] Jules Michelet, *La Mer* (1st pub. 1861, Lausanne: L'Âge d'Homme, 1980), 72.

[22] See Barthes on Michelet's fascination with intermediary life-forms (*Michelet*, 31).

[23] Elie Metchnikoff, *The Nature of Man*, trans. P. C. Mitchell (London: Watts, 1938), 11.

[24] Zoologist and embryologist Elie Metchnikoff (winner of the Nobel Prize and Director of the Pasteur Institute), whose work on bacteriology and pathology led to the establishment of the science of immunology, discovered the role of white blood cells. Proust read his popular scientific text, *Études sur la nature humaine*, and discussed it as early as 1906 in a letter to Antoine Bibesco (*Correspondance*, vi. 57); in 1921 he wrote to Daniel Halévy and referred to Halévy's review of Olga Metchnikoff's biography, *Vie d'Elie Metchnikoff* (ibid. xxi. 678–9).

[25] The sense of near repetition in the narrator's own genealogy—'Peu à peu, je ressemblais à tous mes parents, à mon père qui—de tout autre façon que moi sans doute, car si les choses se répètent, c'est avec de grandes variations—s'intéressait si fort au temps qu'il faisait' (iii. 586)—is redescribed through a botanical, *infusoire*-style analogy: 'Au vrai, comme ces plantes qui se dédoublent en poussant, en regard de l'enfant sensitif que j'avais uniquement été, lui faisait face maintenant un homme opposé . . . un homme ressemblant à ce que mes parents avaient été pour moi' (iii. 615).

asexual reproduction cannot be an infinite process: 'sans la régénération nucléaire qui en est le but et la conséquence, la segmentation ni le bourgeonnement ne sauraient avoir lieu, du moins indéfiniment.'[26] Repetition must, at some point, be not-quite.

But we shouldn't forget that Proust also exploits the repetitious quality of the *infusoires* to enforce the law. In the second passage, the *infusoires* are posited as the building blocks of life, in this case the life of the nation, in order to back up the argument about individual and mass psychology.

A similar tension between the uses and dangers of repetition informs the apparently authoritative analogies that Proust draws from the natural sciences. By extension, these patterns of repetition suggest that if there were to be a natural history of the novel, then repetition would necessarily be evident, but also 'not quite'. A similar solution is suggested by another scientific discipline, chemistry: 'Les combinaisons par lesquelles au cours des générations la chimie morale fixe ainsi et rend inoffensifs les éléments qui devenaient trop redoutables, sont infinies, et donneraient une passionnante variété à l'histoire des familles' (iv. 165). This passionate variety, this variety of the passions, takes the form of a chemical reaction. In *Du côté de chez Swann*, memory is described as a type of pharmacy or laboratory (i. 892), while the phenomenon of involuntary memory is compared to a chemical reaction (i. 50). The infamous *madeleine* dunked in lime tea brings back to the narrator his own preparation of this infusion for his Aunt Léonie; he describes the flowering of the dried lime blossoms, delighting in their beauty and in the 'charmante prodigalité du pharmacien'.

If we stop at this point—having found a variety or abundance akin to that yielded by involuntary memory—we can conclude comfortably with a return to the text's own theories, forgetting all about the not-quite-ness of repetition. But this is to be blinded by the spectacular effects of a chemistry which is closer to alchemy and to neglect the persistent hard work done by the narrator as botanist. The involuntary repetition of Swann's story and the narrator's enforcing of difference seem to indicate a necessary failure to model. In the next section I will move from this idea of modelling as narrative similarity to consider how scientific modelling is more successfully and suggestively manipulated by the narrator, to explore textual and sexual problematics which both escape the repetition of *infusoire* style reproduction and also elude the painterly solutions of *Le Temps retrouvé*.

[26] Gourmont, *Physique de l'amour*, 26.

5.3 Scientific modelling

> Quant au style, je me suis efforcé de rejeter tout ce que dicte l'intelligence pure, tout ce qui est rhétorique, enjolivement et à peu près, images voulues et cherchées . . . pour exprimer mes impressions profondes et authentiques et respecter la marche naturelle de ma pensée.
>
> Proust, *Correspondance*

The use of analogy as a cognitive tool allows the not-quite-ness of repetition to be seen instead as creative misprision. This means shifting from the process of aesthetic to scientific modelling. Scientific modelling had not been formalized as such at the time of *A la recherche*. A 'modèle' was something or somebody to be imitated, whether in an aesthetic or a moral sense; in another sense of the word, 'to' becomes 'ought to', and the model becomes exemplary. 'Modèle' could also designate a scale model or an object to be mass-produced. In all senses modelling has exact reproduction as its aim. 'Modèle' had not yet been coined by scientists to designate what must, in effect, be an inexact reproduction. But if 'scientific modelling'[27] was not available at the time of Proust's writing, traces of it can be found in the attempts of philosophers and scientists to describe a thought process which requires repetition to be not quite. Bergson, in *L'Évolution créatrice*, for example, argues that human intelligence, shaped by evolution, isolates the already known and looks for repetition in the past. Science is seen as having taken this basic operation to the highest level of precision: 'Comme la connaissance usuelle, la science ne retient des choses que l'aspect *répétition*. Si le tout est original, elle s'arrange pour l'analyser en éléments ou en aspects qui soient *à peu près* la reproduction du passé.'[28] For philosophy and the sciences to be revitalized, Bergson proposes, the mind's natural tendency to register repetition of the known must be denied:

> L'introduction du mouvement dans la genèse des figures est à l'origine de la mathématique moderne. Nous estimons que, si la biologie pouvait jamais serrer son objet d'aussi près que la mathématique serre le sien, elle deviendrait à la physico-chimie des corps organisés ce que la mathématique des modernes s'est trouvée être à la géométrie antique.[29]

[27] Of course, this sense of the word 'model' has now passed into common usage. I refer to 'scientific modelling' here and elsewhere to draw attention to its origins in the history and philosophy of science, but also simply to distinguish it from other senses of the word.

[28] Bergson, *L'Évolution créatrice*, 29.

[29] Ibid. 32.

Introducing Bergsonian 'movement' into the use of analogy ('aesthetic modelling') might be said to make of it a scientific model. This model, beyond registering similarity, allows prediction and extension. It also uses misprision creatively. Scientists contemporary with Proust, while not concerned with the virtues or otherwise of *modelling*, were simply discussing it under another name: *analogy*. As Einstein and Infeld claim in *The Evolution of Physics*:

> It has often happened in physics that an essential advance was achieved by carrying out a consistent analogy between apparently unrelated phenomena. . . . The association of solved problems with those unsolved may throw new light on our difficulties by suggesting new ideas. It is easy to find a superficial analogy which really expresses nothing. But to discover some essential common feature, hidden beneath a surface of external differences, to form, on this basis, a new successful theory, is important creative work.[30]

The turn of the century saw the polarization of a debate centring on the validity of analogy in science.[31] The terms of that debate were still being reproduced in the 1960s to structure similar arguments about modelling.[32]

The history of debate around the use of metaphor in science is not dissimilar in its anxieties to the debate around hypothesis. The anxiety about metaphor differs primarily in that it raises questions about the function of language in science. As James Bono argues: 'Popular and professional images of science, reinforced by philosophical traditions stretching back to Plato and Bacon, differentiate between a science striving to "mirror Nature" and literature enmeshed, if not mired, in language.'[33] Metaphors used in science might introduce 'inappropriate, nonliteral meanings . . . contaminating the precise and stable meanings science attempts to discover behind the terms it uses'.[34] As with hypothesis, such fears may be dealt with by the normative view that, once a law has been articulated—that is, when a speculative

[30] Albert Einstein and Leopold Infeld, *The Evolution of Physics* (Cambridge: Cambridge University Press, 1938), 286.

[31] Valéry considers the problematic of finding models in the field of the new physics: 'Mais du jour où l'enceinte des éléments apparemment rigides et inertes a été violée—où l'atome s'est ouvert montrant l'énergie interne—l'explication physique a été atteinte. Le monde de l'expérience *directe* n'a plus de modèles à nous offrir' (cited in Crow, *Paul Valéry: Consciousness and Nature*, 162).

[32] See Mary Hesse, *Models and Analogies in Science* (London: Sheed and Ward, 1963), on which the following account of the Duhem–Campbell debate is based.

[33] James J. Bono, 'Science, Discourse, and Literature', in *Literature and Science*, ed. S. Peterfreund (Boston: Northeastern University Press, 1990), 59.

[34] Ibid. 62.

metaphor may be translated into a non-figurative, theoretical statement—then the metaphor itself may be discarded. The belief that theories may be purged of their origins in metaphor depends, of course, on the belief that scientific language has a privileged relationship with the real, or, according to Barthes's characterization, that science disposes of a slave language, a transparent medium allowing the absolute expression of ideas.[35] That metaphor might have helped shape and even have been instrumental in forming those ideas endangers such a relationship. Apparently stable theories may have at their origin a metaphor which was once susceptible to a range of different readings and applications. That the meaning has been temporarily 'fixed' does not prevent the metaphor from being reopened to its primary speculative state. The languages of science and literature are no longer so clearly demarcated: in both, language shapes and articulates thought. 'Language is not a passive instrument but an active engagement.'[36]

Black's answer to these concerns, and specifically to the anxiety that 'recourse to models smacks too much of philosophical fable and literary allegory to be acceptable in a rational search for the truth',[37] is, paradoxically, intuition. The modeller must have an intuitive grasp of the potential and limits of her analogy.[38] And I will return to this paradox in the concluding section of this chapter. For now I would like to illustrate the concerns discussed above by focusing on a localized instance of the model debate.

As physicists in the latter half of the nineteenth century abandoned their search for mechanical models of the ether as explanations of the phenomena of light and electromagnetism, they were forced to reconsider the place and form of analogy, to rethink the process of modelling itself. The theoretical suppositions (those deriving from Newtonian physics) which gave rise to these mechanical models ultimately rendered both implausible. Discrepancies and contradictions

[35] 'Pour la science, le langage n'est qu'un instrument, que l'on a intérêt à rendre aussi transparent, aussi neutre que possible, assujetti à la matière scientifique . . . qui, dit-on, existe en dehors de lui et le précède' (Roland Barthes, 'De la science à la littérature', in *Le Bruissement de la langue* (Paris: Seuil, 1984), 14).

[36] N. Katherine Hayles, 'Complex Dynamics in Literature and Science', in *Chaos and Order* (Chicago: University of Chicago Press, 1991), 5.

[37] Black, *Models and Metaphors*, 231.

[38] For Poincaré, describing the movement of mathematical induction from the particular to the general (*La Valeur de la science*, 30–1), analogy is the tool which is used by intuition in the formulation of law, or 'le sentiment direct de ce qui fait l'unité d'un raisonnement, de ce qui en fait pour ainsi dire l'âme du fait et la vie intime'.

in these theories were off-loaded on to the models and became clearly visible, as Einstein and Infeld describe:

In order to construct the ether as a jelly-like mechanical substance physicists had to make some highly artificial and unnatural assumptions. . . . The artificial character of all these assumptions, the necessity for introducing so many of them all quite independent of each other, was enough to shatter the belief in the mechanical point of view.

And further:

In the attempt to understand the phenomena of nature from the mechanical point of view throughout the whole development of science up to the twentieth century, it was necessary to introduce artificial substances like electric and magnetic fluids, light corpuscles, or ether. The result was merely the concentration of all the difficulties in a few essential points.[39]

The failure of these models necessitated a debate on their usage and validity. As Macintyre describes: 'One of the signs that a tradition is in crisis is that its accustomed ways for relating seems and is begin to break down.'[40] Varying degrees of investment in such analogies were held: for Maxwell, the ether was simply a 'heuristic convention'; for Kelvin, 'real matter'.[41] Models could be read according to different conventions; they might be seen as realistic, or as a loose caricature. They might be literally constructed, but, more often, simply involved 'talking in a certain way'. In other words, the crisis of explanation in physics had precipitated a methodological debate. This may be characterized by the positions adopted by Campbell and Duhem for and against the use of models.

In his *La Théorie physique* of 1914, the French physicist and philosopher Pierre Duhem attacked the practice of modelling.[42] His argument contrasts two types of scientific mind, the 'Continental' and the English, representing the former as abstract, logical, systematizing,

[39] Einstein and Infeld, *Evolution of Physics*, 123–5.

[40] A. Macintyre, 'Epistemological Crises, Dramatic Narratives and the Philosophy of Science', in *Paradigms and Revolutions*, ed. G. Cutting (Notre Dame, Ind.: University of Notre Dame Press, 1980), 60.

[41] See Black, *Models and Metaphors*, 227–8.

[42] Both Duhem and Poincaré may be loosely categorized in the conventionalist philosophical tradition; see 'Hypothesis' (pp. 97–9 above). However, the reactions of these two scientists to Édouard Le Roy's article 'Un positivisme nouveau' (1901) are indicative of the range of positions adopted within the conventionalist 'camp'. Both Poincaré and Duhem are listed in Le Roy's article as representatives of the 'nouvelle critique des sciences'. Poincaré's response to this article criticized its extreme conventionalism, or 'nominalism' (this forms part 3 of *La Valeur de la science*), and in turn caused Duhem to defend his accepted position within the 'nouvelle critique'.

and geometric, the latter as visualizing, imaginative, and incoherent: Pascal's 'esprit géométrique' is superior to the 'esprit de finesse', who indulges in the dubious process of modelling: 'Theory is for him [the English physicist] neither an explanation nor a rational classification of physical laws, but a model of these laws, a model not built for the satisfying of reason but for the pleasure of the imagination. Hence, it escapes the domain of logic.'[43] Duhem acknowledges analogy's role as a valuable tool and a respectable method of discovery, but only with the proviso that it be purged of all imaginative power. By this he means that the two domains related by analogy must first have been formulated as 'abstract systems'. Models are criticized as incoherent and superficial, tending to distract the mind from its search for logical order.

English physicist Norman Robert Campbell replied indirectly to Duhem's attack in his *Physics, the Elements* (1920). His defence of models is structured around two principal lines of argument. In the first he claims that, as an explanation, a theory must provide intellectual satisfaction, which entails an intelligible interpretation in terms of a model, as well as mathematical intelligibility and 'perhaps' the formal characteristics of simplicity and economy. This tends to relegate the model to its illustrative role, and it is the second line of argument which asserts the necessary cognitive function of models in science. The dynamic character of theories, according to Campbell, means that they are constantly being extended and modified to account for new phenomena. Without a model, a theory can less easily reach out to make predictions in new domains. Poincaré describes this from a broader perspective in *Science et méthode*:

> Les grands progrès du passé se sont produits lorsque deux de ces sciences se sont rapprochées, lorsqu'on a pris conscience de la similitude de leur forme, malgré la dissemblance de leur matière, lorsqu'elles se sont modelées l'une sur l'autre, de telle façon que chacune d'elles pût profiter des conquêtes de l'autre. (p. 35)

And Peirce actually characterizes what he calls the 'higher planes' of science as accessible only to 'those who succeed in adapting the methods of one science to the investigation of another': 'Darwin adapted to biology the methods of Malthus and the economists; Maxwell adapted to the theory of gases the methods of the doctrine of chances, and to electricity the methods of thermodynamics. Wundt

[43] Pierre Duhem, *The Aim and Structure of Physical Theory*, trans. P. Wiener (Princeton: Princeton University Press, 1954), 81.

adapted to psychology the methods of physiology [etc.]'.[44] Campbell's own conclusion in response to Duhem's attack is that

> Analogies are not 'aids' to the establishment of theories; they are an utterly essential part of theories, without which theories would be completely valueless and unworthy of the name. It is often suggested that the analogy leads to the formulation of the theory, but that once the theory is formulated the analogy has served its purpose and may be removed or forgotten. Such a suggestion is absolutely false and perniciously misleading.[45]

The origins of the model debate are couched in almost literary terms—is analogy a mere ornament, an illustration, or is it a valid cognitive tool, necessary to the growth and sustenance of theory?

5.4 A correspondence course in modelling

Although Proust did not engage in the study of contemporary science, he was acutely aware of the metaphoric potential of scientific discourse. His correspondence provides the medium for an exchange not unlike the process of modelling outlined above, an exchange in which Proust provides the the intuitive model and his correspondents provide the analogies from their area of expertise, which in the case of the following examples is in some aspect of the sciences. Proust's letters tend to detail a phenomenon, often an aspect of human (and particularly social) behaviour; he then pares down the description of this phenomenon until he captures its essential characteristics and/or dynamic, at which point he asks his correspondent whether anything similar occurs in their field—botany, say, or geometry. In June–July 1913, for example, Proust consulted both Max Daireaux[46] and André Foucart[47] about the phrase 'comme dans le dessin en perspective d'un solide, une de ses faces opposées au spectateur'. 'Pouvez-vous rendre cette phrase correcte, je veux dire qu'elle ne contienne pas de *monstruosité*', he asks the latter.[48] The phrase occurs in *A l'ombre des jeunes filles en fleurs* as a description of M. de Norpois, in whose eyes, the narrator notes, 'ce regard vertical, étroit et oblique (comme, dans le dessein en perspective d'un solide, la ligne fuyante d'une de ses faces)', so leading irresistibly into the generalization 'regard qui s'adresse à cet

[44] Peirce, *Collected Papers*, vii. 66.

[45] Cited in Hesse, *Models and Analogies*, 129.

[46] Letter shortly after 18 June 1913, in *Correspondance*, xii. letter 92.

[47] Letter of July 1913, ibid. xxi. letter 486.

[48] Ibid. 652.

interlocuteur invisible qu'on a en soi-même' (i. 470). In the same letter to Foucart, Proust plunders his acquaintance's knowledge for other correspondences in the sciences:

Ce qui est beaucoup moins important et que nous pourrons laisser pour plus tard: Comment s'appelle ce qui fait que la rotation de la terre n'est pas exactement ce qu'elle serait si . . . (déclinaison?) et comment s'appelle ce qu'il y a de plus complet pour mesurer le temps (je suppose une horloge prodigieuse comme il doit y en avoir dans les observatoires marquant tout ce qu'elle peut marquer d'astronomique etc.). Le temps exact s'appelle le *temps vrai* n'est-ce pas. *Y a-t-il d'autres mots*.[49]

In a letter of 27/8 June 1920 to the duchesse de Guiche, Proust parodies his own method. He recounts an anecdote which is a classic instance of social snobbery and which has, of course, already been accounted for and made familiar by the Proustian laws of desire, jealousy, and indifference. But he does not classify the anecdote under any of these headings; instead, he defamiliarizes it, and, assuming that an analogous phenomenon exists in some field of science, he asks the duchesse if her husband can supply him with its 'nom scientifique':

Dites-lui que par un phénomène bizarre dont il connaît sûrement le nom scientifique, qu'il sera si gentil de m'apprendre, depuis que j'ai écrit que le nom de Murat ne pouvait être égalé à celui de Gramont et que j'ai célébré les grandeurs de la maison d'Aure, la Princesse Murat me dit encore bonjour, mais le Duc de Gramont a entièrement cessé.[50]

Proust also corresponds directly with the duc de Guiche on such matters. In a letter of 17 June 1921, Proust praises Guiche's knowledge of science, 'cette *terra incognita* des sciences où je sais que vous êtes maître'.[51] There follows a discussion of telepathy, which Proust claims should be a common phenomenon; during the war he invented a series of events 'que je ne pouvais savoir, qui souvent n'avaient pas encore eu lieu, et qui se sont trouvés minutieusement réalisés dans la vie'. Yet this in turn does not provide an explanation of telepathy; rather:

Je crois qu'elle est une conséquence logique de prémisses vraies. Est-ce qu'il n'y a pas un théorème qui dit: quand deux triangles semblables etc., eh bien je crois que cette géométrie est vraie aussi pour l'humanité, et qu'en ne s'écartant pas d'un raisonnement juste on trouve naturellement avec la précision la plus subtile ce que la vie contrôle ensuite, à l'étonnement irréfléchi du lecteur informé.[52]

49 Ibid. 653.
50 *Correspondance*, xix. 327–8.
51 Ibid. xx. 348.
52 Ibid. 348–9.

This exchange is not only an example of Proust's concern to find new models from different fields—in this case, geometry—to express the precision of a calculation; it also displays his desire for what makes a scientific model fruitful, and indeed powerful. The qualities of extension and prediction are desirable for his field, the field of 'humanité'.

Painterly modelling is also a concern of the correspondence, notably as a result of the insatiable curiosity of many of Proust's acquaintances about *clefs*. Was Charlus modelled on Robert de Montesquiou, for example? In a letter to Montesquiou, Proust dismisses such identification of 'real' characters, claiming that 'même pour les choses inanimées (ou soi-disant telles), j'extrais une généralité de mille réminiscences inconscientes'.[53] In an earlier letter to Jacques de Lacretelle Proust is more specific, claiming that there is no single key for any of his characters, but rather eight or ten, 'de même pour l'église de Combray, ma mémoire m'a prêté comme "modèles" (a fait poser), beaucoup d'églises'.[54] The redundancy of such painterly models is then illustrated by a comically hyperbolic list of the 'originals' of every monocle to appear in *A la recherche*. This is worth quoting in full:

> Je puis vous dire que (Soirée Saint-Euverte) j'ai pensé pour le monocle de M. de Saint-Candé à celui de M. de Bethmann . . . , pour le monocle de M. de Forestelle à celui d'un officier frère d'un musicien qui s'appelait M. d'Ollone, pour celui du général de Froberville au monocle d'un prétendu homme de lettres une vraie brute que je rencontrais chez la Princesse de Wagram et sa sœur et qui s'appelait Mr de Tinseau. Le monocle de M. de Palancy est celui du pauvre et cher Louis de Turenne qui ne s'attendait guère à être un jour apparenté à Arthur Meyer si j'en juge par la manière dont il le traita un jour chez moi. Le même monocle de Turenne passe dans le *Côté de Guermantes* à M. de Bréauté je crois.

The list even spills over into a postscript, where Proust notes that the profusion of monocles means that some characters are forced to share the same model: 'Je vois car décidément la réalité se reproduit par division comme les infusoires, aussi bien que par amalgame, [que] le monocle de M. de Bréauté est aussi celui de Louis de Turenne.' This transposition through a biologic analogy itself neatly indicates the potential of scientific modelling over its mimetic counterpart.

[53] Letter of 17 May 1921, Correspondance, xx. 281.
[54] Letter of 20 Apr. 1918, ibid. xvii. 193–5.

5.5 Metaphor or model?

Modelling privileges the cognitive potential of metaphor. And as part of the expansive, dilatory movement of retroduction, it has been seen that metaphor and maxim are speculative partners. What is described above as a 'correspondence course' reveals the technique in process in those cases where some form of science provides the model, and these represent some of the most spectacular, and also self-conscious, instances of model building in *A la recherche*. Such borrowings may result in an isolated and elaborate conceit. Virtanen's article 'Proust's Metaphors from the Natural and Exact Sciences', for example, locates the following elaborate metaphor from hydrostatics: the narrator encounters Elstir in the company of the 'jeunes filles':

> Désormais inévitable, le plaisir de les connaître fut comprimé, réduit. . . . Des lois aussi précises que celles de l'hydrostatique maintiennent la superposition des images que nous formons dans un ordre fixe que la proximité de l'événement bouleverse. Elstir allait m'appeler . . . la contraction du plaisir que j'avais auparavant cru avoir était due à la certitude que rien ne pouvait plus me l'enlever. Et il reprit, comme en vertu d'une force élastique, toute sa hauteur, quand il cessa de subir l'étreinte de cette certitude, au moment où . . . je vis Elstir . . . leur dire au revoir. (ii. 211)

Although we find the analogy repeated elsewhere, it does not develop beyond its function of illustration—borrowing from the sciences with a certain degree of complexity, or preciosity, does not make of it a model, for the characteristics of extension and prediction are lacking.[55] This can be contrasted with metaphors drawn from astronomy and optics,[56] botany, and geology, which are used repeatedly throughout the text, as Virtanen suggests, 'to unify the diverse materials of which the novel is composed'. 'Unify' is misleading, in that it suggests that metaphors from these disciplines are used always in the same

[55] Specialist knowledge can, however, revive commonplace, or 'dead', metaphors. As Black illustrates, the metaphor 'man is a wolf' may take on a quite different meaning if 'a naturalist who really knows wolves [tells] us so much about them that *his* description of man as a wolf diverges quite markedly from the stock uses of that figure' (*Models and Metaphors*, 43). In isolation, the comparison of young girls with flowers in bud is a commonplace; the following metaphor, also comparing girls with flowers, is not: 'Hélas! dans la fleur la plus fraîche on peut distinguer les points imperceptibles qui pour l'esprit averti dessinent déjà ce qui sera, par la dessication ou la fructification des chairs aujourd'hui en fleur, la forme immuable et déjà prédestinée de la graine . . . Même mentalement, nous dépendons des lois naturelles beaucoup plus que nous ne croyons et notre esprit possède d'avance comme certain cryptogame, comme telle graminée les particularités que nous croyons choisir' (ii. 245).

[56] See Shattuck, *Proust's Binoculars*.

way, motivated by the same underlying theory. Instead, we might think of such webs of metaphor as what Black terms a 'conceptual archetype': that is, a 'systematic repertoire of ideas by means of which a given thinker describes, by *analogical extension*, some domain to which those ideas do not immediately and literally apply'.[57] By means of their dispersal and interaction with *maximes*, such metaphors function as fruitful models, illustrating, modifying, and pushing forward theory, or 'law'.[58]

This sense of analogy as more than illustration, as necessary to theory, and vice versa, is particularly pertinent to the narrator's technique in the opening section of *Sodome et Gomorrhe*. And the technique is dramatized as the narrator, fresh from his botany lesson with the duchesse de Guermantes (but already armed with considerably more specialist knowledge than she could plausibly give him) happens upon both model (orchid and bee) and object of investigation (Charlus and Jupien, or 'homosexuality').

5.6 *Sodome et Gomorrhe*

> Peut-être, d'autre part, en artiste, sinon en corrompu, Swann eût-il en tout cas éprouvé une certaine volupté à accoupler à lui, dans un de ces croisements d'espèces comme en pratiquent les *mendélistes* ou comme en raconte la mythologie, un être de race différente, archiduchesse ou cocotte, à contracter une alliance royale ou à faire une mésalliance.
>
> (i. 461)

In tracing the movement of the striking botanical metaphor which opens *Sodome et Gomorrhe* across different texts and in successive drafts, associations and suggestions deeply embedded in the passage may be recovered. This tracing reveals not only a shift in the ideas expressed since the original comparison, but also, significantly, a shift in methodology, in the workings and function of metaphor itself. The solitary flower of *Jean Santeuil* ('La digitale dans le vallon') becomes the exotic fertilized orchid of *Sodome et Gomorrhe*. The association with notions of creativity persists throughout: a creativity at first literary,

[57] Black, *Models and Metaphors*, 241.

[58] Gaston notes this practice of modelling. He cites the use of an image from celestial mechanics (iii. 672), involving the concepts of attraction and perpetual motion: 'ici l'utilisation de la physique n'a rien d'ornemental; elle éclaire rétrospectivement toute la page' (*Proust, l'homme des mondes*, 191).

Jean's sympathy with the flower's isolation allowing him to see the composition of a book as a means of escaping his solitude and communing with like minds, but replaced in *Sodome et Gomorrhe* by the botanical and the physical, as Jean's passing comparison becomes a sophisticated metaphor devised by the narrator as a model for homosexual 'fertilization'.[59]

If we turn from the axis of textual genesis to the development within the final version of the novel, we find that the narrator's model is already curiously announced in *Le Côté de Guermantes* by the duchesse (ii. 805–7). Here it is drawn up with clarity and concision. Despite a passing reference to Darwin, her comparison is simply a 'jeu d'esprit', describing the fertilization of plants in human and social terms. But its origins are curious, as the duchesse is simply repeating a comparison made for her by a greater authority, Charles Swann: ' "C'est Swann qui m'a toujours beaucoup parlé de botanique. Quelquefois, quand cela nous embêtait trop d'aller à un thé ou à une matinée, nous partions pour la campagne et il me montrait des mariages extraordinaires de fleurs" ' (ii. 806). Again, Swann acts as literary origin for a theme which is to be repeated, but 'naturally' with significant and superior variation, by the narrator's experience. Swann's analogy is ironic, playful—the duchesse speaks of 'dames' and 'messieurs', of 'fiancés' and 'fiancées', of marriage and visiting cards. The analogy is also straight, redescribing heterosexual relations in society. Again, Swann, the original who always comes second, has been set up. He is the dilettante, suffering from a failure to recognize his inescapable inclusion within these analogies and narratives. His marriage to Odette is seen by the duchesse as effectively excluding him from their society, since it is 'encore beaucoup plus étonnant' (ii. 806) than the marriages between flowers which he once described to her. The basic stories, theories, and, in this case, socially normative analogies are provided by Swann, but gain their value, their revelatory quality, only when reinvented by the narrator as speculative models and as models with implications for the self.

In this case the narrator seems keen to keep apart—to mark his position *outside*, at some distance even, from the scene of modelling. Elsewhere he styles himself as a natural historian, preoccupied now with collecting rare species—Saint-Loup's colouring is, for example,

[59] The wider context of botany in *A la recherche* is discussed by Rina Viers, 'Évolution et sexualité des plantes dans *Sodome et Gomorrhe*', *Europe*, nos 502–3 (Feb./Mar. 1971), 100–13; Diane de Marjerie's *Le Jardin secret de Marcel Proust* (Paris: Albin Michel, 1994) describes and illustrates the botanical imagery of Proust's texts.

'un plumage si étrange, faisait de lui une espèce si rare, si précieuse, qu'on aurait voulu le posséder pour une collection ornithologique' (iv. 281)—and now with taxonomy, as, for example, in this characterization of a woman's face—'une figure ronde comme certaines fleurs de la famille des renonculacées, et au coin de l'œil un assez large signe végétal', which leads to the remark: 'Et les générations des hommes gardant leurs caractères comme une famille de plantes, de même que sur la figure flétrie de la mère, le même signe, qui eût pu aider au classement d'une variété, se gonflait sous l'œil du fils' (iii. 215–16). At the opening of *Sodome et Gomorrhe*, however, a rather different kind of scientific attitude is evident. The narrator literally positions himself as an analyst with a superior vantage-point, also as a voyeur.

On sait que bien avant d'aller ce jour-là (le jour où avait lieu la soirée de la princesse de Guermantes) rendre au duc et à la duchesse la visite que je viens de raconter, j'avais épié leur retour et fait, pendant la durée de mon guet, une découverte, concernant particulièrement M. de Charlus, mais si importante en elle-même que j'ai jusqu'ici, jusqu'au moment de pouvoir lui donner la place et l'étendue voulues, différé de la rapporter. . . . A défaut de la contemplation du géologue, j'avais du moins celle du botaniste. (iii. 3)

The scene and the science are heavily staged. The narrator cites his sources on the fertilization of orchids: Swann, by way of the duchesse's wit, and, significantly, Darwin—significantly, because science is rarely attributed to sources of any kind in *A la recherche*. (Earlier drafts of this passage enlist yet more authorities: 'j'avais lu les livres de Darwin', claims the narrator, 'j'étais allé demander à un professeur de botanique au Museum des échantillons de diverses sortes de pollen' (iii. 1267).) The sense of scientific staging is heightened by the timing of its narration; the episode is of such importance that it has been deferred: 'j'ai jusqu'ici, jusqu'au moment de pouvoir lui donner la place et l'étendue voulues, différé de la rapporter' (iii. 3). The temporal and spatial sealing off of the episode lend the quality of a controlled experiment. Yet the terms of the ensuing comparison—plants and people—are not so clear. Both are physically and implausibly present, and rather than one set providing a description of the other, they interact and are mutually informative. As Kristeva comments in her 'Apologia for Metaphor', Proustian metaphor 'is much more like the reciprocal relationship maintained between the two terms', and, further, 'what is contiguous becomes metaphoric'.[60]

[60] Julia Kristeva, *Proust and the Sense of Time*, trans. S. Bann (London: Faber, 1993), 58 and 63.

Developing the analogy between botany and homosexuality frees up the ensuing discussion. Various discourses had been developed around this topic—or perhaps it would be more accurate to say that these discourses had created their subject, but it was not this that Proust wanted to discuss. These ways of speaking about homosexuality included the sensationalist reporting of a series of high-profile cases which put on trial the sexuality of prominent figures (the Wilde case is briefly alluded to (iii. 17)), and the direct essayistic and often apologetic line adopted by novelists. Choosing a botanical metaphor as a starting-point allows Proust to arrive at a different kind of homosexuality: the discourses of the sensational and the essayistic are still present, but they are styled differently, the subject demanding an implausible aesthetic of its own, 'à eux les romans d'aventure les plus invraisemblables semblent vrais', 'cette vie romanesque, anachronique' (iii. 19).[61]

The choice of science also has a legislative impulse. Proust had already defended the lesbian Montjouvain scene by comparing his creative work with that of the scientist. Removing this episode, as was requested by Louis de Robert, would constitute the falsification of an experiment: 'Je ne peux . . . modifier le résultat d'expériences morales dont je suis obligé de donner communication avec une bonne foi de chimiste.'[62] The next section will survey the 'science' which establishes male homosexuality: chemistry is replaced by botany.

5.7 Botany: the state of the field

On veut que la physique et la chimie nous donnent la clef de tout.

Bergson, *L'Évolution créatrice*

According to the novel's plan as it stood in 1912, the passage on homosexuality preceded *Le Temps retrouvé* (then the third volume), so implying an intimate link between sexual and aesthetic revelation. With the

[61] Aldous Huxley, in a letter to Robert Nichols of 18 Jan. 1927, in *Letters of Aldous Huxley*, ed. G. Smith (London: Chatto and Windus, 1969), no. 258, sees *Sodome et Gomorrhe* as a model in a different sense: 'It is good, I think, because it is the first book [*Les Faux-Monnayeurs*] in which Gide has ventured to talk about the one thing in the world that really interests him—sentimental sodomy. Now that Proust has given the world his guide book to the cities of the plain, the other sodomites feel that they can follow suit, without scandal, sheltering themselves behind his precedent.'

[62] Letter of first days of Sept. 1913, in *Correspondance*, xii. 270–1.

subsequent growth of the text, the ubiquitous botanical material becomes prominent instead at a pivotal moment, opening the central volume of *A la recherche*. The recognition of homosexuality now only gestures towards the final aesthetic revelation, becoming instead a revelation of cognition. By this I mean not only that the narrator becomes cognizant of Charlus's and Jupien's sexuality, but further, that the plotting and play, the manipulation of knowledge, that is the drama of cognition is most prominently displayed. The ever growing number of homosexuals to 'come out' is triggered by this. Indeed, the opening of *Sodome et Gomorrhe* will also act as a pivot in my argument, leading (in the next chapter) into an exploration of the narrator's most overtly plotted 'research'—the construction of knowledge and ignorance about homosexuality.

That Proust should make use of botany is not surprising. Written in a non-mathematical language, the life sciences were still directly accessible to the general reader, as physics and chemistry were not. Popularizing texts for the physical sciences, such as those by Eddington and Poincaré, were, of course, available. But in the field of biology, there is a wider spread of texts, scientific (that is, written for the scientific community, but accessible to a general readership), popular, and philosophical. Two such texts have already been cited in the discussion of the *infusoire* metaphors: Michelet's *La Mer* and Metchnikoff's *Études sur la nature humaine*. The *Études* are also the source for M. de Bréauté's exposition on the artificial breeding of the vanilla (ii. 806), which forms part of the duchesse's discussion of the 'mariages extraordinaires de fleurs', and is subsequently readopted and adapted by the narrator in *Sodome et Gomorrhe* (iii. 28). Further references can be traced to Remy de Gourmont and Maeterlinck's work on natural history. The latter's description of 'la fécondation florale' in *L'Intelligence des fleurs* is, for example, the source of Swann's comparison:

> Le jeu des étamines et du pistil, la séduction des parfums, l'appel des couleurs harmonieuses et éclatantes, l'élaboration du nectar, absolument inutile à la fleur, et qu'elle ne fabrique que pour attirer et retenir le libérateur étranger, le messager d'amour, abeille, bourdon, mouche, papillon, phalène, qui doit lui apporter le baiser de l'amant lointain, invisible, immobile.[63]

Gourmont, Michelet, and Maeterlinck, as the above extract indicates, blend the scientific and the lyrical, the animal or botanical and the human, the empirical and the mystical. For, while the crisis of expla-

[63] Maurice Maeterlinck, *L'Intelligence des fleurs* (1st pub. 1907, Paris: Fasquelle, 1950), 3.

nation in the new physics had precipitated a debate on the validity of models, the various branches of the life sciences were practising the kind of linguistic and conceptual exchange advocated by Poincaré and Peirce. In contrast to the revolutionary developments made in physics and mathematics, which required the formulation of radically new laws, the exchanges practised within the life sciences, still operated within the frame of evolutionary theory, a theory capacious enough to encompass new developments—as, for example, the analogy drawn by embryologists between *infusoires* and reproductive cells, which would eventually lead to the study of genetics—but also to allow a revisiting of past speculations. The style of the above passage from *L'Intelligence des fleurs* is closer to Darwin's grandfather Erasmus's lyrical botanical poetry than to the style of *The Origin of Species*. Similarly, Erasmus Darwin's theory of the universal nature of sexual love, from the simplest to the most complex life-forms, is restated in the opening lines of Remy de Gourmont's *Physique de l'amour*, whose project is to 'agrandir la psychologie générale de l'amour, la faire commencer au commencement même de l'activité mâle et femelle, situer la vie sexuelle de l'homme dans le plan unique de la sexualité universelle'.[64] And, as Bowie has indicated, both Freud and Proust 'in their fantasticated accounts of the yearnings felt by unisexual human creatures for their bisexual pre-existence are closer to the scientific world of Erasmus Darwin's *The Loves of the Plants* than to his grandson's *Origin of Species*'.[65] The apparent lack of any dramatic advance—the revisiting, even, of former theories—caused some to regard biology as the 'backward' scientific discipline; as Valéry remarks, 'notre connaissance de la vie est insignifiante auprès de celle que nous avons du monde inorganique'.[66] Valéry's critique of biology extended not only to what he saw as its lack of methodological awareness, but even to the discipline as a whole.[67] As Christine Crow describes, 'Because of the very nature of its necessary abstract divisionism or interruption of

[64] Gourmont, *Physique de l'amour*, 7.

[65] Bowie, *Freud, Proust, and Lacan*, 81. See also Robert Fraser, *Proust and the Victorians* (New York: St Martin's Press, 1994), 202–4.

[66] Cited in Crow, *Paul Valéry: Consciousness and Nature*, 31. Valéry defines 'connaissance' as the power to reproduce/predict certain results by simplification of phenomena 'en opérations imaginaires ou volontaires': see Crow, ibid. 30–47: 'Knowing and Understanding'.

[67] Valéry is sceptical about what he sees as biology's confusion between fact and hypothesis. Nevertheless, he is fascinated by the notion of plants as models of the mind. 'Ils [crystal, flower, shell] nous proposent, étrangement unies, les idées d'ordre et de fantaisie, d'invention et de nécessité, de loi et d'exception' (cited, ibid. 127), and composes botanically imaged maxims which explore moral and aesthetic concerns.

the "wholeness" of life, the activity of "connaître" cannot for Valéry grasp the unity of nature—"le Tout"—of which it is already itself but a single effect.' Valéry's interest in evolutionary theory was further tempered by the aura of dogma and mysticism which was beginning to surround it (in texts such as Gourmont's, which Proust was reading and drawing on). 'La "théorie de l'évolution" ', he writes, 'je n'ai jamais pu la prendre pour autre chose qu'une imagerie.'[68]

Yet the life sciences were to prove innovative by the force and transfer of analogies, their 'imagerie', across disciplinary boundaries.[69] As Sulloway argues in *Freud, Biologist of the Mind*, the late nineteenth and early twentieth century saw the development of Darwin's work and that of other nineteenth-century evolutionary thinkers by those working on the science of mind, not by biologists. Psychoanalysis, then, owes its fundamental theoretical inspirations to biological sources: 'It was Darwin who handed Freud that most powerful instrument—namely, evolutionary theory's stress upon the dynamic, the instinctual, and, above all, the nonrational in human behaviour.'[70] (Freud himself had moved from biology—he was a neuroanatomical specialist on the human nervous system—to psychoanalysis.)

Darwin's influence provided an important scientific sanction for trends in nineteenth-century thought which had previously been considered speculative and philosophical, as, for example, Schopenhauer's work, with its stress on the unconscious and irrational (Schopenhauer is cited in both Maeterlinck's *L'Intelligence des fleurs* and Remy de Gourmont's *Physique de l'amour*). It also constituted a powerful common denominator between Freud, Wilhelm Fliess, and the rise of the sexology movement. Sexual perversions were regarded in a more naturalistic, biological, and especially Darwinian light. On the basis of Darwin's argument that the very first species were hermaphrodites, James Kiernan argued: 'The original bisexuality of the ancestors of the race . . . could not fail to occasion functional, if not organic, reversions when mental or physical manifestations were interfered with by disease or congenital defect'; and, further: 'The lowest animals are bisexual and the various types of hermaphrodism are more or less complete reversions to the ancestral

[68] Crow, *Paul Valéry: Consciousness and Nature*, 34–5.

[69] On the other hand, as Patrick Pollard's account of Remy de Gourmont's writing indicates, the crossing of disciplinary boundaries was also exploited by popularizers to rhetorical effect (*André Gide* (New Haven: Yale University Press, 1991), 68–83).

[70] Frank J. Sulloway, *Freud, Biologist of the Mind* (London: Burnett Books, 1979), 276: see in particular the chapter 'Freud and the Sexologists', 277–319.

type.'[71] Proust read similar arguments in Metchnikoff's *Études sur la nature humaine*, which describes the atrophied male organs in flowers which were once hermaphrodites, and claims that 'at a very remote period, the ancestral vertebrates were hermaphrodites . . . they became divided into males and females only gradually, still retaining in each sex traces of the other sex'.[72] Such theories were equally open to manipulation by anti-homosexual writers, or, as it were, apologists for heterosexuality. Ezra Pound's preface to his translation of Gourmont's *Physique de l'amour*, *The Natural Philosophy of Love* (1926), pushes some of Gourmont's extreme ideas *ad absurdum*.

Valéry's preference for the purer, more spectacular advances of physics and mathematics, his distaste for the natural sciences, his apparent unease at what appears to be simply 'une imagerie', suggest equally why Proust should have been attracted to them. Indeed, Proust describes the importance for literature itself of this kind of boundary crossing. His enthusiasm for Maeterlinck focuses on the way the latter's work brings together philosophy, natural history, and literature:

> J'ai toujours été émerveillé chaque fois que j'ai vu un écrivain arracher un 'genre' littéraire à la technique immémoriale et mensongère où il se momifiait, et en faisait de la vie, y faisait passer, aussi librement que dans un roman ou un essai, toute la vie de sa pensée. Tout récemment la littérature d'histoire naturelle a vu de cette façon s'élever bien au-dessus d'elle, bien en dehors d'elle, la *Vie des Abeilles*.[73]

And Gourmont makes similar claims for his project, *Physique de l'amour*, as a necessary updating of the *moralistes*' approach to psychology by way of contemporary science: 'Il n'est pas indifférent de connaître le mécanisme normal de l'amour, puisqu'une des prétentions des moralistes est d'en régler les mouvements. . . . Ceux qui ont inventé la morale naturelle connaissaient fort peu la nature.'[74]

The opening of *Sodome et Gomorrhe* needs to be seen against the background of this pre-paradigmatic period—that is, against both the cross-fertilization of biology/sexology and psychoanalysis and that of

[71] James Kiernan, 'Sexual Perversion and the Whitechapel Murders' (1888), cited in Sulloway, *Freud*, 292.

[72] Metchnikoff, *Nature of Man*, 19 and 47.

[73] Letter to Mme de Pierrebourg, shortly after 6 June 1913, in *Correspondance*, xii. 195.

[74] Gourmont, *Physique de l'amour*, 83–4. In his introduction, Gourmont claims that the *moralistes*' approach to psychology is outdated, and consequently invalid, if it fails to take science into account. His project, then, is to redescribe and analyse human sexuality by considering it as part of the evolution and variety of sexuality in the natural world.

literature and science. The narrator's model will be seen both to parody and to explore such speculations. This is also evident linguistically; for, as a consequence of this disciplinary cross-fertilization, a stable or consensual language for speaking about homosexuality had yet to be established. Instead, competing discourses coexisted, often borrowing from and heavily influenced by biology, in particular the work of Darwin. *Sodome et Gomorrhe* draws on, and also caricatures, this nascent and chaotic discourse on homosexuality.

5.8 Genesis of the model

> To be natural is such a very difficult pose to keep up.
>
> Oscar Wilde, *An Ideal Husband*

> La nature veut tout. Elle est complaisante à toutes les activités et ne refuse aucune analogie à aucune de nos imaginations.
>
> Remy de Gourmont, *Physique de l'amour*

In an episode in *Jean Santeuil*, Jean and Henri are walking in the countryside when Jean, losing sight of his companion, notices 'au fond de la gracieuse vallée, sur une tige élancée une digitale violette, habitante silencieuse et brillante de ce lieu' (p. 470). Here botany is present as metaphor rather than model. The metaphor gives rise to general reflections: in a ubiquitous move from the particular to the general, the flower is 'si isolée comme fleur périssable, mais si grande comme pensée durable de la nature, comme type si vaste de la vie' (p. 471). Jean compares his sense of isolation with that of the flower, and concludes that if he were to write a book, he might communicate with a world 'plein de pensées pareilles à la mienne' (p. 471).

Science, in this episode, is simply a means of categorization. Henri's recognition of the flower interrupts Jean's emotional response. But the response is in any case limited, the metaphor contained and controlled: Jean likens himself to the flower simply in that he feels a sense of isolation, and from the comparison recognizes that literature may enable him to escape his condition through the spiritual contact with a community of like minds, past and present. Once formulated, this conclusion exists independently of its original stimulus; it speaks of spiritual contact rather than fertilization, of the mind, not the body, and does not involve process, whether of communication or of creativity. The potentially phallic significance of the flower goes unnoticed, as does its medicinal power—the magical effects, both curative and toxic, of the foxglove caused it to be nicknamed 'doigt de fée'. In *Sodome et Gomorrhe*, these other terms—the body, fertilization, process—have expanded the metaphor, making of it a model, which is bound up not only with the polemics of homosexuality, but also with aesthetics. Science allows this expansion. Through his correspondence with the *curé* of Illiers, Proust had discovered Gaston Bonnier's manual of botany. Further references have been identified in the following texts by Darwin (which Proust read in translation): *The Various Contrivances by which Orchids are Fertilised by Insects* (1862), *The Effects of Cross and Self-Fertilisation in the Vegetable Kingdom* (1876), *The Different Forms of Flowers* (1877), and by Maeterlinck, *L'Intelligence des fleurs* (1907).[75]

Early sketches for this passage reveal the initial use of the metaphor as frame rather than continuous model.[76] The narrator, at the window overlooking the courtyard, watches bees pollinating the sophora; the meeting between M. de Guercy (subsequently renamed the baron de Fleurus before becoming Charlus (iii. 1024–5)) and Borniche (here, ironically, a florist) is then reported in far less detail; and only after this does he revisit and reappropriate the sophora as an analogy: 'Et comme les fleurs du sophora . . . ainsi un être existait aussi rare que notre sophora, pour qui la fleur rêvée était un monsieur plus âgé que lui'; the note is then added 'La digitale dans le vallon' (iii. 938). From this transitional passage (*Jean Santeuil* was clearly in Proust's mind, associated, if not yet worked in, with the now overriding theme of homosexuality) the analogy is problematized, made more 'scientific', in the sense that it becomes a speculative model, resulting in the maxims and case histories of homosexuality. Ricoeur's redescription of modelling as linguistic performance is part of a commentary on Max Black's work on metaphor, but it is also peculiarly appropriate to Proust's botanical-homosexual model:

> To describe a domain of reality in terms of an imaginary theoretical model is a way of seeing things differently by changing our language about the subject of our investigation. This change of language proceeds from the construction of a heuristic fiction and through the transposition of the characteristics of this

[75] See iii. 1269, n. 1.

[76] Esquisse II. *Le Marquis de Guercy*, from cahier 51, June–July 1909 (iii. 934–42).

heuristic fiction to reality itself. . . . Thanks to this detour through the heuristic fiction we perceive new connections among things.[77]

In the final version of *Sodome et Gomorrhe I* the implausible encounter between the two pairs—bee and orchid, Charlus and Jupien—is the heuristic fiction which reveals new connections. The speculative extension of the model through an abundance of the exotically natural finally allows purchase to be made on the subject, the 'hommes-femmes', thus enabling a paradigm shift from botany to homosexuality. In a sense this process is familiar: according to Proust's claim to 'recreate the evolution of thought', we are made party to a phenomenological narrative of discovery; yet here the process is more explicitly staged, and speculative thought itself becomes a spectacle.[78]

Provocatively and, of course, implausibly, both subject and model are present, viewed by the voyeuristic narrator. Nature has been transplanted from the deserted, mountainous setting of *Jean Santeuil* to the confines of the courtyard of the Guermantes's *hôtel*. Here the narrator-botanist settles down to observe: 'Le petit arbuste de la duchesse et la plante précieuse exposés dans la cour avec cette insistance qu'on met à faire sortir les jeunes gens à marier, et je me demandais si l'insecte improbable viendrait, par un hasard providentiel, visiter le pistil offert et délaissé' (iii. 3–4). The model is first introduced as a simple analogy. Jupien is 'enraciné comme une plante', then adopts 'des poses avec la coquetterie qu'aurait pu avoir l'orchidée pour le bourdon providentiellement survenu' (iii. 6). Eventually, the narrator is able to classify Jupien as a *lythrum salicaria*, or purple loosestrife, a flower discussed by Darwin in *The Different Forms of Flowers* as unusual, because self-fertilization is not only undesirable for it, but, in fact, impossible.[79]

And while, from the very inception of the model, botanical detail is added, it also gives rise to alternative speculative comparisons. The theory of cross-fertilization is 'supported' by examples drawn from

[77] Paul Ricoeur on Max Black, in *Interpretation Theory* (Fort Worth, Tex.: Texas Christian University Press, 1976), 67.

[78] The 'de-camping' of the episode—Jupien is no longer a florist, Charlus is no longer Fleurus—which in earlier drafts had punningly put homosexuality centre-stage, means that the narrator, albeit shiftily, comes clean about the subject of his observations. Instead, the speculative process of modelling takes centre-stage. Still, at the moment of revelation, Proust cannot resist transforming Charlus with the touch of a magic wand.

[79] 'Nature has ordained a most complex marriage arrangement, namely a triple union between three hermaphrodites', writes Darwin of the purple loosestrife (*The Different Forms of Flowers* (London: John Murray, 1877), 138). See in particular pp. 137–8 of ch. 4, 'Heterostyled Trimorphic Plants'.

human physiology, examples which are decreasingly technical and result in almost moralistic utterances:

> Comme une antitoxine défend contre la maladie, comme le corps thyroïde règle notre embonpoint, comme la défaite vient punir l'orgueil, la fatigue le plaisir, et comme le sommeil repose à son tour de la fatigue, ainsi un acte exceptionnel d'autofécondation . . . fait rentrer dans la norme la fleur qui en était exagérément sortie. (iii. 5)

Reversing the terms of the original comparison, the human is now used to figure the botanical. Indeed, the model comes to be characterized by its very reversibility; reviving the duchesse de Guermantes's original analogy, the meeting of Jupien and Charlus is compared to the 'préludes rituels' or 'fêtes' preceding a marriage. The model is also characterized by its fertility:[80] it allows a movement from the vegetable to the human to the animal, as Charlus and Jupien are redescribed, as were Mlle Vinteuil and her lover, as two birds. For, once the model is extended, nature becomes richly various: 'La multiplicité de ces comparaisons est elle-même d'autant plus *naturelle* qu'un même homme, si on l'examine pendant quelques minutes, semble successivement un homme, un homme-oiseau ou un homme-insecte, *etc.*' (iii. 8; emphasis added). In this revision of nature as the object of science, it has become 'empreinte d'une étrangeté, ou si l'on veut d'un naturel' (iii. 7). And when Charlus and Jupien leave the courtyard, the former 'sifflant comme un gros bourdon, un autre, un vrai celui-là entrait dans la cour' (iii. 8): nature's reappearance is comically artificial.

The *invraisemblance* of the passage has less to do with the metamorphoses accorded by the narrator's fertile imagination as with this construction of nature as part of the speculative staging of cognition. The dramatic moment of 'révélation', when the narrator realizes that Charlus is homosexual, allows a pause in the speculative movement. But the suspense of this moment too has been undermined by previous pointed non-disclaimers, informing the reader that this is a '(simple comparaison pour les providentiels hasards, quels qu'ils soient, et sans la moindre prétention scientifique de rapprocher certaines lois de la botanique et ce qu'on appelle parfois fort mal l'homosexualité)' (iii. 9). It has been undermined too by an aesthetic

[80] 'It is in fact a great virtue of a good model that it does suggest further questions, taking us beyond the phenomena from which we began, and tempts us to formulate hypotheses which turn out to be experimentally fertile. . . . It is this suggestiveness, and systematic deployability, that makes a good model something more than a simple metaphor' (Toulmin, *Philosophy of Science*, 38–9).

revelation which is obviously central for the narrator, but occurs backstage for the reader, and to which I will return in the next section. This moment in which Charlus 'becomes' homosexual is, then, less about revelation, than about a Kuhnian revolution—'dès le début de cette scène une révolution, pour mes yeux dessillés, s'était opéré' (iii. 15)—, part of the drama of retroduction and redescription. As Arbib and Hesse argue, 'Scientific revolutions are, in fact, metaphoric revolutions, and theoretical explanation should be seen as metaphoric redescription of the domain of phenomena.'[81] Here, the model appears to have yielded a stable subject: the 'hommes-femmes' are a race as distinct as the 'homme-oiseau' and 'homme-insecte' referred to previously. And now that the laws of homosexuality provide the informing theory, allowing a 'straight' purchase on the subject, the model is discarded. The narrator switches faculties—from amateur botanist to a chair in homosexual studies (as Brichot remarks, 'si jamais le Conseil des facultés propose d'ouvrir une chaire d'homosexualité, je vous fais proposer en première ligne' (iii. 811)). The 'hommes-femmes' exordium presents a 'colonie orientale, cultivée, musicienne, médisante' (iii. 33), informed by new maxims and a new system of classification, 'ces différentes classes répondent, tout autant qu'à des types physiologiques divers, à des moments successifs d'une évolution pathologique ou seulement sociale' (iii. 21); supplemented by new case-studies and illustrations; defined by a new aesthetic, in which, of course, *invraisemblance* is key (iii. 21). The guise of the naïve observer, who experiments with many different modes, is now replaced by that of the assured specialist, who in a leisured and scholarly fashion discourses upon his subject. He draws case-studies from an apparently vast fund of similar histories, 'Laissons pour le moment de côté ceux qui . . .' (iii. 22), and constructs imaginative illustrations of certain laws, 'Le jeune homme que nous venons d'essayer de peindre. . .' (iii. 23). He indicates that revisions may be necessary: a theory about the rarity of two homosexuals meeting which has only just been established is interrupted by a more experienced voice: 'Enfin—du moins selon la première théorie que j'en esquissais alors, qu'on verra se modifier par la suite' (iii. 17). The stagy precision of the 'modelling' passage is replaced by what appears to be an infinitely expanding discussion of Sodom, one which—the reader is told—will in turn need to be revised in the light of the narrative to

[81] Michael Arbib and Mary Hesse, *The Construction of Reality*, cited in Bono, 'Science, Discourse, and Literature', 70.

follow.[82] Through a new metaphorical basis in the botanical model, the representation of a different culture is made possible, one which is richly various and artificially natural. This is the cognitive effect of the pairing of orchid (or purple loosestrife) and bee, not that they provide an effective model for elucidating homosexuality as such, but rather that they escape the dangerous repetition of the *infusoires*' reproduction.

But the metaphor which has given birth to the subject may still be said partly to constitute, and thereby to have introduced instability into, it. Or, as Bono, developing the arguments of Arbib and Hesse, suggests, 'scientific change, rather than representing an inexplicable gestaltlike change, as with Kuhn and Foucault, can be rooted in the destabilizing tendencies inherent in a scientific language'.[83] In other words, the 'fix', or purchase, on the subject accorded by language means that it is always subject to redescription. Charlus, 'touché par une baguette magique', has undergone a magical transformation; but through the *general* topic of homosexuality, this change may be inverted. The theories, case studies, and *caractères* of homosexuality may be redescribed by the narrator, who is himself a hybrid, 'a human herbalist, a moral botanist'. In one such *caractère* the narrator characterizes and categorizes the solitary homosexual, by comparing him to a 'méduse stérile qui périra sur le sable', to a flower, and to an insect. These analogies in turn cause a digression away from the subject, back to methodological concerns about how we perceive the natural: 'Méduse! Orchidée! Quand je ne suivais que mon instinct, la méduse me répugnait à Balbec; mais si je savais la regarder, comme Michelet, du point de vue de l'histoire naturelle et de l'esthétique, je voyais une délicieuse girandole d'azur' (iii. 28).[84] And the digression allows the original botanical model literally to be revisted: 'M. de Charlus m'avait distrait de regarder si le bourdon apportait à l'orchidée le pollen qu'elle attendait depuis si longtemps' (iii. 29). This

[82] 'Au reste j'exagérais beaucoup alors, devant cette révélation première, le caractère électif d'une conjonction si sélectionnée . . . ces êtres d'exception que l'on plaint sont une foule, ainsi qu'on le verra au cours de cet ouvrage, pour une raison qui ne sera dévoilée qu'à la fin' (iii. 32).

[83] Bono, 'Science, Discourse, and Literature', 78.

[84] This apologetic metaphor draws on Michelet's description of the jellyfish, or medusa, in *La Mer* (pp. 99–105). It is first used by Proust to discuss lesbianism in an early piece entitled 'Avant la Nuit' (published in *La Revue blanche*, Dec. 1893): 'Chez les natures vraiment artistes l'attraction ou la répulsion physique est modifiée par la contemplation du beau. La plupart des gens s'écartent avec dégoût de la méduse. Michelet, sensible à la délicatesse de leurs couleurs, les ramassait avec plaisir' (in *Jean Santeuil*, 170).

return to the model introduces the most detailed 'scientific' discussion of 'les ruses les plus extraordinaires que la nature a inventées' (iii. 29),[85] and these 'ruses' described in a technical botanical language are matched point by point with equivalents from the narrator's now established archive on homosexuality.[86]

There is a tension, then, between the fix on homosexuality as subject arrived at by way of the botanical model and the fertility and reversibility of the original model. This is characterized by Bono in his redescription of metaphor as a site of exchange: 'rather than ineluctably resulting in anarchic instability—a chaotic flux of meanings—such exchanges, I want to suggest, function within, or rather create, an "ecological" network driven by the tension-fraught need or desire both to "fix" meanings, and to disrupt, generate and transform them.'[87] The fix which comes through redescribing the subject as homosexuality is temporary. The instability and energy of the language which describes this subject are artificially contained by the narrator's overly authoritative gestures and by the break which separates the first section of *Sodome et Gomorrhe* from the rest of the volume (the structure of this volume is exceptionally strict; epigraphs are used, and chapter divisions headed by summaries). Yet, despite these measures, this is a topic which, we are warned, will spill over into the remainder of the novel, and from its localized first appearance assume grand proportions: 'Laissons enfin pour plus tard ceux qui ont conclu un pacte avec Gomorrhe. Nous en parlerons quand M. de Charlus les connaîtra. Laissons tous ceux, d'une variété ou d'une autre, qui apparaîtront à leur tour' (iii. 25).

If nature, through botany, is constructed and, indeed, revisited in this way—by which I mean that there is both an actively speculative use of the model, but also an involuntary collapsing back into it—we should bear in mind that this very instability characterized the 'state of

[85] The narrator's exclamations here recall stylistically Darwin's descriptions, as, e.g., in *The Effects of Cross and Self-Fertilisation*: 'Cross-fertilisation is also ensured in many cases, by mechanical contrivances of wonderful beauty, preventing the impregnation of the flowers by their own pollen' (p. 2); and in *The Various Contrivances by which Orchids are Fertilised by Insects* (ist pub. 1862, London: John Murray, 1877): 'The Orchideae exhibit an almost endless diversity of beautiful adaptations' (p. 282).

[86] 'Les ruses les plus extraordinaires que la nature a inventées . . . ne me semblaient pas plus merveilleuses que l'existence de la sous-variété d'invertis destinée à assurer les plaisirs de l'amour à l'inverti devenant vieux: les hommes qui sont attirés non par tous les hommes, mais—par un phénomène de correspondance et d'harmonie comparable à ceux qui règlent la fécondation des fleurs hétérostylées trimorphes comme le *Lythrum salicaria*—seulement par les hommes beaucoup plus âgés qu'eux' (iii. 29–30).

[87] Bono, 'Science, Discourse, and Literature', 73.

the field' (as outlined above). Botany was exploited by popularizers, as by scientists, to classify the 'obscure middle zone of sexuality'; and as Malcolm Bowie's readings of Proust and Freud indicate, it operated across what in any case must be loosely termed 'scientific' and 'literary' texts.[88] The opening of *Sodome et Gomorrhe* exposes this disciplinary cross-fertilization, and parodies the voice of scientific authority. Proust's modelling undoes the metaphors which were common currency in arguments for and against the naturalness of homosexuality: exposing the metaphorical status of these 'scientific' arguments, it questions in particular the use of metaphors which depend on a commonplace definition of the natural. Nature—in Proust's text—is characterized by what are usually defined as its opposites—artificiality, manipulability, implausibility. The natural is no longer what is self-evident, but the reverse. Defining nature as *invraisemblable* is, of course, not just to do with plausibility, whether in an aesthetic or a scientific sense: the *vraisemblable* also designates what is morally acceptable.

In a sense—and quite wildly, then—Proust's botanical model frees up what it is possible to say about homosexuality. It also suggests a curious use of science which plays on the notions of authority and revelation. Proust's commentary on Maeterlinck's *La Vie des abeilles* (cited above) suggests his own ambition for the use of science as a means of exploring how we think—'la vie de la pensée'—rather than using science as an authoritative means of avoiding having to think.

5.9 The aesthetic model

If the botanical model frees up the representation of homosexuality (and this is of course something many readers of Proust have questioned), it is also instrumental in preventing a discussion of aesthetics. While not upstaged, the revelatory drama of the passage is undermined by a competing moment of aesthetic revelation: 'Mes réflexions avaient suivi une pente que je décrirai plus tard et j'avais *déjà* tiré de la ruse apparente des fleurs une conséquence sur toute une

[88] 'If "male" and "female" were no longer available to the observer of human sexuality as an efficient system of classes, then the reason for their shortcomings was not to be sought in the recent history of European culture, nor in the changing pressures which that culture placed upon the sexual instinct, but in the early history of biological species. The journey back through biological time led not to an Eden of bipolar sexual difference but to a primordial hermaphrodism' (Bowie, *Freud, Proust, and Lacan*, 78).

partie inconsciente de l'œuvre littéraire, quand je vis M. de Charlus qui ressortait de chez la marquise' (iii. 5, emphasis added). The revelation around which this passage is staged is defused and diffused; but this is equally, if differently, true of this aesthetic recognition. It is utterly unspectacular, makes a sudden and unexpected non-appearance, is then deferred, and retrospectively not explicitly referred to, as one might have expected, among the 'aesthetic laws' of *Le Temps retrouvé*. Certain aesthetic issues relating to homosexuality are indeed dealt with in this particular passage, but they are confined to questions of representation and *vraisemblance*.

The narrator's model suggests both that seeing is believing and that knowledge helps us to see more. That this model should quite literally be present creates the tension, described above, between nature and artifice. But the literalness also complicates the question of how seeing can be believing if what you are being shown isn't the whole story, and if the person who's doing the showing draws your attention to the fact that you can only look at one thing at a time. In this scene the model is literally present alongside its referent. Our attention is drawn from the one to the other. When with the narrator we are observing one pair, we are often made aware that our vision of the other is obscured. We do not know if the bee has fertilized the orchid, because the narrator has been looking at Jupien and Charlus. Both pairs are at one time or another lost from view.

If seeing is knowing, we might then ask what not-seeing is. Is it simply the opposite—that is, ignorance? or naïvety? Is there something that connects what the narrator does not allow us to see, with what he is, literally, unable to see because he is looking at something else. What is not seen is, first, the aesthetic revelation; second, the sexual activities of Jupien and Charlus, who are lost from sight though not from sound; and finally, the bee perhaps pollinating the orchid.

What is also not seen in this passage is the narrator's spying on the others. Female homosexuality was viewed in the opening volume of *A la recherche* in a similar moment of voyeurism. Here the voyeurism is redescribed as scientific, 'à défaut de la contemplation du géologue, j'avais du moins celle du botaniste' (iii. 3), as if the narrator were simply maintaining an objective viewpoint. After the revelation of homosexuality, much of the drama of the passage is invested in how the narrator can get a closer look at what is going on, with all the risks that relinquishing his vantage-point entails—the risk of being seen, the risk of implication. And these are risks which are rhetorically and literally played up. When Jupien and Charlus disappear into Jupien's workshop, the narrator, rather than taking advantage of what he describes as an undercover route, chooses to make himself visible, and runs straight across the courtyard. He has dropped the guise of botanist at this stage, comparing himself instead to a combatant in the Boer War. His risk taking is in line with the aesthetic of the event, for it is, he claims, highly implausible. It is as if the narrator wishes to risk visibility, and wishes us to see him taking this risk—that is, to see his body in a narrative which is constantly pointing at the bodies of others. What is gained from the risk running is, of course, not a better vantage-point, but the sound of Jupien and Charlus's encounter: their subsequent conversation is not elucidated for the reader, it is simply reported. Proust's narrator seems to be saying that if you can't show, there is nothing to tell: the subject viewed in modelling has, in a sense to be silent, as are the flowers. The verbal elaboration which takes place—in particular, that of the final, exuberantly digressive passage on homosexuality—is the narrator's property. This is a further means of drawing a line, a distance between subject and object, of maintaining the detached, objective gaze of the scientist—a distance which is then wilfully and riskily compromised.

If we saw this risk taking as in some way related to the speculations which are enabled by the model, we might ask why does the narrator wish his body to be implicated, and yet not seen (other than by the reader). In earlier versions of this episode, aesthetics and botany implicate the narrator's body in a different style of speculation.[89] Here the style is genuinely, rather than archly, speculative, characterized by hesitant self-questioning and the interweaving of tentative analogies and fragments of memory ('Quand à Combray . . .', 'A Balbec quand j'avais vu . . .'). The aesthetic theory which is developed here is also shot through with science, stylistically recalling Darwin in its repeated exclamations of delight in the beauty and multiplicity of laws. The narrator's argument is that literature should have as its ideal the deciphering and representation of the laws of the unconscious, laws similar to those governing the behaviour of plants ('toutes ces belles lois' (iii. 1269)); but laws which, equally, are the prerequisite for this form of artistic creation.[90] If man is 'le lieu d'une aussi grande infinité

[89] I refer here to the two typescripts of *Sodome et Gomorrhe I*. See Compagnon's notes, iii. 1261–2.

[90] See also the description of the fertilization of Morel's literary style by the mannerisms of Bergotte's conversation: 'Cette fécondation orale est si rare que j'ai voulu la citer ici. Elle ne produit, d'ailleurs, que des fleurs stériles' (iv. 347).

de lois merveilleuses et géniales' (iii. 1269), laws of which he remains ignorant, the artist distinguishes himself by the ability to make conscious 'un petit fragment de ces lois . . . inconscientes' (iii. 1270). And this ability, in turn, is described as instinctive: 'Cette sorte de coopération physiologico-spirituelle qu'exige la production d'une œuvre, une sorte d'instinct inconscient du cerveau le pousse à réserver ses forces pour l'intuition, pour le souvenir des intuitions, et à laisser échapper les faits purement matériels' (iii. 1270). The artist is seen as developing a different way of knowing, an epistemology 'autre que rationnelle et scientifique'. Whereas the physiologist or the chemist 'n'arrivent à connaître que du dehors, étudiant l'évolution de nos organes, le rôle de nos sécrétions, l'autodéfense de nos cellules, comme ils étudieraient, aussi étrangères à eux-mêmes, les anthères d'une fleur dolichostylée' (iii. 1269), the artist is working from the inside. His deciphering of the laws of the unconscious is itself elucidated by a curious evolutionary metaphor: the artist is to develop the faculty of perceiving these laws directly, so that they become, in a sense, self-reflexive, or as Proust writes, 'à ce qu'elles se connaissent elles-mêmes' (iii. 1270), as if the artist were developing a different kind of eye. Rather than perceiving the self from the outside as if one were studying 'les anthères d'une fleur dolichostylée', this eye would look inwards: 'elles (les belles lois aveugles) se doublent de conscience, elles deviennent réfléchissantes, comme s'est faite au-dessous du front notre chair là où elle est devenue des yeux' (iii. 1270). The evolutionary metaphor suggests at once the artist's privileged position—he is selected by nature for his ability to read the laws of the unconscious (this is what his instinct is reserving him for)— and the enormity of his task, for, once selected, he has actively to develop this 'unconscious eye': 'rendre conscient, faire se formuler à nous ce qui d'abord est inconscient, n'est pour nous exactement rien, cela semble impossible' (iii. 1270–1).

In the final text, these arguments appear as verbal echoes. The following botanical metaphor of *Le Temps retrouvé* suggests the instinctive nature of the artistic production:

> Cette vie, les souvenirs de ses tristesses, de ses joies, formaient une réserve pareille à cet albumen qui est logé dans l'ovule des plantes et dans lequel celui-ci puise sa nourriture pour se transformer en graine, en ce temps où on ignore encore que l'embryon d'une plante se développe, lequel est pourtant le lieu de phénomènes chimiques et respiratoires secrets mais très actifs. (iv. 478)

Robert Fraser has compared this image of 'autofécondation' to Darwin's conclusion in *The Effects of Cross-Fertilisation in the Vegetable Kingdom*, that, 'after several generations of intense cross-fertilization nature will occasionally intervene to maintain a proper balance by one exceptional act of self-fertilization'.[91] A more likely source, perhaps, is Remy de Gourmont's *Physique de l'amour*, in which what he terms 'sexual cannibalism' is described by way of the same image: 'Il y aurait dans le mâle des éléments assimilables nécessaires au développement des œufs, à peu près comme l'albumen des graines, plantule avortée, est nécessaire à la nourriture de l'embryon végétal, plantule survivante.'[92] Without this source, the metaphor of *Le Temps retrouvé* is, despite its apparent botanical precision, an archetypal image.[93] It suggests the passive or, rather, instinctive nature of artistic creation. Proust does rework Gourmont's violent characterization of plant development to focus on the apparently passive and unconscious, or instinctive, work of the plant, but the image of plant cannibalism is also appropriated to inform the argument from aesthetic production (the writer's life consumed by his book) through to the reader's consumption of the book (and indirectly of the writer's life): 'ceux qui se nourriraient ensuite . . . ignoreraient, comme ceux qui mangent les graines alimentaires, que les riches substances qu'elles contiennent ont été faites pour leur nourriture, avaient d'abord nourri la graine et permis sa maturation' (iv. 478). And the latent violence of this self-consumption will be discussed in the penultimate chapter.

The powerful originality of the aesthetic-botanical model of the drafts lies not in the notion of *consumption*, but the effort beyond this to analyse and decipher the laws of this instinctive *production*. The narrator, as scientist of the unconscious, is both subject and object,

[91] Fraser's précis in *Proust and the Victorians*, 236.

[92] Gourmont, *Physique de l'amour*, 156–7.

[93] Plant growth has been used 'as an image of the growth of meaning, as a metaphor of mind, as an analogue for the maturation of the work of art, a historical paradigm, a philosophical analogy, and similarly as a centre of what Valéry calls "Mythique ou mythologie végétative / Rites et coûtumes de la vie végétative"'. Valéry also considers the chance germination of an idea by way of this analogy: 'Je me demande comment il peut arriver que l'une de ces graines se fixe et entre en germination. Il faut qu'elle attende un jour de pluie,' and 'ce petit moment hors de moi est un germe, ou se projette comme un germe. Tout le reste de la durée le développe ou le laisse périr' (Crow, *Paul Valéry: Consciousness and Nature*, 164–6). Proust makes similar use of the image in the drafts of the cahier 2 as the editors paraphrase: 'quand le moi du créateur est envahi par la joie qui accompagne une idée originale, le moment d'inspiration ressemble à une graine. Cessant de germer dans l'atmosphère trop sèche de l'intelligence, elle est ressuscitée par l'humidité et la chaleur de la vérité' (iv. 1269).

scientist and nature, inside and outside the laws—'ses belles lois aveugles, les plus merveilleuses parties de nous-mêmes' (iii. 1270). The implications of this epistemological position for the analyses of the modelling scenarios (the painterly analogy and the narrator–Swann relationship) in the early stages of this chapter are clear. Where writers such as Valéry might question the epistemological correctness of life analysing itself, seeing in this the limitations of biology as a discipline, Proust chooses to position his own reading of science on these boundaries as a new science of man. For the claim made is that it will elucidate not only the mind of the artist, but also the laws of 'amour propre' (see p. 24 above): 'lifting the veil of the unconscious' on 'les lois qui dirigeant l'imagination, mais dirigeant aussi l'amour-propre, sont divines chez les poètes mais aussi chez les sots' (iii. 1270). His discussion of intuition and its laws includes, and indeed reclassifies, what will become the most spectacular instance of unconscious work, involuntary memory: 'L'effort est long, semble devoir rester toujours inutile. Et pourtant n'arrive-t-il pas dans notre esprit qu'il y a des choses que nous voyons tout d'un coup sortir tout entières de rien, créées *ex nihilo*, dans la réminiscence par exemple' (iii. 1271). Speculative references to involuntary memory in these drafts are not included in the botanical-homosexual context of *Sodome et Gomorrhe*, but reserved instead for *Le Temps retrouvé*, allowing the narrator to arrive at a set of spectacular aesthetic laws, in which sexuality, desire, and jealousy are transcended. The botanical model suggests a more persistent, less dramatic link, in which both homosexuality and the unconscious tap into the phylogenetically archaic in man. It functions as a 'conceptual archetype' evident in the recurring fragments of botanical imagery, and I will return to this with reference to *Albertine disparue*. Yet the model is not universally applicable—the next chapter will explore its failure to elucidate the topic of female homosexuality, under the more general notion of the construction of ignorance.

6

KNOWLEDGE AS REVOLUTION AND REVELATION

C'est épouvantable, le vice est devenu une science exacte!

Proust to Paul Morand

Nobody's sexuality is straightforward in *A la recherche*. Or perhaps this law could be more accurately phrased to state that characters fascinate because their sexuality is ambivalent. The text alternately speculates about who will 'come out' next and is shocked by revelations of homosexuality. Hypotheses are framed, and models designed, to address such questions, sustaining the text's speculative impulse. One might say that Foucault has accustomed us to this. Indeed Eve Kosofsky Sedgwick makes this very gesture in the opening pages of her study, *Epistemology of the Closet*: 'In accord with Foucault's demonstration, whose results I will take to be axiomatic, that modern Western culture has placed what it calls sexuality in a more and more distinctively privileged relation to our most prized constructs of individual identity, truth and knowledge, it becomes truer and truer that the language of sexuality not only intersects with but transforms the other languages and relations by which we know.'[1] The nature of this intersection has been explored in the mapping of Chapter 4, 'Hypothesis', in which we saw that latent in the tracery of speculation is the reduction to questions of sexuality, but that to reduce the text to an 'original desire' for knowledge about sexuality is to collapse it back into the commonplace book (a book of laws with the desire taken out of it), performing a reduction which the text itself repeatedly fails to stage. This failure is bound up with other determining discourses, particularly those of cognition. For if sexuality is one of the key questions— perhaps *the* key question—in this study of science in *A la recherche*, we need to look at the structures and performances of knowledge and ignorance by which it is determined. The chapter will begin by considering the asymmetry of knowledge which characterizes the

[1] Eve Kosofsky Sedgwick, *Epistemology of the Closet* (London: Harvester Wheatsheaf, 1991), 13.

opposition between Sodom and Gomorrah. This analysis of the Proustian discourses on male and female sexuality in terms of both the rhetoric and cultural context is then developed by a consideration of their hermeneutic unravelling in an attempt to answer the questions: Why is this a story about knowledge, and what kind of story is being told here? This chapter describes the most spectacular modes of knowing in *A la recherche*: knowledge as revolution and revelation.

Barthes's formulation of a law encompassing both sexuality and cognition in *A la recherche* also works with the elements of reduction, shock, and inversion. He reads homosexuality as a subset of the more general statement 'Le renversement est une loi',[2] according to which the subject may always flip over to an opposite version of the self. 'On comprend alors pourquoi l'éthos de l'inversion proustienne est la surprise: c'est l'émerveillement d'un retour, d'une jonction, d'une retrouvaille, (et d'une réduction).' While I would want to question the notion of reversibility (given the relentless and irreversible proliferation of homosexuality from *Sodome et Gomorrhe*, the central point of *A la recherche*), the terms of Barthes's equation are illuminating. While hypothesis fails repeatedly to connect with experience, knowledge is gained by revelation. And Barthes describes this revelatory knowledge but carefully avoids the term 'révélation', prefering 'renversement', 'retour', 'retrouvaille'. For the revolutionary nature of knowledge about sexuality is a discovery, but, above all, a return; it is strikingly new, and just a repetition. Cognition itself, rather than sexuality as such (although it will be seen that these are difficult to keep apart), would seem to behave according to the law of 'renversement'.

How might revelation be mapped in *A la recherche*? The revelatory moment is nothing new for the reader of Proust, since *A la recherche* is hung upon that final aesthetic revelation which is presaged throughout the text and which enables the writing of the book (Beckett's *Proust* provides a parodic list of such aesthetic revelations and near revelations).[3] The revelation of involuntary memory functions as a divine disclosure, redeeming the life of the narrator-as-artist. This moment is itself set against a background of what might be termed 'empirical revelation': the narrator's progress through the novel has traditionally

[2] Roland Barthes, 'Une idée de recherche', in *Recherche de Proust*, ed. G. Genette and T. Todorov (Paris: Seuil, 1980), 38. Where the *moralistes* use the classic 'ne que' to describe the real self masked by appearances, Proust substitutes 'une syntaxe concomitante: la princesse est aussi une maîtresse de bordel: nouvelle syntaxe, qu'il faudrait appeler métaphorique' (ibid.).

[3] Beckett, *Proust*, 23–5.

been described as one of 'Bildung', or enlightenment (as, for example, his desiring, then becoming disabused of the various 'salons' and 'côteries'). Moments of revelation are absorbed into, recuperated by, this progression from naïvety to detachment. But the mechanism of revelation itself is in a sense anti-progressive, not always recuperable as this reading would wish, and the effect of the interplay between 'Marcel' and his older and wiser narrating self results both in that sudden illumination which is the desired effect of La Rochefoucauld's *maximes* and in comedy. In this case, revelation might be described as an abrupt encounter with the real, an encounter which subsequently allows the narrator to categorize and theorize his newly discovered topic. The comic revelation of Legrandin's character operates according to this mechanism, the 'real' in this case being the sight of Legrandin's buttocks as he bends over to kiss a lady's hand, then straightens himself:

> Ce redressement rapide fit refluer en une sorte d'onde fougueuse et musclée la croupe de Legrandin que je ne supposais pas si charnue; et je ne sais pourquoi cette ondulation de pure matière, ce flot tout charnel, sans expression de spiritualité et qu'un empressement plein de bassesse fouettait en tempête, éveillèrent tout d'un coup dans mon esprit la possibilité d'un Legrandin tout différent de celui que nous connaissions. (i. 123)

From the observation of this physical detail, the recognition and classification of Legrandin as a snob, 'un saint Sébastien du snobisme' (i. 127), emerges, and the narrator proceeds to maximize on the topic of snobbery.

Against this background of revelations, minor and redemptive, enlightening and comic, the episodes of homosexual revelation are plotted to stand out. They might tautologically be termed 'cognitive' revelations, because they demonstrate, as these other categories of revelation do not, a self-reflexive concern with the mechanism of disclosure, the nature of the truth disclosed, and its subsequent interpretation, verification, and evaluation.

The opening of *Sodome et Gomorrhe* might be described as the most overtly constructed and puzzling instance of such cognitive revelation in which the narrator's switch from ignorance to expertise camps up the narrative of the phenomenology of discovery. The heuristic device of the botanical model allows the reader to share in this process, to become, as it were, knowingly naïve. Revelation then allows the narrator suddenly to acquire a vast authority on the subject of homosexuality and to introduce the reader to a new world of maxims, histories, and behavioural patterns. And indeed he speaks with a voice of such authority, such energetic authority, that it must be checked, returned to the *récit*—into which it will subsequently make repeated incursions. The narrator's initial references to himself as a geologist and a botanist have led into what seems to be a theory-laden experiment, a demonstration even, not just a set of naïve observations. And it is a demonstration which prepares the reader, handing over a typology, laws, and case-studies in readiness for the *récit* to come.

Revelatory encounters which fall into the range of the narrator's speculation are of a different kind. Here the revelation is its own guarantee; the fact of Albertine's friendship with Vinteuil's daughter is revelatory because it is 'quelque chose que mon esprit n'aurait su inventer, mais que j'appréhendais obscurément' (iii. 500). Whereas *knowledge* of male homosexuality appears, *ex nihilo*, in the hands of the narrator, revelations about lesbianism, which are in fact always revelations about Albertine, are not theorizable, categorizable. All that appears *ex nihilo* is the binary hypothesis about Albertine's sexuality. And no model exists whereby this speculation might be refined or elucidated. When the narrator hires two women to 'model' the possibly lesbian activities of Albertine and Andrée, they can only provide, as it were, a real-life copy—or rather, a copy of one of the narrator's two hypotheses.

Modelling depends on the visual. Where Montjouvain and the opening of *Sodome et Gomorrhe* are subject to the narrator's voyeuristic gaze, the lesbian modelling of *Albertine disparue* is paradoxically redescribed as if it were occurring in another room and could only be heard. The narrator is unable to elucidate 'la signification d'un bruit original, expressif d'une sensation que nous n'éprouvons pas. Si on l'entend d'une pièce voisine et sans rien voir, on peut prendre pour du fou rire ce que la souffrance arrache à un malade qu'on opère sans l'avoir endormi' (iv. 130). The scene is further described as if it were a performance behind stage curtains: 'le rideau baissé à tout jamais pour les autres qu'elle-même sur ce qui se passe dans le mystère intime de chaque créature' (iv. 131). The narrator's vision is, of course, temporarily and literally obscured during his observation of the meeting of Charlus and Jupien, but his revelation is unaffected, and he simply concludes that, 'il y a une chose aussi bruyante que la souffrance, c'est le plaisir' (iii. 11).

No analogical transfer of knowledge, no modelling *between* male and female homosexuality, is undertaken in *A la recherche* (although transfers of anxiety are multiple). Kristeva, in *Le Temps sensible*, attempts such a transfer by way of the botanical model, which she extends from its specific application to allow for every sexual permutation: 'Méduse, orchidée, homme ou femme, dit en substance Proust, nous sommes tous bisexués.' It is then applied specifically to Albertine: 'Tout change si l'on transpose sur elle la théorie florale de la sexualité hermaphrodite, que Proust développe à propos de Charlus, mais qu'il veut universelle.'[4] This extension of Proust's analogy might be seen as evidence of an understanding of the practice of scientific modelling. Kristeva is taking the text's model, the conceptual archetype of botanical analogies and imagery, and its partner theorizing on the topic of sexuality, and applying it to new areas. But can the extension of a localized model so simply be accorded the status of a truth? Why 'Proust' might wish the theory to be universal ('qu'il veut universelle') is difficult to ascertain. Does he really claim ('dit en substance Proust') that we are 'all bisexual'? For now the differences are all one, and the vast, seemingly insuperable distance separating Sodom from Gomorrah is forgotten. This is the distance between the infinite body of theory and facts (case histories, fables, myths, typologies) on male homosexuality and the aporia that is lesbianism. Or, as Philippe Sollers suggests in his contrast between the 'complexité sournoise' of Gomorrah and the 'surface' of Sodom: 'Gomorrhe est infiniment plus troublante, noire, détournée, que Sodome . . . A l'agitation bavarde de Sodome, correspondent le silence et la dérobade de Gomorrhe.'[5]

Kristeva's reading, in which lesbianism seems to vanish as it merges into bisexuality, simply echoes the drama of the narrator's own attempts to map Gomorrah. In the narrator's mental landscape, lesbianism ceases to form a category in its own right, a category to which laws could be attributed. By its very fluidity and ambiguity it also threatens the pure 'race' of homosexuals outlined in the exordium, for which Charlus is already nostalgic (iii. 800).

6.1 Revelation and the archive: male homosexuality

The revelations of Sodom have an immediate certainty. The magical transformation of Charlus yields an abundance of knowledge. The

[4] Kristeva, *Le Temps sensible*, 110 and 97 respectively.

[5] Philippe Sollers, 'Proust et Gomorrhe', in *Théorie des exceptions* (Paris: Folio, 1986), 77.

revelations of both the baron and Saint-Loup seem retrospectively to confer on them a psychological unity. Sexuality is a key to complete understanding of these characters, and ensures an absolute accordance of sign and meaning, of *signifié* and *signifiant*:

> Maintenant l'abstrait s'était matérialisé, l'être enfin compris avait aussitôt perdu son pouvoir de rester invisible et la transmutation de M. de Charlus en une personne nouvelle était si complète que . . . tout ce qui avait paru jusque-là incohérent à mon esprit, devenait intelligible, se montrait évident comme une phrase. (iii. 16)

Inversely, marginal figures find confirmation in the typology established in *Sodome et Gomorrhe I* as, for example, M. de Vaugoubert and his wife, whose self-transformation to suit her husband maps back into the world of plants and insects: 'si la femme n'a d'abord pas les caractères masculins, elle les prend peu à peu pour plaire à son mari, même inconsciemment, par cette sorte de mimétisme qui fait que certaines fleurs se donnent l'apparence des insectes qu'elles veulent attirer' (iii. 46).

Such is the communality of knowledge about male homosexuality that even the narrator's exordium is repeated by another expert, Charlus, who makes similar claims to scientific objectivity: 'il n'y a que les généralités qui m'intéressent, je vous parle de cela comme de la loi de la pesanteur' (iii. 806). While the narrator's exordium on Sodom is triggered by Charlus, Charlus's performance is triggered by Gomorrah. Mlle Vinteuil and her friends are, he claims, 'd'une terrible réputation . . . Elles sont amies de toute une bande terrible, tout ça doit se réunir dans des endroits affreux' (iii. 799). Moreover, Charlus's claims to scientific objectivity and abstraction are undermined and ridiculed because we know of his very self-interested passion for the particular: ' "Cependant, moi qui suis un curieux, un fureteur, j'en ai connu, et qui n'étaient pas des mythes. Oui, au cours de ma vie j'ai constaté (j'entends scientifiquement constaté, je ne me paie pas de mots) deux réputations injustifiées" ' (iii. 800). The narrator takes a back seat at this performance, handing over the part of false *ingénu* to Brichot, who desires to 'set the baron talking on his favourite subject' as part of Mme Verdurin's scheme to separate Charlus from Morel. The cruel comedy of this excursus lies in its timing: Charlus, blind to the fact that society has already classed him as a 'tante' and is well aware of his passion for the violinist, is the victim of his own authoritative digression on the topic of homosexuality—a digression which not only exposes the sexuality he seeks to mask, but also prevents him from joining Morel and allows Mme Verdurin to close her trap.

Brichot, feigning astonishment at the baron's expertise, sees Charlus as 'un de ces rares voyants d'une vérité que personne ne soupçonne autour d'eux' (iii. 801), and, in keeping with the baron's own rhetoric of scientific justification, compares him to Urbain Le Verrier. According to Brichot, both have made discoveries which have been verified only retrospectively. This is no chance comparison. The shorthand 'l'existence de la planète de Leverrier' encodes the word-play which the naming of the planets would evoke. Le Verrier's discovery of Neptune in 1846 was deduced from calculations based on an orbit of Uranus. The terms 'urning' and 'uranism', which allude to Plato's *Symposium*, were coined by Carl Heinrich Ulrichs to designate homosexuality. As Gide's *Corydon* indicates, 'Remarquez je vous prie que Schopenhauer et Platon ont compris qu'ils devaient, dans leurs théories, tenir compte de l'uranisme.'[6] Brichot's passing comparison appears superficially to belong to that set of analogies which refer to science with the intention of celebrating and justifying intellectual creativity (as, for example, the Vinteuil–Lavoisier comparison, the notion that Elstir's paintings reveal new scientific laws, or indeed the narrator's own claims to scientificity). Yet the encoding of the particular—'uranisme'—undermines the status of Charlus's artful and personal science.

In this respect Charlus is no different from the lovers (namely, Swann and the narrator), who, throughout *A la recherche*, attempt to cloak their desire for the particular in a passion for the general, the abstract, for scientific knowledge. What distinguishes him is not so much the style of his desire as the rhetorical performance of it. Yet, if Charlus's scholarly excursus on homosexuality gives him away at every turn, what are the implications for the narrator's exordium on the same subject? There is a curious absence of narratorial intervention at this stage. The narrator is unusually eager to indicate the genuine kindness of Charlus, the sincerity of the baron's friendship for him. He describes the setting, Madame Verdurin's salon, in an aesthetic digression couched in the language of involuntary memory and metaphor: 'quelque élément général, commun à plusieurs apparences et plus vrai qu'elles, qui de lui-même éveillait toujours en moi un esprit intérieur et habituellement ensommeillé, mais dont la

[6] Gide, *Corydon* (1st pub. 1920, Paris: Gallimard, 1925), 61.

remontée à la surface de ma conscience me donnait une grande joie' (iii. 788). He then proceeds to assess, at some length, his own character and most strikingly his own moral sense in order to arrive at the conclusion: 'Je n'avais aucune opinion sur la mesure dans laquelle le bien et le mal pouvaient être engagés dans les relations de Morel et de M. de Charlus, mais l'idée des souffrances qu'on préparait à M. de Charlus m'était intolérable' (iii. 795). Despite these disclaiming and distancing narratorial gestures, there is no disguising the curious relation between the bravura digressions of these two characters, as if Charlus and the narrator were fellow experts vying for the chair in homosexual studies ironically proposed by Brichot (iii. 811).

This complicity between Charlus and the narrator is never acknowledged. The narrator takes on the part of passive and anxious listener to Charlus's performance, and only once transposes knowledge of homosexuality (Charlus's statistics indicating the number of homosexuals in society) to the partner field of lesbianism. Yet, the narrator's exordium was cut short with the suggestion that here was an infinite body of material, and, despite his claim that 'je vis dans l'abstrait, tout cela ne m'intéresse qu'à un point de vue transcendantal' (iii. 806), Charlus's excursus is made up of very particular facts and figures. Both the exordium and the Charlusian archive are characterized by their energetic disorder, by their seemingly infinite extendability. Curiously, too, Charlus had offered to make his archive available to the naïve narrator of *A l'ombre des jeunes filles*:

> J'ai souvent pensé, monsieur, qu'il y avait en moi, du fait non de mes faibles dons, mais de circonstances que vous apprendrez peut-être un jour, un trésor d'expérience, une sorte de dossier secret et inestimable, que je n'ai pas cru devoir utiliser personnellement, mais qui serait sans prix pour un jeune homme à qui je livrerais en quelques mois ce que j'ai mis plus de trente ans à acquérir et que je suis peut-être seul à posséder. (ii. 583)

The complicity is reinforced by the Swann narrative. The narrator is author of '*Un* amour de Swann'; Charlus, effectively, of 'plusieurs'. Both have insider knowledge of two key areas—the emblematic story of heterosexual love and the body of information and narratives on homosexuality—and the former is, according to Charlus's account, necessarily bound up with the latter (Swann 'dont les tendances si opposées avaient été toujours connues' and Odette, discovered by Charlus at a club, 'dans son demi-travesti' (iii. 803)). Through the homosexual lens held up by Charlus, Swann's story is no longer emblematic, but trails off as part of the all-engulfing homosexual archive: 'Enfin, vous n'allez pas commencer à me faire raconter l'histoire de Swann, nous en aurions pour dix ans, vous comprenez, je connais ça comme personne' (iii. 804). Charlus may, at first, seem to parrot the narrator, but perhaps the reverse is true. For the baron, as is revealed by his synthetic approach to the Swann story (of which he and Odette are the origin; the origin of the narrator's version is Swann himself), has access to a still greater fund of material than does the narrator.

Yet Charlus's disadvantage is made to lie precisely in his expertise. His archive might be described as an 'entassement du particulier', whereas the narrator's observations always tend towards the law, 'c'est à la cime même du particulier qu'éclôt le général'.[7] The degree of abstraction which, Charlus claims, justifies his own knowledge is strikingly absent from his excursus. The narrator's exordium is not an archive, as is Charlus's, but rather a collection of case-studies, character sketches in the style of La Bruyère, theories, and maxims. Whereas Charlus both quotes La Rochefoucauld and includes him among his ancestors (iii. 808), the narrator practices a form of independent moralizing which enables him to knit Charlus back into his analysis. Indeed, Charlus's excursus is undermined from the outset by the narrator's moralistic commentary. The baron may generalize expansively on the topic of homosexuality, but he sees his own example as exempt from such abstractions: 'M. de Charlus taxait d'inversion la grande majorité de ses contemporains, en exceptant toutefois les hommes avec qui il avait eu des relations et dont, pour peu qu'elles eussent été mêlées d'un peu de romanesque, le cas lui paraissait plus complexe' (iii. 802).

Charlus's superiority at the level of the particular is in effect undermined by the narrator's ability to rise above sexual mores, and accede to a higher level of generality. At this level, the over-arching laws of desire pertain, and the legislator's strength and weakness are determined by his ability at once to formulate these laws and to recognize his subjection to them (as we will see in the next chapter's analysis of *Albertine disparue*). Charlus might exclude himself and his lovers from his own laws, but he is subsequently drawn back in by the narrator, and included in more general examples in the style of La Bruyère which portray heterosexual couples. The narrator cites the 'viveurs' who claim not to believe in women's honour, yet exempt their own

[7] Letter to Daniel Halévy, 19 July 1919, in *Correspondance*, xviii. 334.

mistresses from this rule. This generalization against false or dishonest generalizers—those not prepared to feel the force of their own maxims—also critiques the level at which their generalizations operate. Their categories are felt to be overly simplistic: 'ce sentiment de la vie qui fait que dès qu'on s'approche des êtres, des existences, les étiquettes et les compartiments faits d'avance sont trop simples' (iii. 802). And the narrator is careful to cover his own practice here: he vacillates between an affective response—his horror at the cruelty of Mme Verdurin's revenge, his sympathetic presentation of Charlus's kindness—and a cooler moralistic appraisal of Charlus as 'raseur comme un savant', 'assujetti comme un maniaque' (iii. 809).

Whereas the creative scientist-artists are characterized by their certainty of discovery, their speculation, experimental method, and discovery of law, the topic of homosexuality is Charlus's 'spécialité', whose origins in the personal he is at pains to conceal. And, as the narrator is eager to indicate, the common currency of this knowledge of homosexuality, with its stories and histories, is always susceptible to being subsumed into a higher set, the formulation of Sodom's typology, case-studies, and laws, and beyond this into the still more general category of the laws of desire. Access to this higher category of laws—laws which are not in free circulation, but are hard won, always formulated painfully under the force of the personal, of 'souffrance'—is reserved for the narrator, and is triggered by the gap in the Charlusian archive.

The painfully parodic and personal nature of Charlus's excursus would seem retrospectively to confirm the status of the narrator's own exordium. Yet it also connects at the level of the particular, with the story of the narrator's pursuit of Albertine. For the stability of Charlus's archive is endangered by new developments in homosexual practice. These developments are towards a greater fluidity and ambiguity in sexual relationships. Women are implicated for the first time. Although it is the narrator's reference to Mlle Vinteuil which has provoked the discussion, Charlus's response is to enumerate a purely male, even virile, lineage (amongst whom women may find protectors), and he is horrified that women might even have knowledge of (male) homosexuality. The narrator's exordium, which also excludes lesbianism, promises the reader that more will be learnt about this topic from Charlus: 'Laissons enfin pour plus tard ceux qui ont conclu un pacte avec Gomorrhe. Nous en parlerons quand M. de Charlus les connaîtra' (iii. 25); but the baron proves just as puzzled by this subject.

On discovering that Morel plays the role of both homosexual and lesbian, 'la jalousie de M. de Charlus n'avait plus de raison de se borner aux hommes que Morel connaissait, mais allait s'étendre aux femmes elles-mêmes' (iii. 720). Charlus's anxious questioning is echoed by the narrator's: ' "Qu'est-ce que la femme peut représenter d'autre à Albertine?" pensais-je, et c'était bien là, en effet, ma souffrance' (iii. 811). Both the narrator and Charlus exclude lesbianism from their repertoire. Both know of its existence and have access to it—the narrator's first specific interpretation of Albertine is structured around the hetero/homosexual opposition, and Charlus has a long-established friendship with Odette. Yet neither is able to speak with authority on the subject; neither admits the transposition of knowledge from male to female homosexuality. Indeed, it seems doubtful that lesbianism even exists as a subject.

6.2 Revelation and aporia: female homosexuality

> Ignorance and opacity collude or compete with knowledge in mobilizing the flows of energy, desire, goods, meanings, persons.
>
> Kosofsky Sedgwick, *Epistemology of the Closet*

The plotting of the narrator's relationship with Albertine necessarily depends on the aporia that is lesbianism. Yet a series of lesbian revelations parallel the homosexual revolution which opens *Sodome et Gomorrhe*, and they take place against a backdrop of female homosexuality which is quite distinct from its male counterpart.

Lesbianism is emblematized by Montjouvain. Isolated thematically from the intense concern with homosexuality which develops out of *Sodome et Gomorrhe*, it is also isolated theoretically, since the scene which establishes the lesbian relationship between Mlle Vinteuil and her friend is elucidated by a theory of sadism, not sexuality. Only with the narrator's speculation about Albertine does the episode assume its emblematic function. Consequently, Mlle Vinteuil and her lover become archetypes, since, unlike male homosexuality, lesbianism has no lineage, no history. Whereas male homosexuality, found amongst the working classes, also teems with representatives from the aristocracy, both past (as outlined by Charlus) and present (the baron himself, Saint-Loup, the prince de Guermantes), lesbians are always 'demi-mondaines' or members of the bourgeoisie (Léa, Bloch's sisters); there is no 'duchesse' or 'princesse de Guermantes' to be found in this group. The Oscar Wilde case is referred to in *Sodome et Gomorrhe*, as are other cases involving male homosexuals, notorious in their time. No women were involved in cases such as these. Save for the Montjouvain pair, the sexuality of many of the female characters of *A la recherche* is ambiguously styled: there is speculation about Mme Verdurin and Odette,[8] about the 'jeunes filles'—could Andrée and Albertine be lovers, and what does the testimony of the 'blanchisseuse' signify? The identities of these characters remain unresolved. Such questions are, it could be argued, set up to be dismissed: the narrator's fascination with Albertine's sexuality is simply the expression of his jealousy, Proust claimed, and a similar claim might be made to cover Swann's suspicions about Odette. But rather than accepting the text's justification, in particular for the Albertine story, as just another episode on the way to aesthetic revelation and redemption, I want to explore the styling and significance of the dramatic opposition between male and female homosexuality. The subheading of this section is 'female homosexuality'; but, for the nature of the aporia described by Kosofsky Sedgwick to become apparent, we need to begin by characterizing further the nature and content of the text's archive on male homosexuality. A little patience is requested from the reader, who might at this stage object that beginning in this way, delaying still further the representation of lesbianism, in itself repeats the oppositional schema suggested by the text's own pairing, 'Sodome et Gomorrhe', and reinforces the traditional placing of lesbianism on the margins of male homosexuality. Once the nature of the opposition has become clear, the aporia will, as it were, take centre-stage.

A la recherche might, in fact, be described as a repository of *idées reçues* on male homosexuality. The sudden acquisition of knowledge at the opening of *Sodome et Gomorrhe* is presented as revelatory; but, according to Rivers's study *Proust and the Art of Love*, these laws were, for the most part, commonplaces of the time, familiar to the first readers of *A la recherche*. Rather than presenting revolutionary findings, they re-present the debris of the competing and collaborating discourses, legal, literary, journalistic, scientific, and pseudo-scientific which sought to define homosexuality.[9]

A great number of medical studies date from the beginning of the

[8] For a discussion of this see Kristeva, *Le Temps sensible*, 85–93.

[9] See Rivers, *Proust and the Art of Love*, and idem, 'The Myth and Science of Homosexuality in *A la recherche*'.

period 1895–1909, a period which, starting with the trial of Oscar Wilde, saw a series of scandalous court cases exposing often important public figures as homosexual. The scientific study of the 'field' in turn established its own 'laws of homosexuality', which, though ostensibly descriptive, were potentially as prescriptive as those of the legal system, and also had the potential for legal reform: German sexologist Carl Heinrich Ulrichs, a pioneer in this field, used the medical claim that homosexuality was a hereditary abnormality to campaign for a legal revision.[10] Law statements on male homosexuality proliferated. The scandalous court cases provoked 'a swelling tide of controversy which encompassed science, politics, literature, journalism and social conversation'.[11] Popular works capitalized on this notoriety, purporting to reveal the causes and psychology of homosexuality, and often using the maxim to do so. Remy de Gourmont's column, 'Dialogues des Amateurs', dealing with such issues was published in the *Mercure de France*, of which Proust was a regular reader.[12] The medical background of Proust's family gave him still greater access to what might tentatively be called more seriously scientific material. Two colleagues and friends of his father, Dr Ambroise Tardieu (1818–79) and Dr Paul Brouardet (1837–1906), were leading French authorities on the subject; both were also homophobic. However, science was often simply used as a justification for prurient curiosity (much in the style of Charlus's claims to disinterested knowledge).

Rivers traces a number of borrowings from, and allusions to, common contemporary theories in *A la recherche*. These include the notion of homosexuality as hereditary illness (Charlus and Jupien are described as predestined by 'remote heredity'; the male Guermantes are a 'perverted' family, and only the heterosexual duc is 'spared') and the distinction between modern and classical, nervous and conventional homosexuality. The very mode of the narrator's exordium, its 'ideas, imagery, enumerative, distributive style', may be seen to 'derive from writing on homosexuality contemporary to Proust',[13] while the epigraph to *Sodome et Gomorrhe*—'Première apparition des hommes-femmes'—is derived from Carl Heinrich Ulrichs's theory that the homosexual has 'the soul of a woman enclosed in the body of

[10] See Sulloway, *Freud*, 280–2. In France, where the legal system was less oppressive than in Germany and England, there were no homosexual apologists arguing vigorously for legal reform. See Pollard, *André Gide*, 129–30, and also ch. 7, 'Medico-Legal Attitudes'.

[11] Rivers, *Proust and the Art of Love*, 144.

[12] Ibid. 138–9.

[13] Ibid. 169.

a man'. Yet, having completed this identification, Rivers is led to the simple conclusion that 'by speaking of the "aunt", the "third sex", and the "man-woman" as if these concepts embodied general truths about homosexuality, Proust presents a seriously distorted picture'.[14] Rivers's critical reconstruction of a context in defence of homosexuality blinds him to the text's rhetorical performance of such knowledge, to the possibility of parody and pastiche, to the style of hypothesizing and modelling, in which 'the range of risky analogies deployed . . . shows Proust at full stretch imaginatively, in his attempt to represent and rehabilitate these outlawed sexual practices'.[15]

This performance sets the endlessly chattering taboo of male homosexuality against the aporia of lesbianism, the repetition, variation, and expansion of the archive against the repetition of a failure to establish any significant body of knowledge at all. Yet received wisdom on lesbianism was available.[16] The contextualizing approach adopted by Rivers fails here—he quotes the lack of 'lesbian types' in *A la recherche*,[17] and, when drawing on contemporary (pseudo-)scientific texts for information about male homosexuality, neglects their treatment of women; the dramatic opposition which the text stages between male and female homosexuality is dissolved by refering to lesbianism as 'androgyny'.

Rivers and Proust's narrator might be described as complicit in their approach, save that the former is at most mildly puzzled by the absence of lesbianism, and the latter excessively preoccupied with it. The legalities of homosexuality are of interest here. Of the proliferating discourses on male homosexuality, the legal and scientific approaches were the most authoritative and the most complicit. Prominent political and public figures might be brought to trial simply because it was alleged that they were homosexual, but the often crucial justification for the case being brought at all was that their

[14] Rivers, *Proust and the Art of Love*, 187.

[15] Edward Hughes, 'The Mapping of Homosexuality in Proust's *Recherche*', *Paragraph*, 18/2 (1995), 160.

[16] Proust himself was at one time treated by Doctor Sollier, a specialist in the psychopathology of women, who held 'advanced views' on the statistics of female homosexuality (George D. Painter, *Marcel Proust*, rev. enlarged edn (London: Chatto and Windus, 1989), ii. 53).

[17] Attention is drawn to Mme de Vaugoubert and Mme d'Huxelles (see Charlus's 'excursus'), both of whom have masculine traits which cause them to marry homosexual men: 'In neither case is there any hint that these masculine wives of homosexually oriented men have lesbian tendencies. Indeed, the narrator proposes a complicated series of reasons for the mannishness of such women, among which lesbianism is conspicuous by its absence' (Rivers, *Proust and the Art of Love*, 290 n. 85).

sexuality endangered national security. Women did not signify at this political and public level; the law did not even recognize female homosexuality as such. This is not to say that lesbianism was any less of a threat or a fascination; indeed, the fact of its being removed from the public stage made its potential effects all the more insidious. Attempts to map 'Gomorrah' resulted in titillating travel guides, such as Ali Cottignon's *Paris vivant: la corruption à Paris* (1889) and Léo Taxil's *La Corruption fin-de-siècle* (1891), which localized the phenomenon in tones of scandalized outrage, and whose professed aim was to expose the depravity of decadent society. These and other such texts are described in Catherine van Casselaer's study *Lot's Wife*, which remains true to the sensationalist appeal of its sources, claiming that the 'Paris of the belle-époque' was 'the undisputed capital of world lesbianism'.

Whereas male homosexuality was most powerfully defined and contested by legal and scientific discourses, lesbianism signified more ambiguously through the scientific and the literary. Scientific texts drew upon literature, and in particular on the peculiarly French tradition of literature about 'the lesbian'. Literature in turn absorbed the current, often modish theories of science. Many texts, including apologetic or justificatory works written by lesbians, operate in a middle ground where references to science and literature carry equal currency. Havelock Ellis admits to the use of literary example; Natalie Barney, who draws on a wide range of authors, from Shakespeare to Whitman, notes that 'les livres de physiologie traitent d'exemples parfois moins poétiques, et autrement définis' and defends her practice of extensive literary quotation: 'Si j'ai choisi mes exemples plutôt dans la littérature, c'est que les êtres doués d'expression se racontent avec plus de subtilité et d'étendue, et dans une forme plus acceptable'.[18]

The effect of this ambiguous relationship between the scientific and literary discourses which sought to define the lesbian is above all generative. By 1900, numerous studies of both male and female homosexuality had appeared; between 1898 and 1908, in Germany alone, more than a thousand articles and books on the subject were published, a figure which indicates the number of garrulous Charlusian experts in the field.[19] The very first of these publications was a case-study by Carl von Westphal, a German psychiatrist, in

[18] Barney, *Pensées d'une amazone* (Paris: Émile Paul, 1920), pp. xiv–xv.
[19] Faderman, *Surpassing the Love of Men*, 248.

1869. The subject of the study was identified as a 'congenital invert'; her lesbianism was not acquired, but was 'the result of hereditary degeneration and neurosis'. Once identified, this new type was quickly established, and many similar studies soon followed. The impact in France, whose literary tradition had already encompassed representations of female homosexuality—the title character of Théophile Gautier's *Mlle de Maupin* remained the prototype of lesbianism for decades after its publication in 1835—was even greater. As Faderman summarizes:

> French 'concern' developed earlier, perhaps because the French aesthete writers from the 1830's on delighted in exploring whatever had the potential to astound the bourgeoisie . . . and flaunted exotic images of sex between women in their poetry and prose. Combined later with the 'knowledge' furnished by the sexologists and the annoyance of feminism, French anxiety about the potentials of female alliances rose to a fever pitch by the end of the century.[20]

Julien Chevalier's study *L'Inversion sexuelle* expresses this anxiety in its unusual investigation of both heredity and environment as possible causes of female homosexuality.[21] Despite the persuasiveness of the environmental argument, it was generally accepted that the lesbian belonged to 'the third sex'; her condition was inherited, not acquired, and was read as a sign of degeneration. Richard von Krafft-Ebing, in his study *Psychopathia Sexualis* (1886), pointed out that lesbianism was due to 'cerebral anomalies', the sign of 'an inherited diseased condition of the central nervous system'. Havelock Ellis, heavily influenced by Krafft-Ebing's work, reinforced the stereotype of lesbian morbidity. Chevalier's is one of the rare attempts to read a relationship between women's emancipation and sexual tendencies, to theorize this into 'environmental' or 'acquired lesbianism'. Sexologists were, on the whole, unable or unwilling to delineate what might count as 'scientific' data, and their theorizing is characterized by false leaps from the singular to the general, and vice versa, repeatedly taking the peculiarly singular as general, and the general as insignificant or 'fake'.[22]

20 Faderman, *Surpassing the Love of Men*, 238.

21 See Catherine van Casselaer's discussion, *Lot's Wife* (Liverpool: Janus Press, 1986), 12.

22 Ellis, for example, had difficulty reconciling his 'congenital taint' theory with evidence that environment seemed to play a significant part in determining sexuality. Conceding that the women's movement may well promote lesbianism, he then adds the proviso that this is only a 'spurious imitation'; a 'true' lesbian is determined by hereditary factors, yet the women's movement might well 'promote hereditary neurosis'. Elsewhere it is argued that the 'true lesbian' has a 'more or less distinct trace of masculinity'. In his case-studies, how-

To those lesbian authors who wished to define and justify themselves and their writings with reference to their gender, the scientificity of such studies (and the general chaos of the 'field') was perhaps less interesting than was its potential for manipulation. German author Elisabeth Dauthendey, for example, manipulates the congenitalist theory in support of the naturalism of female homosexuality. In her 1906 pamphlet *The Uranian Question and Women*, Dauthendey lists the 'facts' of lesbianism, as, for example, '1. Uranianism is no one's fault since it is due to a disorder of empirical natural laws. 2. Like all other deformities or functional disorders, it deserves compassion and not contempt. 3. It is definitely compatible with intellectual functioning. 4. It is never the result of exterior causes or training but always congenitally conditioned.'[23]

Whereas Dauthendey is preoccupied with science as a means of absolving guilt—heredity means that lesbianism is 'no-one's fault'—American writer Natalie Barney takes a wider and bolder approach, ironizing and critiquing questions of guilt and science, and flamboyantly manipulating the scientific-literary middle ground. Natalie Barney's work is striking for its appropriation of a form rarely used by women writers, whether gay or straight, of any period: notably the aphorism and the fragment. Her three volumes—*Éparpillements* (1910), *Pensées d'une amazone* (1920), *Nouvelles pensées de l'amazone* (1939)—might be described as laying down the law on female homosexuality; as such they are the perfect guidebooks for Proust's narrator. In the style of the *moralistes*, she does not order or otherwise tabulate her *maximes*—they are loosely collected under headings such as 'Les sexes adverses', 'Choses de l'amour', 'Pages prises aux romans que je n'écrirai pas', 'Autres éparpillements'—which in this case has the additional effect of reflecting the chaotic variety of discourses on homosexuality. Barney covers the topics of hermaphrodism, the literary representation of homosexuality, the sensational public reports of lesbianism, the work of sexologists such as Havelock Ellis, and so on—in other words, all the topics to which one would expect to find an accretion of 'laws' at this time. On spiritual hermaphrodism, for example, she writes: 'Il semble naturel que des êtres, nés de deux sexes, portent parfois leurs

ever, Ellis often admits that 'the general conformation of the body is feminine'. Contrary to the majority of his case-studies, Ellis tried to associate lesbianism with transvestism, and referred to unique and bizarre cases (clinical histories were at first difficult to obtain) as 'in most respects so typical' of the 'true lesbian'. See Faderman's account of this mis-theorizing, *Surpassing the Love of Men*, 241–8.

[23] Cited, ibid. 316.

doubles attributs mélangés. Hommes par le corps, femmes par l'esprit, ou le contraire, ou une fraction du contraire, variables à l'infini. Il y a des androgynes d'esprit aussi bien que de corps';[24] on the response of the general public, '"Il n'y a donc pas de détails libidineux?"—murmure en lui-même le public oiseux, désappointé, avec une nuance de reproche.—Ce public, à l'esprit vide, est généralement dépravé';[25] and in criticism of the Baudelairean stereotype of the lesbian: 'Il a fallu que le romantisme vienne ajouter l'innovation de ses "femmes damnées" pour galvaniser d'un semblant de "vice" infernal ces couples féminins.'[26]

The writings of Barney and Proust might be described as major signifiers in the intense activity of mapping and maximizing on homosexuality which was being carried out by numerous writers living in Paris at this time. (Studies such as Shari Benstock's *Women of the Left Bank* (1987) and Andrea Weiss's *Paris Was a Woman* (1997) document the female, mostly lesbian contribution to this area; paradoxically, no such study details the male counterpart; information can instead be found in single author criticism, such as Patrick Pollard's *André Gide: Homosexual Moralist.*) The correspondence between Proust and Barney indicates a mutual awareness of this shared activity, and a certain curiosity—although each attributes the curiosity to the other. According to George Wickes's biography of Barney, *The Amazon of Letters*, their correspondence was initiated by Proust, who, having read the *Pensées*, 'decided to pursue his research on Sapphic love by conferring with an author of such expertise'. The letters themselves suggest a different order of events, with Barney initiating the correspondence by sending Proust a copy of her *Pensées* bearing the dedication: 'A Marcel Proust dont la compréhension mérite cet exemplaire non expurgé—entre les pages 72 et 73—des "Pensées d'une Amazone" où il se trouvera nommé. Attentivement, Natalie C. Barney.'[27] Proust's reply expresses his customary hyperbolic praise: 'votre livre est ravissant et profond et fait honte aux miens'. More interesting is his comparison of Barney's 'doux chant' and the tone of *Sodome et Gomorrhe* (still in preparation), in which 'la paix divine des *Bucoliques*, du *Banquet*, la

[24] This (xi) and the following fragments are from 'Le procès de Sapho', (i–xxxiv), in *Pensées d'une amazone* (inserted between pp. 72 and 73).

[25] Ibid. xvi.

[26] Ibid. xxii. Proust, however, in a letter to Barney, expresses his admiration for the 'audacity' of Baudelaire's treatment of lesbianism in the *Épaves* (22 Oct. 1920, in *Correspondance*, xix. 289).

[27] Cited, ibid. xix. 256.

liberté de Lucien, n'y règnent pas mais plutôt le sombre désespoir des deux vers de Vigny'.[28] Barney's dedication wittily inscribes the threat of censorship: she sends Proust 'cet exemplaire non expurgé'—the central section to which she refers as 'non expurgé' and which anticipates *Sodome et Gomorrhe* is entitled 'Le procès de Sapho'; it is paginated separately with roman numerals (separated, therefore, from the arabic pagination of the remainder of the text) and includes reviews by male readers.[29] Proust, by contrast, writes explicitly that he is fearful of the public's response to his representation of homosexuality: 'Le goût est devenu bien sévère. En publiant prochainement *Sodome et Gomorrhe*, je renonce—avec allégresse—à tous les honneurs futurs.'[30]

The ensuing correspondence is generated by their failure to meet in person.[31] Proust claims his ill health as the reason, and reiterates that their meeting be 'anti-mondain'; Barney presided over a salon which Proust seems to have been eager to avoid. Barney, perhaps frustrated by this prevarication, finally writes a near incomprehensible letter (Proust describes it, perhaps euphemistically, as 'presque entièrement illisible'), which plays on such 'Proustian' theories as 'the multiple self', mystifying and twisting them to imply a spiritual intimacy: 'Que cela est difficile de continuer après un commencement; mais ne sommes-nous pas plus multiples que notre être inconnu? Et ne pouvons nous diversifier et intensifier nos aspects? . . . Je pouvais être celle-ci ou celle-là, nous voici confrontés par nous-mêmes—limités à nous aussi.'[32] The eventual meeting, at Barney's 'Temple à l'amour', reads as a parody of the narrator's attempts in *A la recherche* to track lesbianism. According to Wickes's biography, Proust was 'too nervous to broach the topic he wanted to discuss', while Barney was 'unable to interrupt the flow of his chatter about high society in order to bring it around to the subject of lesbianism';[33] or, as she herself records in *Aventures de l'esprit* (1929): 'En vain j'essayais de l'entraîner sur un terrain encore inexploré entre nous—il préférait se réfugier près des carillons belges du rire de Mme de Guermantes et autres plaisanteries mondaines qu'il avait dû souvent conter avec succès.'[34]

[28] Letter of 1/2 May 1920, ibid. xix. 255.

[29] See Shari Benstock, *Women of the Left Bank: Paris, 1900–1940* (Austin, Tex.: University of Texas Press, 1987), 297.

[30] Letter of 22 Oct. 1920, in *Correspondance*, xix. 543.

[31] Letters of 22 Oct. 1920, ibid. letter 289; 3 Nov. 1920, ibid. letter 309; 28 Jan. 1921, ibid. xx. letter 37; 29 Jan. 1921, ibid. xx. letter 38.

[32] Letter of 24 Dec. 1920, ibid. xix. 687.

[33] George Wickes, *The Amazon of Letters* (London: W. H. Allen, 1977), 179.

[34] Barney, *Aventures de l'esprit* (Paris: Émile Paul, 1929), 67.

Barney had anticipated Proust's treatment of lesbianism in the forthcoming *Sodome et Gomorrhe*:

> '*La femme aura Gomorrhe et l'homme aura Sodome*'.
> '. . . *Et se jetant, de loin, un regard irrité,*
> *Les deux sexes mourront, chacun de son côté.*'
> Mais que ceux qui craignent la fin de l'espèce se rassurent!
> 'Les deux sexes mourront, chacun de son côté'
> lorsqu'ils ne se jetteront plus '*un regard irrité*' . . .
> Nous sommes encore loin de cette entente indifférente qu'il nous est permis de supposer entre Gomorrhe et Sodome (qu'en doit dire prochainement Marcel Proust?).[35]

As she records in the sketch entitled 'Marcel Proust', of her *Aventures de l'esprit*, she was disappointed by *Sodome et Gomorrhe*, and, unsurprisingly, found his 'Gomorrheans' unbelievable: 'Je les [Gomorrhéennes] trouve surtout invraisemblables! . . . Même en les approchant des connaissances qu'il peut avoir de "l'amour qui ne dit pas son nom", Proust ne saurait avoir aucun rapport avec ces mystères.'[36] Proust's title seems to have misled Barney, as the above fragment indicates, to expect some conciliatory gesture between male and female homosexuality. The opposition between archive and aporia which *A la recherche* styles suggests that Proust's representation is more interested in the epistemological dilemma posed by the proliferating discourses which attempt to establish sexuality as a subject than in the plundering and manipulating of those discourses to apologetic ends.

The figure of Sappho is emblematic of this difference. For ironically, but aptly, the only scrap of lesbian culture to reach *A la recherche* takes the form of the drowned Sappho (iii. 197). The narrator has always visualized Albertine against the seascape of Balbec. The revelation of her connection with Mlle Vinteuil resurrects the image of Montjouvain—'Derrière Albertine je ne voyais plus les montagnes bleues de la mer, mais la chambre de Montjouvain où elle tombait dans les bras de Mlle Vinteuil' (iii. 501). Later she is set against the superimposed images of both seascape and Montjouvain. When, under the pressure of the narrator's interrogation, Albertine threatens to drown herself, 'La mer sera mon tombeau', 'Comme Sapho' is Marcel's reply. This slight reference would seem to refer to Ovid's canonical version of the myth (15th Epistle of the *Heroïdes*), according to which Sappho, 'transformed into the archetypal abandoned woman, physically humiliated', her sexuality 'normalized', kills her-

[35] Barney, *Pensées*, xviii. [36] Barney, *Aventures*, 74.

self for love of a man, Phaon.[37] However, reworkings of the Sappho myth by writers contemporary with Proust suggest an alternative interpretation. These reworkings are described by Benstock as 'an important lesbian feminist enterprise'—'the recovery of Sappho as a woman's poet whose writings celebrated female love and friendship'.[38] That this was a contested and contentious site is indicated by the title of the censored section of Natalie Barney's *Pensées*, 'Le procès de Sapho' (the section in which Proust's *Sodome et Gomorrhe* is anticipated), while her choice of the epigrammatic form reinforces the sense that Barney is 'laying down the law'. Further reworkings include Renée Vivien's 'La Mort de Psappha' and Barney's 'Équivoque' in *Actes et entr'actes*. The effect of these texts is to restore Sappho's homosexuality ('nineteenth-century male writers (many of them homosexual) had appropriated Sappho as a figure of concupiscence and equated Sapphic love with female decadence'[39]); consequently, Sappho's suicide is described as provoked by unrequited love of a woman.[40] The ambiguity of the narrator's remark—it could refer either to the canonical Ovidian 'straight' retelling or to contemporary lesbian rewritings—is typical of the ambiguous presence of lesbianism in the text. Yet the sharp exchange between Albertine and Marcel in which the reference is made is perhaps most telling in its brevity, posing as it does this glimpse of a lesbian history and culture on the point of suicide. Proust's Sappho fragment is set incongruously against the vast expanses of male homosexuality.

At once avoiding the currency of feminist lesbian rewriting and breaking with the traditional place of reference, Lesbos, used by Baudelaire and others, Proust chooses to define lesbianism through its biblical origin, establishing an unprecedented link with Gomorrah. McGinnis's article 'L'Inconnaissable Gomorrhe' cites some rare late nineteenth-century instances of Gomorrah used in a lesbian context, but notes that these examples retain the traditional meaning, 'symbole de tout vice ou péché contre nature', rather than being specific to lesbianism.[41] Indeed, the term 'gomorrhéen, -enne' first gains its association with female homosexuality after the publication of *A la recherche*. McGinnis also draws attention to the fact that lesbianism has

[37] Joan de Jean, *Fictions of Sappho 1546–1937* (Chicago: University of Chicago Press, 1989), 7.

[38] Benstock, *Women of the Left Bank*, 281.

[39] Ibid.

[40] De Jean, *Fictions of Sappho*, 284–5.

[41] R. McGinnis, 'L'Inconnaissable Gomorrhe', *Romanic Review*, 81 (1990), 92–104.

traditionally been on the margins of male homosexuality—the biblical story of Gomorrah is not narrated. Genesis 18–19 tells of Yahweh's destruction of the cities of the Plain as a punishment for the vice of the men of Sodom; Gomorrah's inhabitants also die in the rain of fire and sulphur, but their sin is not described.

Proust's retelling of the biblical narrative in *Sodome et Gomorrhe I* repeats this pattern, and provides the template for the representation of male and female homosexuality in *A la recherche*. Sodom is both originary *and* historicized; the rhetorical performance of the archive spills over into the texts which follow, and the 'parade of Sodom', to borrow Sollers's phrase, becomes central to the society of *A la recherche*. Gomorrah is always on the margins, inaccessible to the desire for knowledge (expansion, interpretation), locked in a traumatic origin, whose effects are felt only in their basic repetition. This binary opposition between archive and aporia is suggested by the very title of the central volume of *A la recherche, Sodome et Gomorrhe*. Indeed, the Albertine texts, *La Prisonnière* and *Albertine disparue*, are subtitled *Sodome et Gomorrhe III* (suggesting a parallel structure to the 'Côté de Guermantes' and 'de chez Swann' of the opening volumes, male homosexuality now providing the first of the two *côtés*, lesbianism the second). Proust's coining of this term has the effect of fixing and isolating Gomorrah as origin; it also evacuates it of any meaning other than its original moral content.

That lesbianism was a subject which attracted, rather than repelled aphorism, but whose magnetism Proust chose—even in this renaming—to ignore, is not to join Barney in her criticism, but rather returns us to the dynamics of the text itself. For the narrator, wilfully ignorant, is exceptionally unable to 'lay down the law' in this area. Rather than tapping into the wealth of popular misinformation, as he does for male homosexuality, he taps again and again into an original anxiety which fails to generate such theories. This repetition is still presented as a narrative of revelation, albeit a repetitious and sterile revelation.

The only certainty is conferred by Montjouvain; all else collapses into ambiguity, speculation. And while the remembrance of Montjouvain is repeated, as emblem, each remembrance is a revolution without progression. The narrator, looking back on his pursuit of Albertine, is still unable to translate her sexuality into knowledge or law:

Je ne connaissais qu'imparfaitement la nature suivant laquelle j'agissais; aujourd'hui j'en connais clairement la vérité subjective. Quant à sa vérité objective, c'est-à-dire si les intuitions de cette nature saisissaient plus exactement que mon raisonnement les intentions véritables d'Albertine, si j'ai eu raison de me fier à cette nature et si au contraire elle n'a pas altéré les intentions d'Albertine au lieu de les démêler, c'est ce qu'il m'est difficile de dire. (iii. 850)

Knowledge is prevented by a Heisenbergian involvement with the subject. As the enquirer disfigures the object of enquiry, so the latter becomes impossible to establish, comes to represent in fact the aporia by which lesbianism is defined. The fascination of Montjouvain is that it explains nothing, yet appears to give a glimpse of the subject intact, viewed by the naïve narrator, not yet disfigured by desire.

Only Cottard, as 'disinterested' observer and analyst, attempts to elucidate lesbianism. His excess of scientific neutrality is set in an emblematic and parodic episode entitled 'la danse contre seins' (iii. 191). Whereas Montjouvain contains no explicit reference to lesbianism, Cottard's analysis centres farcically on pinning down lesbian behaviour through science. To establish his 'medical fact' that women are most prone to orgasm by stimulation of the breast, and, in this case, the connection of the fact with lesbianism, an elaborate series of chance happenings occurs. The 'chance' breakdown of the narrator's tram means that he must stop in Incarville. He then, by chance, meets Cottard, whose train has also, by chance, broken down, and who has been forced to stay longer in Incarville, where he happened to be visiting patients. Cottard accompanies the narrator to the casino where Albertine and her friends are spending the afternoon. The narrator, all too innocently, describes the 'tumulte de jeunes filles', many of whom are dancing together. But 'chance'—the chance that the narrator terms Cottard's 'bad upbringing' and his forgetting to bring his pince-nez—causes the doctor to react quite differently to the sight of Albertine and Andrée dancing together: '"J'ai oublié mon lorgnon et je ne vois pas bien, mais elles sont certainement au comble de la jouissance. On ne sait pas assez que c'est surtout par les seins que les femmes l'éprouvent. Et voyez, les leurs se touchent complètement"' (iii. 191).

In earlier drafts (Esquisse XVII, iii. 1081–2) of the Andrée–Albertine waltz scene, it is Elstir who makes this remark; a note then follows that Cottard should replace him: 'c'est comme docteur, comme vue médicale que Cottard me fera remarquer l'attitude des jeunes filles dansant'. The voice, albeit jocular and titillating, of medical authority is placed to speak within an implausible setting of chance circumstance. It is the only pronouncement of its kind, supplemented by no further remarks; the narrator, at this point, barely reacts, making brief reference to his 'mal' and 'trouble cruel'. Yet this baroque episode framing its piece of 'evidence' is interpreted retrospectively by the narrator as provoking his future investigation, his 'cruelle méfiance . . . naquit d'une remarque de Cottard' (iii. 190). Overly anxious to attribute his hypothesis to science, the narrator forgets that his 'cruelle méfiance' was already attributed to the first emblematic scene, Montjouvain.

Montjouvain occurs long before the revelations of male homosexuality. It stamps itself, as emblem, on the child's mind, and later functions as foreknowledge. And it is repeated as such, rendering impotent the powers of transformation, of metamorphosis, which the narrator's knowledge and imagination wield throughout, becoming literally emblematic; for the narrator visualizes Albertine's lesbianism by putting her in the frame, the setting of Montjouvain: 'Derrière la plage de Balbec, la mer, le lever du soleil, que maman me montrait, je voyais . . . la chambre de Montjouvain où Albertine . . . avait pris la place de l'amie de Mlle Vinteuil' (iii. 513–14). This process of superimposition and repetition has the effect of embalming Albertine, as Duras's own elegiac image describes:

> Soirées écrites, embaumées dans l'écrit, dorénavant lectures sans fin, sans fond. Albertine, Andrée étaient leurs noms. Qui dansaient devant lui déjà atteint par la mort et qui cependant les regardait, et qui cependant qu'il était là, devant elles, déchiré, anéanti de douleur, écrivait déjà le livre de leur passé, de leur rencontre, de leurs regards noyés qui ne voyaient plus rien, de leurs lèvres séparées qui ne disaient plus rien, de leurs corps embrasés de désir, le livre de l'amour ce soir-là à Cabourg.[42]

Montjouvain divides vice from virtue, homosexuality from heterosexuality—or rather, lesbianism from heterosexuality. For these categories are pre-imposed as a code for interpreting Albertine's behaviour. They constitute the moral knot described in 'Hypothesis', and seem not to apply to male homosexuality, where vice and virtue are temporarily discarded to allow for a purely 'scientific' discussion, then re-enter in the complex revelation of Saint-Loup. What is curious is that the original elucidation of Montjouvain is not concerned with sexuality as such; its theorization explores the notion of sadism, but in complex moral terms which are far from the strict

[42] Marguérite Duras, *L'Été 80* (Paris: Minuit, 1980), 18.

antithetical divisions according to which the narrator later structures his enquiry. These initial terms invoke an almost exclusively affective model of vice and virtue; morality is coded according to its effect on others, whether painful or pleasurable. This acutely sensitized space is the register for moral values. Vinteuil's daughter and her lover are described as 'des êtres si purement sentimentaux, si naturellement vertueux que même le plaisir sensuel leur paraît quelque chose de mauvais, le privilège des méchants' (i. 162); sadism involves a performance of cruelty and pleasure in which goodness is identified with 'souffrance'. Only retrospectively does the scene become set according to the stark and simplistic equation wherein homosexuality equals vice, and heterosexuality, virtue. This is the partner equation to the binary hypothesis. 'Souffrance' is the key word, the term whereby the narrator establishes contact with the subject, and enters this acute space of affects. The voyeur, by contrast, stands free of his subject and of moral considerations: his observation and, subsequently, classification or theorization are enabled by this detachment. The concluding sentence of the Montjouvain passage describes and proscribes such detachment as indifference: 'cette indifférence aux souffrances qu'on cause et qui, quelques autres noms qu'on lui donne, est la forme terrible et permanente de la cruauté' (i. 163). Once Montjouvain is no longer viewed (viewed as the spectacle of lesbianism) but internalized (as a morality and subsequently an epistemology of affects), the narrator at once ceases to be indifferent, and relinquishes the possibility of knowledge: he can only register and attempt to theorize those affects he experiences.

When the revelation of Albertine's lesbianism occurs, then, it affords no sudden expansion into a rich realm of new knowledge, stories, laws. It is simply a return, the shock of repetition. But this repetition is described as yielding the excitement of an intellectual discovery: 'Nous pouvons avoir roulé toutes les idées possibles, la vérité n'y est jamais entrée, et c'est du dehors, quand on s'y attend le moins, qu'elle nous fait son affreuse piqûre et nous blesse pour toujours' (iii. 499). The recall of Montjouvain imposes itself with the certainty of involuntary memory. Its image 'emmagasinée' is resurrected. And the knowledge gained through this is part of a causal chain: 'j'avais dangereusement laissé s'élargir en moi la voie funeste et destinée à être douloureuse du Savoir' (iii. 500). Knowledge about male homosexuality may, it appears, be acquired wholesale, and is cause for celebration. The cause of knowledge about lesbianism is vicious; it implicates the voyeur (no innocent bystander or even objective scientist), and, despite painful research, merely returns the narrator to its origins. Rather than the revelation and sudden acquisition of knowledge, we feel here the force of revelation on a mind already primed and needing only this 'intermittence du cœur' to justify its pursuit whereby the narrator is thrown into an affective relationship with knowledge and with the law. This is described as 'un sentiment presque orgueilleux, presque joyeux, celui d'un homme à qui le choc qu'il aurait reçu aurait fait faire un bond tel qu'il serait parvenu à un point où nul effort n'aurait pu le hisser' (iii. 500).

This movement is later described by the image of the sea, the rising and falling of waves during a storm:

> Ce n'est que pendant que nous souffrons que nos pensées, en quelque sorte agitées de mouvements perpétuels et changeants, font monter comme dans une têmpete, à un niveau d'où nous pouvons la voir, toute cette immensité réglée par des lois, sur laquelle, postés à une fênetre mal placée, nous n'avons pas vue, car le calme du bonheur la laisse unie et à un niveau trop bas. (iv. 475)

Painful revelation, it is suggested, gives access to laws—or, at least, the turbulence experienced by the self gives a sudden vista of them. The involuntary movement described in this metaphor may be contrasted with the placing of the voyeur, who, like the narrator spying on Mlle Vinteuil and her lover, or on Charlus and Jupien, has chosen his position: in such cases it should follow that the choice is not propitious to generality. The window voluntarily chosen is 'mal placée', in the sense that it separates the self from the natural world. Sheltered from its force—literally insensitive to its laws—the observer is unable to perceive them. 'Suffering', by contrast, 'opens a window on the real and is the main condition of it'.[43]

Now there is a paradox here, in that those scenes of voyeurism in which the narrator enjoys a very superior vantage-point do yield many laws: notably the laws of sadism and of homosexuality. What the passage quoted above suggests is that the viewing of such scenes offers an, as it were, flattened, two-dimensional viewing of the law; the internalization of this metaphor allows an expansion into three dimensions as the narrator's own thoughts become part of the turbulent seascape he has previously observed. Now the self is registering the law affectively, has become, in part, the subject of exploration. Just as the sensitized self was the gauge of morality in the Montjouvain

[43] Beckett, *Proust*, 16.

scene, so here it is suggested that knowledge, and the laws which structure it, must be measured affectively.

It is no coincidence that Proust first used the metaphor of the stormy seascape to figure Baudelaire's lesbian poems, the *Épaves*. Proust describes the effect of restoring these poems to *Les Fleurs du mal*, the text from which they they were cut, as follows: 'Elles reprennent leurs places entre les plus hautes pièces du livre comme ces lames altières de cristal qui s'élèvent majestueusement après les soirs de tempête et qui élargissent de leurs cimes intercalées l'immense tableau de la mer.'[44]

Gomorrah remains a *terra incognita*, whereas Sodom is a parade: the narrator is the forewarned, yet ignorant, witness of Montjouvain and also the naïve yet knowledgeable observer of the opening of *Sodome et Gomorrhe*. The stylized model and rich knowledge of male homosexuality is simply stripped away to reveal the suffering, desiring mind dealing with the scant raw materials of experience:

> C'est souvent seulement par manque d'esprit créateur qu'on ne va pas assez loin dans la souffrance. Et la réalité la plus terrible donne en même temps que la souffrance la joie d'une belle découverte, parce qu'elle ne fait que donner une forme neuve et claire à ce que nous remâchions depuis longtemps sans nous en douter. (iii. 500)

This charting for the first time of an unknown country is a figure often used to describe the gathering of knowledge. It occurs, for example, in *A l'ombre*, where women as/in landscapes are desired. In *Sodome et Gomorrhe I* the landscape of Sodom is charted,[45] but its partner city, Gomorrah, is an enigma. Albertine was mapped by her homeland, Austria—'sa singularité géographique, la race qui l'habitait, ses monuments, ses paysages, je pouvais les considérer comme dans un atlas' (iii. 504); now this must be effaced, replaced by a lesbian landscape, unknown, perhaps unknowable. And whereas Sodom is allowed to expand, Gomorrah/Trieste is, for the narrator, 'une cité maudite que j'aurais voulu faire brûler sur-le-champ et supprimer du monde réel' (iii. 505).

Suppression and expansion; the narrator's quest both repeats itself (the shock of recognition has yet to play itself out) and yields new laws.

[44] 'A propos de Baudelaire', in *Contre Sainte-Beuve*, 631–2.

[45] See Hughes, 'Mapping of Homosexuality', which considers how 'the strains of European colonialism, and also questions of ethnic and national identity that were in such sharp focus at the time of the First World War, colour the depiction of sexuality which Proust's narrator offers' (p. 148).

Not the laws of Gomorrah, but reflections on cognition and desire, reflections beyond the pursuit of sexual difference. Lesbianism is, according to the narrator, prolific and ambiguous, seeming to border on bisexuality. Maxims to this effect are invariably paired with scenarios in which women meet by chance, and immediately recognize each other, so swift and keen is their desire: 'Les gomorrhéennes sont à la fois assez rares et assez nombreuses pour que, dans quelque foule que ce soit, l'une ne passe pas inaperçue aux yeux de l'autre' (iii. 853). The illustrative anecdote describes a dinner attended by the narrator, two male friends, and their wives: the women 'ne furent pas longues à se comprendre, mais si impatientes de se posséder'. Again, the narrator is in the position of voyeur; his friends remain unaware of the women's behaviour; from this scenario, he jumps forward in time to sketch in the remainder of the history. The lack of detail and the speed with which the illustration is given contrast strikingly with the precise, slow-motion narration which opens *Sodome et Gomorrhe.* We are simply told of the facility with which lesbian relations may occur: 'Gomorrhe était dispersée aux quatre coins du monde' (iii. 533), while another restaurant anecdote is unwittingly comic in its description of the striking homogeneity of a group of ten lesbians: 'Mais la Gomorrhe moderne est un puzzle fait des morceaux qui viennent de là où on s'attendait le moins' (iii. 597).

Paradoxically, the above maxim occurs in a passage in which the narrator tries—again, and in vain—to decipher Albertine's sexuality. For there is a disjunction between 'expérience' and intuition, between the law desired and the resulting level of generality: 'Si les faits particuliers—que seuls l'expérience, l'espionnage, entre tant de réalisations possibles, feraient connaître—sont si difficiles à trouver, la vérité, en revanche, est si facile à percer ou seulement à pressentir' (iii. 596). This disjunction is illustrated by the text's subsequent slippage between the particular and the general. If the individual facts of experience are impossible to establish, the fictions, exempla, and laws of the Proustian *doxa* are easily accessible. Theorizing through these *topoi* has a therapeutic effect, numbing the narrator to the unassimilable affects which are the substance of his revelations. In one such instance the narrator, ever suspicious, notices that Albertine's gaze seems to be attracted only by young women who pass by, yet his response to this suspicion is to digress: he generalizes by way of the topic of cuckolded husbands, their recognition of their wife's infidelity, and their jealousy—which in turn demands more 'facts'. 'Mais il faut un dossier plus matériellement documenté pour établir une scène de jalousie' (iii. 597), claims the narrator somewhat implausibly, given his eloquence on the subject elsewhere. How will the woman respond when found out? Two generalized possible responses are given: 'Certes il y a des amours . . .', and 'Mais combien d'autres . . .' (iii. 597–8). And so the hypothesis about Albertine's lesbianism is defused, diffused over a series of heterosexual exempla, which in turn give way to topics where sexual preference is irrelevant, the Proustian *topoi* of lying and jealousy.[46] Albertine and also the *récit* are returned to briefly, but again her person is quickly absorbed by generality. Her eyes 'appartenaient à la famille de ceux qui'; this in turn allows a definition of type, 'ces êtres-là sont des êtres de fuite', and category, 'signe correspondant à ce qu'en physique est le signe qui signifie vitesse' (iii. 599). Within these generalities exists another infinite range of possible particularities: 'Le champ infini des possibles s'étend, et si par hasard le réel se présentait devant nous, il serait tellement en dehors des possibles que, dans un brusque étourdissement, allant taper contre ce mur surgi, nous tomberions à la renverse' (iii. 600). Reality is so other that it cannot be figured, and if presented as such, has the effect of, quite literally, bowling the narrator over, bringing the generative mode of speculation to a dead end. This encounter returns the narrator briefly to the space of affects, which requires always to be resolved by therapeutic maximizing.

Both the over-general, over-hasty maxims on Gomorrah and the digressive movement mapped above are typical of the laws formulated by the narrator in pursuit of lesbianism/Albertine. Rather than the careful detail which maps Sodom, the narrator shoots past such possible material, glimpsing only crowds of potential lesbians on the way, and quickly arriving at that superior vantage-point from which he enjoys the global aspect of the laws of desire and cognition. Even, for example, at the moment of the Montjouvain revelation, the narrator begins to speculate on the possibility of forgetting Albertine and, having included her case amongst those of all past mistresses ('les maîtresses que j'ai les plus aimées'), reflects on the properties of love as a natural phenomenon:

On aurait dit qu'une vertu n'ayant aucun rapport avec elles leur avait été accessoirement adjointe par la nature, et que cette vertu, ce pouvoir simili-

[46] See Emma Wilson (*Sexuality and the Reading Encounter* (Oxford: Oxford University Press, 1996) on this topic: 'Reading Albertine's Sexuality; or, "Why Not Think of Marcel Simply as a Lesbian?" ', pp. 60–94.

électrique avait pour effet sur moi d'exciter mon amour . . . Comme par un courant électrique qui vous meut, j'ai été secoué par mes amours, je les ai vécus, je les ai sentis: jamais je n'ai pu arriver à les voir ou à les penser. (iii. 511)

The affective revelation is displaced into the binary hypothesis: is Albertine lesbian or not? And from this, in turn, speculatory maxims are generated around and away from the original topic. This tendency is still further exaggerated at points of extreme tension—namely, when the narrator is on the verge of some important discovery about Albertine's sexuality. The most heightened sequence of such near-revelations occurs towards the end of *La Prisonnière*, shortly before Albertine's departure. The sequence begins with Albertine's unwitting use of the expression 'casser le pot',[47] which she interrupts, but which the narrator subsequently completes. The revelatory quality of this exchange lies in its being involuntary. Albertine's use of the phrase is a verbal slip, while the narrator's completion of Albertine's words also appears to be unwitting: 'Et tout d'un coup deux mots atroces, auxquels je n'avais nullement songé, tombèrent sur moi: "le pot"' (iii. 842). More than this, the narrator describes himself as the victim of knowledge; the words fall on him as if he were being assaulted by them. Yet, as this revelation and its affective, rather than cognitive force, 'après le sursaut de la rage, les larmes me venaient aux yeux' (iii. 843), are absorbed into the narrator's web of interrogation and interpretation, the impact is lost. The truth of the revelation might be guaranteed by its involuntariness, but still the narrator desires a confession from Albertine. He sets traps to confirm his suspicions about her sexuality, and when she falls into them, giving further involuntary confirmation of the narrator's suspicions, his desire for, and violent attempts to force, a confession are only heightened. The tissue of commentary and maxims which supplements this episode suggests that the clumsy and painful exchanges between the narrator and Albertine are recuperable through the laws of the passions. At this level, the specifics of sexuality ('la vérité subjective' (iii. 850)) do not register: the particular situation becomes simply another example of a general law ('la vérité objective' (ibid.))—in this case, the lover's duplicity. Ironically, this topic is illustrated by the example of Charlus:

Le cas d'une vieille femme maniérée comme était M. de Charlus . . . ce cas rentre dans une loi qui s'applique bien au-delà des seuls Charlus, une loi d'une

[47] Trans. as 'get myself b...' in *The Captive*, trans. C. K. Scott Moncrieff, T. Kilmartin, and D. J. Enright (London: Chatto and Windus, 1992), 385.

généralité telle que l'amour même ne l'épuise pas tout entière; nous ne voyons pas notre corps que les autres voient, et nous 'suivons' notre pensée, l'objet qui est devant nous, invisible aux autres. (iii. 847)

Homosexuality is effectively reintroduced, but neutralized, as just another 'caractère', then as another 'case' of the still more general Proustian law of perspective. This generalization in turn allows the narrator (by way of a parenthetical reflection on the novelist's art) to reach the projected and no longer painful conclusion that at the end of his research he will fail to decipher Albertine (iii. 850).

This is the shape of the aporia which is female homosexuality. Theory on lesbianism never moves beyond the most basic of laws, and never becomes a tool of recognition. The fact that lesbianism eludes the narrator's maxims, that it escapes typology and borders on bisexuality, aligns it with the apparent breakdown in social types and structures. This is represented by the rise of the probably lesbian, possibly bisexual Mme Verdurin from the bourgeoisie to the aristocracy to become the 'princesse de Guermantes'. An ever-growing number of sexual and social permutations and combinations arise, as the syntax of the following phrase suggests:

Car dans les rapports qu'ils [les invertis] ont avec elles, ils jouent pour la femme qui aime les femmes le rôle d'une autre femme, et la femme leur offre en même temps à peu près ce qu'ils trouvent chez l'homme, si bien que l'ami jaloux souffre de sentir celui qu'il aime rivé à celle qui est pour lui presque un homme, en même temps qu'il le sent presque lui échapper, parce que, pour ces femmes, il est quelque chose qu'il ne connaît pas, une espèce de femme. (iii. 24)

Yet this aporia is actively and profusely occupied with the formulation of laws so general that they bypass the specifics of female homosexuality, and move straight to the all-encompassing laws of desire, deceit, jealousy, and forgetting. The aporia which (as will be seen in the next chapter) is the end-point of this mapping of the text might be redescribed as an arena, since it is the site of epistemic play, at once needy and aggressive.

6.3 Narratives of revelation

The neat schematization of this conclusion in which aporia is set against archive is one means of mapping revelation in *A la recherche*, but it neglects the readerly sense of revelation as narrative. We might question what kind of hermeneutic expectations these narratives encourage. For there is no single end-point, no one moment at which the aporia becomes an arena. Instead, we are led along multiple paths of revelation, none of which can be developed into knowledge *per se*, but can only be displaced into the arena—where both knowledge and morality signify purely in terms of affects. This is why the narrator so often registers the moment of revelation physically—describes his body forced into motion, displaced, overcome—the passive recipient not so much of knowledge of something outside himself, but simply of its affect. 'L'habitude de penser empêche parfois d'éprouver le réel, immunise contre lui, le fait paraître de la pensée encore. Il n'y a pas une idée qui ne porte en elle sa réfutation possible, un mot le mot contraire' (iv. 182). The affect signifies simply by indicating the real presence of something beyond the self, by allowing the self to register an objective reality, a world not yet subject to the distortions of the mind. The theory of sadism which elucidates the observation of Montjouvain informs the narrator's epistemology: he desires to be violated, overcome, affected—paradoxically as a first step towards objective knowledge, but one which can never be developed beyond the affect, since this would entail what is tellingly described in the above quotation as the immunization of thought.

His compulsive speculation requiring always to remain in that middle ground between the posing of the enigma and its resolution, the narrator does not want to solve the Albertine mystery; as his response to her interrogation ironically indicates: '*P.-S.—Je ne réponds pas à ce que vous me dites de prétendues propositions que Saint-Loup (que je ne crois d'ailleurs nullement en Touraine) aurait faites à votre tante. C'est du Sherlock Holmes. Quelle idée vous faites-vous de moi?*' (iv. 39). For the Albertine narratives repeatedly frustrate our expectations of what Barthes has defined as the 'hermeneutic code': 'L'ensemble des unités qui ont pour fonction d'articuler, de diverses manières, une question, sa réponse et les accidents variés qui peuvent ou préparer la question ou retarder la réponse; ou encore: de formuler une énigme et d'amener son déchiffrement.'[48] Brooks's model of the plot, while describing basically the same pattern, has more to say about what it feels like as a reader to occupy the middle ground of a text governed by this hermeneutic code in which 'the questions and answers that structure a story, their suspense, partial unveiling, temporary blockage, eventual resolution, with the resulting creation of a "dilatory space"—

[48] Barthes, *S/Z*, 24.

the space of suspense—which we work through what is felt to be, in classical narrative, the revelation that occurs when the narrative sentence reaches full predication'.[49] Such narratives are, Brooks argues, read 'in a spirit of confidence, and also a state of dependence, that what remains to be read will restructure the provisional meanings of the already read'.[50] It could be argued that this failure of plot is a typical feature and concern of modernist texts. Marcel's enquiry proves the impossibility of narratives to which the function of revelation is prescribed, resulting instead in a multiplicity of variants (the narratives and laws of the arena) digressing from the central, empty topic (lesbianism). What it is also possible, and perhaps more fruitful, to say is that there is perhaps no other modernist narrative which so overtly draws attention to its desire and failure, again and again, to find meaning. Just as the aporia is no blank, or, as Kosofsky Sedgwick describes, 'ignorance and opacity collude or compete with knowledge in mobilizing the flows of energy, desire, goods, meanings, persons',[51] so the failure of plot is not simply a failure; it fails in a particular style, and this style determines its significance.

Brooks's 'dilatory space' is in effect represented by the 'arena', the space of epistemic enquiry and variation to which there is no end-point, no solution. It is not a case of 'temporary blockage' or even 'partial unveiling'; often the object itself is completely lost from view. This occurs both on a limited scale and more generally, as we find that the enquiry pre-dates the Mlle Vinteuil-Albertine revelation/'intermittence du cœur', continues right up to *Le Temps retrouvé*, and is unaffected by Albertine's death. Proust effectively creates a narrative of revelation which is just that—a narrative about revelation, but evacuated of the meaning we would expect revelation to bring. The *repetition* of this narrative only heightens this effect. We become familiar with the narrator's response, at once (and this 'at-once-ness' indicates both the simultaneity and the interpenetration of the two modes) affective—'souffrance'—and intellectual—the joy of discovery. We become familiar, too, with the playing out of such moments—that is, with the shape the narrator's enquiry will take. The confessions and testimonies which he receives are always uncertain and contradictory, of necessity ambiguous. Swann's story provides no key; it only rehearses similar suspicions. 'La réalité est donc quelque

49 Peter Brooks, *Reading for the Plot* (Oxford: Oxford University Press, 1984), 18.

50 Ibid. 23.

51 Sedgwick, *Epistemology of the Closet*, 4.

chose qui n'a aucun rapport avec les possibilités, pas plus qu'un coup de couteau que nous recevons avec les légers mouvements des nuages au-dessus de notre tête' (i. 357): this physiological description of Swann's speculations about Odette sets a precedent for what will become the affective-sadistic epistemology of the narrator. The narrator's investigations are even accompanied by the following disclaimer: 'Quant à sa vérité objective, c'est-à-dire si les intuitions de cette nature saisissaient plus exactement que mon raisonnement les intentions véritables d'Albertine . . . c'est ce qu'il m'est difficile de dire' (iii. 850).

Proust confirms this lack of resolution in a letter to Binet-Valmer, 'ce que je vous ai peut'être dit, et c'est exact, c'est que ce Gomorrhéisme ne sera pas plus marqué [que] dans *Un Amour de Swann*. C'est la jalousie du héros pour Albertine.'[52] There is a lack of both suspense and of that other mark of the hermeneutic code, the spirit of confidence (on the part of both reader and narrator) that questions will, in the end, be answered.

Yet the plotting of knowledge about male homosexuality also diverges from the expectations of the hermeneutic code: there is a plenitude and repetition of knowledge about male homosexuality which mirrors the repetitious absence of knowledge about lesbianism. The revelation scene of the opening of *Sodome et Gomorrhe* is, in terms of its yield of knowledge, revelatory only for the young narrator. Charlus's sexuality has already been unambiguously referred to in 'Un amour de Swann', where Swann is described as 'heureux toutes les fois où M. de Charlus était avec Odette. Entre M. de Charlus et elle, Swann savait qu'il ne pouvait rien se passer' (i. 310). Other such pointers are listed in Terdiman's *The Dialectics of Isolation*, and, as he indicates, when the last such clue is given, 'we are only forty pages from the Baron's meeting with Jupien, and nothing can surprise us anymore'.[53] Despite the narrator's preoccupation with questions of

[52] Letter of shortly after 4 June 1921, in *Correspondance*, xx. 315. This apparently simple explanation belies the complexity and force of jealousy and its links with knowledge and creativity. See Bowie, *Freud, Proust, and Lacan*, 45–66; Nicolas Grimaldi, *La Jalousie* (Arles: Actes Sud, 1993); Christie McDonald, 'Republications', in *Reading Proust Now*, ed. M. A. Caws and E. Nicole (New York: Peter Lang, 1990), 197–222. This letter should also be regarded with some suspicion given Proust's further remarks on the status of 'sodomisme'; he claims that, after *Sodome et Gomorrhe*, it will not recur, or, rather, it will only recur in an unequivocally comic or cruel form, 'et plus jamais en action'; again he states that it will appear less and less often 'sauf un peu avant la fin dans une terrible scène'. This series of attempts to play down the presence of male homosexuality in the text, each followed by a qualification, serves only to point up its continuing significance.

[53] Richard Terdiman, *The Dialectics of Isolation* (New Haven: Yale University Press, 1976), 128.

interpretation, neither the absence nor the fullness of knowledge complies with the expectations of the hermeneutic code. Sodom is always present; Gomorrah is always an enigma.

The drama of this binary opposition is persuasive. The narrator's objective and ironic distance ensures his revelatory knowledge about male homosexuality; his affective involvement with Albertine prevents such resolution—in both cases the epistemic moments of revelation are highly memorable. How, then, does Saint-Loup fit into this scheme? Saint-Loup is, in fact, 'outed' at the very end of *Albertine disparue*, at a time when the desire to ascertain Albertine's sexuality has all but faded. This ought to be a charged moment. Saint-Loup, 'purest' of Guermantes, early friend of the narrator, turns out to be a *tante*—and yet it is easily forgotten. 'One hardly notices that Saint-Loup changes completely thrice,' notes Clive Bell in his 1928 study of *A la recherche*.[54] The episode is absorbed into the surrounding 'events', placed as it is between the preoccupation with Albertine's sexuality and the aesthetic revelations of *Le Temps retrouvé*.

The revelation of Saint-Loup is absolute—in this it is characteristic of the representation of male homosexual identity in *A la recherche*. Characteristic too is the resulting transparency of the character: the knowledge that Saint-Loup is gay is applied retrospectively to elucidate puzzling episodes—such as the confrontation with the journalist and, shortly after this, Saint-Loup's violent reaction to the propositions of a man who approaches him in the street. Where Saint-Loup differs is that his character, unlike that of his uncle Charlus, required no supplementary explanation. The episodes to which Saint-Loup's homosexual identity offer an explanation were also initially explicable in a heterosexual context. Both readings are plausible.

The Saint-Loup revelation seems to occur at a point of interference in the Sodom-Gomorrah schema, at a point of dead, if reluctant, certainty. It is introduced through a conversation between the narrator and his mother during a train journey, and in its backwards-forwards scanning movement—now the narrator anticipates the marriage, now he looks back on its unhappy outcome—its revelatory nature is already undermined. The first hint is given in the form of gossip, the kind of gossip desired by the narrator in his research into Albertine. The narrator regrets that neither Saint-Loup nor Charlus have informed him of the forthcoming marriages. There is no apparent transition between this and the anonymous reporting of

[54] Clive Bell, *Proust* (London: Hogarth Press, 1928), 46.

reactions from the local brothel to these 'nouvelles mondaines', the hostess of which provides the information that Saint-Loup is 'comme ça' (iv. 241). But this charged gossip is simply planted in the text; it leads to no speculation. Only fifteen pages later, by which time the narrator is visiting an unhappily married Gilberte, do we learn that she is 'trompée par Robert, mais pas de la manière que tout le monde croyait' (iv. 256). Robert is described 'en vrai neveu de M. de Charlus' in a sentence which trails off, and is, literally, left incomplete. This is not the pain of gaining new vistas of knowledge described in the Albertine revelation, nor the joyous expansion of *Sodome et Gomorrhe I* where 'une erreur dissipée nous donne un sens de plus'. Instead, there is dead certainty, a dullness of response—'une peine infinie'—to an unambiguous truth: 'Mais j'avais été malheureusement aiguillé vers la vérité, vers la vérité qui me fit une peine infinie, par quelques mots échappés à Jupien' (iv. 256).

Slight speculation is aroused around the two agents of revelation, Jupien and Aimé: the narrator questions whether Saint-Loup was already homosexual during the first stay at Balbec. But it is a despairing speculation, which recognizes its own impotence; the narrator's desire to preserve an idyllic past friendship (Jupien's claim that Saint-Loup's homosexuality is recent, 'personne n'était plus opposé de nature à ces choses-là' (iv. 257)) is constantly interrupted by reminiscences which disturb. According to Aimé, Saint-Loup's homosexuality is 'archiconnu', and was in evidence during the narrator's first year at Balbec (iv. 259). Yet Aimé's disclosure is no forced confession, but is itself remembered by the narrator as forming part of a conversation during a short (and unspecified) stay at Balbec. The conversation had at the time made the narrator unhappy ('me rendit fort malheueux'), yet he remembers too Saint-Loup's unusual observation of the waiters, which is now seen to betray 'un ordre de curiosités et de recherches entièrement différent' (iv. 259). This, the narrator's slight and melancholy speculation, is accompanied by an attempt to generalize away from the topic—on the limited viewpoint of the individual, the impossibility of encompassing the variety of nature; yet neither of these modes are pursued with the energetic neediness which characterizes their presence in the Albertine narrative—ultimately both simply point back to a misreading.

For in Saint-Loup we encounter a deeply problematic figure in the schema Sodom versus Gomorrah. 'Si blond, d'une matière si précieuse et rare' (iv. 265), presented as a Guermantes who cannot escape his aristocratic origins, Saint-Loup is then forced to undergo an 'évolution physiologique'. But the evolution is, paradoxically, a regression responding to immediate heredity and also reaching beyond to a primitive, perhaps even an originary, homosexuality. 'Tare', 'stigmates extérieurs', the horrified response contained within these terms comically belies the claim that, 'Personnellement, je trouvais absolument indifférent au point de vue de la morale qu'on trouvât son plaisir auprès d'un homme ou d'une femme' (iv. 264). The creative imagination finds itself at a dead end; there is no way out here, as the vain attempts to maximize on the *topos* of homosexuality indicate (this will become possible, if not entirely comfortable, once the knowledge has been assimilated and categorized in *Le Temps retrouvé*; see e.g. iv. 315).[55] There is a failure to connect: this is no serendipitous discovery, for the knowledge has come too late, and the self is mourned as much as is the idealized Saint-Loup:

> Ce dont nous n'avons pas eu l'intuition directe, ce que nous avons appris seulement par d'autres, nous n'avons plus aucun moyen, l'heure est passée de le faire savoir à notre âme; ses communications avec le réel sont fermées; aussi ne pouvons-nous jouir de la découverte, il est trop tard. (iv. 266)

The narrator wants to feel the pain of this revelation, rather than its 'peine'. He needs 'Suffering . . . to open a window on the real'. Saint-Loup is too close to the narrator for this revelation of his identity to register other than affectively (there can be none of the pleasure, whether of the taxonomist or of the caricaturist, that is taken in the identification of Charlus), yet not close enough for the affect to resonate, to signify. The knowledge comes late; it is both clumsy and indirect.

The redundancy of the Saint-Loup revelation—it is not styled as part of the narrator's binary schema—does, however, signify in the patterns of repetition and subversion which we have been tracing throughout this chapter. For the explanation of Saint-Loup's homosexuality introduces repetition by way of a new, and deeply pessimistic, 'scientific' language. Whereas Darwin's fertilization of orchids

[55] The recuperation of apparently trivial details into the overall schema, once this has been established, at times reads as a parody of 'intellectual work'. However, both Darwin and Freud shared this capacity to make meaningful the seemingly insignificant (see Sulloway, 'Darwin and Psychoanalysis', in *Freud, Biologist of the Mind*, and Bowie, *Freud, Proust, and Lacan*, 77). Popularizers of the new sexology, such as Remy de Gourmont, exaggerate this trait, as Ghéon's review of *Physique de l'amour* indicates: 'There is no detail so strange, whether it belongs to mole, bull or oyster, for him not to draw from it a piquant generalization applied to us'; cited in Pollard, *André Gide*, 69.

provides the model for the homosexuality of Charlus and Jupien, the language of fated heredity and of evolution as degeneracy explains that of Saint-Loup. This language had already been invoked to justify what the narrator sees as uncharacteristic of Saint-Loup—the malicious vulgarity of the latter's remarks about Bloch, for example, is attributed to his aristocratic ancestors: 'Il devait y avoir dans ces moments-là, qui sans doute ne revenaient qu'une fois tous les deux ans, éclipse partielle de son propre moi, par le passage sur lui de la personnalité d'un aïeul qui s'y reflétait' (ii. 693). Now the revelation of his homosexuality redescribes the pattern of revelation as return. Like the narrator, Saint-Loup is caught up in repetition. Unlike the narrator, he is caught up in a repetition to which the justificatory language of heredity and origins is ascribed, 'une sorte de répétition involontaire d'un geste ancestral' (iv. 263).

Originary repetition might also describe the recurrence of the emblematic scene of Montjouvain. Justifying this scene to the scandalized first readers of 'Combray', Proust claimed that it was fundamental to the structure of the novel as a whole, and that its significance would, with the publication of the subsequent volumes of *A la recherche*, become apparent. In other words, repetition would allow the scene to signify. On the one hand, the immediate textual justification of Montjouvain—the laws of sadism—has allowed us to define the Heisenbergian aporia-arena in which revelation can only register repeatedly and affectively. This will be the subject of the next chapter.

What I would like to consider is the possibility that the repetition of Montjouvain (its early placing in the novel, its repetition as hallucinatory image, its resistance both to interpretation and to being played out through a connecting narrative) might relate in some way to the repetition of the language of heredity introduced through Saint-Loup.[56] If this were the case, it might allow us to understand the phenomenon of repetition more generally in the novel, to ascertain a different and more fundamental type of structural importance.

If heredity is understood as repetition, we can begin to understand why homosexuality should be the locus of such anxiety, of the anxiety about repetition as reversion or return. While Saint-Loup's homosexuality is specifically posited as aristocratic, the repetition of an

[56] The language of heredity *per se* is of course used prior to this revelation, notably to explain the narrator's own inherited characteristics; but this usage is particularly striking because of what we might call its 'ancestral' force, and also because it is the sole and deeply pessimistic explanation given for Saint-Loup's sexuality.

ancestral gesture, the narrator of the exordium proposes that it might be fundamental, might relate to human origins, since it derives from 'cet hermaphroditisme initial dont quelques rudiments d'organes mâles dans l'anatomie de la femme et d'organes femelles dans l'anatomie de l'homme semblent conserver la trace' (iii. 31). This explanation is at once more modish and more ancient than Proust's biblical narrative, which informs the naming of the homosexual origins of *Sodome et Gomorrhe*—more modish in that 'by 1905 the bisexual theory of homosexuality [was] advocated by most of Europe's leading sexologists: including Krafft-Ebing, Ellis, Kurella, Moll, Féré, Hirschfeld, Weininger, Herman, Freud'.[57] According to this theory, homosexuality might be seen as 'an atavistic depravity'—hence Kiernan's argument that the 'original bisexuality of the ancestors of the race . . . could not fail to occasion functional, if not organic reversion when mental or physical manifestations were interfered with by disease or congenital defect';[58] but it was increasingly perceived to be biogenetic. The explanation is also more ancient, in that the myth of originary bisexuality derives from Plato (the division of the androgynes producing the two sexes); more ancient too in that it refers beyond the biblical myth to the prehistory of man.

Mythology and science also coincide in Elstir's depiction of the poet as androgyne:

> Les Muses étaient représentées comme le seraient des êtres appartenant à une espèce fossile mais qu'il n'eût pas été rare, aux temps mythologiques, de voir passer le soir . . . Quelquefois un poète, d'une race ayant aussi une individualité particulière pour un zoologiste (caractérisée par une certaine insexualité), se promenait avec une Muse, comme, dans la nature, des créatures d'espèces différentes mais amies et qui vont de compagnie. (ii. 714–15)

Similarly, the narrator's observation of homosexuality, through a botanical lens, leads to an 'aesthetic recognition',[59] which is ultimately suppressed and reserved for *Le Temps retrouvé*, in which art is theorized as originating from involuntary memory. This displacement allows *A la recherche* to conclude by narrating its own genesis, or, to put it more accurately, to posit the moment of its conception as a moment of doubling.

[57] Sulloway, *Freud*, 295.

[58] Cited, ibid. 292.

[59] Fraser's reading suggests a provocative reversal of this sequence: 'It is not in fact until he has observed the homo-erotic dalliance of Charlus and Jupien that the narrator is able, in retrospect, to construe the Montjouvain episode at all' (*Proust and the Victorians*, 222).

The scientific theories and myths of an originary bisexuality provide Proust with a repertoire of figures of doubling and splitting as a means—at least at one level—of recuperating repetition: repetition is the myth which informs the prehistory of the novel. But it is the confluence of such figures in sexology and another scientific area, the study of heredity, which makes them particularly powerful. While sexologists were positing an originary bisexuality, biologists were analysing evolutionary development on a different scale—namely, the reproduction of cells through internal division and repetition. This analysis of heredity by Weismann, De Vries, and others is the foundation of modern genetic theory. For, while the notion of reproduction by cell splitting was not in itself original, Weismann had made the necessary conceptual leap in recognizing that only innate characteristics could be transmitted from generation to generation, and that the heredity of acquired characteristics was impossible: 'L'enfant était pensé comme la continuation de ses parents, une sorte de prolongation externe de leurs développements. Maintenant, l'enfant ressemble à ses parents parce qu'il est l'effet des mêmes causes qui leur ont donné naissance et qui sont restées inchangées.'[60] Both groups, biologists and sexologists, were in favour of the argument for innate over acquired characteristics. But the biologists were also fascinated, as was Proust, by the potential of the *infusoires* as a model for human reproduction—indeed, for the reproduction of all life-forms—since they demonstrably reproduce by splitting, by creating a replica of the original. As Weismann described in his lecture of 1883, 'De l'hérédité': 'Nous avons donc, de la sorte, pour la reproduction des êtres multicellulaires le même processus que pour celle des animaux unicellulaires; une division continue de la cellule germinative.'[61]

According to Brooks's model, repetition occurs centrally in the narrative, 'between blindness and recognition, between origin and ending'.[62] These scientific models and theories suggest that repetition is at the origin of life itself, whether it be on an evolutionary scale or at the microscopic level of the single cell, and that beyond this point of origin the repetition continues—as Metchnikoff indicates, 'Those cells, the function of which is to secure reproduction of the species, are, like unicellular organisms, potentially immortal.'[63] Repetition in *A la recherche* simply recurs; there is no release into some final moment

[60] Lenay (ed.), *La Découverte des lois de l'hérédité*, 165.
[61] Weismann, 'De l'hérédité', 174.
[62] Brooks, *Reading for the Plot*, 107.
[63] Metchnikoff, *Nature of Man*, 165.

of recognition. Moreover, what is repeated, and indeed repeatedly revealed, pertains in some way to origins. We might even say that origins in *A la recherche* signify as such because of their capacity to repeat or replicate. The key originary figure located in the previous chapter is Swann, whose allegiance with the *infusoires* indicates his potential for dangerously prolific self-replication. Repetition, in the sense of self-replication, is not always easily assimilable, for it relates also to the text's self-consciousness about its own origins; it might even be described as a working method, the unit of growth *par excellence*. As Calvino describes: 'Not even Marcel Proust managed to put an end to his encyclopedic novel, though not for lack of design, since the idea for the book came to him all at once, the beginning and the end and the general outline. The reason was that the work grew denser and denser from the inside through its own organic vitality.'[64]

These accounts of the origins of life and the evolution of the sexes explain the potency of repetition in *A la recherche*. There is an unspoken and powerful affinity between the new science of heredity as genetics, which explained the origins of life as a form of splitting and replication; the myth and science of homosexuality, Plato's myth locating the origins of homosexuality in the androgyne and foreshadowing the 'modern' scientific account of an originary bisexuality; and finally, Proust and his narrator's sense of self-reproduction. The myth and science of repetition as originary creation would seem at one level to justify the novel's sense of its own construction—hence the association of homosexuality and androgyny with art described in the images and narratives cited above—at another to explain the proliferation of homosexuality/bisexuality in *A la recherche*. Yet creative repetition suggests too—and this is Calvino's point—that all this world, these maxims and *caractères*, this *récit*, might be the fabulation of the mind, a mind which, unaffected by external forces, might simply continue to replicate itself, producing ever more fantastic variations. In this sense, repetition undermines the very notion of construction, of creative elaboration, and most importantly of the attempt to get beyond the self. For the image of reproduction through self-splitting is also one of confinement, entrapment, sameness; this is the middle zone of affects and repetition and the subject of the next chapter.

[64] Italo Calvino, *Six Memos for the Next Millenium*, trans. P. Creagh (London: Jonathan Cape, 1992), 110.

7
THEORY-LADEN *SOUFFRANCE*

> Pareillement me sentais-je troublé devant cet étrange règne de la cristallisation qu'est le monde de la pierre. Ici plus rien de la flexibilité de la fleur qui au plus ardu de mes recherches botaniques, fort timidement—d'autant mieux—ne cessa jamais de me rendre courage: 'Aie confiance, ne crains rien, tu es toujours dans la vie, dans l'histoire.'
>
> Proust, ' "L'Affaire Lemoine" par Michelet'

If the story of knowledge traced in the previous chapter is spectacular and revelatory, staging the dramatic tension between archive and aporia and sustained by an intense speculation about sexuality, its resolution is through an entropic narrative of cognition,[1] characterized by loss of energy, increasing disorder, and, above all, the failure of significance. This failure is not the disorder of the aporia, whose energetic opposition to the archive on male homosexuality constantly charges it with the potential for meaning. Rather it is the failure of even this opposition, the failure of questions of sexuality, to signify. As *Albertine disparue* opens, the speculation about Albertine's sexuality has not been resolved, but its irresolvability is no longer meaningful; the conclusion of this volume sees the unwanted revelation of Saint-Loup, blurring and confounding the oppositional schema, signifying only inasmuch as it reinforces the sense of disintegration.

The potential of the homosexual body to endow meaning is lost; in its place the sensitized and suffering body of the narrator becomes central. Whereas knowledge of the homosexual body depends on the visual—hence the series of spectacular revelations—the narrator's body registers affectively, viscerally. The cognitive narrative which results is necessarily entropic: the acute registering of each affect must be followed by a dispersal, a lessening of the pain. At first the narrator attempts to preserve his suffering as a privileged mode of knowing—according to a perverse epistemological hygiene, he must 'garder sa

[1] 'Entropic' is used metaphorically here to suggest the competition between energy and disorder which determines the trajectory of the moralistic discourse in *Albertine disparue*.

souffrance franche' (iv. 13). There is an infusion of the discourses of physiology and epistemology. 'Souffrance' is theory-laden.

The trajectory described by the narrative of *souffrance* moves from charged moments of painful revelation into the negative capability[2] of *Albertine disparue.* Paradoxically, this most maxim-laden, theory-laden of texts is also that in which meaning as such drains away, in which significance is lost. The moralistic discourse becomes prominent at this point because—exceptionally—it has become both the substance, the action of the text, and its commentary. Indeed, physical acts register only for their effect on the mind: the first action of *Albertine disparue* occurs when the narrator stands up—'Je me levai pour ne pas perdre de temps, mais la souffrance m'arrêta: c'était la première fois que je me levais depuis qu'Albertine était partie' (iv. 13) and this minor movement is significant for provoking a new train of speculation. Albertine's disappearance is immediately translated into an energetic and chaotic mode of speculation and generalization; there is no disjunction between past events and commentary, but only layers of commentary and analysis in this direct reportage of the narrator's *souffrance.* As the loss is felt less keenly, so the text moves through crude speculation and generalization to a more sophisticated, but also more subdued, synthetic mode of therapeutic maximizing.

For to describe suffering as theory-laden is to suggest not only the epistemological value which the narrator ascribes to this experience, but also, more simply, to designate the loss of innocence. The disappearance of Albertine revives the Proustian commonplaces. Jealousy, habit, and desire, key terms in what might be called the repertoire of normative Proustian laws, the laws of the passions, are revisited. The narrator recognizes the repetition of laws which he has repeatedly established himself, yet also keenly feels his *souffrance* to be singular and original: 'quelle chose originale, atroce, inconnue, quel mal entièrement nouveau' (iv. 8). This sense of being both outside and inside, at once laying down the law and subject to its forces, results in what Gillian Beer has termed 'a painful play of energies between the scrupulous disclosures of law and the passionate unanswerable needs of human beings'.[3] What makes for the particular acuity of the play in

[2] Keats's term describes the quality which, in his eyes, is most necessary to write 'great literature' (Dec. 1817, letter 22): '*Negative Capability*, that is when man is capable of being in uncertainties, Mysteries, doubts, without any irritable reaching after fact and reason' (*The Letters of John Keats*, ed. M. B. Forman (London: Oxford University Press, 1952), 71). See also Weidlé, *Die Sterblichkeit der Musen*, 262.

[3] Gillian Beer, 'Plot and the Analogy with Science in Later Nineteenth-Century

this instance is the location within one individual of an awareness of the particular and the general. Whereas in Eliot, Hardy, and Zola (the late nineteenth-century novelists analysed by Beer) it falls to the narrator to recognize and describe the laws to which the characters fall victim, Proust's narrator is at once legislator and victim—his story is the story of this awareness.

This, the 'negative capability' of *Albertine disparue*, is both the counterpart and the reversal of the typically Proustian—reversal, that is, of the abundant, synthetic and, most characteristically, metaphor-laden text. *Albertine disparue* might still be qualified as abundant, yet its richness is of a different kind. Maxims proliferate within this middle zone of affects, which is demarcated by the pain of, and subsequent indifference to, the loss of Albertine. 'C'est sans aucun doute dans *Albertine disparue* qu'on rencontre le plus grand nombre de maximes générales, isolables et qui, rassemblées bout à bout, donneraient l'idée la plus complète et la mieux définie du système de Proust.'[4] Crémieux's review suggests the abundance of the Albertine maxims, but not their animation in this now needy relation with the law.

Again, the notion of return is key: the narrator's return to some of the earliest Proustian commonplaces; Proust's return in *Albertine disparue*, the last section of the novel to be reworked before his death, to some of the earliest and most persistent themes of *A la recherche*, notably the 'intermittences du cœur'; our return, in focusing on what has traditionally been read as the most moralistic, or maxim-laden, volume of *A la recherche*, to many of the key questions about 'Proust as *moraliste*' with which this study began, questions which will be revisited now both in the light of the scientific model and as an extension into the arena of affective epistemology described in the previous chapter.

The exclamatory maxim which opens *Albertine disparue* heralds this revisitation of the regulative Proustian commonplaces: 'Comme la souffrance va plus loin en psychologie que la psychologie!' (iv. 3). The repertoire of terms is revised, primarily that of 'l'habitude'. From its introduction in the opening pages of 'Combray', 'habit' has acquired a familiar resonance. Here it emerges as a new force: 'J'avais une telle habitude d'avoir Albertine auprès de moi, et je voyais soudain un nouveau visage de l'Habitude.' The capitalization informs the melodramatic and aesthetic language of the subsequent clauses, as they

Novelists', in *Comparative Criticism*, ed. E. Shaffer (Cambridge: Cambridge University Press, 1980), 136.

[4] Crémieux, 'Nouveauté d'*Albertine disparue*', 217.

seek to redefine the originality of this familiar concept. The narrator claims that he had always considered habit to be 'un pouvoir annihilateur qui supprime l'originalité et jusqu'à la conscience des perceptions' (iv. 4), a normative definition which is refashioned to particularize and visualize the latent personification—Habit becomes a vengeful goddess whose powers exceed the distillation of any maxim; this 'divinité redoutable', once encrusted in the narrator's heart, now tears itself away. In this inauguration of a new negative abundance, the narrator is 'fécondé par le chagrin' (iv. 495).

The initial maxim 'Comme la souffrance va plus loin en psychologie que la psychologie!' is preceded by the exclamation 'Mademoiselle Albertine est partie!' This, the trigger to *Albertine disparue*, echoes throughout the opening section of the novel.[5] And just as here it is paired with what might be termed a sloganistic maxim, so in the following pages generalizing sentences are pared down, strengthened, repeated. These formulations, pronounced with both bravado and neediness, are in turn indicative of the maxim's fall from grace, the debilitation of the sententious discourse. For the narrator has become a 'petit corps féminin', the particular suffering individual who at once feels the law's force and struggles to regain the power to enunciate and reformulate it. The argument that 'l'intelligence n'est pas l'instrument le plus subtil, le plus puissant, le plus approprié pour saisir le vrai' (iv. 7) is, for example, abbreviated to 'C'est la foi expérimentale' (and simply 'Foi expérimentale' in the Laget edition, p. 347). Albertine's flight becomes 'Fugitive parce que reine, c'est ainsi' (iv. 9), while the passage describing the reduction of Albertine to nothing more than a name concludes with a cluster of striking, emblematic phrases: 'Proportions minuscules de la figure de la femme, effet logique et nécessaire de la façon dont l'amour se développe, claire allégorie de la nature subjective de cet amour' (iv. 17). These phrases might be read as the shorthand jottings of the *moraliste*, who, weary of his formulations, does not have the energy or the belief to expound his theory on the nature of love at length yet again. In fact, they conclude a passage which both performs and describes the process of condensation. The narrator claims that he can no longer visualize Albertine, that she is reduced simply to a name which he can do

[5] Terdiman notes the development of this phrase: 'the repetition and progressive modification of the obsessional sentence whose primitive, paradigmatic form we have already seen at the heart of the crisis: "Albertine est morte", which re-echoes twelve times in the twenty pages following its first appearance, and ten times more in the remaining sixty pages' (*Dialectics of Isolation*, 208).

nothing but repeat; and this monotonous cry transforms him into a mythological bird, 'un oiseau pareil à celui de la fable dont le cri redisait sans fin le nom de celle qu'homme, il avait aimée' (iv. 16). The transitional generalization of this experience, 'On se le dit et, comme on le tait' (iv. 16), takes us inside the mind to find nothing but a wall scrawled over and over again with Albertine's name. Albertine has disappeared ('je n'apercevais pas son corps'), the repetition of her name is '[un] besoin sans cesse renaissant, mais à la longue, une fatigue', and the narrator's suffering is relocated in habit and habit broken. The sequence of maxims which allows this, most Proustian of conclusions is itself reformulated to settle on the emblematic phrases quoted above, as if the narrator cannot quite bear the reduction of his singular suffering to the commonplace.

The mobile and synthetic qualities of this passage are exemplary of the negative abundance of *Albertine disparue*, and stand in sharp contrast to the crude, self-deluding analysis which is the narrator's immediate response to Albertine's departure. Such analysis is often given in the present tense, and is pared down by virtue of its simple syntax—many sentences consist of a single main clause—and conversational style, as in the reading of Albertine's letter. The conclusions reached in this mode are similarly simplistic; taking Swann and Odette's relationship as his model, the narrator sees Albertine's flight as blackmail. But for the most part these are only the initial stages of what will become a far more complex analysis. The passage following directly on from Albertine's letter, for example, reports the narrator's response in the present tense—'Tout cela ne signifie rien me dis-je' (iv. 5)—and, comically, his decision to lure her back with gifts of a Rolls-Royce and a yacht. In the edition established by Laget, this episode reads as a parody of the hyper-speculative imagination (*La Fugitive*, 345–6).[6] The narrator surmises that this vast expense would deplete his resources, such that after some years he would be forced to commit suicide. The transition from present to past tense—'C'est la décision que je pris' (ibid.)—marks the beginning of a different train of speculation. The subsequent maxims and analyses focus on the loss not of Albertine, but of the self. The narrator's death is figured as stasis, the specific loss of movement of thought: 'ce serait fini pour moi de penser toutes ces choses qui défilaient sans cesse dans mon esprit', and 'ma pensée s'arrêterait pour toujours' (ibid.). From economic abundance and the promise of recovering Albertine there is a transi-

[6] See discussion in Ch. 1, p. 29.

tion to a sense of mourning for the self. Projecting the inevitable loss of such speculation and theorizing about Albertine, here the (absent) topic of this rhetorical performance about loss is to project the self as an 'appareil vide'. Suffering must be preserved, habit warded off, if this new, privileged relation with the law is to be maintained. The narrator not only intends to respect the originality of his suffering, he wishes to 'garder sa souffrance franche' and 'se coucher avec sa douleur' (iv. 13). And this momentary falling away, the fear that, once 'souffrance' subsides, there will be nothing more to be said, haunts *Albertine disparue I*.

The stabilization of response as the narrator assimilates knowledge of Albertine's departure allows a return from emblem and exclamation to the more characteristic synthetic mode, and exempla and metaphors are reintroduced. The accumulated perceptions, sensations, and memories around Albertine also suggest the accumulation of analysis, image and example, which now cluster around the original experience of loss:

> Bref Albertine n'était, comme une pierre autour de laquelle il a neigé, que le centre générateur d'une immense construction qui passait par le plan de mon cœur. Robert, pour qui était invisible toute cette stratification de sensations, ne saisissait qu'un résidu qu'elle m'empêchait au contraire d'apercevoir. (iv. 22)

These two sentences introduce a passage which explores the commonplace 'love is blind', itself a subset of the repeatedly established Proustian law that vision by its very nature is subjective and distorts. The digressive exploration of the topic is triggered by Saint-Loup's disappointed reaction to Albertine's photograph, his surprise that such a woman could have caused so much suffering. In a relaxed, discursive style, the narrator works through and dismisses various commonplace maxims on the nature of love, to reach the key formulation for this passage. The change in style is dramatic. Where before we would have expected an emblematic statement, here the maxim unfolds gradually through striking imagery, as if still exploring its own implications. The lover's perception is distorted by the accumulation of sensation around the woman, and this accumulation is described as 'l'énorme œuf douloureux qui l'engaine', an image which by its compression brings together the botanical ('engainé' suggests the sheath around a plant shoot or stem) and the mammalian to suggest a desire at once maternal and predatory. To supplement this image, the woman is compared to a fountain covered in snow, and finally (but still within the same sentence) the lover's perception is described as 'aussi loin du point où les autres le voient qu'est loin le soleil véritable de l'endroit où sa lumière condensée nous le fait apercevoir dans le ciel'. The following sentences are composed of discursive generalizations expanding the theme: hidden by the distortions of the lover's gaze, 'la chrysalide de douleurs et de tendresses', the woman is changing, 'les pires métamorphoses de l'être aimé'. To illustrate such a 'différence d'optique', the narrator draws examples from previous narratives (iv. 23)—Odette's cruel significance for Swann as contrasted with her appearance as the 'dame en rose' for the narrator's great-uncle; the narrator's own view of 'Rachel quand du seigneur', Saint-Loup's mistress—and even projects his own experience as a future such example in this category. Whereas Swann's life is seen as the classic example of this law—'Cette dissemblance, toute la vie d'un amant . . . toute la vie d'un Swann la prouvent' (iv. 24)—Elstir's love for Odette offers, quite literally, the most striking illustration—'que l'amant se double d'un peintre comme Elstir et alors le mot de l'énigme est proféré, vous avez enfin sous les yeux ces lèvres que le vulgaire n'a jamais aperçues dans cette femme' (ibid.). The language of optics enables the intellectual gymnastics ('par une gymnastique inverse') of this digression. There is an occasional intrusion of physiological terminology, reminding us of the particularity of the narrator's *souffrance*: Albertine has become the narrator's 'apport cardiaque et mental' (iv. 24); his suffering is 'vibratile' (iv. 23), a term most often found in biology to describe whatever can be set in vibration—namely, the cilia of protozoa and of course infusoria—but also according to late nineteenth-century medical usage 'se dit d'une douleur dans laquelle il semble au malade que ses nerfs sont en vibration'.[7] Yet the digression is largely unaffected by these intrusions, and continues to assimilate the narrator's story as yet another example of the archetypal lover's experience. A description of how Albertine's appearance has changed slips through a subordinate clause from the particular to the general: 'et cela suffit; ce qu'on aime est trop dans le passé . . .'. The passage again attempts to conclude by paring itself down, emblematizing the woman as 'ce signe où se résume la personnalité permanente d'une femme, cet extrait algébrique, cette constante' (iv. 24); but this is belied by the syntax of the reinstated synthetic mode. For this conclusion is expressed in a single sentence of approximately twenty lines, which moves from the particular, the

[7] See entry for 'vibratile' in the *Larousse grand dictionnaire*.

narrator's experience of Albertine, through the pivotal clause 'et cela suffit', to a series of maxims which crystallize as a *caractère* in the style of La Bruyère ('cela suffit pour qu'un homme attendu dans le plus grand monde . . .' (iv. 24)).

The generalizing force of this passage is dependent on a number of recurrent strategies: textual example (drawing on past case histories), 'fictional' example, the *caractère*, sententious discourse, emblematic image, and mythology (Albertine as Helen of Troy). Such references to Greek myth may be slight, and often parodic, yet the perspective of literary generality which they offer has the effect of grounding *A la recherche* in the archetypal stories of the passions. Maximizing has resumed its therapeutic function, 'que penser d'une façon générale, qu'écrire, est pour l'écrivain une fonction saine et nécessaire dont l'accomplissement rend heureux' (iv. 480–1), and by *Le Temps retrouvé*, even *souffrance* will be mythologized: 'Les chagrins sont des serviteurs obscurs, détestés, contre lesquels on lutte, sous l'empire de qui on tombe de plus en plus, des serviteurs atroces, impossibles à remplacer et qui par des voies souterraines nous mènent à la vérité et à la mort' (iv. 488).

Souffrance emerges from these readings of *Albertine disparue* as theory-laden, not only because it entails a revisiting of the Proustian commonplaces, but also as key to the text's narration and conceptualization of knowledge. *Souffrance* is part of the theory of affective epistemology which was traced in the previous chapter, and which Proust develops as the 'intermittences du cœur'.

The 'intermittences du cœur' is a memory of the sensitized and suffering body, or, as the narrator more elliptically relates, 'aux troubles de la mémoire sont liées les intermittences du cœur' (iii. 153). Intermittence represents the counterpart of 'mémoire involontaire'. Both types of memory are involuntary; both result from physical memory—that is, the physical recall of a sensation. This characteristic is the marker of their truth, of the aesthetic truth of the former, the epistemological truth of the latter. Both require translation. 'Je retrouvais dans un souvenir involontaire et complet la réalité vivante. Cette réalité n'existe pas pour nous tant qu'elle n'a pas été recréée par notre pensée' (iii. 153) is the narrator's reaction, not, as one might expect, to involuntary memory, but to the first experience of intermittence. These two styles of involuntary memory seem to be distinguishable only by their effect, whether they cause pain or pleasure. Intermittence occurs only twice in the course of the novel, both instances are in *Sodome et Gomorrhe* (iii. 152–60, the death of the grandmother; iii. 497–515, the revelation of Albertine and Montjouvain); but it will be seen that the *modus operandi* and, indeed the slogan for the Albertine texts which are, as it were, written under the auspices of intermittence, is *souffrance*.

The opposition between 'mémoire involontaire' and 'intermittence', between aesthetics and epistemology, was discussed by Proust when, in 1915, his friend André Foucart, whom he consulted for information on science, wrote an 'essai' imitating the madeleine episode, but in which the sensation triggering involuntary recall is painful, not pleasurable. Proust wrote to Foucart and thanked him for what he terms an analytical masterpiece, 'ce chef-d'œuvre d'analyse'.[8] The timing of this exchange, after the publication of *Du côté de chez Swann* (1913) and some time before the publication in 1922 of *Sodome et Gomorrhe II*, is such that Foucart would have been unaware of the 'intermittences du cœur' schema.

'Ce qui fait *l'originalité absolue* de votre étude, et c'est à mon avis un peu *son défaut*, c'est que la sensation est une *douleur*' (emphasis added). Proust points out that what distinguishes his work from Foucart's is that the madeleine–tilleul moment is not simply pleasurable but is '[un] plaisir d'un ordre assez profond', or 'la béatitude': this mode of involuntary memory has intellectual value 'avec les vues qu'il ouvrira sur des choses assez importantes', but does not risk becoming 'un simple exercice d'adresse et de dissection'. Proust's subsequent backtracking for fear of offending Foucart is more revealing than this rather weak defence of his own work. Of course, he counters, he is not suggesting that Foucart's piece is simply a sterile work of analysis; nor is the analysis of pain in any way lesser than that of pleasure: in fact, the reverse is true: 'Je crois même exactement le contraire, parce que je crois que nous mettons hélas plus de nous-même dans la souffrance et qu'ainsi l'analyse y trouve une substance plus riche, des vérités plus essentielles (et encore pour d'autres raisons).'

Proust's conclusion, that Foucart's essay is 'autre chose que la mienne et en son genre, un indispensable modèle', is the nearest he gets to admitting that he had long since devised his own counterpart to 'mémoire involontaire'. Indeed, the hesitancy, and even caginess, of his reaction to Foucart's work suggests that Proust was still working through the implications of these styles of memory triggered by pain and pleasure: the working note, 'Travail: recherche de ce qu'il y a de

[8] Letter of 18 Nov. 1915, in *Correspondance*, xxi. 665–6.

profond dans le plaisir', is already made in the *Carnet de 1908*.[9] What is clear is Proust's acknowledgement of 'intermittence': that is, of the intellectual value of an involuntary memory whose trigger is pain. The parenthetical and enigmatic 'et encore pour d'autres raisons' suggests Proust's indecision at this stage as to how the competing and contrasting schemas of 'intermittence' and 'mémoire involontaire' should be resolved.

'Les Intermittences du cœur' was in 1912 proposed as the title for the novel as a whole. But, as Antoine Compagnon's analysis of the genesis of *Sodome et Gomorrhe* indicates, the term itself dates back to the very earliest drafts of *A la recherche*, pre-dating the aesthetic theory of involuntary memory: 'Quelques notations autobiographiques du Carnet 1, dès ses premiers feuillets du début de 1908, avant l'essai sur Sainte-Beuve et la définition de la mémoire involontaire comme théorie du roman, annonçaient le thème des "intermittences du cœur" ' (iii. 1227). By the 1912 drafts, these 'intermittences' constitute the second element of what Compagnon designates as 'le jeu de la sensualité et du sentiment de culpabilité' (iii. 1231). In this instance the elements of 'le jeu' are the narrator's mourning for his grandmother—he dreams of her during a trip to Italy—and his desire and pursuit of the Baronne Putbus's 'femme de chambre'. After the war, Proust redistributes this material. Albertine replaces the 'femme de chambre', but this results in a cross-over between the 'jeu' and the oppositional schema of 'Sodome et Gomorrhe'—the revelation of her link with Montjouvain—which is figured as a second instance of 'intermittence'. The narrator's second stay at Balbec is effectively framed by chapters which in his 1918 plan, published in the first edition of *A l'ombre des jeunes filles* (see iii. 1233), Proust entitles 'Les Intermittences du cœur I' and 'II'.[10] The simple play-off between guilt and sensuality has been replaced by a sequential patterning whose significance is more difficult to determine. By the publication of *Sodome et Gomorrhe* the markers of the 1918 plan have disappeared: the first chapter has been reduced to the final subsection of *Sodome et Gomorrhe II, III*; the second is no longer a chapter, nor is it named as an instance

[9] Proust, *Le Carnet de 1908*, ed. P. Kolb (Paris: Gallimard, 1976), 64.

[10] In a letter to Lionel Hauser of 28 Apr. 1918 (*Correspondance*, xvii. letter 83) Proust rejects the former's theory that physical and mental good health are prerequisites for genius, claiming that, on the contrary, this has become the function of sickness: 'Je ne sais plus si c'est Bergson ou Boutroux qui a dit que le roseau pensant ploie encore plus sous le poids de la pensée que sous le poids de la matière. Mais je crois que, ne fût-ce que par la valeur créatrice de la souffrance, la maladie physique est (dans nos jours dégénérés) presque une condition de la force intellectuelle un peu géniale' (p. 215).

of 'intermittence' (whether as the title of a subsection or during the course of the episode itself). The genesis of the 'intermittences' is one of gradual effacement from the surface of the text. What remain are the strong structural and internal links between the episodes: structural simply in that they open and close the stay at Balbec, internal in that the two 'intermittences' are interpreted by the narrator as causally linked, the recall of Montjouvain being specifically referred to as a punishment for the death of the grandmother. Repetition allows the 'intermittences' to signify.

A similar process of effacement is evident in Proust's rejection of his 'titre primitif', 'Les Intermittences du cœur', in favour of *A la recherche du temps perdu*. The following letter to Bernard Grasset explains the decision:

Ce changement vient de ce que dans l'intervalle j'ai vu annoncé un livre de M. Binet Valmer intitulé *le Cœur en désordre*. Or cela doit être une allusion au même état morbide qui caractérise les cœurs intermittents. Je réserverai à un simple chapitre du deuxième volume le titre: *Les intermittences du cœur*.[11]

Proust's anxiety draws attention to two rather different aspects: the first is simply to do with originality—the provisional title sounds too close to that already chosen by Binet-Valmer. But the second, the claim that both refer to the 'même état morbide', seems less plausible. Proust's title suggests a play with medical terminology, which the more romantic 'cœur en désordre' does not. 'Morbide' is the key here, when read not as relating to a medical condition, but as abnormal or unhealthy in the decadent sense of 'littérature morbide'. Proust had already attempted to distance his work from Binet-Valmer's when, during his attempts to find an editor the previous year, he alerted Gaston Gallimard to the possibility that those parts of *A la recherche* which portray homosexuality might cause offence, but stressed that it was still far from falling into the category of a 'monographie spéciale comme le *Lucien* de Binet-Valmer par exemple'.[12]

Paradoxically, a closer verbal echo of Proust's 'intermittences du cœur' is Maeterlinck's usage of the simple 'intermittences'. Maeterlinck does not propose 'intermittences' as a title, but coins the term in his essay 'L'Immortalité', and, as Compagnon indicates (iii. 1432), his usage has clear parallels with Proust's: 'On dirait que les fonctions de cet organe par quoi nous goûtons la vie et la rapportons à nous-

[11] Letter after mid-May 1913, *Correspondance*, xii. 177. See also Proust's letter to Louis de Robert, July 1913, ibid. xii. letter 103.

[12] Letter shortly after 6 Nov. 1912, ibid. xi. 287.

mêmes, sont intermittentes, et que la présence de notre moi, excepté dans la douleur, n'est qu'une suite rapide et perpétuelle de départs et de retours.'[13] 'L'Immortalité' was published in *L'Intelligence des fleurs*, one of the key texts consulted by Proust for the botanical model of *Sodome et Gomorrhe*. Ironically, Proust rejects the Binet-Valmer link for fear that *A la recherche* might be seen as just another book about homosexuality, yet his subsequent reading and reworking of *L'Intelligence des fleurs* will effectively knit the text back into the most spectacular instance of homosexuality in the novel, *Sodome et Gomorrhe I*. The complexity of these rejections and reworkings is compounded by the timing of Proust's letter to Grasset; his refutation of the 'cœur en désordre'–homosexuality link occurs before the insertion in 1915 of the Montjouvain–Albertine recognition, the second 'intermittence' which will reveal Albertine's possible homosexuality.

The complex genesis of the 'intermittences', sketched here only in part (a comprehensive account is given in Antoine Compagnon's introduction to *Sodome et Gomorrhe*, iii. 1185–261), is revealing for the ever-increasing density of homosexual reference and the interweaving of this into the original schema of the 'intermittences du cœur'. For while intermittence may be described as a 'theme', dating back to the conception of *A la recherche* and becoming less significant as the novel develops, it also originates and persists as a structuring device, or, as I have termed it here, a 'schema'. As the text grows, so new schemas are devised to shape and dramatize, sometimes to narrate (Proust at one stage envisages his novel as a sequence of mornings, at another as a sequence of stops on a train journey), often to conceptualize; hence the oppositional pairs: the two 'côtés', Swann and Guermantes, Sodom and Gomorrah. The evolution of these schemas is such that the revelation of Albertine–Montjouvain signifies both as part of the oppositional pairing of Sodom and Gomorrah and as part of the sequential 'intermittences du cœur'. Occurring at a point of interference between these two schemas, which represent the epistemological and the affective, the connection of Albertine with Montjouvain is at once a revelation and a moment of painful recall. The patterns of interference are key, for it is here that the language of affects, of physiology and epistemology intersects with—indeed, is described as causally related to—the representation of homosexuality. As the double meaning of the 'état morbide' suggests, homosexuality might signify on the side of decadence or physiology. The following

[13] Maeterlinck, *L'Intelligence des fleurs*, 290.

close readings of the 'intermittences', how they relate to each other and subsequently to *Albertine disparue*, will develop the concept of an affective epistemology, to consider the style and significance of the body's suffering.

'Bouleversement de toute ma personne' (iii. 152). The syntactical effect of this first intermittence is startling. There is no introduction, no explanation, no verb, just this signal of the abrupt shift from the narrator's arrival at Balbec to the heart of this painful recall. The narrative which then follows describes, not the 'intermittence du cœur' itself, but a 'crise de fatigue cardiaque' (later, Albertine will be described as an 'apport cardiaque et mental' (iv. 24)). Attempting to suppress his pain, the narrator bends over to take off his shoes. This action provokes the 'intermittence': 'His life is switched over to another line and proceeds, without any solution of continuity, from that remote moment of his past when his grandmother stooped over his distress.'[14] Just as the narration of the instances of involuntary memory plays on the disparity between the overwhelming experience of recall and the triviality of its cause—cake dunked in tea, say, or tripping on an uneven paving stone—so here there is a disparity between the simple action of taking off shoes and the immense pain of recall, the resurrection of the narrator's grandmother. Beckett (whose *En attendant Godot* opens with Estragon's painful and painfully tragicomic attempts to remove his shoes) considered this first 'intermittence' 'perhaps the greatest passage that Proust ever wrote'.[15]

'Les intermittences du cœur . . . [font] allusion dans le monde moral à une maladie du corps.'[16] As Proust's elliptical definition suggests, the 'intermittences' are marked from the outset by a confusion of the physiological and the psychological, of body and mind, in which the only constant is pain. Memory is not registered externally, visually, but is inhaled: 'ma poitrine s'enfla, remplie d'une présence inconnue, divine' (iii. 152–3). The tears which the narrator now weeps, saving him from 'la sécheresse de l'âme', echo the 'watering' and flowering of the dessicated lime-flowers in that initial instance of involuntary memory. The 'intermittences' too are contingent: the 'cadre de sensations'—in this case a moment of distress and fatigue similar to that experienced during his first visit to Balbec—summons up a past self. Where the expansive plenitude of 'mémoire involontaire' allows both

[14] Beckett, *Proust*, 27.
[15] Ibid. 25.
[16] Letter to Eugène Fasquelle, 28 Oct. 1912, ibid. xi. 257.

a resurrection of, and escape from, the self, here the sense of plenitude is felt tightly against the confines of the body, and the experience of recovery entails a recognition of loss: 'Je ne faisais que de le découvrir parce que je venais, en la sentant [ma grand-mère] pour la première fois, vivante, véritable, gonflant mon cœur à le briser, en la retrouvant enfin, d'apprendre que je l'avais perdue pour toujours' (iii. 154–5). 'Aux troubles de la mémoire sont liées les intermittences du cœur' (iii. 153). The 'intermittences du cœur' allow an escape from time, but, rather than leading into the full and mobile world of involuntary memory, they result in a blocked and recurrent repetition: 'aussitôt que j'avais revécu, comme présente, cette félicité, la sentir traversée par la certitude, s'élançant comme une douleur physique à répétition, d'un néant qui avait effacé mon image de cette tendresse, qui avait détruit cette existence' (iii. 155). Now it could be argued (as Compagnon does, iii. 1227) that these 'intermittences' are the negative counterpart of involuntary memory because they are never 'sublimated'; in other words, the narrator does not attempt to derive from them an aesthetic theory. And yet, at the end of this first 'intermittence', the narrator is already recognizing not its aesthetic but its epistemological potential, respecting 'l'originalité de ma souffrance', desiring to be subject to its laws:

> Si ce peu de vérité je pouvais jamais l'*extraire*, ce ne pourrait être que d'elle, si *particulière*, si *spontanée*, qui n'avait été ni tracée par mon intelligence, ni infléchie ni atténuée par ma pusillanimité, mais que la mort elle-même, *la brusque révélation de la mort, avait comme la foudre creusée en moi*, selon un graphique surnaturel, inhumain, *comme un double et mystérieux sillon.* (iii. 156, emphasis added)

This is no sublimation towards metaphor and style, the laws of aesthetics; but it describes that moment at which the narrator enters the arena, at which a breach is made in the world of habit, and habitual thought no longer provides immunity against the real. This revelation, as do those pertaining to Albertine–Montjouvain, brings with it a desire to interpret, to 'extraire la vérité'. Unlike the Albertine revelation, however, no speculation is involved: the 'truth' which the narrator wants to extract is simply the experience of loss, his grandmother's death.

The conclusion of this episode is not couched in the high language of epistemology, aesthetics, or ethics, but is expressed as the sentimental desire that the narrator might be reunited with his grandmother in heaven. Yet the narrator imagines this meeting as curiously indirect, mediated through the 'cloison', that thin dividing wall which separated him from his grandmother at Balbec, and on which he would knock to signal his *souffrance* and his need of her. In other words, the narrator remembers a form of suffering which might be communicated and alleviated. Now that his grandmother has gone, suffering simply registers. Indeed, the narrator's body absorbs past selves and others such that they become difficult to distinguish: 'cette souffrance de son cœur ou plutôt du mien; car comme les morts n'existent plus qu'en nous, c'est nous-mêmes que nous frappons sans relâche quand nous nous obstinons à nous souvenir des coups que nous leur avons assenés' (iii. 156). No longer a mode of communication, suffering is internalized as a violence done to the self. The 'trois petits coups' have become a 'douleur physique à répétition'.

Kaufmann's reading of Proust's correspondence is illuminating on this question of the resonance of suffering: ' "I cause suffering, therefore I am"—Proust loses, with his mother, the depository of his own pain, the possibility of finding and knowing himself through the pain he causes her . . . Thus, long before Albertine, suffering is the fugitive in Proust's life. He is constantly *A la recherche de la douleur perdue*.'[17] Once suffering ceases to signify as a means of communication, it has to signify differently; such is Marcel's recognition at the loss of his grandmother, for his suffering no longer resonates, whether through the 'cloison' or as the reflection of pain and sympathy on the faces of another, but is internalized. The narrator's Baudelairean response to this painfully internalized memory—'que s'enfonçassent plus solidement encore en moi ces clous qui y rivaient sa mémoire'—subsequently finds release in the hyperbolic imagery of the second intermittence, in which *souffrance* is projected on to the spectacle of the rising sun:

> Le sanglant sacrifice que j'allais avoir à faire de toute joie, chaque matin, jusqu'à la fin de ma vie, renouvellement solennellement célébré à chaque aurore de mon chagrin quotidien et du sang de ma plaie, l'œuf d'or du soleil, comme propulsé par la rupture d'équilibre qu'amènerait au moment de la coagulation un changement de densité, barbelé de flammes comme dans les tableaux, creva d'un bond le rideau derrière lequel on le sentait depuis un moment frémissant et prêt à entrer en scène et à s'élancer, et dont il effaça sous des flots de lumière la pourpre mystérieuse et figée. (iii. 512–13)

Whereas the corporeal internalization of the first 'intermittence' is

[17] Kaufmann, *Post Scripts*, 140.

mapped as a visceral landscape, 'pour y parcourir les artères de la cité souterraine, nous nous sommes embarqués sur les flots noirs de notre propre sang' (iii. 157), the suffering of the second is wide-ranging, mobile: 'C'était une *terra incognita* terrible où je venais d'atterrir, une phase nouvelle de souffrances insoupçonnées qui s'ouvrait' (iii. 500). But the release is only partial: Montjouvain is described as visually superimposed on the Balbec seascape, Albertine is both outside and inside the narrator: 'les mots: "Cette amie, c'est Mlle Vinteuil" avaient été le Sésame, que j'eusse été incapable de trouver moi-même, qui avait fait entrer Albertine dans la profondeur de mon cœur déchiré' (iii. 512). The narrator has in a sense become the 'cloison', the register of his own suffering. The projection of this *souffrance* on to an apocalyptic sunrise is followed by the simple statement 'I could hear myself crying', as if the narrator were looking back at himself as part of the same spectacle. The 'intermittence' which resurrects Montjouvain allows the partial release of the internalized *souffrance* of the first episode, and allows the narrator's suffering to signify again through the speculation which was the subject of the previous chapter.

Souffrance, not 'intermittence', opens *Albertine disparue*: but it is a suffering which the narrator is careful to qualify as 'mon chagrin, le chagrin qui n'est nullement une conclusion pessimiste librement tirée d'un ensemble de circonstances funestes, mais la reviviscence intermittente et involontaire d'une impression spécifique, venue du dehors, et que nous n'avons pas choisie' (iv. 14), for this volume describes the third and final section of the 'intermittences' sequence. 'La réalité qui s'imposait à moi m'était aussi nouvelle que celle en face de quoi nous mettent la découverte d'un physicien' (iv. 7); Albertine's departure is revelatory, because it signifies as part of the affective-epistemological mode—'quelle chose originale, atroce, inconnue, quel mal entièrement nouveau' (iv. 8), exclaims the narrator. The style of the revelation is violently abrupt.[18] Crystallization is the metaphor which describes the process; the revelation is 'dure, éclatante, étrange, comme un sel cristallisé, par la brusque réaction de la douleur' (iv. 4). Stendhal's metaphor, 'Ce que j'appelle cristallisation, c'est l'opération de l'esprit, qui tire de tout ce qui se présente la découverte que l'objet aimé a de nouvelles perfections',[19] is reworked here to describe not the

[18] 'Proust's meaning does not emerge from the slowly "dawning consciousness" which always announces psychological revelation in the Realists. The movement in *La Fugitive* is violent, primitive' (Terdiman, *Dialectics of Isolation*, 200).

[19] Stendhal, *De l'amour* (1st pub. 1822, Paris: Garnier Flammarion, 1965), 35. See

cumulative crystallization of love, but the experience of loss as the sudden precipitation of a crystal from a supersaturated solution. The revelation is also described as a process of condensation, and these metaphors are matched by the new necessity and energy with which maxims are formulated. Yet the revelation does not yield elucidation, but simply a return to an old habit of a different kind. The well-worn hypothetical mode, which the narrator is already tentatively revisiting in the opening pages of *Albertine disparue*, interrupts the present-tense speculation that Albertine's departure is a sign of her impatience to be married:

> C'est cela l'intention de son acte, me disait ma raison compatissante; mais je sentais qu'en me le disant ma raison se plaçait toujours dans la même hypothèse qu'elle avait adoptée depuis le début. Or je sentais bien que c'était l'autre hypothèse qui n'avait jamais cessé d'être vérifiée. (iv. 6)

The loss of Albertine, described as 'entièrement nouveau', leads back into the blocked speculation about her sexuality. For, where *Sodome et Gomorrhe I* is experimental and richly imaged, described coyly by the voyeuristic narrator, here the revolution is internal, the narrator physically implicated in his experience of law. 'Le sillon de la foudre' (iv. 8) is an exact verbal echo of the effect of the first 'intermittence du cœur': 'la brusque révélation de la mort, avait comme la foudre creusée en moi, selon un graphique surnaturel, inhumain, comme un double et mystérieux sillon' (iii. 156). Still the narrator clings to 'l'originalité de ma souffrance', again he fails to make this suffering signify other than through the spectacle of his own suffering body, on which the 'sillon de la foudre' is scored. Physical action in *Albertine disparue I* is delegated to other characters; the narrator's body serves simply to register loss. There is no coy reaching for possible models, and under the force of the present, the only representation is a direct reportage of the mourning self, until the synthetic mode is reinstated, and the narrator returns to those 'éléments connus', the repetitions and commonplaces of the archetypal lover's experience.

For here the loss of Albertine is simply that: experienced in time rather than lifted out of it through involuntary memory. *Albertine disparue* narrates the process of mourning, of coming to terms with the loss, not of Albertine, but of that mode in which suffering can signify.

also Virtanen on crystallization in *A la recherche* as picturing 'those sudden shifts in human behaviour which seem inexplicable but are actually the result of a slow accumulation of silently working causes' ('Proust's Metaphors', 1041).

Les liens entre un être et nous n'existent que dans notre pensée. La mémoire en s'affaiblissant les relâche, et, malgré l'illusion dont nous voudrions être dupes et dont, par amour, par amitié, par politesse, par respect humain, par devoir, nous dupons les autres, nous existons seuls. L'homme est l'être qui ne peut sortir de soi, qui ne connaît les autres qu'en soi, et, en disant le contraire, ment. Et j'aurais eu si peur, si on avait été capable de le faire, qu'on m'otât ce besoin d'elle, que je me persuadais qu'il était précieux pour ma vie. (iv. 34)

This extract concludes a passage which both describes and enacts the dangers of an excess of therapeutic maxims. The narrator has claimed that the loss of Albertine means that every sensation, whether internal or external, is linked with her. This statement triggers a series of reflections which speak of the experience of loss, of desire, of satisfaction, resulting in a concentrated local instance of the meditation on these topics which constitutes *Albertine disparue.* But, by the final maxim, 'L'homme est l'être . . .', a point of such solipsism has been reached that the original stimulus to this theorizing—that is, the painful sensation of loss—has disappeared, and indifference threatens. For if there is no desire left, there is no novel, only a single master maxim—and this dead point triggers a reflex from fear at the loss of loss, 'Et j'aurais eu si peur', back to narrative, here a narrative of loss and mourning.

No longer recuperable as a story about sexuality, or as a moment of intermittence which would make this loss significant, Albertine's disappearance eludes the schemas whose genesis we traced at the beginning of this section—and while this failure to signify, this non-recuperability might be described as an extension of the process of effacement which is the genesis of the 'intermittences', it is also the logical end-point of this entropic narrative of cognition, which has moved from the initial crystallization of *souffrance* to the synthetic and therapeutic maximizing which subsequently embalms Albertine and becalms the narrator.

The ambivalence which operates more widely in *A la recherche* between what have been tagged Newtonian and Heisenbergian philosophies of science is relinquished in these passages of theory-laden *souffrance* to explore the consequences of an extreme enactment, a caricature even of the latter. The narrator's suffering entails an affective and self-implicating relationship with knowledge, such that the body demands not merely to be taken into account as a factor of distortion, but in which it becomes the only and absolute register of knowledge. The bodies of others—their capacity for suffering, their death even—cease to signify independently; the knowledge gained is burdened with guilt.

J'aurais dû chercher à comprendre son caractère . . . et peut-être . . . j'aurais évité de prolonger, entre nous avec cet acharnement étrange [et mon invariable pressentiment,] ce conflit qui avait amené la mort d'Albertine. Et j'avais alors, avec une grande pitié d'elle, la honte de lui survivre. Il me semblait, en effet, dans les heures où je souffrais le moins, que je bénéficiais en quelque sorte de sa mort, car une femme est d'une plus grande utilité pour notre vie, si elle y est, au lieu d'un élément de bonheur, un instrument de chagrin, et il n'y en a pas une seule dont la possession soit aussi précieuse que celle des vérités qu'elle nous découvre en nous faisant souffrir. Dans ces moments-là, rapprochant la mort de ma grand-mère et celle d'Albertine, il me semblait que ma vie était souillée d'un double assassinat que seule la lâcheté du monde pouvait me pardonner. (iv. 78; in brackets, Laget edn, 402)

This passage hesitates between simply formulating another maxim about knowledge (an anti-feminist maxim about the epistemological value of suffering) and assuming responsibility for the means by which this knowledge is gained—and this hesitation is startling because we have become accustomed to a mode of cognition which is passive and involuntary. The melodramatic language in which the narrator becomes an agent, 'soiled by a double murder', and takes responsibility for his body and actions in the world, breaks through the web of maximizing and speculation, challenges the reader. The abruptness of this challenge marks the degree to which we have become versed in the language of involuntariness—whether it be the involuntariness of knowledge, or the theory-ladenness of *souffrance*—which, in a sense, isolates the body and ultimately releases it, for removing the possibility of volition absolves the narrator of guilt.

For the body is otherwise theory-laden—constructed by the Proustian commonplaces, those fundamental laws of the passions which are established in the opening pages of 'Combray'. These laws, the laws of habit, desire, jealousy, are couched in a physiological vocabulary deriving from the deterministic and analytic language of the passions developed by the *moralistes*. Yet these are not the only laws, and this not the only language, which constructs *souffrance*. The narrator's body is shot through with theories drawn in various scientific languages—the languages of cell biology, chemistry, heredity, botany, and immunology. The body is 'le lieu d'une aussi grande infinité de lois merveilleuses et géniales' (iii. 1269).[20]

[20] Richard W. Saunders's recent study, *Metamorphoses of the Proustian Body* (New York:

Key to this construction is the chemical model of the mind. Memory is initially described as a pharmacy, subsequently as an experimental laboratory: 'car nous trouvons de tout dans notre mémoire: elle est une espèce de pharmacie, de laboratoire de chimie, où on met au hasard la main tantôt sur une drogue calmante, tantôt sur un poison dangereux' (iii. 892). Habit too has a place in this pharmacy of the passions: 'l'habitude abêtissante qui pendant tout le cours de notre vie nous cache à peu près tout l'univers et dans une nuit profonde, sous leur étiquette inchangée, substitue aux poisons les plus dangereux ou les plus enivrants de la vie quelque chose d'anodin qui ne procure pas de délices' (iv. 124). The first experience of involuntary memory is characterized by a sense of expansion and well-being; the dried lime-flowers, prescribed for Aunt Léonie, blossom again, and the narrator exclaims at the 'charmante prodigalité du pharmacien'. In the second instance, the benign authority of the pharmacy is absent; the mind has become a laboratory in which random experiment threatens the therapeutic effects of the drugs it contains. Searching his memory for information about Albertine, the narrator chances on poison.[21]

The key element in the pharmaceutical laboratory is the *tilleul*; there is no equivalent drug for the 'intermittences du cœur'. But if we were to reinvent the Proustian pharmacy, that drug, also a flower, might be the datura.

Datura was the main constituent of the powder regularly burnt and inhaled by Proust to relieve the symptoms of his asthma: 'Qu'elles soient blanches, dorées ou sanguines, les corolles fascinantes des fleurs du datura, les fameuses trompettes des anges, sont aussi belles que sont toxiques ses fruits, qui l'ont fait dénommer par les uns "l'arbre de paradis" et par d'autres "l'herbe du diable ou des sorciers".'[22] Whereas the appearance of the dried lime-flower is unprepossessing, blossoming only once when steeped in water, which releases its curative—and largely sedative—powers, the beauty of the datura belies the poisonous fruit which it produces. Its flowers, when dried, burnt, and

Peter Lang, 1994), analyses the significance of the body in *A la recherche*, but specific attention is not paid to the role of scientific discourse.

[21] This opposition between 'intermittence' and 'mémoire involontaire' is not merely metaphoric. Proust's schema in fact anticipates recent theories of affective and biological modes of memory. See François-Bernard Michel's analysis in *Proust et les écrivains devant la mort*, 71–81.

[22] Ibid. 54–5. Michel documents fully both the drugs and the medical books consumed by Proust.

inhaled, have a terrifying hallucinogenic effect. As the tree of paradise—that is, the tree of knowledge—the datura represents the negative counterpart of the *tilleul*. Éluard described it as the 'flower which dare not speak its name': 'Datura, roi honteux d'avoir / régné sans dire son nom.'[23]

Proust's ritual inhalations of this anti-asthmatic powder would begin as soon as he got up; they took place in the small corridor linking his bedroom to the bathroom. According to Céleste, the inhalations, or 'fumages', lasted up to six or seven hours, and she might even be asked to collect another box of powder, 'alors la chambre était pleine d'une fumée à couper au couteau'; she prepared the 'fumages', but Proust would measure out the powder himself 'pour la doser à sa volonté'. For each inhalation, a new box was opened. According to Céleste, Proust feared that, once opened, the powder could become dusty—although the paper sachet inside the box prevented any risk of this. Consequently, each 'fumage' involved the inhalation of twenty-five times the prescribed amount of powder: 'Avec une boîte, il inhalait d'un coup la fumée de 20 grammes d'extraits de feuilles et 0,75 gramme de fruits, soit 135 mg d'alcaloïdes. Les toxicologues sont formels: à cette dose, on n'échappe pas aux effets toxiques.'[24] The effects of such intoxication—and Proust favoured the Legras powder, the most concentrated in datura—include intellectual excitation resulting in sensory hallucinations, a disorientation in time and space, euphoria or attacks of anxiety and depression, dilation of the pupils disturbing vision, an abnormally rapid heartbeat, loss of muscular strength, and dizziness leading to loss of muscular co-ordination.

In *A la recherche* the datura is classified as a sleep-inducing drug: 'le jardin réservé où croissent comme des fleurs inconnues les sommeils si différents les uns des autres, sommeil du datura, du chanvre indien, des mutiples extraits de l'éther, sommeil de la belladone, de l'opium, de la valériane' (ii. 385–6). This classification forms part of an extensive digressive and speculative passage on sleep, memory, and dreams, of which the guiding maxim is: 'Il en est du sommeil comme de la perception du monde extérieur. Il suffit d'une modification dans nos habitudes pour le rendre poétique' (ii. 384). These flowers are not burnt and inhaled; they are touched and made to blossom, in the fashion of the 'tilleul', only then releasing the 'arôme de leurs rêves particuliers' for the 'inconnu prédestiné'. This is not the desperate

[23] Paul Éluard, cited in Michel, 56. [24] Ibid. 58.

recourse of the invalid; 'prédestiné' has far happier and, indeed, aesthetic associations with, for example, the meeting of Charlus and Jupien ('profondément sélectionné' (iii. 29)), and of course with the occurrence of 'mémoire involontaire' itself.

Moreover, both the drugs of the 'jardin réservé' and the narrator's sleep itself are described through botanical imagery. Like the chemical model of the mind, the botanical model suggests that the body is always passive, simply the place in which reactions and metamorphoses occur, in which laws may be observed, and, at most, in which experimentation may be conducted. Here the narrator's sleep mimes the characteristics of the drug; he becomes plant-like: 'je me sentais attaché à un sol invisible et profond par les articulations, que la fatigue me rendait sensibles, de radicelles musculeuses et nourricières', deeply and physically embedded in the ground of memory, 'là où nos muscles plongent et tordent leurs ramifications et aspirent la vie nouvelle, le jardin où nous avons été enfant' (ii. 390). And the analysis of these deep-rooted physical memories is compared to an archaeological excavation.

Whereas the *souffrance* of the 'intermittences' schema is seen to have epistemological value, throwing the narrator into a conflictual relationship with the world and demanding to be interpreted, the laws of science through which the body is also constructed are not subject to such scrutiny. Yet there is an anxiety that, however potent these laws might appear, the body should not be trapped in the deterministic languages of science. Whereas the ancestral and homosexual bodies of others—namely, the Guermantes—may be thus determined, the narrator's body is traversed but not pinned down in this way. The claims made for a visceral memory of the body in the passage cited above are immediately covered by the proviso: 'Mais on verra combien certaines impressions fugitives et fortuites ramènent bien mieux encore vers le passé, avec une précision plus fine, d'un vol plus léger, plus immatériel, plus vertigineux, plus infaillible, plus immortel, que ces dislocations organiques' (ii. 391). That the reader should be alerted to the 'better' type of involuntary memory at this stage in the text indicates this anxiety about the potency of these deterministic languages of science to construct the body. A similar tension is evident in the exordium of *Sodome et Gomorrhe*, when the narrator's aesthetic revelation emerges from the tracery of botanical and biological imagery, only to be deferred until the conclusive and transcendent moment of *Le Temps retrouvé*, the moment at which the aesthetic theories of 'mémoire involontaire' will release the body from the materiality of scientific law and restore it to its singularity.

In *Le Temps retrouvé*, *souffrance* still pertains. Although it could be argued that suffering, and indeed mortality, is now attributed to others in the often cruel and caricatural exposition of the 'bal des têtes', yet it also predominates in the second half of the narrator's aesthetic exposition,[25] where, despite the transcendent release of the narrator's body through 'mémoire involontaire', repeatedly, overwhelmingly, we encounter the term *souffrance* as the necessary partner to notions of artistic creativity. The artist experiments with his suffering: 'Certes nous sommes obligé de revivre notre souffrance particulière avec le courage du médecin qui recommence sur lui-même la dangereuse piqûre' (iv. 484).[26] The *moraliste*-style 'foule de vérités relatives aux passions, aux caractères, aux mœurs' is discovered partly in *souffrance*. 'Chaque personne qui nous fait souffrir peut être rattachée par nous à une divinité dont elle n'est qu'un reflet fragmentaire' (iv. 477). In this Platonic schema, the level of divinity, the 'Idée', represents the joyful abstraction to which suffering gives access. Achieving this level is, for the writer, therapeutic, 'une fonction saine et nécessaire' (iv. 481). A writer lacking imagination may none the less become a great novelist if he is is able to create from the substance of his suffering (iv. 479–80); similarly, 'l'œuvre à laquelle nos chagrins ont collaboré peut être interprétée pour notre avenir à la fois comme un signe néfaste de souffrance et comme un signe heureux de consolation' (iv. 482); and again, 'on ne souffre plus de son amour en travaillant que comme de quelque mal purement physique où l'être aimé n'est pour rien, comme d'une sorte de maladie de cœur' (iv. 483). Suffering in its role as prerequisite to the creation of art is simply the lover's unhappiness, and is resolved by its sublimation into a Platonic realm of Ideas.

The well-known botanical metaphor, in which the novel is represented as an embryonic plant, 'le lieu de phénomènes chimiques et respiratoires secrets mais très actifs', nourished by the life of its writer, has as its logical conclusion the writer's death 'comme la graine, je

[25] Kaufmann, in his study of Proust's correspondence, suggests a link between the accelerating decline of Proust's health and the writing of *A la recherche*: 'As it grows less and less inhabitable and less and less presentable, his body becomes a barrier that the years will render almost insurmountable . . . His body becomes an unpresentable, elusive third party preventing all form of meeting between Proust and the rest of the world' (*Post Scripts*, 33–4).

[26] In the correspondence we find an ironic reversal of this metaphor: Proust refers increasingly to the injections without which he could not continue to write, as in his letter to Charles Maurras (beginning of May 1921, in *Correspondance*, xx. letter 119).

pourrais mourir quand la plante se serait développée' (iv. 478). Read against the background of the *tilleul*/datura discussion, the logic of this metaphor is heavily ironic. Images of the suffering body take over towards the end of this development of an aesthetics of pain. And yet, as the body becomes literally (not metaphorically) present for the first time, so the reader experiences, through syntax and imagery, this 'lifting' of the sentence, which before had been only weakly described as the movement from pain towards 'abstraction', 'generality', or 'the Idea':

> Le chagrin finit par tuer. A chaque nouvelle peine trop forte, nous sentons une veine de plus qui saillit, développe sa sinuosité mortelle au long de notre tempe, sous nos yeux. . . . Mais puisque les forces peuvent se changer en d'autres forces, puisque l'ardeur qui dure devient lumière et que l'électricité de la foudre peut photographier, puisque notre sourde douleur au cœur peut élever au-dessus d'elle, comme un pavillon, la permanence visible d'une image à chaque nouveau chagrin, acceptons le mal physique qu'il nous donne pour la connaissance spirituelle qu'il nous apporte; laissons se désagréger notre corps, puisque chaque nouvelle parcelle qui s'en détache vient, cette fois lumineuse et lisible, pour la compléter au prix de souffrances dont d'autres plus doués n'ont pas besoin, pour la rendre plus solide au fur et à mesure que les émotions effritent notre vie, s'ajouter à notre œuvre. (iv. 485)

This eulogy of suffering is worth quoting in full as syntax and imagery here enact the argument. The sentence moves away from the body, focusing instead on the process of transformation; the models used suggest heat and light, dynamic movement, and by the time (literal reading time) we have returned to the subject, it is as a plea for the body to disintegrate, to be allowed to enter into this model of the transformation of forces, to become 'lumineuse et lisible'.[27] Where the 'intermittences' schema depends on a painful contact between self and world, and is modelled according to what might be called the 'principle of the conservation of suffering'—'Comme le mal que j'avais fait à ma grand-mère, le mal que m'avait fait Albertine fut un dernier lien entre elle et moi et qui survécut même au souvenir car, avec la conservation d'énergie que possède tout ce qui est physique, la souffrance n'a même pas besoin des leçons de la mémoire' (iv. 107)—and where others remain trapped in the deterministic languages of science; this model of the transformation of forces releases the

[27] In reply to questions posed by André Lang on the 'roman d'analyse', Proust establishes the necessary part of both mind and body in the literary representation of the unconscious: 'Pour réussir ce travail de sauvetage, toutes les forces de l'esprit, et même du corps, ne sont pas de trop' (second half of Oct. 1921, ibid. xx. 497).

narrator, and the singularity of his body, freed of these laws and schemas, is restored through art. A similar scientific analogy describes the release of Bergotte:

> Le génie, même le grand talent, vient moins d'éléments intellectuels et d'affinement social supérieurs à ceux d'autrui, que de la faculté de les transformer, de les transposer. Pour faire chauffer un liquide avec une lampe électrique, il ne s'agit pas d'avoir la plus forte lampe possible, mais une dont le courant puisse cesser d'éclairer, être dérivé et donner, au lieu de lumière, de la chaleur. Pour se promener dans les airs, il n'est pas nécessaire d'avoir l'automobile la plus puissante, mais une automobile qui, ne continuant pas de courir à terre et coupant d'une verticale la ligne qu'elle suivait, soit capable de convertir en force ascensionnelle sa vitesse horizontale. (i. 544–5)

But it is an artful kind of science—a scientific metaphor—which allows this release, and in the next chapter it will be seen that scientists contemporary with Proust were devising similar models of the mind and body to account for creativity.

8

SERENDIPITY

Cette immense et très singulière rhapsodie de la connaissance.

Gaëtan Picon, *Lecture de Proust*

If *A la recherche* is a rhapsody of knowledge, it also entails, as the previous chapter has described, the failure of reason and the loss of the desire to know. This 'Negative Capability, that is when man is capable of being in uncertainties, Mysteries, doubts, without any irritable reaching after fact and reason'[1] is the end-point of the narrative of cognition which develops out of the 'intermittences' schema into *Albertine disparue*, and which explores the extremes of an affective and self-implicating epistemology. Knowledge in *A la recherche* is revelatory and involuntary; it overwhelms the narrator, and is respected for its generative, transformative effect. But in contradistinction to the revelations which open *Sodome et Gomorrhe* and which establish the significance of the homosexual body, the painful crystallization of *Albertine disparue* suggests the contraction and solipsism of a mode of knowing which is located viscerally in the body of the self as both subject and object of enquiry. 'Mémoire involontaire' is part of this same repertoire of the involuntary and revelatory; yet, as the counterpart to the narratives of breakdown, of solipsism and loss, it constitutes, as we have seen in the previous chapter, an instance of miraculous and luminous recall, allowing the release of the body through art.

The initial work of this study, 'Proust as *moraliste*', involved a different kind of revisionary reading against the 'thèse' of the 'roman à thèse' which *A la recherche* claims it is not, but which has established a tradition of how to read Proust and informed a hand-me-down version of the quintessentially Proustian for those who do not read him. What I want to do now is revisit the 'theory' of 'mémoire involontaire', not for its results—that is, not as signifying aesthetic redemption—but rather, as the most spectacular instance of a series of metaphors and maxims which, throughout *A la recherche*, attempt to describe the nature of creative work, most spectacular because this is

[1] Keats, *Letters*, 71.

the moment at which the text performs its own conception and explains the conditions of its production.

Scientists contemporary with Proust were also narrating, speculating on, and attempting to theorize and justify the place of unconscious work: as Poincaré exclaims in *La Valeur de la science*: 'Deviner avant de démontrer! Ai-je besoin de rappeler que c'est ainsi que se sont faites toutes les découvertes importantes!'[2] The placing of the self as both subject and object of science in *A la recherche* echoes Poincaré's belief that science needs to analyse itself as process: 'D'une part, la science mathématique doit réfléchir sur elle-même et cela est utile, parce que réfléchir sur elle-même, c'est réfléchir sur l'esprit humain qui l'a créée'.[3]

Poincaré's account of the rhetoric and dynamics of scientific law (see chapter 1, section 6) traces its origin to the unconscious, but an unconscious which is variously described: at one extreme as instinctive and primitive, at the other as aesthetic and revelatory. It is this second, serendipitous type of unconscious work which bears the closest resemblance to Proust's 'involuntary memory'. Good mathematicians, it is argued, must have good memories; but memory is effective only when informed by an intuition of mathematical order. At this point in the argument, the text shifts from discursive to narrative mode. The previously impersonal theoretician begins to tell his story.

The story is strikingly familiar to the reader of Proust. It begins with a description of Poincaré's efforts to find a particular 'analogous function'. He has been working hard all day, experimenting with various 'combinaisons'. In the evening he drinks a cup of black coffee, something he does not usually do, and is kept awake by it: 'Les idées surgissaient en foule; je les sentais comme se heurter, jusqu'à ce que deux d'entre elles s'accrochassent, pour ainsi dire, pour former une combinaison stable' (p. 51). The next morning he has solved the problem. All that remains is for the results to be written up. Poincaré's second example describes how, on leaving Caen for a geology course, 'les péripéties du voyage' cause him to forget his mathematical research. But, getting into the bus, 'Au moment où je mettais le pied sur le marche-pied, l'idée me vint, sans que rien dans mes pensées antérieures parût m'y avoir préparé, que les transformations dont

[2] Poincaré, *La Valeur de la science*, 153.

[3] Poincaré, *Science et méthode*, 31. All further page references, unless otherwise indicated, are to *Science et méthode*.

j'avais fait usage pour définir les fonctions fuchsiennes étaient identiques à celles de la géométrie non-euclidienne' (p. 51). Again, some physical experience seems to trigger the appearance of the solution to a thought process begun earlier, but interrupted and shelved. These solutions always present themselves with 'les mêmes caractères de brièveté, de soudaineté et de certitude immédiate' (p. 52); they are, Poincaré suggests, indicative of a long period of unconscious work, 'signes manifestes d'un long travail inconscient antérieur' (p. 53).

Before considering Poincaré's theories on the nature of what we would call 'serendipity', I would like to juxtapose his second 'story' with an episode from *Le Temps retrouvé*. The narrator is on his way to the 'matinée des Guermantes', having, after repeated efforts, given up any idea of becoming a writer; he is forced to jump out of the way of an advancing carriage, stumbles, and

> Au moment où, me remettant d'aplomb, je posai mon pied sur un pavé qui était un peu moins élevé que le précédent, tout mon découragement s'évanouit . . . Comme au moment où je goûtais la madeleine, toute inquiétude sur l'avenir, tout doute intellectuel étaient dissipés. Ceux qui m'assaillaient tout à l'heure au sujet de la réalité de mes dons littéraires et même de la réalité de la littérature se trouvaient levés comme par enchantement. (iv. 445)

'Au moment où' marks for scientist and artist a moment of happy certainty, a recognition triggered by the unconscious: what in *A la recherche* are described as 'anti-intellectual' forces assuage the doubts and frustrations of conscious thought. Where Proust's phrase 'par enchantement' suggests a magical transformation, Poincaré's description, in which his thoughts resemble a group of molecules attempting to find a stable structure, already suggests the attempt to conceptualize and understand the phenomenon of serendipity. Yet, common to both accounts is the interaction of conscious and unconscious thought, in which the former effectively frames the latter. The work of the unconscious must be preceded and stimulated by conscious thought. In Proust's account a process of translation follows; in Poincaré's the revelatory moment is subject to verification and orderly formulation, a stage which is noted as particularly difficult, since the laws are intuited rather than formulated, 'se sentent plutôt qu'elles ne se formulent'.

What Poincaré terms the 'machine inconsciente, mise en branle' is variously interpreted. The model presented by *A la recherche* is of memories constantly present in the unconscious, but inaccessible until triggered by an analogous sensation. Poincaré offers two alternatives. The first of these is surprisingly Lacanian: the unconscious resembles conscious thought—'il n'est pas purement automatique, il est capable du discernement, il a du tact, de la délicatesse; il sait choisir, il sait deviner' (p. 56)—but is in fact superior to its conscious counterpart, which, having started work on a problem that it is incapable of solving, triggers the unconscious to complete the solution.

Poincaré's preferred model, however, is that of an automatic unconscious (pp. 58–62). Here the conscious work applied to a problem again acts as a trigger to the unconscious. In response, the unconscious, working infinitely faster than the conscious, comes up with a multitude of solutions, one of which may be correct. Its mechanistic nature does not allow it, as in the previous example, to *choose* the correct solution; so Poincaré's second model acquires a type of membrane, a 'sensibilité esthétique', providing a dividing line between conscious and unconscious. If the right 'combinaison' is formed in the unconscious, it will hit the membrane, be picked up by the 'sensibilité esthétique', and enter consciousness (see diagram).

combinaisons automatiquement formulées	combinaisons heureuses
l'inconscient (no known limits)	le conscient étroitement borné

sensibilité esthétique
crible délicat

The diagram shows Poincaré's alternative model. When the mind is truly at rest, the elements of the problems to be solved remain attached to the 'wall' of the unconscious; once activated, the elements are detached, and start to move about: 'Ils sillonnent dans tous les sens l'espace, j'allais dire la pièce où ils sont enfermés, comme pourrait le faire, par exemple, une nuée de moucherons ou, si l'on préfère une comparaison plus savante, comme le font les molécules gazeuses dans la théorie cinétique des gaz' (p. 60).[4] It is the abundance, but also the random nature, of the combinations resulting from this movement which are likely to produce the solution. In this model we have a more orthodox divide between the conscious, representing 'la discipline,

[4] Valéry was familiar with Poincaré's work on creativity, and drew on it to describe the process of poetic composition in which words break through to consciousness 'comme des bulles d'une masse pâteuse travaillée par des gaz'; he also compares this process with osmosis and describes an aesthetic membrane, similar to Poincaré's, between conscious and unconscious, 'une mystérieuse paroi semi perméable' (cited in Crow, *Paul Valéry: Consciousness and Nature*, 189–90).

l'attention, la volonté', and the unconscious, characterized by 'la liberté, l'absence de discipline, le désordre né du hasard'.

Both Proust and Poincaré use models of the unconscious in an attempt to explain the nature of their particular intellectual activity. Here both invoke the unconscious as part of a process of revelation and its translation. For Poincaré the elegant formulations of mathematics are attainable only through the innate aesthetic sensibility of the scientist, the activity of the unconscious allowing the formation of law;[5] in *A la recherche* we find a similar aesthetic revelation about the stylistic importance of metaphor. Both writers describe the sensation caused by these moments of unconscious creativity as a sense of doubling:

> Il semble que, dans ces cas, on assiste soi-même à son propre travail inconscient, qui est devenu partiellement perceptible à la conscience surexcitée et qui n'a pas pour cela changé de nature. (p. 62)

> Au vrai, l'être qui alors goûtait en moi cette impression la goûtait en ce qu'elle avait de commun dans un jour ancien et maintenant, dans ce qu'elle avait d'extra-temporel, un être qui n'apparaissait que quand, par une de ces identités entre le présent et le passé, il pouvait se trouver dans le seul milieu où il pût vivre, jouir de l'essence des choses, c'est-à-dire en dehors du temps. (iv. 450)

The narrator's experience of 'doubling' is described as a moment of resurrection (iv. 451), and the genesis of the novel depends on this recognition; Poincaré's description concludes a chapter which deals with the creative processes of mathematics. Both, however, play themselves out through speculation about the nature of this unconscious 'work' and its creative potential. Indeed, what we think of as the aesthetic theorizing which follows the sequence of involuntary memories is more accurately described as a prolonged speculation on the aesthetic uses of memory, and beyond this, a collection of hypotheses on what would be needed to supplement a book based on the experience of 'mémoire involontaire'. The experience proposes itself as a puzzle to the narrator: 'Saisis-moi . . . et tâche à résoudre l'énigme de bonheur que je te propose' (iv. 446). And his attempts to find the answer are genuinely speculative in both their narration and

[5] Valéry writes on the aesthetics of science: 'Si l'on fait abstraction des connaissances qui n'expriment qu'un pouvoir certain d'action extérieure, le savoir restant n'est évalué que par une sorte de jugement "esthétique", qui lui donne vie et vigueur en chacun, et définit pour chacun sa vérité. Même la condition de non-contradiction, de conformité aux lois logiques, n'est en dernière analyse qu'une condition esthétique' (in reply to the question 'Les Sciences de l'esprit sont-elles essentiellement différentes des Sciences de la Nature?', *La Revue de Synthèse*, Oct. 1931, cited in Crow, *Paul Valéry*, 36).

their exposition, containing many parenthetical lists, attempts to model ('ma mémoire . . . ne faisait que combiner entre eux des éléments homogènes' (iv. 452)), hesitations, and all the rhetorical markers of the attempt at once to interpret the intuition, but also to convince both self and reader. These aesthetic speculations—attempts to answer both the riddle of involuntary memory and, once this has been resolved and stylistically translated as metaphor (iv. 468), attempts to find the supplements required to 'make a book'—might be seen as the performance of what Poincaré describes as 'formulation', the difficult process of translating the intuited solution ('[les lois] se sentent plutôt qu'elles ne se formulent'). Moreover, the scientist's argument in favour of the unconscious, its invaluable role in what might be called 'serendipity', is a powerful relativizer of the apparently anti-intellectual arguments drawn from the experience of involuntary memory. The critique of *Le Temps retrouvé* is directed against 'les vérités que l'intelligence saisit directement à claire-voie dans le monde de la pleine lumière' (iv. 457), but these are truths quite different from those which interest both Poincaré and Proust's narrator, and which, formulated in the unconscious, require translation in order to leave the 'penumbra' and be clearly perceptible. This is the point of cross-over between Poincaré's aestheticization of the scientific imagination and the scientific certainty of Proust's aesthetic conclusion that 'nous ne sommes nullement libres devant l'œuvre d'art . . . mais que préexistant à nous, nous devons, à la fois parce qu'elle est nécessaire et cachée, et comme nous ferions pour une loi de la nature, la découvrir' (iv. 459).

What is important here is the telling of the process, not that the one account is mysteriously similar to the other, but that both seek to explain and justify by reference to involuntary or unconscious mental activity, and that both describe the intuited certainty of the solution which such work reveals. Both, moreover, elaborate alternative, more visceral and biological models of the place of the unconscious in creative work. Poincaré describes 'mathematical instinct' as 'quelque vague conscience de je ne sais quelle géométrie plus profonde, et plus cachée, qui seule fait le prix de l'édifice construit' (p. 158) the laws of which 'se sentent et ne s'énoncent pas' (p. 159). In *La Valeur de la science* this account of an ancient corporeal memory, a memory of the species, is more explicit:

Ces assemblages délicats d'aiguilles siliceuses qui forment le squelette de certaines éponges. Quand la matière organique a disparu, il ne reste qu'une frêle et élégante dentelle. Il n'y a là, il est vrai, que de la silice, mais ce qui est intéressant, c'est la forme qu'a prise cette silice, et nous ne pouvons la comprendre si nous ne connaissons pas l'éponge vivante qui lui a précisément imprimé cette forme. C'est ainsi que les anciennes notions intuitives de nos pères, même lorsque nous les avons abandonnées, impriment encore leur forme aux échafaudages logiques que nous avons mis à leur place.[6]

It is this which provides continuity at times of dramatic change: theories may be disproved, done away with, replaced, reinvented. But there is a different order of law, more ancient, more persistent, less spectacular than that formulated by the latest advances of science. And these ancient laws are perpetuated by man's physical relation to them. As Poincaré describes in *Science et méthode*, 'Une association nous paraîtra d'autant plus indestructible qu'elle sera plus ancienne. Mais ces associations ne sont pas, pour la plupart, des conquêtes de l'individu, puisqu'on en voit la trace chez l'enfant qui vient de naître: ce sont des conquêtes de la race' (p. 107). Like Proust's, Poincaré's accounts of the unconscious and its place in creative intellectual work are multiple; there is no *one* law of the unconscious: its theorization is supplemented by the stories of personal experience and by speculative models.

Why might both Proust and Poincaré wish to narrate and conceptualize artistic and scientific creativity? Why do both attempt to do so by reference to thought processes which might collectively be described as 'non-rational', and which might variously be listed as unconscious, instinctive, involuntary, corporeal, visceral even? We can begin to understand these similarities by first considering the traditional dissimilarities between art and science: namely, the different rhetorical strategies by which the two cultures seek to justify themselves. For, as Gillian Beer argues in 'Forging the Missing Link', 'Forms of knowledge do not readily merge; they may be askance or cross-grained. But that does not imply failure. Disanalogy can prove to be a powerful heuristic tool. Indeed, it is important not too readily to pair particular disciplines since that ignores indirection, the shared and dispersed other forms of experience and knowledge active in the time.'[7]

[6] Poincaré, *La Valeur de la science*, 29. Compare Proust's description of a genetic-botanical memory: 'soit que je l'évoquasse par mimétisme et association de souvenirs, soit aussi que les délicates et mystérieuses incrustations du pouvoir génésique eussent en moi, à mon insu, dessiné comme sur la feuille d'une plante, les mêmes intonations, les mêmes gestes, les mêmes attitudes qu'avaient eus ceux dont j'étais sorti' (iii. 615).

[7] Gillian Beer, 'Forging the Missing Link' (Cambridge: Cambridge University Press, 1992), 5.

In neither account does the unconscious provide a straightforward guarantee; nor does either propose one single form of it, although in Proust's case this tends to be obscured by the spectacular effects of 'mémoire involontaire' in its claim to break free from the pain and desire which characterize all other forms of creative memory in the text. But the status of Poincaré's account is particularly striking. For to find claims of this kind, justifications even, in a scientific text breaks with a rhetorical tradition founded on the exclusion of the subjective, the personal, the aesthetic. The statement that 'Science as an existing, finished [corpus of knowledge] is the most objective, most unpersonal [thing] human beings know, [but] science as something coming into being, as aim, is just as subjective and psychologically conditioned as any other of man's efforts' might be considered a truism; but its very formulation reveals something significant about the state of science as a discipline.[8] For statements made within the scientific community tend to be formulated according to the public rhetoric of verification and falsification, experiment and observation. In this context of justification, appeals to intuition simply have no place. Indeed, science has long relied upon an unspoken notion of intuition, as Martha Nussbaum defines:

> The Stoic philosopher Zeno argued that all our knowledge of the external world is built upon the foundation of certain special perceptual impressions: those which, by their own internal character, their own experienced quality, certify their own veracity. From (or in) assent to such impressions, we get the cataleptic condition, a condition of certainty and confidence from which nothing can dislodge us. On the basis of such certainties is built all science, natural and ethical. (Science is defined as a system of *katalēpseis*.)[9]

The assumption underlying this system is that man is in harmony with nature, and can therefore intuit nature's laws. Goethe's brief description of the place of intuition in science in the section entitled 'Galileo Galilei' of his treatise on colour, *Zur Farbenlehre* (1810)—'Alles kommt in der Wissenschaft auf das an, was man ein Aperçu nennt, auf ein Gewahrwerden dessen, was eigentlich den Erscheinungen zum Grunde liegt. Und ein solches Gewahrwerden ist bis ins Unendliche fruchtbar' ('Everything in science depends on what one calls an insight, a coming into awareness of what really lies behind appearances. And such a coming into awareness is infinitely fruitful')[10]—

[8] Einstein, cited in Holton, *Thematic Origins of Scientific Thought*, 6–7.

[9] Nussbaum, *Love's Knowledge*, 265.

[10] Goethe, *Zur Farbenlehre*, ed. M. Wenzel (Frankfurt: Deutscher Klassiker Verlag, 1991), 689; my trans.

suggests an uncomplicated relationship between self and world, and might be contrasted with Poincaré's lengthier account and exploration of serendipity.

Poincaré does not tag the revelations of unconscious work in this way, does not call them by any one name, such as 'serendipitous', because he is more concerned with exploring the diverse styles of intuition, the various models according to which it might work. *Science et méthode* was written at a time of scientific revolution, a moment at which science was reaching out to describe a world beyond that available to sense experience which might be described as counter-intuitive. This revolution saw, if not the collapse, then the limitation, of those theories which had formed the foundations of modern science: namely, Newtonian physics and Euclidean geometry.[11] The view of a harmoniously predictable and causal nature was threatened by the discoveries of subatomic and astrophysics, which represented a reality beyond that of everyday experience, 'a "meta-world" which was not describable in Newtonian terms':

> This 'meta-world' was . . . composed of decentred, multi-dimensionally fluctuating energies . . . far from being linear or continuous with itself, that 'meta-world' was observed to involve leaps, jerks, gaps, irregularities and discontinuities. Finally, within this 'meta-world' the principle of causality seemed not to apply, and classical space and time changed from independent and absolutely valid grids of reference into concepts which were relative to the velocity of the object observed and the location of the observer.[12]

Poincaré's categorization of intuition as either primitive or aesthetic represents an attempt to understand the relation of the scientist to these worlds in which different laws of science pertain—our physical, primitive intuition of the laws of the experiential everyday, as opposed to the aesthetic, even disembodied, unconscious which informs the laws of the extra-sensory world of the new physics. This categorization is a pragmatic gesture which was in no way characteristic of the culture as a whole, pragmatic both in the sense that it attempts to delimit areas in which different scientific laws might pertain, and also in that it might be described as occupying the middle ground, somewhere between the positions adopted by leading figures such as Einstein and Heisenberg. The theory construction of the former was still motivated by 'the "classical" aims and characteristics of science'.[13]

[11] Described by Poincaré in *La Valeur de la science*, ch. 8: 'La Crise actuelle de la physique mathématique'.

[12] Sheppard, 'Problematics of European Modernism', 14–15.

[13] Gerald Holton characterizes these aims as 'primacy of formal rather than materialistic

Einstein would not admit Poincaré's pragmatic division whereby different laws applied to different areas, but wanted to find a totalizing theory, as he describes in 'Theoretical physics':

From the very beginning there has always been present the attempt to find a unifying theoretical basis for all these single sciences, consisting of a minimum of concepts and fundamental relationships, from which all the concepts and relationships of the single disciplines might be derived by logical process. This is what we mean by the search for a foundation of the whole of physics. The confident belief that this ultimate goal may be reached is the chief source of the passionate devotion which has always animated the researcher.[14]

Moreover, Poincaré's categorization, in making the assumption that both objectivity—the scientist's ability to view nature as a spectacle apart from the self—and correspondence between self and world are possible, is also at odds with the Heisenbergian position. For the distortion and unpredictability of the world described by the new physics is in part due to the very impossibility of such separation and correlation. As Heisenberg describes, 'for the sciences of nature, the subject matter of research is no longer nature in itself, but nature subjected to human questioning, and to this extent man, once again, meets only with himself'.[15]

In short, the reality suggested by the 'new physics' upset the tacit assumptions of correspondence between the human *logos* and the natural world, and this in turn changed scientific discourse. Scientists had to start speaking about the nature of intuition, reflecting on scientific process and creativity, as Nietzsche's call for a more honest account of intellectual creativity suggests:

Man muß nicht Wissenschaftlichkeit affektieren, wo es nicht Zeit ist, wissenschaftlich zu sein; aber auch der wirkliche Forscher hat die Eitelkeit von sich zu tun, eine Art von Methode zu affektieren, welche im Grunde noch nicht an der Zeit ist. Ebenso Dinge und Gedanken auf die er anders gekommen ist, nicht mit

explanation; unity or unification, and cosmological scale (applicability of laws throughout the total realm of experience); logical parsimony and necessity; symmetry; simplicity; causality; completeness; and invariance' ('Do Scientists Need a Philosophy?', *TLS*, 2 Nov. 1984, 1234). In *Thematic Origins of Scientific Thought*, Holton contrasts the themata, or thematic concepts, of the seventeenth and eighteenth centuries with those of the twentieth: 'In the language of physics alone we find the rise in the last six decades of terms such as radioactive decay, or decay of particles; displacement law; fission; spalliation; nuclear disintegration; discontinuity . . . ; dislocation . . . ; indeterminacy, uncertainty; probabilistic (rather than classically deterministic) causality' (p. 79).

[14] Einstein, 'Considerations Concerning the Fundaments of Theoretical Physics', *Science*, 91 (24 May 1940), 487.

[15] Cited in Aldous Huxley, *Literature and Science* (London: Chatto and Windus, 1963), 65.

einem falschen Arrangement von Deduktion und Dialektik zu 'fälschen' . . . Man soll die *Tatsache*, wie uns unsere Gedanken gekommen sind, nicht verhehlen und verderben. Die tiefsten und unerschöpftesten Bücher werden wohl immer etwas von dem aphoristischen und plötzlichen Charakter von Pascals *Pensées* haben.

(One must not affect scientificity when it is not yet time to be scientific; but even the true researcher must overcome the vanity of affecting a kind of method, for which, in fact, the time has not yet come. In the same way, things and thoughts at which he arrives by other means should not be 'falsified' by a false arrangement of deduction and dialectics . . . One should not conceal and corrupt the facts about how our thoughts come to us. The deepest and most inexhaustible books will probably always have something of the aphoristic and sudden character of Pascal's *Pensées*.)[16]

It is no coincidence that Peirce's revival of the notion of 'retroduction', the forgotten Aristotelian inference describing science in process, occurred at this time—'It is certain that the only hope of retroductive reasoning ever reaching the truth is that there may be some natural tendency toward an agreement between the ideas which suggest themselves to the human mind and those which are concerned in the laws of nature'[17]—and, as this quote suggests, that he was anxious about the nature of an intuition which had itself become the object of scientific study.

One conclusion to be drawn from these developments is simply that, in its attempts to understand the nature of scientific process and creativity, science became more porous to other disciplines and discourses—porous both in the sense that it might embrace, albeit speculatively, the work of the new sciences of man (psychology, sexology, psychoanalysis, and so on), and also in that, considered as creative work, as a way of understanding the world, it bears a greater resemblance to art. We have seen this porosity in the cross-over between Proust and Poincaré: where *A la recherche* looks to science at key moments of justification, and as a way of describing the creative process, *Science et méthode* looks to aesthetics.[18] These patterns of cross-over suggest that art and science were seeking in each other new forms of self-understanding, and further, that both, in considering the place of memory, of the body, of heredity, were speculating over a common range of new scientific models. The traditional relationship whereby literature borrows from and is dependent on science's prestige is

[16] Nietzsche, *Versuch einer Umwertung aller Werte*, cited in Krüger, *Über den Aphorismus*, 95; my trans.

[17] Peirce, *Collected Papers*, I. 81.

[18] See Ch. 1, sect. 6, and Ch. 2.

replaced by a new mutuality in which the relative statuses of the 'two cultures' are deeply bound up with each other.

This cross-over has rhetorical consequences. A new way of speaking about science develops as scientific discourse ventures out of its traditional context of justification into that of discovery—although it could also be argued that this second context is simply a new area in which justification of a rather more general kind is negotiated.[19] For the novel to describe cognitive process is not so unusual: the *Bildungsroman* might be considered to describe just this, and *A la recherche*, despite its 'anti-intellectual' arguments, has been defined by some critics as such. Yet, as we have seen, Proustian narratives of cognition do not follow the incremental patterns of the *Bildungsroman*. Rather, new narrative patterns emerge both from the performance of cognition—the staging of the self as scientist—and from the retroductive model which informs the interaction of maxim, metaphor, and *récit*, and whose modulations define the relationships between self and world, and between self and law. We see these laws in the process of formulation, subject to the pressures of desire, of pain, of mind and body; formulated as speculations, as dogma; reformulated as alternative law statements, and tested as models, which privilege the cognitive potential of metaphor. The text desires for itself the generality, the laws, of science, yet is anxious to remain particular. The one is always threatening to collapse into the other, and this has a generative effect—from it new narratives of cognition emerge. The interaction might also be described as an infusion of the particular and the general, or, to develop this metaphor with greater precision, we might think of the abundance of *A la recherche* as a supersaturated and unstable solution of the particular, out of which, at any moment, a law might crystallize—this crystal might grow, the law might continue to accumulate partner maxims and metaphors, or it might simply dissolve back into the solution of the *récit*. Where scientific discourse is modified by the importation of a personal voice, of narratives, of speculative models describing creativity and intuition, literature is affected in terms of style and structure.

[19] The claims of scientific language to have, as it were, a privileged relation with the real are also subject to revision. See Richard Sheppard's article 'Problematics of European Modernism', which cites the example of Heisenberg and Bohr's first meeting in the early summer of 1920. In response to Heisenberg's question about the nature of the language he was using to describe atomic and subatomic relationships, Bohr replied: 'We must be clear that, when it comes to atoms, language can be used only as in poetry. The poet, too, is not nearly so concerned with describing facts as with creating images and establishing mental connections' (p. 28).

A la recherche is perhaps exemplary in its exploration of cognition at the level of both style, the retroductive interaction of the general and the particular, and structure, the performance of knowledge. But other literary texts contemporary with *A la recherche* show similar concerns, as, for example, the work of Paul Valéry, whose notes on poetic creativity both describe and syntactically enact the dialogue between intuition and logic. Valéry was impressed by Poincaré's texts, and his use of the notion of precipitation, also the terms 'mécanique ou logistique', suggest that he had accounts of scientific creativity in mind:

> Ainsi, un précieux poème ne peut résulter ni d'une sorte d'abandon et de descente spontanée de l'esprit; ni de l'application d'une formule d'opérations. Mais spontanément il en apparaît des fragments, quelques arêtes éclairées, un commencement qui semble bien le commencement prédestiné de quelque chose—ou un dernier mot, etc.
>
> Et, mais, d'autre part, il y a une mécanique ou logistique. Ce qu'on appelle comme on peut: intuition, est une solution—parfois née avant le problème qu'elle délie—et alors, on en déduit le problème, le demande . . . Spontanée, c.-à-d. non tant soudaine qu'obtenue par une voie non analytique. Conséquence sans chemin *apparent*. C'est l'apparence ou la non apparence du chemin. Précipité chimique.[20]

The syntactical effect of describing retroduction, Valéry's use of notation rather than continuous discursive prose, is significant. Generalizing statements alone are inappropriate in this new relationship between reason and intuition, between the particular and the general. A theoretical language interrogating itself would appear not only suspect but also inadequate. New forms are needed, a new style which will express the particular and the general, the intuitive and the logical, the non-rational and the rational. A similar process of interrogation can be read in Nietzsche's fragments, which speak explicitly of a need to investigate intellectual process, but also enact this concern in their form and syntax: although seemingly self-contained, they are often unfinished, provocative, inviting expansion.

The hermeneutic mode of *A la recherche* connects with both fragmentary and discontinuous forms such as these, and also with the work of other novelists of the period. Thomas Mann's encyclopaedic *Der Zauberberg* (1924) is a case in point, as are the novels of Musil and Woolf. These writers all experiment with new narrative structures in which the particular and the general—that is, the *récit* and maxim–

[20] Cited in Crow, *Paul Valéry: Consciousness and Nature*, 213. See also p. 186.

metaphor—interact. Both *Zauberberg* and Musil's unfinished novel, *Der Mann ohne Eigenschaften* (1930, 1932), for example, share with *A la recherche* the tendency to essayism. Yet in both, the passages of theory and *récit* are held in ironic tension, rather than integrated.[21] Woolf's attempt to bind theory and fiction by means of alternate chapters in her penultimate work, *The Pargiters*, is ultimately abandoned, and she writes instead a novel, *The Years* (1937), and an essay, *Three Guineas* (1938).[22] The critical language generally used to address these texts is revealing, for it defines the interaction of the particular and the general as that of theory and fiction, essay and novel, terms which indicate the tendency of these oppositional modes to remain discrete—whereas describing the phenomenological generality of *A la recherche* has required a variety of terms—maxim, law, theory, *caractère*, hypothesis, case history, and model—which cannot be separated from the *récit* as such; nor can this generality be separated from the self whose story it tells. This story might encompass narratives in which cognition fails, but it also describes moments of revelation, documents archives, discerns laws. Whereas Musil describes the mind 'peer[ing] forth' from 'the almost hourly growing body of facts and discoveries' and the body 'grow[ing] away from the inner being' such that 'there is

[21] Critics have focused on the way in which Musil's work violates boundaries between art and science (but also between the rational and the intuitive, philosophy and literature, and so on) in his effort to break down polarized thinking. David S. Luft (*Robert Musil and the Crisis of European Culture*) lists titles characteristic of this approach: *Dichtung und Erkenntnis, Mathematik und Mystik, Fiktion und Reflexion, Ratio und 'Mystik', Identität und Wirklichkeit, Studien zur Antimonie von Intellekt und Gefühl, Dichtung und Wissenschaft* (p. 3). Luft's own approach to such dichotomies is by way of 'essayism': 'The leading writers of the generation of 1905 believed that the tasks of philosophy, literature and cultural criticism had converged, and they shared the preference for hybrid forms, between metaphysics and the novel, which I call essayism' (p. 20). See ch. 2, 'Between Science and Art: 1905–1911', and also Anne Longuet Marx's comparative study, *Proust, Musil* (Paris: Presses Universitaires de France, 1986). Peter Smith's forthcoming study of German literature and the world-view of science in the nineteenth and twentieth centuries (Oxford: Legenda) includes a discussion of science in Musils's earlier novel *Törleß* entitled, 'Beyond the *Logos* of Science: Musil's *Die Verwirrungen des Zöglings Törleß*'.

[22] Woolf worked on *The Pargiters* from 1932 to 1935; she began rewriting it as *The Years* in 1935. *Three Guineas* was begun in 1936. *The Years* was published in 1937 and *Three Guineas* in 1938. As Mitchell A. Leaska describes in his introduction to *The Pargiters* (London: Hogarth Press, 1978): 'The "Novel-Essay" would have been for Virginia Woolf a new and profoundly challenging experiment in form, calling into action both the creative and the analytical faculties almost simultaneously. More important, it would have committed her in the Essay portions to the very difficult task of adopting and sustaining a brand of rhetoric alien to her artistic temperament—the pressure of granite against rainbow' (p. vii). See also Grace Radin, *Virginia Woolf's 'The Years'* (Knoxville, Tenn.: University of Tennessee Press, 1981).

no central point where they all unite',[23] the mind and body of the Proustian self are central, still the locus of meaning.

Critics of Woolf and Musil have interpreted this failure to synthesize in terms of the political context: Musil believed that the failure of his generation to work out some kind of balance between intellect and feeling had led directly to the First World War,[24] the strength of Woolf's politicized feminist response to the Second World War necessitated the split between theory and fiction. In Musil's case, however, this could also be interpreted in epistemological terms. For what I have termed a failure to synthesize, and what might equally be considered a variation on the retroductive model, is not only performed but also described by the text:

> The well known incoherency of ideas, with their way of spreading out without a central point, an incoherency that is characteristic of the present era and constitutes its peculiar arithmetic, rambling about in a multitude of things, from a hundred possibilities to yet a thousand others, and always without a basic unity.[25]

The increasing cumulation and fragmentation of knowledge is described here as if it were impersonal, as if the self were no longer able to give significant shape and purpose—indeed, as if ideas led an existence independent of that self. The maxims of *Der Mann ohne Eigenschaften* also indicate an awareness of laws which are not modelled on the individual, but according to the patterns of technology and mass society; as, for example, the claim that 'zoology makes it clear that a sum of reduced individuals may very well form a totality of genius'.[26] Finally, Musil's sense that scientific development has brought about a divorce between the senses and the intellect—'They go as fast as the wind, and if they have sharp eyes they are eagle-eyed, not giant-refractor-eyed. Their feelings have not yet learnt to make use of their intellect, and between these two faculties there lies a difference in development almost as great as that between the appendix and the meninx dura mater'[27]—might be contrasted with the accessibility, both sensual and intellectual, of all scales of reference to the Proustian self.

For the Proustian self is both particular and general; both the

[23] Musil, *The Man without Qualities*, trans. E. Wilkins and E. Kaiser (London: Picador, 1988), i. 179.

[24] Luft, *Robert Musil and the Crisis of European Culture*, 100.

[25] Musil, *Man without Qualities*, i. 17.

[26] Ibid. i. 30.

[27] Ibid. i. 37.

subject and object of exploration—inhabited by hypothesis, shot through with scientific and moralistic laws which make of it a pharmacy, a laboratory, an archaeological site, a plant, a group of cells. This is the nature of Proust's encyclopaedism: the natural world still offers a system of correspondences of which the self is a part and through which it can navigate by way of metaphor and maxim. It is no coincidence that this system makes little direct reference to the new physics. For, while the text's hermeneutic narratives explore, often parodically, the epistemological concerns and consequences of the scientific revolution, they are set against a backdrop of metaphors drawn principally from the life sciences and which collaborate with maxims to elaborate a web of laws and correspondences. Working out the relationship between the two modes, narrative and metaphoric, is to understand the paradox with which this study of Proust's science began: namely, that it is both Newtonian and Heisenbergian, desiring for itself the authority and stability of law, yet impossibly subjective. The same affective and self-implicating relationship of self and world which distorts and blocks the narrator's enquiries is the necessary foundation to a new area of scientific enquiry in which subjectivity and self-reflexivity are key. As Freud suggested, both the physical and behavioural sciences had undergone a paradigm shift: 'Das Unbewußte ist das eigentlich reale Psychische, *uns nach seiner inneren Natur so unbekannt wie das Reale der Außenwelt und uns durch die Daten des Bewußtseins eben so unvollständig gegeben wie die Außenwelt durch die Angaben unserer Sinnesorgane.*'[28] ('The unconscious is the true psychical reality; *in its inner nature it is as much unknown to us as the reality of the external world, and it is as incompletely presented by the data of consciousness as is the external world by the communications of our sense organs.*'[29]) Proust suggests that the artist, by virtue of his very ability to be both subject and object, scientist and nature, inside and outside the law—'ses belles lois aveugles, les plus merveilleuses parties de nous-mêmes' (iii. 1270)—can develop this science of the unconscious.

A la recherche might be described as an updating of the *moralistes'* science of man, in that it aims to discern the laws of the unconscious mind, the laws of 'amour propre', 'les lois qui dirigeant l'imagination, mais dirigeant aussi l'amour-propre, sont divines chez les poètes mais aussi chez les sots' (iii. 1270). But it is an updating which foregrounds

[28] Freud, *Die Traumdeutung* (1st pub. 1900), vol. 2 of *Studienausgabe*, ed. A. Mitscherlich, A. Richards, and J. Strachey (Frankfurt: Fischer, 1972), 580.

[29] Freud, *The Interpretation of Dreams*, in *Standard Edition* (London: Hogarth Press and The Institute of Psychoanalysis, 1975), v. 613.

scientific method (the artist is described as developing a different way of knowing, an epistemology 'autre que rationnelle et scientifique') and which borrows from science, from evolutionary theory, to define itself (the artist is selected to evolve an inward-looking eye with which to observe the laws of the unconscious). According to this revision, the scientist is, Proust argues, limited in his position as external observer, whereas the science of the artist is to be absolutely implicated: 'cette sorte de coopération physiologico-spirituelle qu'exige la production d'une œuvre, une sorte d'instinct inconscient du cerveau le pousse à réserver ses forces pour l'intuition, pour le souvenir des intuitions, et à laisser échapper les faits purement matériels' (iii. 1270).

This discussion, from which the artist emerges as a scientist of the unconscious, is itself buried in the 'genesis' of the text, available only through a work of excavation, an analysis of the prehistory of *A la recherche*—to borrow from the range of metaphors devised by Proust to characterize the nature of his own creative work. The specifically scientific language of this earlier discussion is absent from those rare traces of it which remain in the final text, as, for example, this more general description of the artist as 'researcher':

> Grave incertitude, toutes les fois que l'esprit se sent dépassé par lui-même; quand lui, le chercheur, est tout ensemble le pays obscur où il doit chercher et où tout son bagage ne lui sera de rien. Chercher? pas seulement: créer. Il est en face de quelque chose qui n'est pas encore et que seul il peut réaliser, puis faire entrer dans sa lumière. (i. 45)

Where science does persist is (as we have seen in Chapter 5) in the web of metaphors, albeit stripped of the speculative and theoretical support system of the drafts, metaphors as, for example,

> Cette vie, les souvenirs de ses tristesses, de ses joies, formaient une réserve pareille à cet albumen qui est logé dans l'ovule des plantes et dans lequel celui-ci puise sa nourriture pour se transformer en graine, en ce temps où on ignore encore que l'embryon d'une plante se développe, lequel est pourtant le lieu de phénomènes chimiques et respiratoires secrets mais très actifs. (iv. 478)

This web of metaphors and maxims cast in the pharmaceutical, biological, and moralistic language of involuntariness suggests that the self is structured and determined by laws which are part of a larger system of correspondences, of what Edmund Wilson terms 'a gigantic dense mesh of complicated relations: cross-references between different groups of characters and a multiplication of metaphors and similes connecting the phenomena of infinitely varied fields—biological, zoological, physical, aesthetic, social, political and financial'.[30]

What compounds this interconnectedness are the themata not of the spectacular new physics, but of biology. These themata, or thematic concerns, are repetition, multiplication, infinite splitting, and division—and their underlying or informing law might be Gourmont's statement that 'L'homme n'est pas au sommet de la nature; il est dans la nature, l'une des unités de la vie, et rien de plus'.[31] Proust's *infusoires* metaphor is key to understanding these patterns of connection between self and world and, as it were, the infusion of the particular and the general in *A la recherche.* For Proust posits the *infusoires*, these single-celled water creatures, as the building-blocks of the human body, of the nation-state, of life itself. Capable of causing planetary extinction, the *infusoires* also explain the multiplication of monocles in the text. The laws of their behaviour inform those of human activity, national conflict, rock formation, and the writing of novels. The *infusoires* are emblematic of the wild range of reference and connection in *A la recherche*, in which habitual temporal and spatial scales are done away with, as Proust's metaphors dip in and out of plant and animal life, the micro- and the macroscopic, the prehistoric and the futuristic. The language of the *moralistes* is blended with that of science in this description of Aunt Léonie's bedroom as a teeming mass of *infusoires*, or in this case 'myriads of protozoa':

> C'étaient de ces chambres de province qui—de même qu'en certains pays des parties entières de l'air ou de la mer sont illuminées ou parfumées par des myriades de protozoaires que nous ne voyons pas—nous enchantent des mille odeurs qu'y dégagent les vertus, la sagesse, les habitudes, toute une vie secrète, invisible, surabondante et morale que l'atmosphère y tient en suspens. (i. 48–9)

In this characteristically Proustian movement between the particular and the general, the *infusoires* are used to suggest that the seemingly insignificant or 'microscopic' life can hold all human passions ('mille odeurs', 'toute une vie'): but this usage also suggests biology's adoption of the *infusoires* as a model for the behaviour of human reproductive cells. The *infusoires* reproduce by internal division, and, as Metchnikoff indicates, 'Those cells, the function of which is to secure reproduction of the species, are like unicellular organisms, potentially immortal.'[32]

This model posits the potentially infinite splitting of the *infusoires* as

[30] Wilson, *Axel's Castle*, 158.

[31] Gourmont, *Physique de l'amour*, 8–9.

[32] Metchnikoff, *Nature of Man*, 165.

the origin of life itself, whether on an evolutionary scale or at the microscopic level of the single cell, be it reproductive or cancerous. It suggests a non-hierarchical model of evolution, a model which is also adopted by Remy de Gourmont in his *Physique de l'amour*, at the centre of which are the *infusoires* and from which all other life-forms radiate out: 'Il faut donc laisser de côté la vieille échelle dont les évolutionnistes gravissent si péniblement les échelons. Nous imaginerons, métaphoriquement, un centre de vie d'où rayonnent les multiples vies divergentes, sans tenir compte, passée la première étape unicellulaire, des subordinations hypothétiques.'[33] This model, in describing an alternative, non-linear version of evolution facilitates the interconnectedness which we see in *A la recherche*, allowing people to be seen as plants and steam trains as woolly mammoths (iv. 459). It also facilitates theories of sexuality both within *A la recherche* and as developed by sexologists and biologists contemporary with Proust. These theories connect the laws of botany with those of homosexuality; they also move beyond the androgyne of Plato's myth of origins to what Darwin posits as an originary hermaphrodism. As the narrator of the exordium summarizes, 'les invertis, qui se rattachent volontiers à l'antique Orient ou à l'âge d'or de la Grèce, remonteraient plus haut encore, à ces époques d'essai où n'existaient ni les fleurs dioïques ni les animaux unisexués, à cet hermaphroditisme initial dont quelques rudiments d'organes mâles dans l'anatomie de la femme et d'organes femelles dans l'anatomie de l'homme semblent conserver la trace' (iii. 31).

Within the evolutionary model informed by the proliferating, self-splitting *infusoires*, the primitive and the sophisticated are connected; homosexuality is a reversion, and in *A la recherche* a repeated reversion, to an ancient androgyny; the doubling of the narrator informs a new science of cognition, and his doubling in involuntary memory a new aesthetic. These disparate figures are not connected by a linear narrative or argument, but by the themata of repetition, doubling, and splitting. All pertain to origins and to creation. Repetition as doubling is the myth which informs the prehistory of the novel.

Repetition might also reveal itself as uncontrollably prolific reproduction: the incessant proliferation of the text within the confines of its original structure, which is Proust's writing practice:

> Not even Marcel Proust managed to put an end to his encyclopedic novel, though not for lack of design, since the idea for the book came to him all at once, the

[33] Gourmont, *Physique de l'amour*, 10.

beginning and end and the general outline. The reason was that the work grew denser and denser from the inside through its own organic vitality.'[34]

A la recherche takes from science both the strength and the fragility of law, the authority and the neediness of the subject, a delight in proliferating particularity and in paring down to general structures and schemas. For it connects with the philosophy and substance of two very different scientific world-views: the life sciences, in particular the emerging study of genetics, and the new physics, so that the self is at once separated from the world, and the story of the attempt to overcome this separation describes the failure, incapacity, involuntariness, neediness, and comic frailty of cognition, but is also part of a larger system of correspondences, of a lawlike nature which is sensually and intellectually accessible. Or, as Proust more succinctly notes, 'Les puissantes intuitions de mon esprit, même un soir d'épuisement ou de mort. Principe de renouvellement qu'est la vérité.'[35] From these cognitive themata, in Proust's shorthand, 'puissantes intuitions', 'mort', 'principe de renouvellement', 'vérité', grows a new hybrid form—a novel of non-linearity, which repeats and regenerates itself, performing taxonomic and moralistic variations, retelling old stories and revisiting and uncovering new maxims, a text which is at once encyclopaedia and commonplace book, *science et méthode*.

[34] Calvino, *Six Memos*, 110.

[35] Proust, *Le Carnet de 1908*, 59.

BIBLIOGRAPHY

TEXTS BY PROUST

A la recherche du temps perdu, Bibliothèque de la Pléiade (4 vols), under the general editorship of Jean-Yves Tadié, Paris: Gallimard, 1987–9.

La Fugitive, ed. Thierry Laget (3 vols), vol. 3, Paris: Robert Laffont, 1987.

Contre Sainte-Beuve, Bibliothèque de la Pléiade, ed. Pierre Clarac and Yves Sandre, Paris: Gallimard, 1971.

The Captive. The Fugitive, trans. C. K. Scott Moncrieff, Terence Kilmartin, and D. J. Enright, vol. 5 of *In Search of Lost Time* (6 vols), London: Chatto and Windus, 1992.

Jean Santeuil, preceded by *Les Plaisirs et les jours*, Bibliothèque de la Pléiade, ed. Pierre Clarac and Yves Sandre, Paris: Gallimard, 1971.

Le Carnet de 1908, ed. Philip Kolb, Cahiers Marcel Proust 8, Paris: Gallimard, 1976.

Correspondance de Marcel Proust, ed. Philip Kolb (21 vols), Paris: Plon, 1970–93. Unless otherwise indicated, page numbers are given.

OTHER PRIMARY TEXTS

Barney, Natalie Clifford, *Actes et entr'actes*, Paris: Sansot, 1910.

—— *Éparpillements*, Paris: Sansot, 1910.

—— *Pensées d'une amazone*, Paris: Émile Paul, 1920.

—— *Aventures de l'esprit*, Paris: Émile Paul, 1929.

—— *Nouvelles pensées de l'amazone*, Paris: Mercure de France, 1939.

—— *Traits et portraits*, Paris: Mercure de France, 1963.

Barthes, Roland, *Roland Barthes par Roland Barthes*, Paris: Seuil, 1975.

—— *Fragments d'un discours amoureux*, Paris: Seuil, 1977.

Bergson, Henri, *L'Évolution créatrice* (1907), Paris: Presses Universitaires de France, 1994.

—— *La Pensée et le mouvant* (1938), Paris: Presses Universitaires de France, 1993.

Bernard, Claude, *Introduction à l'étude de la médecine expérimentale* (1865), ed. F. Dagognet, Paris: Flammarion, 1984.

Calvino, Italo, *Six Memos for the Next Millenium* (1988), trans. Patrick Creagh, London: Jonathan Cape, 1992.

Campbell, Norman Robert, *Physics, the Elements*, Cambridge: Cambridge University Press, 1920.

Colomb, Georges (Christophe), *Les Facéties du sapeur Camember* (1896), Baume-les-Dames: Armand Colin, 1984.

—— *L'Idée fixe du savant Cosinus* (1899), Baume-les-Dames: Armand Colin, 1984.

Darwin, Charles, *The Various Contrivances by which Orchids are Fertilised by Insects* (1862), London: John Murray, 1877.

DARWIN, CHARLES, *The Effects of Cross and Self-Fertilisation in the Vegetable Kingdom*, London: John Murray, 1876.

—— *The Different Forms of Flowers*, London: John Murray, 1877.

DESCARTES, RENÉ, *Œuvres et lettres*, Bibliothèque de la Pléiade, ed. André Bridoux, Paris: Gallimard, 1952.

DUHEM, PIERRE, *The Aim and Structure of Physical Theory*, trans. Philip Wiener, Princeton: Princeton University Press, 1954.

DURAS, MARGUÉRITE, *L'Été 80*, Paris: Minuit, 1980.

EDDINGTON, ARTHUR, *The Nature of the Physical World* (1928), London: J. M. Dent, 1942.

EINSTEIN, ALBERT, 'Considerations Concerning the Fundaments of Theoretical Physics', *Science*, 91 (24 May 1940), 487–92.

—— and INFELD, LEOPOLD, *The Evolution of Physics: The Growth of Ideas from the Early Concepts to Relativity and Quanta*, Cambridge: Cambridge University Press, 1938.

FREUD, SIGMUND, *Die Traumdeutung* (1900), vol. 2 of *Studienausgabe*, ed. Alexander Mitscherlich, Angela Richards, and James Strachey, Frankfurt: Fischer, 1972.

—— *The Interpretation of Dreams*, trans. under the general editorship of James Strachey, in collaboration with Anna Freud, assisted by Alix Strachey and Alan Tyson, in *Standard Edition* (24 vols), vol. 5, London: Hogarth Press and The Institute of Psychoanalysis, 1975.

GIDE, ANDRÉ, *Corydon* (1920), Paris: Gallimard, 1925.

GOETHE, JOHANN WOLFGANG, *Zur Farbenlehre* (1810), Bibliothek Deutscher Klassiker, ed. M. Wenzel, Frankfurt: Deutscher Klassiker Verlag, 1991.

GOURMONT, REMY DE, *Physique de l'amour: Essai sur l'instinct sexuel* (1904), in *Œuvres*, vol. 3, Paris: Mercure de France, 1930.

HEISENBERG, WERNER, *The Physicist's Conception of Nature*, trans. A. J. Pomerans (*Das Naturbild der heutigen Physik*, 1955), London: Hutchinson, 1958.

HUXLEY, ALDOUS, *Literature and Science*, London: Chatto and Windus, 1963.

—— *Letters of Aldous Huxley*, ed. Grover Smith, London: Chatto and Windus, 1969.

KEATS, JOHN, *The Letters of John Keats*, ed. M. B. Forman, London: Oxford University Press, 1952.

LA BRUYÈRE, JEAN DE, *Les Caractères*, ed. R. Garapon, Paris: Classiques Garnier, 1962.

LANDAU, NICOLAS, *Aphorismes*, Paris: Imprimés pour Alain Brieux, ses amis et ceux de Nicolas, 1985.

LA ROCHEFOUCAULD, FRANÇOIS, DUC DE, *Maximes*, ed. J. Lafond, Paris: Gallimard, 1976.

MAETERLINCK, MAURICE, *L'Intelligence des fleurs* (1907), Paris: Fasquelle, 1950.

MERLEAU-PONTY, MAURICE, *Éloge de la philosophie* (1953), Paris: Gallimard, 1960.

—— *Signes*, Paris: Gallimard, 1960.

METCHNIKOFF, ELIE, *The Nature of Man: Studies in Optimistic Philosophy*, trans. P. Chalmers Mitchell, revised and updated by Charles M. Beadnell (*Études sur la nature humaine: Essai de philosophie optimiste*, 1903), London: Watts, 1938.

MICHELET, JULES, *La Mer* (1861), Lausanne: L'Âge d'Homme, 1980.

MONTAIGNE, MICHEL DE, *Essais* (3 vols), ed. A. Micha, Paris: Flammarion, 1979.

MUSIL, ROBERT, *The Man without Qualities*, trans. E. Wilkins and E. Kaiser (*Der Mann ohne Eigenschaften*, vol. 1, 1930, vol. 2, 1932, vol. 3 posthumously), London: Picador, 1988.

PASCAL, BLAISE, *Pensées*, ed. L. Lafuma, Paris: Seuil, 1962.

PEIRCE, CHARLES SANDERS, *Collected Papers of Charles Sanders Peirce*, Cambridge, Mass.: Belknap Press; vols 1–6, ed. C. Hartshorne and P. Weiss, 1931–5; vols 7 and 8, ed. A. W. Burks, 1958 (references indicate volume number, followed by paragraph number).

POINCARÉ, HENRI, *La Science et l'hypothèse* (1902), Paris: Flammarion, 1968.

—— *La Valeur de la science* (1905), Paris: Flammarion, 1914.

—— *Science et méthode* (1908), Paris: Flammarion, 1920.

—— *Dernières pensées*, Paris: Gallimard, 1913.

POUND, EZRA, Foreword to Remy de Gourmont, *The Natural Philosophy of Love* (1926), in *Modernism: An Anthology of Sources and Documents*, ed. Vassiliki Kolocotroni, Jane Goldman, and Olga Taxidou, Edinburgh: Edinburgh University Press, 1998, 379–82.

PROUST, ADRIEN, *L'Hygiène du neurasthénique*, Paris: Masson, 1897.

RUSSELL, BERTRAND, *The Scientific Outlook*, London: George Allen and Unwin, 1931.

STENDHAL, *De l'amour* (1822), Paris: Garnier Flammarion, 1965.

VALÉRY, PAUL, *Œuvres*, Bibliothèque de la Pléiade (2 vols), vol. 2, ed. Jean Hytier, Paris: Gallimard, 1960.

WEISMANN, AUGUST, 'De l'hérédité', trans. Henry de Varigny ('Über Vererbung', 1883), in *La Découverte des lois de l'hérédité*, ed. C. Lenay, Paris: Presses Pocket, 1990, 167–212.

WOOLF, VIRGINIA, *To the Lighthouse* (1927), London: Granada, 1985.

—— 'Phases of Fiction', in *Granite and Rainbow*, New York: Harcourt Brace, 1958, 93–145 (1st pub. in *The Bookman*, April, May, and June 1929).

—— 'On Being Ill' (1930), in *The Moment*, London: Hogarth Press, 1947, 14–24.

—— *The Pargiters: The Novel-Essay Portion of The Years*, ed. Mitchell A. Leaska, London: Hogarth Press, 1978.

CRITICAL, BIOGRAPHICAL, AND REFERENCE WORKS ON PROUST

ADORNO, THEODOR W., 'Kleine Proust-Kommentare', in *Noten zur Literatur*, vol. 2, Frankfurt: Suhrkamp, 1961, 95–109.

—— *Notes to Literature* (2 vols), vol. 1, trans. Shierry Weber Nicholsen, New York: Columbia University Press, 1991.

BARNES, ANNIE, 'Proust lecteur de Pascal', *Bulletin de la Société des amis de Marcel Proust*, 27 (1977), 392–409.

BARTHES, ROLAND, 'Une idée de recherche', in *Recherche de Proust*, ed. G. Genette and T. Todorov, Paris: Seuil, 1980, 34–9.

—— 'Longtemps je me suis couché de bonne heure', in *Le Bruissement de la langue*, Paris: Seuil, 1984, 313–25.

BECKETT, SAMUEL, *Proust*, New York: Grove Press, 1931.

BÉHAR, SERGE, *L'Univers médical de Proust*, Paris: Gallimard, 1970.

BELL, CLIVE, *Proust*, London: Hogarth Press, 1928.

BENJAMIN, WALTER, 'Zum Bilde Prousts', in *Über Literatur*, Frankfurt: Suhrkamp, 1969, 72–86.

—— *Illuminations*, trans. Harry Zohn, London: Fontana, 1992.

BERSANI, JACQUES (ed.), *Les Critiques de notre temps et Proust*, Paris: Garnier, 1971.

BILLY, ROBERT DE, *Marcel Proust, lettres et conversations*, Paris: Éditions des portiques, 1930.

BISSON, L. A. (ed.), *Literature and Science: Proceedings of the Sixth Triennial Congress 1954*, Oxford: Blackwell, 1955.

—— 'Proust and Medicine', in *Literature and Science*, Oxford: Blackwell, 1955, 292–8.

BOWIE, MALCOLM, *Freud, Proust, and Lacan: Theory as Fiction*, Cambridge: Cambridge University Press, 1987.

BRUNET, ÉTIENNE, *Le Vocabulaire de Proust* (3 vols), Geneva: Slatkine, 1983.

CARTER, WILLIAM C., *The Proustian Quest*, New York: New York University Press, 1992.

CATTAUI, GEORGES, 'Proust et les sciences', in *Literature and Science*, ed. L. A. Bisson, Oxford: Blackwell, 1955, 287–92.

CHAMBERS, ROSS, 'Gossip and the Novel: Knowing Narrative and Narrative Knowing in Balzac, Mme de Lafayette and Proust', *Australian Journal of French Studies*, 23 (1986), 212–33.

COMPAGNON, ANTOINE, *Proust entre deux siècles*, Paris: Seuil, 1989.

CORTIE, RONALD and ODETTE (eds. and trans.), *Marcel Proust On Life, Love and Letters*, London: Cecil Woolf Publishers, 1988.

CRÉMIEUX, BENJAMIN, 'Le sur-impressionisme de Proust', from *Vingtième siècle* (1924), in *Les Critiques de notre temps et Proust*, ed. J. Bersani, Paris: Garnier, 1971, 31–5.

—— 'Nouveauté d'*Albertine disparue*', *La Nouvelle Revue française* (hereafter *NRF*), 26 (1 Feb. 1926), 216–24.

CURTIUS, ERNST-ROBERT, 'Marcel Proust', *NRF*, 20 (1 Jan. 1923), 262–6.

—— 'Du relativisme proustien', (from the German, *Französischer Geist im neuen Europa*, 1925), in *Les Critiques de notre temps et Proust*, ed. J. Bersani, Paris: Garnier, 1971, 36–40.

DELEUZE, GILLES, *Marcel Proust et les signes*, Paris: Presses Universitaires de France, 1964.

DIAMANT, NAOMI, 'Judaism, Homosexuality and other Sign Systems in *A la recherche*', *Romanic Review*, 82 (1991), 179–92.

DUCHÊNE, ROGER, *L'Impossible Marcel Proust*, Paris: Éditions Robert Laffont, 1994.

ERICKSON, JOHN D., 'The Proust–Einstein Relation: A Study in Relative Point of View', in *Marcel Proust: A Critical Panorama*, ed. Larkin B. Price, Urbana, Ill.: University of Illinois Press, 1973, 247–76.

ERMAN, MICHEL, *Marcel Proust*, Paris: Fayard, 1994.

FERNANDEZ, RAMON, 'Note sur l'esthétique de Proust', *NRF*, 31 (1 Aug. 1928), 272–80.

FRAISSE, LUC and RAIMOND, MICHEL, *Proust en toutes lettres*, Paris: Bordas, 1989.

FRASER, ROBERT, *Proust and the Victorians*, New York: St Martin's Press, 1994.

GASTON, GILBERT, *Proust, l'homme des mondes*, Paris: Kimé, 1993.

GRAHAM, VICTOR, 'Proust's Alchemy', *Modern Language Review*, 60 (1965), 197–206.

—— *The Imagery of Proust*, Oxford: Blackwell, 1966.

GRÉSILLON, ALMUTH, LEBRAVE, JEAN-LOUIS, and VIOLLET, CATHERINE, ' "Quand tous mes autres moi seront morts . . ." Réflexions sur l'hologramme proustien', in *Proust à la lettre: les intermittences de l'écriture*, ed. by the above-named authors, Tusson: Du Lérot, 1990, 109–39.

GRIMALDI, NICOLAS, *La Jalousie: étude sur l'imaginaire proustien*, Arles: Actes Sud, 1993.

GUENETTE, MARK D., 'Le loup et le narrateur: The Masking and Unmasking of Homosexuality in Proust's *A la recherche*', *Romanic Review*, 80 (1989), 229–46.

HEPP, NOÉMI, 'Le dix-septième siècle de Marcel Proust dans *La Recherche du temps perdu*', *Travaux de linguistique et de littérature*, 17/2 (1974), 121–44.

HODSON, LEIGHTON, *Marcel Proust, the Critical Heritage*, London: Routledge, 1989.

HUGHES, EDWARD, 'The Mapping of Homosexuality in Proust's *Recherche*', *Paragraph*, 18/2 (1995), 148–61.

JALOUX, EDMUND, 'Sur la psychologie de Marcel Proust', *NRF*, 20 (1 Jan. 1923), 151–61.

KRISTEVA, JULIA, *Proust and the Sense of Time*, trans. S. Bann, London: Faber, 1993.

—— *Le Temps sensible: Proust et l'expérience littéraire*, Paris: Gallimard, 1994.

LEY, HERBERT DE, *Marcel Proust et le duc de Saint-Simon*, Illinois Studies in Language and Literature 57, Urbana, Ill.: University of Illinois Press, 1966.

LONGUET MARX, ANNE, *Proust, Musil: Partage d'écritures*, Paris: Presses Universitaires de France, 1986.

MCDONALD, CHRISTIE, 'Republications', in *Reading Proust Now*, ed. Mary Anne Caws and Eugène Nicole, New York: Peter Lang, 1990, 197–222.

—— *The Proustian Fabric*, Lincoln, Nebr., and London: University of Nebraska Press, 1991.

MCGINNIS, REGINALD, 'L'Inconnaissable Gomorrhe: à propos d'*Albertine disparue*', *Romanic Review*, 81 (1990), 92–104.

MARCH, HAROLD, *The Two Worlds of Marcel Proust*, London: Oxford University Press, 1948.

MARJERIE, DIANE DE, *Le Jardin secret de Marcel Proust*, Paris: Albin Michel, 1994.

MARTIN-CHAUFFIER, LOUIS, review of *Le Côté de Guermantes*, *NRF*, 16 (1 Feb. 1921), 204–8.

MEIN, MARGARET, 'Le général et le particulier dans l'œuvre de Marcel Proust', *Bulletin de la Société des amis de Marcel Proust*, 20 (1970), 976–93.

—— *A Foretaste of Proust*, Farnborough: Saxon House, 1974.

MICHEL, FRANÇOIS-BERNARD, *Proust et les écrivains devant la mort*, Paris: Éditions Grasset et Fasquelle, 1995.

MIGUET, MARIE, 'L'hermaphroditisime dans l'œuvre de Proust', *Bulletin de la société des amis de Marcel Proust*, 32 (1982), 561–74.

O'BRIEN, JUSTIN (ed.), *The Maxims of Marcel Proust*, New York: Columbia University Press, 1948.

PAINTER, GEORGE D., *Marcel Proust: A Biography*, rev. enlarged edn, 2 vols, London: Chatto and Windus, 1989.

PAULTRE, ROGER, *Marcel Proust et la théorie du modèle*, Paris: Nizet, 1986.

PICON, GAËTAN, *Lecture de Proust*, Paris: Mercure de France, 1963.

PIERRE-QUINT, LÉON, *Proust et la stratégie littéraire: avec des lettres de Marcel Proust à René Blum, Bernard Grasset et Louis Brun*, Paris: Correâ, 1954 (1st edn 1930, entitled *Comment parut 'Du côté de chez Swann', lettres de Marcel Proust*).

QUÉMAR, CLAUDINE, 'Autour de trois avant textes de l'"Ouverture" de *la Recherche*: nouvelles approches des problèmes du *Contre Sainte-Beuve*', *Bulletin d'informations proustiennes*, 3 (1976), 7–29.

RICHARDSON VITTI, ELISABETH, 'Marcel and the Medusa: The Narrator's Obfuscated Homosexuality in *A la recherche du temps perdu*', *Dalhousie French Studies*, 26 (1994), 61–8.

RIVERS, JULIUS EDWIN, 'The Myth and Science of Homosexuality in *A la recherche*', in *Homosexualities and French Literature: Cultural Contexts, Critical Texts*, ed. G. Stambolian and E. Marks, Ithaca, NY: Cornell University Press, 1979, 262–78.

—— *Proust and the Art of Love: The Aesthetics of Sexuality in the Life, Times, and Art of Marcel Proust*, New York: Columbia University Press, 1980.

RIVIÈRE, JACQUES, 'Marcel Proust et la tradition classique', *NRF*, 14 (1 Feb. 1920), 192–200.

—— Obituary notice of Proust, *NRF*, 19 (1 Dec. 1922), 641–2.

ROSE, PHYLLIS, *The Year of Reading Proust: A Memoir in Real Time*, London: Vintage, 1998.

SAUNDERS, RICHARD W., *Metamorphoses of the Proustian Body: A Study of Bodily Signs in 'A la recherche du temps perdu'*, New York: Peter Lang, 1994.

SHATTUCK, ROGER, *Proust's Binoculars: A Study of Memory, Time and Recognition in 'A la recherche du temps perdu'*, London: Chatto and Windus, 1964.

SOLLERS, PHILIPPE, 'Proust et Gomorrhe', in *Théorie des exceptions*, Paris: Folio, 1986, 75–9.

SOUPAULT, ROBERT, *Marcel Proust du côté de la médecine*, Geneva: Plon, 1967.

SPITZER, LEO, 'La complexité dans l'appréhension du monde' (extract from

Stilstudien, 1928), in *Les Critiques de notre temps et Proust*, ed. J. Bersani, Paris: Garnier, 1971, 40–9.

STRAUS, BERNARD, *The Maladies of Marcel Proust: Doctors and Disease in his Life and Work*, New York: Holmes and Meier, 1980.

TADIÉ, JEAN-YVES, *Proust et le roman: essai sur les formes et techniques du roman dans 'A la recherche du temps perdu'*, Paris: Gallimard, 1971.

—— *Marcel Proust Biographie*, Paris: Gallimard, 1996.

THIBAUDET, ALBERT, 'Marcel Proust et la tradition française', *NRF*, 20 (1 Jan. 1923), 130–9.

VANDÉREM, FERNAND, 'Les lettres et la vie', *La Revue de France*, 7 (15 June 1921), 845–9.

VETTARD, CAMILLE, 'Correspondance: Proust et Einstein', *NRF*, 19 (1 Aug. 1922), 246–52.

VIERS, RINA, 'Évolution et sexualité des plantes dans *Sodome et Gomorrhe*', *Europe*, nos 502–3 (Feb./Mar. 1971), 100–13.

VIRTANEN, REINO, 'Proust's Metaphors from the Natural and the Exact Sciences', *PMLA*, 69 (1954), 1038–59.

WINTON, ALISON, *Proust's Additions: The Making of 'A la recherche du temps perdu'* (2 vols), Cambridge: Cambridge University Press, 1977.

OTHER SECONDARY TEXTS

ABRAMS, M. H., *The Mirror and the Lamp: Romantic Theory and the Critical Tradition*, Oxford: Oxford University Press, 1953.

BALAVOINE, CLAUDINE, 'Bouquets de fleurs et colliers de perles: sur les recueils de formes brèves au XVIe siècle', in *Les Formes brèves de la prose et le discours discontinu: XVIe–XVIIe siècles*, ed. Lafond, Paris: Vrin, 1984, 51–71.

BARTHES, ROLAND, *Michelet par lui-même*, Paris: Seuil, 1954.

—— *S/Z*, Paris: Seuil, 1970.

—— 'La Rochefoucauld: "Réflexions ou Sentences et Maximes"', in *Le Degré zéro de l'écriture, suivi de Nouveaux essais critiques*, Paris: Seuil, 1972, 69–88.

—— 'De la science à la littérature', in *Le Bruissement de la langue*, Paris: Seuil, 1984, 13–20.

BEER, GILLIAN, 'Plot and the Analogy with Science in Later Nineteenth-Century Novelists', in *Comparative Criticism*, ed. Elinor Shaffer, Cambridge: Cambridge University Press, 1980, 131–49.

—— *Darwin's Plots: Evolutionary Narrative in Darwin, George Eliot, and Nineteenth-Century Fiction*, London: Ark Paperbacks, 1985.

—— *Arguing with the Past: Essays in Narrative from Woolf to Sidney*, London: Routledge, 1989.

—— 'Forging the Missing Link. Interdisciplinary Stories', Inaugural Lecture, 18 Nov. 1991, Cambridge: Cambridge University Press, 1992.

——'Wave Theory and the Rise of Literary Modernism', in *Open Fields: Science in Cultural Encounter*, Oxford: Oxford University Press, 1996, 295–318.

Bennington, Geoffrey, *Sententiousness and the Novel: Laying Down the Law in Eighteenth-Century French Fiction*, Cambridge: Cambridge University Press, 1985.

Benstock, Shari, *Women of the Left Bank: Paris, 1900–1940*, Austin, Tex.: University of Texas Press, 1987.

Bercé, Yves-Marie (ed.), *Destins et enjeux du XVIIème siècle*, Paris: Presses Universitaires de France, 1985.

Bono, James J., 'Science, Discourse, and Literature: The Role/Rule of Metaphor in Science', in *Literature and Science*, ed. S. Peterfreund, Boston: Northeastern University Press, 1990, 59–89.

Brooks, Peter, *Reading for the Plot*, Oxford: Oxford University Press, 1984.

Carou, Marie, *Lectures bergsoniennes*, Paris: Presses Universitaires de France, 1990.

Casselaer, Catherine van, *Lot's Wife: Lesbian Paris 1890–1914*, Liverpool: Janus Press, 1986.

Christie, John and Shuttleworth, Sally (eds), *Nature Transfigured*, Manchester: Manchester University Press, 1989.

Compagnon, Antoine, 'La brièveté de Montaigne', in *Les Formes brèves de la prose et le discours discontinu*, ed. J. Lafond, Paris: Vrin, 1984, 9–25.

Crow, Christine, *Paul Valéry: Consciousness and Nature*, London: Cambridge University Press, 1972.

Culler, Jonathan, *Barthes*, Glasgow: Fontana, 1983.

Davidson, Hugh M., *Pascal and the Arts of the Mind*, Cambridge: Cambridge University Press, 1993.

Delft, Louis van, *Le Moraliste classique: essai de définition et de typologie*, Geneva: Droz, 1982.

Desfougères, Anne-Marie, 'Des moralistes à la psychanalyse', in *Destins et enjeux du XVIIème siècle*, ed. Y.-M. Bercé, Paris: Presses Universitaires de France, 1985, 241–51.

Dijkstra, Bram, *Idols of Perversity: Fantasies of Feminine Evil in Fin-de-Siècle Culture*, New York and Oxford: Oxford University Press, 1986.

Dollimore, Jonathan, *Sexual Dissidence: Augustine to Wilde, Freud to Foucault*, Oxford: Clarendon Press, 1991.

Donnellan, Brendan, *Nietzsche and the French Moralists*, Bonn: Bouvier, 1982.

Faderman, Lilian, *Surpassing the Love of Men*, New York: Women's Press, 1981.

Genette, Gérard, *Figures 1*, Paris: Seuil, 1966.

Gross, John, *The Oxford Book of Aphorisms*, Oxford: Oxford University Press, 1983.

Hall, A. Rupert, 'Le XVIIe siècle et nous: le cas des sciences physiques', in *Destins et enjeux du XVIIème siècle*, ed. Y.-M. Bercé, Paris: Presses Universitaires de France, 1985, 253–60.

Hayles, N. Katherine, *The Cosmic Web: Scientific Field Models and Literary Strategies in the Twentieth Century*, Ithaca, NY: Cornell University Press, 1984.

——'Complex Dynamics in Literature and Science', in *Chaos and Order: Complex*

Dynamics in Literature and Science, ed. N. Katherine Hayles, Chicago and London: University of Chicago Press, 1991, 1–33.

——'Deciphering the Rules of Unruly Disciplines: A Modest Proposal for Literature and Science', in *Literature and Science*, ed. Donald Bruce and Anthony Purdy, Amsterdam and Atlanta, Ga.: Rodopi, 1994, 25–48.

HERWIG, M. C. W., 'Exakte Literatur und schöne Wissenschaft: Naturwissenschaft in Thomas Manns *Der Zauberberg*', Oxford, unpublished M.Phil. thesis submitted 1998.

JAY, KARLA, *The Amazon and the Page: Natalie Clifford Barney and Renée Vivien*, Bloomington, Ind.: Indiana University Press, 1988.

JEAN, JOAN DE, *Fictions of Sappho 1546–1937*, Chicago and London: University of Chicago Press, 1989.

JORDANOVA, LUDMILLA (ed.), *Languages of Nature*, London: Free Association Books, 1986.

KAHN, CHARLES H., *The Art and Thought of Heraclitus: An Edition of the Fragments with Translation and Commentary*, Cambridge: Cambridge University Press, 1979.

KAUFMANN, VINCENT, *Post Scripts: The Writer's Workshop*, trans. D. Treisman, Cambridge, Mass.: Harvard University Press, 1994.

KERN, STEPHEN, *The Culture of Time and Space 1880–1918*, Cambridge, Mass.: Harvard University Press, 1983.

KINLOCH, DAVID P., *The Thought and Art of Joseph Joubert 1754–1824*, Oxford: Clarendon Press, 1992.

KRÜGER, HEINZ, *Über den Aphorismus als philosophische Form*, Munich: edition text + kritik, 1988.

LAFOND, JEAN, 'Les formes brèves de la littérature morale aux XVIe et XVIIe siècles', in *Les Formes brèves de la prose et le discours discontinu: XVIe – XVIIe siècles*, ed. Jean Lafond, Paris: Vrin, 1984, 101–22.

LEVINE, GEORGE (ed.), *One Culture*, London: University of Wisconsin Press, 1987.

LEY, HERBERT DE, *The Movement of Thought*, Urbana, Ill. and Chicago: University of Illinois Press, 1985.

LUFT, DAVID S., *Robert Musil and the Crisis of European Culture 1880–1914*, Berkeley, Los Angeles and London: University of California Press, 1980.

MOORE, W. G., 'Scientific Method in the French Classical Writers', in *Literature and Science*, ed. L. A. Bisson, Oxford: Blackwell, 1955, 150–7.

NEMER, MONIQUE, 'Les intermittences de la vérité. Maxime, sentence ou aphorisme: notes sur l'évolution d'un genre', *Studi francesi*, 26 (1982), 484–93.

NEUMANN, GERHARD (ed.), *Der Aphorismus: zur Geschichte, zu den Formen und Möglichkeiten einer literarische Gattung*, Darmstadt: Wissenschaftliche Buchgesellschaft, 1976.

NUSSBAUM, MARTHA, *Love's Knowledge: Essays on Philosophy and Literature*, New York and Oxford: Oxford University Press, 1990.

ORR, LINDA, *Jules Michelet: Nature, History, and Language*, Ithaca, NY: Cornell University Press, 1976.

PETERFREUND, STUART (ed.), *Literature and Science: Theory and Practice*, Boston: Northeastern University Press, 1990.

POLIAKOV, LÉON, *Le Mythe aryen: essai sur les sources du racisme et des nationalismes*, Paris: Calmann-Lévy, 1971.

POLLARD, PATRICK, *André Gide: Homosexual Moralist*, New Haven and London: Yale University Press, 1991.

RADIN, GRACE, *Virginia Woolf's 'The Years': The Evolution of a Novel*, Knoxville, Tenn.: University of Tennessee Press, 1981.

RICARDOU, JEAN, *Nouveaux Problèmes du roman*, Paris: Seuil, 1978.

RICOEUR, PAUL, *Interpretation Theory: Discourse and the Surplus of Meaning*, Fort Worth, Tex.: Texas Christian University Press, 1976.

ROBINSON, CHRISTOPHER, *Scandal in the Ink*, London: Cassell, 1995.

ROGER, JACQUES, 'Actualité de la science du XVIIe siècle', in *Destins et enjeux du XVIIème siècle*, ed. Y.-M. Bercé, Paris: Presses Universitaires de France, 1985, 261–70.

ROUSSEAU, GEORGE S., 'Literature and Science: The State of the Field', *Isis*, 69/249 (Dec. 1978), 583–91.

ROUSSET, JEAN, *Forme et signification: essais sur les structures littéraires de Corneille à Claudel*, Paris: Corti, 1962.

SCALES, DEREK P., *Aldous Huxley and French Literature*, Sydney: Sydney University Press, 1969.

SCHALK, FRITZ, 'Das Wesen des französischen Aphorismus' (1933), in *Der Aphorismus*, ed. G. Neumann, Darmstadt: Wissenschaftliche Buchgesellschaft, 1976, 75–111.

SEDGWICK, EVE KOSOFSKY, *Epistemology of the Closet*, London and New York: Harvester Wheatsheaf, 1991.

SHEPPARD, RICHARD, 'The Problematics of European Modernism', in *Theorizing Modernism: Essays in Critical Theory*, ed. S. Giles, London: Routledge, 1993, 1–51.

SILVERMAN, KAJA, *Male Subjectivity at the Margins*, New York and London: Routledge, 1992.

SMITH, PETER D., 'German Literature and the Scientific World-View in the Nineteenth and Twentieth Centuries', *Journal of European Studies*, 27 (1997), 389–415.

SPINK, J. S., 'Form and Structure: Cyrano de Bergerac's Atomistic Conception of Metamorphosis', in *Literature and Science*, ed. L. A. Bisson, Oxford: Blackwell, 1955, 144–50.

STERN, JOSEPH PETER, 'Eine literarische Definition des Aphorismus', in *Der Aphorismus*, ed. G. Neumann, Darmstadt: Wissenschaftliche Buchgesellschaft, 1976, 226–79.

SULLOWAY, FRANK J., *Freud, Biologist of the Mind*, London: Burnett Books, 1979.

TERDIMAN, RICHARD, *The Dialectics of Isolation: Self and Society in the French Novel from the Realists to Proust*, New Haven: Yale University Press, 1976.

WEBER, EUGEN, *France: fin de siècle*, Cambridge, Mass. and London: Harvard University Press, 1986.

WEIDLÉ, WLADIMIR, *Die Sterblichkeit der Musen*, trans. K. A. Horst, Stuttgart: Deutsche-Verlags-Anstalt, 1958.

WEISS, ANDREA, *Paris Was a Woman: Portraits from the Left Bank*, London: Pandora, 1995.

WEST, REBECCA, *The Court and the Castle: A Study of the Interactions of Political and Religious Ideas in Imaginative Literature*, London: Macmillan, 1958.

WHITWORTH, MICHAEL, 'Physics and the Literary Community 1905–1939', Oxford, unpublished D. Phil. thesis submitted 1994.

WHYTE, LANCELOT LAW, *The Unconscious before Freud*, London: Tavistock, 1962.

WICKES, GEORGE, *The Amazon of Letters: The Life and Loves of Natalie Barney*, London: W. H. Allen, 1977.

WILSON, EDMUND, *Axel's Castle: A Study in the Imaginative Literature of 1870–1930* (1931), New York: Macmillan, 1991.

WILSON, EMMA, *Sexuality and the Reading Encounter: Identity and Desire in Proust, Duras, Tournier, and Cixous*, Oxford: Oxford University Press, 1996.

HISTORY AND PHILOSOPHY OF SCIENCE

BARNES, BARRY, *Scientific Knowledge and Sociological Theory*, London and Boston: Routledge and Kegan Paul, 1974.

BLACK, MAX, *Models and Metaphors: Studies in Language and Philosophy*, Ithaca, NY: Cornell University Press, 1962.

CUTTING, GARY (ed.), *Paradigms and Revolutions: Appraisals and Applications of Thomas Kuhn's Philosophy of Science*, Notre Dame, Ind.: University of Notre Dame Press, 1980.

GIEDYMIN, JERZY, *Science and Convention: Essays on Henri Poincaré's Philosophy of Science and the Conventionalist Tradition*, Oxford: Pergamon, 1982.

GROSS, ALAN G., *The Rhetoric of Science* (1990), Cambridge, Mass. and London: Harvard University Press, 1996.

HANSON, NORWOOD RUSSELL, *Patterns of Discovery: An Inquiry into the Conceptual Foundations of Science*, Cambridge: Cambridge University Press, 1958.

HESSE, MARY, *Models and Analogies in Science*, London: Sheed and Ward, 1963.

HOLTON, GERALD, 'Do Scientists Need a Philosophy?', *TLS*, 2 Nov. 1984, 1231–4.

—— *Thematic Origins of Scientific Thought: Kepler to Einstein*, rev. edn, Cambridge, Mass. and London: Harvard University Press, 1988.

HOWE, SUSAN, 'Renunciation is a P[ei]rcing Virtue', in *Profession 1998*, New York: MLA, 1998, 51–61.

JACOB, FRANÇOIS, *La Logique du vivant: une histoire de l'hérédité*, Paris: Gallimard, 1970.

—— *The Possible and the Actual*, New York: Pantheon, 1982.

KELLER, EVELYN FOX, *Reflections on Gender and Science*, New Haven and London: Yale University Press, 1985.

KOYRÉ, ALEXANDRE, *Newtonian Studies*, Chicago: University of Chicago Press, 1968.

KUHN, THOMAS, *The Structure of Scientific Revolutions*, enlarged 2nd edn, Chicago and London: University of Chicago Press, 1970.

LENAY, CHARLES (ed.), *La Découverte des lois de l'hérédité*, Paris: Presses Pocket, 1990.

LOSEE, JOHN, *A Historical Introduction to the Philosophy of Science*, 3rd edn rev. and enlarged, Oxford and New York: Oxford University Press, 1993.

MACINTYRE, A., 'Epistemological Crises, Dramatic Narratives and the Philosophy of Science', in *Paradigms and Revolutions*, ed. G. Cutting, Notre Dame, Ind.: University of Notre Dame Press, 54–74.

MAYR, ERNST, *The Growth of Biological Thought: Diversity, Evolution and Inheritance*, Cambridge, Mass. and London: Belknap Press, 1982.

THUILLIER, PIERRE, *D'Archimède à Einstein: les faces cachées de l'invention scientifique*, Paris: Fayard, 1988.

TOULMIN, STEPHEN, *The Philosophy of Science* (1953), London: Hutchinson, 1960.

REFERENCE

LALANDE, ANDRÉ, *Vocabulaire technique et critique de la philosophie*, 8th edn rev. and enlarged, Paris: Presses Universitaires de France, 1960.

LAPLANCHE, JEAN and PONTALIS, J.-B., *The Language of Psychoanalysis*, London: Hogarth Press and The Institute of Psychoanalysis, 1973.

Larousse grand dictionnaire universel du XIXe siècle (1866–79), Paris and Geneva: Slatkine, 1982.

SCHATZBERG, WALTER, WAITE, RONALD A., and JOHNSON, JONATHAN K., *The Relations of Literature and Science: An Annotated Bibliography of Scholarship 1880–1980*, New York: MLA, 1987.

INDEX